A Traveller's Guide to

ABORIGINAL B.C.

A Traveller's Guide to

ABORIGINAL B.C.

CHERYL COULL

BEAUTIFUL
BRITISH COLUMBIA
Magazine

Whitecap Books
Vancouver / Toronto

Copyright © 1996 by Cheryl Coull
Maps copyright © 1996 by Stuart Daniel/Starshell Maps and Cheryl Coull
Whitecap Books
     Vancouver/Toronto
Beautiful British Columbia Magazine

The information in this book is true and complete to the best of our knowledge.
All recommendations are made without guarantee on the part of the author or
publishers. The author and publishers disclaim any liability in connection
with the use of this information. For additional information please contact
Whitecap Books Ltd., 351 Lynn Avenue, North Vancouver, BC, V7J 2C4; or
Beautiful British Columbia, 929 Ellery Street, Victoria, BC, V9A 7B4.

Edited by Elaine Jones
Copy-edited by Elizabeth McLean
Cover design by Warren Clark
Cover photograph by Dorothy Haegert
Interior design by Margaret Ng
Typeset by Margaret Ng
Photo credit abbreviations: BCARS (B.C. Archives and Records Service);
     RBCM (Royal British Columbia Museum).

Printed and bound in Canada.

Canadian Cataloguing in Publication Data

Coull, Cheryl, 1957–
     A traveller's guide to aboriginal B.C.

     Includes bibliographical references and index.
     ISBN 1-55110-402-4

     1. Indians of North America—British Columbia. 2. Indians of North America—
British Columbia—Antiquities—Guidebooks. 3. Historic sites—British Columbia—
Guidebooks. 4. British Columbia—Guidebooks. I. Title.

E78.B9C68 1996   971.1'00497   C95-911139-5

Contents

Foreword

Skeena pole.
CREDIT: JOHN LUTZ

There is a word in our Wsanec language—*kwagwatul*, which means "talking together." The time has come for this. The first Europeans came to live among us when my grandmother was a child. Now I am a great-grandfather, and still, very little is known of our history and values. Few people appreciate that we have always lived here, that we are still here, that we put back into the land what we take from it. Like our neighbours, we have dreams for healthy communities sustained by the same forest and fisheries resources that sustain them. We too hope our children will become doctors, lawyers, professors. We must start by talking together. The more we share of our history and values, the more people will realize we have a right to talk about our future.

—*Gabriol Bartleman, Wsanec elder*

Nuxalk dancers in Hamburg, Germany, in 1886. Their year-long tour was arranged by a Norwegian ship captain who met them on the Pacific northwest coast. While in Germany, they met anthropologist Franz Boas, who became enthralled with their traditions and subsequently visited their territories.

CREDIT: RBCM 4606

Acknowledgements

Much of the material you are about to read has never been published before. It comes directly from elders and elders councils, cultural committees, band and tribal councils throughout the province who have generously shared their knowledge, and patiently reviewed my interpretation of it. Also echoed here are the voices of First Nations people no longer with us, who over the last century have worked closely with ethnographers and anthropologists so their knowledge would be available to us now. Other sources include books written recently by First Nations leaders or authorized by band and tribal councils.

Among those who have shared their homes, their salmon, their wisdom, and their enthusiasm in the hopes of creating greater understanding: Albert McHalsie, *Yewal Siya:m* of Ohamil, on the Halq'emeylem people; Michael Nicoll Yahgulanaas and Marcia Crosby on the Haida; Dorothy Alpine, Marian Michell, Leo Williams, and Beverley O'Neil on the Ktunaxa people; Chief Adam Dick, Daisy Sewid-Smith, Kim Recalma-Clutesi, and Andrea Sanborn on the Kwakwa̱ka'wakw people; Gilbert Capot-Blanc on the Treaty 8 peoples; Katherine Robinson on the Nuu-chah-nulth tribes; Madeline Gregoire on the Okanagan people; Darryl Webster on the Nlaka'pamux; Marilyn Napoleon and Larry Casper on the St'at'imc; Patrick Michell and Cam Beck on the Dakelh; Moris Amos on the Haisla people; Ardythe Wilson, Kathy Holland, Art Wilson, and Don Monet on the Gitxsan; Susan Mars-den on the Tsimshian; John Jules on the Sec-wepemc; Robert Greenway on the Tahltan people; Harry Nyce Jr., Charles Mackay, and Shirley Morvin on the Nisga'a people; Margaret Hanuse and Nicki Shaw on the Oweekeno people; Jennifer Carpenter on the Heiltsuk people; Chief Roger William on the Tsilh-qot'in; Abner Thorne on the Hul'qumi'num people; Tom Paul on the Sechelt people; Gabriol Bartleman on the Straits peoples.

Others to be thanked for their considerable contributions are Glen Baptiste, Linda Beltrano, Randy Bouchard, Cindy Carleton, Keith Carlson, Wayne Choquette, Robert Duncan, Guy Dunstan, Marlene Erickson, Graham Everett, Jane Francis, Henry Green, Marjorie James, Bill Jones, Elaine Jones, Dorothy Kennedy, Kim Lawson, Nathalie Macfarlane, Dan Marshall, Bryan McGill, Linda Morrison, Brian Mulloney, Connie Mungall, Maurice Nahanee, Rosemary Neering, Sylvia Olsen, Doug Patterson, Mildred Roberts, Jimmy Scotchman, John Terbasket, Chief J.J. Wallas, Chief Charley Wesley, Barbara Wilson. Thanks also to the many many others not mentioned here.

Thanks to the First Nations Tourism Association of B.C.—Barry Parker and Gary Johnston—for your support from the beginning. Thank you, Dorothy Haegert, for your photographs and encouragement; Stuart Daniel, for your maps; and the Carden Street West Cafe for always having a table.

Finally, thanks to John Lutz, for taking this journey with me.

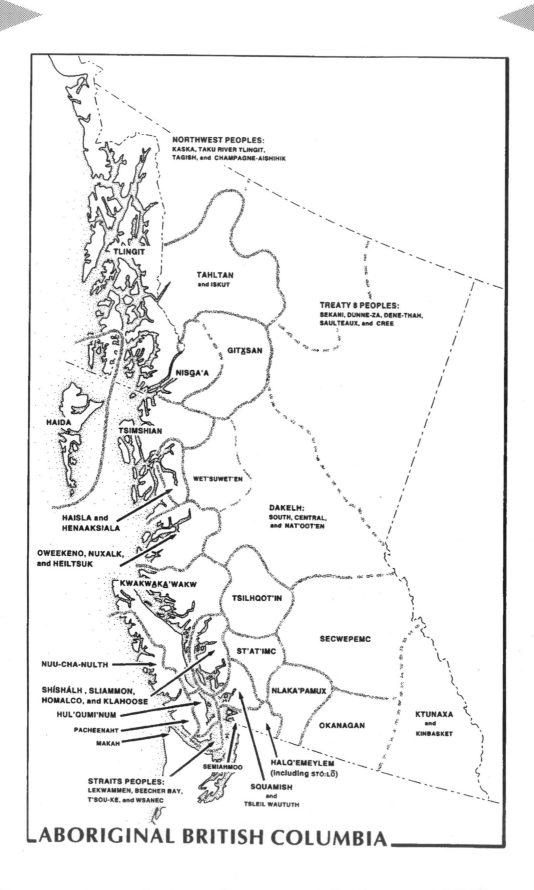

NORTHWEST PEOPLES:
KASKA, TAKU RIVER TLINGIT,
TAGISH, and CHAMPAGNE-AISHIHIK

TLINGIT

TAHLTAN
and ISKUT

TREATY 8 PEOPLES:
SEKANI, DUNNE-ZA, DENE-THAH,
SAULTEAUX, and CREE

GITXSAN

NISGA'A

HAIDA

TSIMSHIAN

WET'SUWET'EN

DAKELH:
SOUTH, CENTRAL,
and NAT'OOT'EN

HAISLA and
HENAAKSIALA

OWEEKENO, NUXALK,
and HEILTSUK

KWAKWAKA'WAKW

TSILHQOT'IN

SECWEPEMC

ST'AT'IMC

NUU-CHA-NULTH

NLAKA'PAMUX

SHÍSHÁLH , SLIAMMON,
HOMALCO, and KLAHOOSE

HUL'QUMI'NUM

OKANAGAN

KTUNAXA
and
KINBASKET

PACHEENAHT

MAKAH

SEMIAHMOO

HALQ'EMEYLEM
(including STÓ:LŌ)

STRAITS PEOPLES:
LEKWAMMEN, BEECHER BAY,
T'SOU-KE, and WSANEC

SQUAMISH
and
TSLEIL WAUTUTH

ABORIGINAL BRITISH COLUMBIA

Introduction

The Road to Aboriginal British Columbia

Before you lies one road, two journeys. One takes you into a new land. The other to an ancient world. It is the new land that is described on official road maps; its tales of explorers, fur traders, and gold rushes are celebrated in ordinary travel guides. The older world, though crowded with peoples, histories, and spirits, and still occupied by the descendants of its original occupants, remains invisible to most who travel through it, and even to many who have lived in its midst for generations.

This is a guide for those who wish to embark on the second journey. It is a journey open to anyone who likes to drive, or be driven, hike, or just travel via imagination to places in British Columbia. We set out simply on the road we drive every day—built over trails people have walked for millennia, tracing rivers etched out or altered by such supernatural beings as Txamsem, the giant Natmuqcin, and the Transformers, Xexa:ls.

This road leads us through one landscape after another: Vancouver Island's west coast, its gentler east coast, the Fraser Canyon, the Okanagan Valley, the mountain-barricaded Kootenays, highlands, plateaus, prairies. These are traditional territories—countries—occupied since the ice age and possibly before that by peoples known collectively to newcomers as aboriginal peoples, Indians, Natives,

First Peoples, or First Nations. They know themselves as Nuu-chah-nulth, Kwakwaka'-wakw, Nlaka'pamux, Okanagan, Ktunaxa, Dunne-za—more than 40 peoples who define themselves by language, history, culture, and changing relationships. Their boundaries often overlap; some flow beyond the borders of what is now the province of British Columbia. Within them are rooted eight language families, dozens of languages, and hundreds of dialects more diverse than those found in Europe.

It would be impossible to find our way without the patience and generosity of hundreds of aboriginal elders and hereditary leaders, elected chiefs, and artists throughout the province. Their willingness to share their knowledge comes from their recognition that what travellers know and understand about them is important. They have been living with policies born out of the impressions of travellers for two hundred years. The Spanish and British who first visited them saw a wilderness for the taking; they did not see the complex societies that were here, founded on time-tested laws, elaborate resource-management systems, profound spirituality, and a rich heritage of material and performing arts. Today's travellers, through their perceptions and their actions, continue to have an impact on the day-to-day lives of aboriginal peoples.

Many First Nations' elders and leaders also see how their perceptions are influencing newcomers to their lands. For at least 10,000 years aboriginal societies flourished: their survival was bound to their ability to perceive and live in accordance with the laws of nature. Stories are told and retold of great floods, volcanic eruptions, salmon runs that failed to appear. These were lessons, say the elders, because people didn't pay attention to what they were doing. Now, as the province's fisheries and forests face an uncertain future, their lessons have relevance to everyone. And there are some hopeful signs that aboriginal perspectives are being respected: a growing number of sacred landscapes have been preserved as parks jointly managed by First Nations and provincial governments; some First Nations' resource-management initiatives are also being implemented.

The question, say the elders, is not how we change the land, but how the land changes us.

You too will feel its power as you visit places described in their stories. You will feel the heat hovering on the barren plains of Nisg̱a'a Lava Bed Memorial Park where two villages lie buried under molten rock. In the hidden crevasse of the Stein River, you might connect directly with what the Nlaka'pamux call *xa'xa*, "the power of nature," or read about it in rock writings left by travellers before you. You will encounter First Nations' communities that are on the Internet but not the road map, looking out to the very confluences where they mark their earthly beginnings, or to the peaks where they found refuge when the flood waters rose.

In this guidebook, emphasis is given to First Nations' communities, cultural and interpretive centres, tours, events, art galleries, and shops where travellers are encouraged to come and learn directly from First Nations people. But also mentioned are communities that have chosen not to open their doors to tourism, or have no facilities yet. They ask simply to be placed within the context of their own culture and landscape, acknowledged by their own name.

Names in themselves connect us with much that is powerful: landmarks we would

normally take no notice of; rivers, mountains, and some of the supernatural beings that inhabit them; the fishing sites, gathering places and ancient villages from which today's towns and cities have taken root. What is offered here is just a sampling. Many of the names, and the stories, traditionally carried in the minds of elders and hereditary leaders have never been recorded on paper. At this moment throughout British Columbia, band and tribal council offices are bustling with researchers, spurred on by the treaty negotiation process begun in 1993. They are interviewing elders, re-examining ethnographic and historical records, mapping every possible contour of the province. Much has been lost. Much is private, and not meant to be known by travellers. Much is waiting to be shared.

This decade has seen an encouraging proliferation of books produced or endorsed by individual First Nations—cultural materials for schools; histories for academic and general audiences. This guidebook finds its place among them as orienteer, placing these materials, and you, the traveller, within the more familiar landscape of British Columbia.

In addition to introducing the peoples, their traditional territories, languages and histories, this guidebook literally puts the aboriginal landscape on the map. Existing road maps leave off most aboriginal communities and other important sites. The 25 maps created for this guide present them along with the roads and highways we are familiar with.

Now, go slowly. Ask questions. Sometimes, just listen. Pay attention to everything—the wind, the detail on a carving, the ripple on the river. There is nothing around you that is not part of aboriginal B.C.

Traditional Territories: Our Home, and Native Lands

Travellers and newcomers to North America have become used to boundaries that are straight lines. British Columbia is an almost

Visitors at Alert Bay, circa 1907.
CREDIT: BCARS 2040

perfect rhomboid, formed by the 49th parallel to the south, the 60th parallel to the north, the Pacific coast to the west. The eastern boundary with Alberta follows the Rocky Mountains northwest, but then cuts a more contrived course due north. These lines are the product of negotiations, in the 1800s, between the colonizing governments of the United States, Russia, and England, and Canada. But all of B.C.'s 948,600 square kilometres have been occupied "since time immemorial" by First Nations peoples, and form their respective traditional territories.

Travellers into aboriginal B.C. may be overwhelmed at first by what appears to be a labyrinth of twisting, intersecting, and sometimes ephemeral lines. The divisions between territories tend to be more like buffer zones than boundaries. What constitutes a territory depends on who is being included within it. For example, we might be referring to all who call themselves Dakelh, or only to those Dakelh who know themselves as Wet'suwet'en. Or, to those Wet'suwet'en who are associated with

a specific *keyoh,* or area, managed by a hereditary leader. Thus it is difficult to state the size of traditional territories, or even to say how many there are within B.C. There is, however, a profound logic underlying the orientation of traditional territories—it is the land itself, and more precisely, its watersheds.

In this guidebook, there are 24 chapters: most focus on one tribal group as they define themselves in these times. Some chapters introduce two or more peoples who share adjacent, or even the same landscapes.

Indian Reserves, Indian Bands, and Tribal Councils

Understanding aboriginal B.C. becomes even more confusing when we overlay the "Indian" landscape—the system of Indian reserves and Indian bands—created by colonial, provincial, and federal governments. The first Indian reserves were established on Vancouver Island in 1850, and by 1897 Indian reserve commissions travelling throughout the province had completed their task (for more, see "The Last Two Centuries," below). The federal *Indian Act* which came into effect in 1876 defined an Indian as someone who belongs to an Indian band, and an Indian band as a group of people living on an Indian reserve. These homogeneous units were administered by federal Indian agents who made all decisions affecting housing, education and health, even marriage and employment, and acknowledged nothing of traditional territories or government systems.

Today, there are 197 Indian bands in B.C. living on about 400 of their 1,650 small reserves. All the reserves together take up 3,440 square kilometres. Of the province's total aboriginal population—170,000 as of the 1991 census—only one-quarter, or 40,500, live on reserves. There are also about 14,000 non-natives living on reserve. Some are married to native people; most are living on land leased from the reserves. Aboriginal people make up 5 percent of B.C.'s total population in 1991. Reserves constitute .37 percent of the province's total land base.

Reserve communities tend to be small, ranging in size from a few families to about 2,000 people. The church is often the most visible landmark—offering the impression of a European-style village in keeping with the intentions of early governments and missionaries. But there is also, often, a more traditional community building—a longhouse or big house—where cultural events, such as potlatches, are held. Also prominent is the band office—headquarters of the chief and councillors, usually elected in accordance with the *Indian Act,* although some bands are returning to traditional systems more workable to them.

Sometimes contemporary reserve villages constitute traditional communities situated at traditional village sites. This can be said of most of the Gitxsan villages of the upper Skeena River. Most of today's Indian bands, however, are an amalgamation of several tra-

ditional villages decimated by smallpox and other plagues shortly after Europeans arrived. A single band may even constitute what is left of an entire cultural group, as in the cases of the Oweekeno, Heiltsuk, and Nuxalk peoples.

Some bands are hard to find—with no cluster of houses around a band office or church. The people of the Cheslatta Carrier Nation, Nee-Tahi-Buhn, and the Xeni Gwet'in of the Nemiah Valley live spread out over the landscape, tending their traplines, their fields, and their herds as they have done for a long time.

And, while many bands remain at traditional village sites, others have moved away to take advantage of new opportunities, working at canneries or mills, or to be closer to schools and hospitals. There are cases too, in which bands have been left with no choice but to vacate traditional sites coveted by newcomers for development.

A band's name may be the name of a tribe, like Kitselas, "people of the canyon," or Gitlakdamix, "the people of the ponds." It may be the name of an ancient place—Skeetchestn, "the meeting place," or Kamloopa, "where the rivers meet." It may be the name of a new place named after a governor, a king, or gold miner—like Douglas, Fort George (now Lheit-Li'ten), or Oregon Jack Creek.

As they stride toward greater self-definition, many bands are choosing not to be called bands, but peoples, tribes, First Nations, or villages. They are reclaiming their traditional names, or adopting new ones that better reflect who they have become.

The majority of Indian bands in B.C. are members of tribal councils. These are contemporary political alliances, usually sharing cultural and linguistic ties. Many have been formed in response to the land question and the need for strength and unity in the pursuit of political and economic independence. There are currently some 40 tribal councils working with about 180 bands. The B.C. Ministry of Aboriginal Affairs publishes *A Guide to Aboriginal Organizations and Services in British Columbia,* which includes a regularly updated list of bands and tribal councils. Contact the Ministry of Aboriginal Affairs, Communications Branch, 1st Floor, 908 Pandora Ave., Victoria, B.C., V8V 1X4. Tel: 356-0330.

How to Use This Guidebook

A PROTOCOL FOR VISITING FIRST NATIONS TERRITORIES AND COMMUNITIES

Traditionally, travellers entering another people's territory acknowledged their hosts and abided by their laws. Among First Nations peoples, this is still protocol, especially in formal situations. Travellers on major routes and thoroughfares can show their respect simply by being aware this is the traditional territory of a particular people.

Along the highway, the first indication you are approaching a First Nations community may be a sign, the band administration office, a glimpse of a longhouse, or carved poles. It may be a row of billboards, which by law can only be erected on lands under federal jurisdiction. Indian reserves fall into this category, and many communities benefit from billboard revenues.

Protocol for visiting communities varies. Some offer a full range of facilities and services, and encourage visitors to come, learn more about their history and culture. Others may have few services but still welcome visitors to drop by band offices. A few very small communities with no visitor services do not encourage visitors. This is usually indicated in the chapters to follow. Except where there are major facilities, such as cultural centres or resorts, or where a major public event is underway, travellers are asked to call or visit local band offices, open weekdays, and seek guidance.

First Nations communities visibly occupy only a part of their reserve land. Many reserves, along major travel corridors or on islands with pleasant beaches, have no build-

ings or other outward sign of ownership. These may be seasonal fishing or berry-picking sites, former villages, or burial places. In some cases, there are signs prohibiting trespassing. In others, travellers may visit or even camp if they first receive permission. Some First Nations have passport systems and a small annual fee is charged.

Generally, populations for each community or band are indicated by two numbers, as in *(Pop. 123/100).* These figures, from the 1991 census, compare the total band population to the number of members who actually live on the reserve(s) belonging to the band in question, or another band. Some communities have provided their own statistics. In most of these cases only one figure, representing the total band population, is given.

Many towns and cities—whose populations are predominantly non-First Nations—are also mentioned. Their histories frequently intersect with those of First Nations communities; tribal council offices and cultural centres are often located in these more urban areas. And many First Nations people live and work here. Relative populations are indicated by *(Pop./ Ab)*—the total population according to the 1991 census, and the number of people who have identified themselves as being aboriginal.

The maps locate First Nations communities relative to the towns and cities familiar to most travellers. They reveal how rivers, mountains, and coastlines define traditional boundaries. The maps have been created solely for guiding travellers through aboriginal B.C., and are not scanctioned by tribal councils, treaty offices, or any government.

The following symbols will guide you from one text entry—one place—to the next.

V First Nations communities, villages
I Places of interest
T Cities and towns
J Important junctions
B Boundaries
? Information

Highlights and events listed after the introduction to each chapter may help you to plan your itinerary.

POWWOWS AND POTLATCHES

Powwows are public events which feature dancing, drumming, and singing groups from all over North America. They are held throughout B.C., but the regalia and dancing reflect plains, more than coastal, traditions. Costumes of brightly coloured headdresses, feather bustles, and beaded moccasins continue to evolve as participants, travelling from one end of the continent to the other on the powwow circuit, influence each other, and compete for prizes. The venue for these events is traditionally a powwow arbour—a circular structure open at the centre, with seating around the edge. The new arbour at Kamloops seats 5,000. The people of the Similkameen Valley also have an elegant new structure just west of Keremeos. The Grand Entry is the most colourful and dramatic moment, with as many as several thousand dancers, men and women, children and grandparents, entering the arbour centre (or community hall) to the resonance of drummers and singers. Specific events will continue for two or three days, with participants camping on the powwow grounds in RVs, tents, and tipis. Craftspeople display their work. Food stands offer hot dogs and ice cream, or buffalo and salmon burgers, and "Indian ice cream" made from wild berries. Some powwows, such as the one hosted by the Mission Friendship Centre for more than two decades, are annual events. In small communities, powwows may be held on a less regular basis.

Potlatches are considered a coastal tradition, though they are also held by Athapaskan-speaking interior peoples in the central and northern parts of B.C. These are singularly private gatherings, hosted by individual families to acknowledge the most important events in life (see "Since the Beginning of Time," below). Most travellers, unless they receive a personal invitation, will not have a chance to

The annual Mission Powwow draws thousands of participants from all over North America.
CREDIT: MISSION FRIENDSHIP CENTRE

witness a potlatch. However, some public events, such as pole-raising ceremonies to celebrate the completion of a new road or bridge, or the opening of a cultural centre, may include elements of a potlatch. The U'Mista Cultural Centre, the Kwagiulth Museum at Cape Mudge, the Royal B.C. Museum, and the University of British Columbia Museum of Anthropology all have excellent exhibits and special programs offering the sights and sounds of potlatches.

FROM TOTEM POLES TO BIRCHBARK BASKETS

The search for rare and beautiful places is often accompanied by a quest for the arts of the people who live there. Art translates the intangible elements of a place into a material form, so travellers can take them home, remember, and share their experiences. Any piece of aboriginal art is a conversation between a "keeper of the culture" and a traveller—so it should come as no surprise that artists are the people travellers are most likely to meet in aboriginal B.C. These encounters may take place in a major gallery or cultural centre where a new masterpiece is being unveiled, or in an artist's workshop or kitchen in a small First Nations community.

The best-known examples of aboriginal art in B.C. are totem poles. These giant sculptures, sometimes the full height of a cedar tree, are actually difficult to take home. In less enlightened times, poles were pirated from traditional villages and transported around the world. Today's travellers take home photographs, and purchase replicas of equal power, but smaller. Full-sized poles are being carved again in villages along the coast after a pause that lasted nearly a century. Some are carved for private use by aboriginal families; others are commissioned by wealthy individuals, corporations, and governments.

The same intricate designs are engraved into gold or silver bracelets and pendants, and in argillite, a rare black slate found on Haida Gwaii. They are also represented on paper, in paintings and prints, on fabric, and even in chocolate. This approach to art is rooted in coastal traditions where objects of daily use— hats, spoons, canoes, even the posts and beams supporting houses—were carved and painted to convey information about the clans, families, or individuals who owned them.

The word totem was apparently derived by Europeans, from the word *ototeman,* in the Ojibway language spoken by aboriginal peoples of eastern North America. It refers to the relationships between clans or families and certain animals or other natural objects— relationships which coastal poles often illustrate. Many of the peoples of B.C.'s coast are organized by clans or family groups that can be traced back to their supernatural origins. The main Tsimshian and Nisga'a clans are Killer Whale, Wolf, Eagle, and Raven. Their Gitxsan neighbours are divided into Fireweed, Wolf, Eagle, and Frog/Raven clans. The Haida clans are Raven and Eagle. The original families of the Kwakwaka'wakw trace themselves to Killer Whale, Grizzly Bear, Thunderbird, and Sun, to name a few. Crests representing these clans and families are just some of the many images often seen in coastal aboriginal art. A carving or painting, whether simple or complex, may also describe an event—the appearance of the first members of a tribe, an epic journey, a joining of tribes, floods and famines. Crests, dances, stories, and songs can only be re-created and interpreted by those who have inherited or been granted the privilege, so every piece of art relates to the stories owned by the artist's family.

Although each pole or bracelet is as individual as the artist who creates it, there are distinctive cultural styles. The Coast Salish peoples are known for their subtle interpretations of the world around them: some of the most interesting examples were, and still are found, on the spindle whorls of their spinning machines (see "X'muzk'i'um," chapter 5). The Kwakwaka'wakw people, conversely, are known for bold presentations: the "world's tallest" totem poles, masks with moving parts. Haida artists are acknowledged for their sense of balance and symmetry.

Some of the best places to see poles are Victoria, Vancouver (UBC Museum of Anthropology), Alert Bay, Old Massett, the Gitxsan villages, and Prince Rupert. At these places, and in other coastal First Nations' communities, noted in the chapters to follow, artists can be found at work in shops and carving sheds, happy to meet visitors.

The arts of interior British Columbia reflect the resources and the traditional lifestyle of the people there. Unlike the coastal groups who maintained more permanent villages, these peoples were more mobile and hence decorated items that travelled with them. Here, we find baskets made from birchbark, garments cut from moose or caribou hide and adorned with intricate beadwork, paintings that reflect their landscapes.

Many interior and coastal artists have their own galleries, or sell their work directly

Detail from a Gitxsan pole. Every piece of art relates to crests and stories belonging to the artist's family.
CREDIT: JOHN LUTZ

from their homes. Some are mentioned in the chapters to follow. Band administration offices can also provide information on local artists. See Further Reading for books offering insight into arts of the northwest coast.

ARCHAEOLOGICAL SITES

If we see a use for, or beauty in, a forest, a river, or a beach, it is likely someone has been there before us—maybe two hundred years ago, a thousand years ago, or more. Archaeological sites are places where people have left behind traces of themselves. These are records of the past written incidentally—depressions and post holes left from cedar lodges built 5,000 years ago, circular depressions from equally ancient kekulis or pit houses, burial mounds, bison jumps, trails, gardens. All along the

coast are thousands of middens—sites where people have been discarding refuse since as far back as the last ice age, about 12,000 years ago. Middens are often but not always open spaces: green spaces with extremely rich black soil mixed with crushed clam and mussel shells. Former interior village and camp sites are marked by food cache pits, fire pits, stone tools broken and discarded. These sites provide archaeologists with information about the tangible aspects of people's lives: where they lived, travelled, died, what they hunted and ate—evidence used sometimes to corroborate that provided by oral historians.

But even archaeologists say archaeology is the study of places archaeologists have been. There are, to date, 20,000 known archaeological sites in B.C., as inventoried by the provincial government's archaeology branch. Most of these are along transportation corridors and riverbanks. Hundreds of thousands of others are believed to exist, especially in rich resource-gathering areas at higher elevations. Of those identified, only a fraction have been studied.

Many archaeological sites continue to be of major significance to First Nations peoples, and they are incorporating some of them into programs for visitors, partly as a way to protect them. East of Vancouver, the Stó:lo Nation has built Xa:ytem National Historic Site and interpretive centre around the remains of an ancient village and important cultural site. They are also guiding tours to burial mounds, pit-house villages and pictographs along the Harrison River; other tours are planned, to the ancient village Aselaw—also known as the Milliken Site—where archaeologists have confirmed 12,000 years of continuous occupation. Meanwhile, the Musqueam people at the mouth of the Fraser River have purchased the real estate built over the famous Marpole Midden near the Vancouver International Airport.

Farther north, Nisga'a Lava Bed Memorial Park provides access and insight into two villages and a landscape buried when a vol-cano erupted 200 years ago. The Tsimshian people of Metlakatla conduct boat tours to several sites around Prince Rupert Harbour. Across Hecate Strait, the Haida Gwaii and Duu Guusd Watchmen protect and offer some inter-pretation of their ancient villages, emptied 150 years ago by smallpox. In the Kitlope Valley, members of the Haisla Nation escort visitors to sites recently spared from logging. The Nla-ka'pamux, who also fought to save their "hid-den valley" from logging, are protectors and interpreters of hundreds of pictographs along the Stein River. Near Nanaimo, Petroglyph Provincial Park protects rock writings. Similar sites throughout the province are vulnerable to development or vandalism.

Many sites are protected simply because people don't know where they are. Others are in danger for the same reason. Anyone finding a site is advised to simply leave it alone and untouched; in most cases it is best to not even report it, unless it seems to be threatened by vandalism or development. In B.C., it is against the law to disturb any archaeological or heritage site whether or not it has been des-ignated, on public or on private land. The existing inventory of sites is used for land-use planning and the management of archaeologi-cal resources. For information, contact the Archaeology Branch, Ministry of Small Busi-ness, Tourism and Culture, 5th Floor, 800 Johnson St., Victoria, B.C., V8V 1X4. Tel: 356-0882.

Since the Beginning of Time

"In the world today, there is a commonly held belief that, thousands of years ago, as the world today counts time, Mongolian nomads crossed a land bridge to enter the western hemisphere, and became the people now known today as the American Indians. The truth of course, is that Raven found our forefathers in a clamshell on the beach at Naikun . . . There is, it can be said, some scanty evidence to support the myth of *the land bridge. But there is an enormous wealth of proof to confirm that the other truths are all valid."*
—Bill Reid, Haida artist

The Stó:lo people of the Fraser River tell us their ancestors were salmon and cedar trees transformed into people. The Ktunaxa people say they were there when the giant Natmuqcin created the Columbia, one of the continent's greatest rivers. From the rocky tip of Vancou-ver Island to the muskeg of the Liard Valley come the histories that say the people and the land *became* together. The stories shared in the following chapters reveal how each people emerged unto themselves on their own dis-tinctive landscape; they also reveal many links between them. All speak, for example, of the great flood, and how its survivors were carried in their canoes to distant regions, often to form new relationships and new tribes.

Although there were traditionally no his-tory books or archives full of official docu-ments, there were, and still are, records of such important events. Ochre pictographs, in the most hidden valleys and inaccessible moun-tain ridges, are testimony of the presence and experiences of First Peoples there. There are poles—house posts, memorial poles, shame poles—where symbols carved into ancient cedar offer many layers of meaning for the few who know how to read them. These are docu-ments, posted in the earth, verifying how peo-ple came to be here, chronicling their achieve-ments from the beginning of time to now.

Until very recently, little was recorded on paper. It was carried from one generation to the next in the language, and the names of people linked with the names of places. Each name, itself a container of information, holds the story of an event or series of events.

More important than the information itself is the historian, who has received it first-hand, then bears the responsibility for how it is interpreted and used, and who hears it. "I was never called by my name," says Gabriol

Bartleman of the Wsanec people. "It was always nephew, grandson . . . When I was very small, they asked me, do you know who your relatives are, who you are? They told me I must never forget that."

Much of this knowledge is considered private. A family's wealth is measured by stories, songs, and dances, and these are not to be spent unwisely.

The grandest presentation of this knowledge is an event called the potlatch. This Chinook Jargon word, "to give," is what the Gitxsan today call the Feast, and the Cowichan people call a Great Deed—to host one is among the greatest accomplishments in a person's life. The different names for the potlatch reflect languages, cultures, and the many occasions—marriage, birth, coming of age, death, the need to undo a wrong done or to honour a good deed done—which require a gathering of witnesses. In times past, messengers "travelled all around the world" by canoe to deliver formal invitations. On the coast, such gatherings were held in winter, in the big house or longhouse, when people returned to their main villages from summer's harvesting. Inland, as among the Dakelh, these meetings were conducted in the summer, when people returned to central fishing sites from hunting grounds throughout their territories.

Before assemblies of up to several thousand people, the host—through words and the presentation of songs, dances, and masks—describes in detail his or her relationship to the land, the people, and its resources. This is also when names are formally passed on. As Gabriol Bartleman explains: "We become our names."

Witnesses are honoured with a feast, and paid. Blankets were one currency traditionally distributed. Coppers, with names like "all-other-coppers-are-ashamed-to-look-at-it," were sometimes broken into pieces, and given as an "unperishable representation of perishable wealth." The potlatch was a demonstration of one's ability to manage resources, and

David and Flora Dawson of Gwa'yi, in Kingcome Inlet, display shield-shaped copper, symbol of a chief's wealth.
CREDIT: DOROTHY HAEGERT

for many, part of an investment system. Today money is given, along with other useful items. An event that in former times may have lasted two or three weeks, nowadays usually spans a weekend. It remains a document, often accompanied by the carving and raising of poles.

Potlatching was outlawed by the federal government in 1884. Some say this was because the colonial government, and the missionaries who supported the ban, did not understand the purpose of the potlatch. They were trying to protect people from giving too much away, and falling into poverty. Others say potlatches were banned because their purpose *was* understood: the jail sentences and confiscation of potlatch masks and coppers was a deliberate attempt to undermine First Nations' histories, government, economic, and spiritual institutions. In many parts of the coast, potlatching continued nonetheless. In 1951, the law against potlatching was quietly deleted from the books.

THE LAST TWO CENTURIES

Where First Nations' histories become somewhat homogenized is after the arrival of Europeans. This story begins in 1763. Looking west of his new colonies on the eastern seaboard, King George III of England acknowledged the multitude of nations and tribes that lay beyond, and he declared they "should not be molested or disturbed in the Possession of such Parts of Our Dominions and Territories as, not having been ceded to or purchased by Us . . ." Over the next century, the now famous Royal Proclamation of 1763 governed land acquisitions from the east coast to the Rocky Mountains.

In the distant and unknown west beyond the Rockies, meanwhile, the European presence was felt before it was seen. Smallpox, a deadly virus spread by direct contact, or by dried particles on blankets or clothing, was delivered to Mexico by the Spanish in the early 1500s; from there it travelled on its own to peoples with no immunity, depopulating a continent. In the 1780s, it reached the people of the lower Fraser River. "The wind carried the sickness among them," recounted Old Pierre, historian of the Katzie people, a century later. "Some crawled away into the woods to die; many died in their homes. Altogether about three-quarters of the Indians perished . . . Not many years later Europeans appeared on the Fraser, and their coming ushered in a new era."

Many who stood to meet the first Spanish and British in the 1790s bore pockmarks of the plague. Over the next few decades, fur traders trickled in by sea and land—as visitors have over the millennia, bringing new ideas and commodities with them. And as long as these newcomers acknowledged the laws of the land, they were welcome; their trading posts became a middle ground, drawing many nations to them. Few but the prophets saw an empire's claims to dominion anchored to these centres.

In 1849, the middle ground shifted. To limit American expansion from the south, the British declared the whole of Vancouver Island, extending far beyond its tiny post of 50 men, a crown colony. James Douglas, chief trader of the Hudson's Bay Company, became governor of territories occupied by Lekwammen, Wsanec, Hul'qumi'num, Pentlatch, Kwakwaka'wakw, and Nuu-chah-nulth peoples.

In apparent compliance with his country's Royal Proclamation, he did make a total of 14 treaties with the Lekwammen and Wsanec peoples of present-day Victoria, the Kwakwaka'wakw of the north island, and the Sney ney mux of Nanaimo, clearing the way for settlement around present-day Victoria, and for access in perpetuity to coal deposits farther north. Yet, for a society that invests so much faith in written history, the processes by which these documents came to be signed remain very much a mystery.

These first and, as it turns out, only treaties west of the Rocky Mountains promised protection of existing villages, and thus formed the basis of B.C.'s first Indian reserves.

In 1857, American and European fortune-seekers, still hungry after the California gold rush, began to follow up rumours of rich deposits to the north. By 1858, Victoria—a trading and gathering place for First Nations up and down the coast—became the main thoroughfare for thousands of Americans, Europeans, and Chinese en route to the Fraser and Thompson rivers on the mainland.

One among these fortune-seekers carried a familiar plague. As soon as the smallpox began to spread among the First Nations trading in Victoria, they were dispersed in a frenzy by colonial authorities. Bound for their home villages up and down the coast, they carried the killer with them. Historians now say it is possible as many as 90 percent of First Nations

Port Alberni residential school in the 1880s. For the next century, more than 20 similar institutions throughout B.C. kept children from their families, cultures, and languages.
CREDIT: BCARS B01058

peoples in British Columbia died in epidemic waves of smallpox, measles, flus, tuberculosis, venereal disease, alcoholism, despair.

As the gold rush proceeded, Governor Douglas—to protect the original inhabitants of the mainland from the miners—established more Indian reserves along the Fraser and Thompson rivers. When B.C. joined Canada in 1871, the responsibility for native welfare fell to the federal government. With land under the jurisdiction of the fledgling province, and Indians under jurisdiction of the federal government, a joint commission travelled throughout First Nations' territories. Not to make treaties, as was being done throughout the rest of the dominion, but simply defining existing villages, some fishing sites, and burial places, and unilaterally allocating less than an average of 20 acres of land per family, to peoples whose economies relied on a vast and integrated resource base—fishing, harvesting,

hunting over hundreds of kilometres, trading.

These reserves were not owned in fee simple by the people sequestered there; rather, they were held in trust by the federal government. Land could be and was subtracted from them, when the governments judged this to be necessary for such purposes as railway or road development. Considerable reductions, or cutoffs, were made in 1913–14, without Indian consent, following a Royal Commission established to review their land holdings.

The process of separating people from their land went hand in hand with the process of separating them from their histories, laws, governments. In 1876, all aboriginal peoples in B.C. became subject to the *Indian Act,* regulating every aspect of their lives.

Missionaries further divided territories into religious zones, redefining peoples as Roman Catholics, Anglicans, Methodists, Presbyterians, members of the United Church or the Salvation Army. Communities were torn apart by the persuasions of ardent preachers maximizing on the failure of traditional medicines to cure the new diseases. Christian utopias—Glen Vowell, Metlakatla, Ayans, Greenville, Meanskinisht—emerged. Fishermen and hunters suddenly became farmers with Christian names. Although some missionaries did support First Nations' leaders in their ongoing attempts to be heard by the colonial government, others were behind such legislation as the anti-potlatch laws in 1884.

Another joint venture was the establishment of residential schools, run by missionaries, funded by the federal government. "In a few years hence, all our boys and girls will speak English, mix with the whites . . . We must endeavour to get them in to School and keep them for a certain number of years," wrote Father McGuckin, among the Secwepemc peoples at Williams Lake. For a full century, from the late 1880s to the 1980s, children from the age of six were forcibly taken from their families to facilities often days away. Desperate homesickness, hunger, head shavings, beatings for speaking so much as a word of their own language, and sexual abuse fill the childhood memories of many people today.

VOICES YESTERDAY AND TODAY

"I ask for the return of my country to me, and that the reserves be no more . . . There was a time when there was no Whiteman in the country, and in those times I had full possession of all the country. What has been done to me with my country would be the other way —I would have measured pieces off for the Whiteman, instead of the Whiteman measuring pieces off for me."

—*Tsukaite, of Blunden Harbour, addressing 1913–1914 Reserve Commission Hearings*

From the moment the fur traders stepped away from their middle ground as visitors to become colonists, there have been declarations, petitions, delegations. In 1850, Wsanec chiefs halted logging in Victoria: they were prepared for war. The Nisga'a travelled to Victoria in 1881 to protest incursions in their territories; three Tsimshian *sm'oogit*, or leaders, formed the first of many delegations to Ottawa in 1885. As early as 1906, First Nations leaders crossed seas, appealing directly to British justice and the colonists' own Royal Proclamation.

The government response: a web of new laws. The years 1927 to 1951 stand out in B.C.'s history as the "period of political prohibition." Fund-raising for the purpose of land claims was illegal. Not until 1947 could First Nations peoples vote in B.C.; not until 1960 in federal elections. In 1949, Nisga'a leader Frank Calder became the first First Nations MLA in British Columbia. In 1973, the Calder Case was the first in a series of landmark trials where Canadian judges ruled aboriginal title to land is rooted in "long time occupation, possession and use" of those lands. The question as to whether that title has been extinguished is still being argued inside and outside the courts. The answer inevitably comes back to 1763, the Royal Proclamation, and First Nations who remind us the land we now call B.C. was not lost in war, it was not sold, it was not given away.

Finally, in 1990, British Columbia joined Canada in a move to abide by its own law and settle the land question. Three years later, the B.C. Treaty Commission extended to First Nations an invitation to join provincial and federal governments at the negotiating table. Most have now submitted formal statements of intent to negotiate treaties. This process will take time, but it is likely that over the next decade, the map of B.C. will have to be redrawn.

Where Salmon Are, People Are

Salmon have flowed like life's blood into every major artery of this province for millennia at the very least. Some say the people came first, and were transformed into salmon. Others describe how Coyote unblocked the Columbia and Fraser rivers so the salmon could make their way up to the people. Coyote even made rapids and rocks and pools so it would be easier to catch them.

Western scientists tell us the "dawn salmon" existed 50 million years ago; another species, 10 to 15 million years ago, weighed 500 pounds, and bore fangs. The modern

Ktunaxa Chief Isadore, centre, in the late 1880s, demanded full possession of his territories.
CREDIT: BCARS 46291

salmon is said to have appeared 2 million years ago, then navigated its way between ice ages.

Hatched from eggs in rivulets and streams, they swim—are swept—down into an expanse of sea and salt. Four years later, they muscle their way back upriver to the precise capillary of their birth, spawn once, and die. After a round trip of thousands of kilometres, at or near the end of their life cycle, they give up what is left of their energies—food for eagles, bears, other fish, for people.

Within the unnatural boundaries of this province, all peoples, except the hunters west of the Rockies, have depended wholly or in good measure on salmon for their survival. Civilizations and trading meccas from the Juan de Fuca Strait to the Taku River, to the 1-kilometre Nadleh River and the 2,000-kilometre Columbia, have grown up around fish-

ing stations, their strength and stability correlating not only with the numbers of salmon that arrive, but with their quality. Salmon, once they enter the river, do not feed. Those caught closer to the sea are fatter, oilier, more nutritious. Those caught farther along are better for drying; but once they have travelled too far they are food only when there is no other choice. Thus it is that the Taku River Tlingit people, who have lived since the fur trade and gold rush days at the headwaters of the 3,185-kilometre Yukon River, continue to return to their ancestral fishing grounds south of the Arctic-Pacific Divide, taking their salmon from the Taku River.

Five species of salmon, each with subpopulations intricately adapted to the environment, arrive in runs from spring to fall. Not all rivers receive all species, but some, like the Fraser, do. The chinook or spring salmon, the largest, can weigh up to 18 kilograms and more. In between are chum, or dog, salmon and coho salmon. Pink, the smallest and most abundant, average about 2 kilograms; they arrive every two years instead of four. The sockeye receives its name from the Straits Salish peoples who traditionally caught it in offshore "reef nets" just before they entered the Fraser River. Upriver, the Stó:lo and Nlaka'pamux peoples waited with their dip nets and gill nets on rocks or on scaffoldings out over the water. Farther still, along the less vigorous tributaries, the Dakelh built weirs, allowing enough salmon through to assure both fish and people a future.

All knew to show the greatest regard for the salmon: to honour the first one to arrive, to return its bones gently to the river. Never to waste: if a speared salmon escaped, there would be no more fishing that day. Hard lessons followed disrespect: floods, bitter winters, volcanic eruptions, salmon runs that never came. The Nuxalk, when escorting the European fur trader Alexander Mackenzie to the sea, routed him around their fishing places, fearing his ghostlike presence would scare away the salmon.

As other fur-seekers entered these territories in the early 1800s they quickly learned not only that their survival depended on salmon, but of its value as a resource, for export. They purchased thousands of fish from the Stó:lo, Secwepemc, St'at'imc, and others, who did not permit the Europeans to catch fish themselves. But by 1888, it was the First Nations who were not to sell their fish, nor even feed themselves without a licence.

The first European-owned cannery opened on the Fraser River in 1866; at the industry's peak in the 1920s, there were seventy canneries all along B.C.'s coast. Early on First Nations men caught the fish; women cleaned them, cut them into can-sized pieces. But, by the mid-1880s, European and also Chinese and Japanese immigrants sought their lucrative positions. Commercial fishing licences were introduced, giving preference to whites; new technologies shifted canneries farther from First Nations' communities; initially, Indians were not permitted to use engine-powered boats. At the same time, new laws limited when, where, and how much First Nations fished for food. The traps, weirs, and reef nets they had used for millennia were banned.

As the century progressed, First Nations spoke out against overfishing, and the dumping of millions of salmon by canneries unable to process them. Against mining, logging, irrigation, pollution, construction of roads, railways and dams blocking migration routes and disturbing spawning beds. The province's greatest ecological disaster was a landslide at Hells Gate on the Fraser River, in 1913, during construction of the Canadian Northern Railway. The Nlaka'pamux describe with great empathy the sight of millions of salmon beating themselves to death in an effort to reach their spawning grounds (see chapter 10). In the wake of this tragedy, between 1919 and 1921, food fishing was banned for over 8,000 First Nations people throughout the entire Fraser River watershed.

B.C.'s rivers today provide food and power for millions, while many First Nations peoples live on reserves without electricity. Their struggle to have access to, and some control over, their salmon fisheries continues. In 1990, the Supreme Court of Canada agreed aboriginal peoples have the right to fish for food, ceremonial, and societal purposes, and that maintaining this is second only to the conservation of salmon. First Nations people are still subject to strict laws, and their allowable catch represents only a fraction of that given commercial and sports fisheries. But for the first time in a century, some First Nations have been granted the privilege of selling a certain portion of their food fish, and are being offered a greater role in fisheries management and enhancement programs.

The link between First Peoples and salmon continues to be expressed in where people live, where they work, what they eat, in their art, stories, and struggles. Its vitality and power is immediately felt by visitors who come to witness age-old ways of catching and preparing salmon at Bridge River, Farwell

Canyon, and Moricetown Canyon. There are traditional salmon camps, barbecues, and restaurants. First Nations–operated spawning channel and hatchery tours are listed in the chapters to follow; the Department of Fisheries and Oceans, 400-555 W. Hastings Street, Vancouver, B.C., V6B 5G3, also publishes a brochure called *Where and When to See Salmon.*

Late summer, early fall is the best time to witness salmon making their final push to their spawning beds. The most celebrated is the Adams River run, peaking every four years (1998, 2002) in late October. Roderick Haig-Brown Provincial Park has viewing platforms and interpretive programs. Other venues include Hells Gate Fishways, Fulton River Spawning Channels, Goldstream and Stamp Falls provincial parks. Brackendale in Squamish territories celebrates the hundreds of eagles that congregate to feed on the salmon.

EULACHON—THE LITTLE SAVIOUR

The Nisga'a called these tiny fish their saviours. They arrived in March or April, before the salmon, sometimes even before the ice broke on their river, to save them from starvation. Like the salmon, this silvery smelt migrates from river to sea and back again. Unlike the salmon, which are strong swimmers, the eulachon depend on the tidewaters to help carry them upriver; they don't get very far before they spawn.

The eulachon bring the river to life after a long winter's sleep. Alvin Nelson of Gingolx, at the mouth of the Nass River, says this is when eagles, sea lions, and killer whales all come, following the little saviours. And people—whole villages of Nisga'a, Haida, Tlingit, Tsimshian, and Gitxsan gathered at Fishery Bay on the lower Nass. In B.C., a dozen rivers, five of them in Haisla territories, once supported eulachon and the people who followed them with their rakes, dip nets, conical nets, and seine nets. Their catch was eaten fresh, smoked, salted, boiled, broiled or fried. Much of it was rendered into oil to be eaten

later, as a condiment, or used a food preservative, and as medicine.

Eulachon oil, packed in cedar boxes, and transported hundreds of kilometres along well-worn "grease trails," was one of the most valuable commodities of a vigorous coast-interior trade economy. The word *eulachon* is part of the Chinook Jargon trade language.

Eulachon fishing continues wherever the eulachon still thrive. On the Nass, the same peoples will still be found in Fishery Bay at winter's end. In Haisla territories, the Kitimat Museum has an excellent display of eulachon fishing and processing technology. On the Fraser, where tidal waters can carry schools 70 kilometres upstream, eulachon are being caught and sold commercially.

Peoples and Languages

Some First Nations people suggest Canadians, struggling with the two languages of their officially bilingual country, might learn something from them. Here, within the boundaries of British Columbia, are eight of the eleven aboriginal languages spoken in all of Canada. Any two are as different from one another as English is from Bengali, both within the Indo-European language family.

Athapaskan is the language spoken by peoples from Alaska to Ontario, south as far as Mexico. Coast Salish is the name given the language spoken by many peoples along the central coast down into present-day Washington State. On the other hand, Haida is spoken only on Haida Gwaii, and no relationship to any language anywhere has been found. The language spoken by the Ktunaxa in their mountain realm is another such rare "isolate."

Within these eight language families are further language divisions. For example, within the Coast Salish language, Halq'emeylem, Squamish, Comox, and Lekwammen are mutually unintelligible. Within these, there are dialects.

Rather than limiting relationships between peoples, these many languages in the past were a means of extending one's reach. Trade networks were strengthened by marriages between peoples: it was not uncommon for individuals to be fluent in three or four, or seven languages.

To facilitate trade, a whole new language developed among the First Nations. It was called Chinook Jargon by European traders who first heard it among the Chinookan people at the mouth of the Columbia River. Initially, Salishan and Wakashan words made up the jargon, but soon French and English, and other indigenous words were added. The entire language consisted of only about 700 words held together by a simple grammar. European traders were able to communicate with people everywhere; surveyors hired Chinook Jargon–speaking natives to work with them. By the beginning of this century, this was the language of business, law, and religion throughout B.C., north to Alaska, and as far south as California. English eventually replaced it, but among the Chinook Jargon words still in use are chinook, tyee, camas, salal, salt chuck, skookum, and high mucka-mucks, "the ones with a lot of grub."

Because aboriginal languages were not, traditionally, written down, much has been lost in the last eight generations to depopulation, the successful efforts of residential schools, the power of television. Many experts wonder how these languages can possibly survive when there are only a handful of elders left who know them as their first. Recognizing the monumental nature of what is being lost in every word—that language, culture, and identity are inseparable—many First Nations have stated among their primary missions, the recovery and preservation of as much as possible. Programs to teach language teachers are increasing. Several First Nations languages, including Kwakwala, Nisga'a, and Yinka Dene (Carrier), are now accepted as accredited second languages in B.C. universities and colleges.

A Note on Spellings and Pronunciations

In this guidebook, readers are being introduced to place names and words from a multitude of aboriginal languages. These languages contain many sounds not familiar to the English tongue or alphabet, and any effort to write them in English offers only an approximation of their pronunciation. Complex orthographies—systems of spelling incorporating symbols and accents for new sounds—are being devised for many of the languages. These are used in teaching and in materials published by respective language groups. A more general use of these orthographies is being encouraged. However, because this guidebook is intended to introduce the most general audiences to a great deal of new information, we are choosing the more basic English spellings wherever they are available. In a few instances, orthographic symbols—underlined letters, colons, and other markings—will appear as the only available or acceptable spellings. See "A Basic Guide to Names," below, for guidance in pronouncing the names of the major cultural groups. Pronunciations are not usually provided for names which appear less often.

What Is In a Name

Haida, in the language of Haida Gwaii, means "people." Many who share the large family of Athapaskan languages know themselves as *Dene*, "people," but are also Dakelh, Carrier, Wet'suwet'en, or Stellat'en. The Halq'emeylem-speaking peoples traditionally knew themselves as *whel mux*, "people of spirit or breath." They are also, specifically, Stó:lo, X'muzk'i'um (Musqueam), Cowichan, and Sne ney mux (Nanaimo) peoples.

The name *Indian*, often still used, originated from a meeting of complete strangers. Christopher Columbus thought he was in India when he first met the indigenous peoples of America. Nearly three centuries later, in 1798, when the British captain, George Vancouver, met coastal peoples from Juan de Fuca Strait to Alaska, he still called them *Indians*.

The *Indians* had many names for the new-comers, depending on their experiences with them. The Wsanec people of Vancouver Island called them "suddenly, they're there." The Nuu-chah-nulth peoples, whom Captain Cook mistakenly named Nootka, called fur traders and those who followed them *mamal-thi,* "people who live in a boat," also implying they had no home. Haida people called them *yaatse haade,* "metal people," or *gomshewa,* "rich at the river mouth," for what they had. The Halq'emeylem-speaking people of the Fraser River called them *xwelitem,* "hungry people," for what they didn't have. The Sec-wepemc called the first fur traders who accept-ed their laws and ways "real whites," to distin-guish them from those who came later. Those who represented the Hudson's Bay Company—British, Hawaiian, French Cana-dian or Iroquois—were "King George Men," while American traders and their employees were "Boston Men." Later, these names distin-guished Britons from Americans.

While colonists and their governments from the mid-1800s to the present have con-tinued to refer to the first peoples simply as *Indians,* ethnographers and anthropologists, more interested in the differences between peoples, derived more specific names from their encounters. Kootenay, Okanagan, Shu-swap, Chilcotin, Tahltan were approximations of what European ears heard people calling themselves or their neighbours. Other names, such as Nootka and Kwakiutl for the Kwak-waka'wakw-speaking peoples were the products of greater confusion. In recent years, in their struggle for a return to self-determination, First Nations peoples are either emphasizing their traditional names as they pronounce them, or are looking to their languages to give their own names to new political identities.

As a result, it is more common now, and generally preferred, to be specific about which people is being referred to and to use their name. When it is necessary to distinguish these peoples of many origins from relative newcomers to this land, First Nations, First Peoples, aboriginal peoples, native peoples, or indigenous peoples are all in common usage.

A Basic Guide to Names

Listed below are the major cultural groups within the boundaries of B.C. according to currently preferred spellings. Non-technical transcriptions accompany those most difficult to pronounce; however, newcomers to these words may still find a huge gap between what they say and what they hear a native speaker saying. The best way to learn these names is to listen closely when in the presence of someone more familiar, and perhaps even ask for a quick lesson. Also included here are names formerly given these groups, and the language families to which they belong.

People	Pronunciation	Have Been Called	Language Family
Haida	Hydah	Haida	Haida
Ktunaxa	Tun-ah-hah	Kootenay	Ktunaxa
Tsimshian		Tsimshian	Tsimshian
Gitxsan	Git-k-san	Tsimshian	Tsimshian
Nisga'a		Tsimshian	Tsimshian
Haisla	Hyzlah	Kitimat	Wakashan
Heiltsuk		Bella Bella	Wakashan
Oweekeno		Kwakiutl	Wakashan
Kwakwaka'wakw	Kwak-wak-ya-wak	Kwakiutl	Wakashan

People	Pronunciation	Have Been Called	Language Family
Nuu-chah-nulth		Nootka	Wakashan
Ditidaht		Nootka	Wakashan
Pacheenaht		Nootka	Wakashan
Tsilhqot'in		Chilcotin	Athapaskan
Dakelh	Da-kelh	Carrier	Athapaskan
Wet'suwet'en		Carrier	Athapaskan
Nat'oot'en		Babine/Carrier	Athapaskan
Sekani		Sekani	Athapaskan
Dunne-za		Beaver	Athapaskan
Dene-thah		Slave(y)	Athapaskan
Tahltan		Tahltan	Athapaskan
Kaska		Kaska	Athapaskan
Tagish		Tagish	Athapaskan
Tutchone	Tuchon-ee	Tuchone	Athapaskan
Nuxalk	Nu-halk	Bella Coola	Coast Salish
Klahoose		Coast Salish	Coast Salish
Homalco		Coast Salish	Coast Salish
Sliammon		Coast Salish	Coast Salish
Sechelt		Coast Salish	Coast Salish
Squamish		Squamish	Coast Salish
*Halq'emeylem		Coast Salish	Coast Salish
*Stó:lo	Staw-low	Coast Salish	Coast Salish
*Hul'qumi'num		Coast Salish	Coast Salish
Pentlatch		Coast Salish	Coast Salish
**Straits		Coast Salish	Coast Salish
St'at'imc	Stat-liem	Lillooet	Int. Salish
Nlaka'pamux	Ing-khla-kap-muh	Thompson/Couteau	Int. Salish
Okanagan		Okanagan	Int. Salish
Secwepemc	She-whèp-m	Shuswap	Int. Salish
Tlingit		Tlingit	Tlingit

* Halq'emeylem is actually the upriver dialect of the language spoken by the people of the Stó:lo Nation. There is also a closely related downriver dialect. Hul'qumi'num is the language spoken by peoples on the east coast of Vancouver Island from Malahat to Nanoose. It is related to Halq'emeylem.

** The Straits Peoples of southern Vancouver Island speak the Lku'ngen or Lekwammen and Wsanec languages.

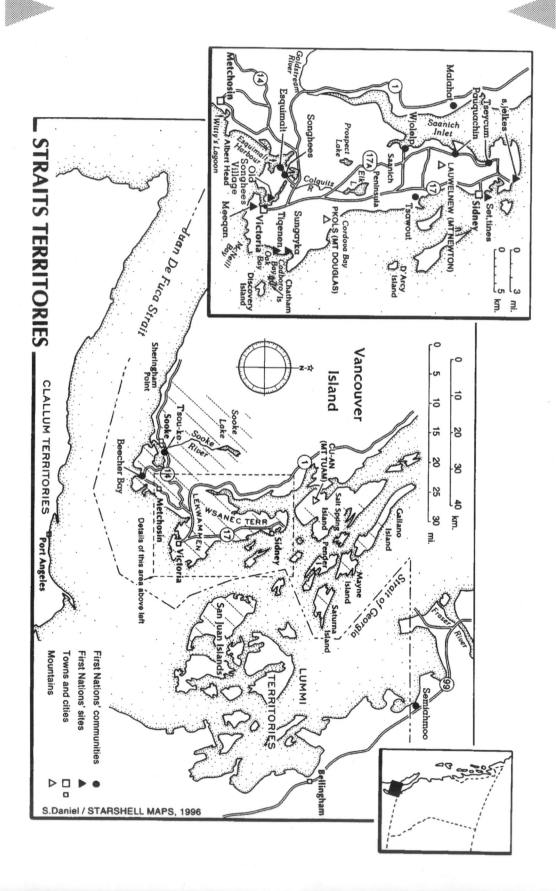

STRAITS TERRITORIES

CLALLUM TERRITORIES

Port Angeles

Juan De Fuca Strait

Vancouver Island

N ☆

0   5   10   15   20   25   30 mi.
0   10   20   30   40   km.

Sheringham Point

Sooke Lake

Tsou-ke
Sooke
Sooke River

Beecher Bay

14

Metchosin

Details of this area above left

LEKWAMMEN

WSANEC TERR

Victoria

17

Sidney

CU-AN (MT TUAM)

Salt Spring Island

Pender Island

Galiano Island

Mayne Island

Saturna Island

Strait of Georgia

San Juan Islands

LUMMI TERRITORIES

Bellingham

Fraser River

99

Semiahmoo

First Nations' communities · □
First Nations' sites ▶ ▫
Towns and cities ▷
Mountains

△   □   ▶   ●
        ▫

S.Daniel / STARSHELL MAPS, 1996

Detail map (upper inset)

Metchosin 14

Goldstream River

Esquimalt

Saanich Inlet

Malahat

Tseycum
Pauquachin

s,jelkes

1

Wjolelp

Saanich

Prospect Lake

Songhees

Colquitz R

17A

Elk L

Peninsula

LAUWELNEW (MT NEWTON)

17

Sidney

Set,tines

Tsewout

Esquimalt Harbour
Old Songhees Village
Albert Head

Witty's Lagoon

Songhees

Meeqan

Victoria

Tigenen
Tiqenen

Sungayka

Oak Bay

Cadboro Bay

Cordova Bay

PKOLS (MT DOUGLAS)

Chatham Is

Chatham Island

Discovery Island

D'Arcy Island

0   3 mi.
0   5 km.

McNeill Bay

Cadboro Bay

CHAPTER 1

The Straits:
Lekwammen, Beecher Bay, T'Sou-ke, and Wsanec

*We bury our ancestors in sacred places and we bury
them near to us; they remain a part of our village . . .
We keep them near so we can watch over them and
they can watch over us . . . Our land holds our ancestors
and our ancestors are a sacred presence.*

—Gabriol Bartleman, Wjolelp elder, Wsanec

The Lekwammen, T'Sou-ke, Beecher Bay, and Wsanec peoples live on the southern tip of Vancouver Island, where it tucks into the mainland so perfectly, you might think the two landforms were once joined together. Other links are suggested too. Here, there are relatively few salmon-spawning streams, and for the people on both sides, the straits—Juan de Fuca and Georgia—are their river. Their eight respective communities on the west "bank" share with their Semiahmoo and Lummi relatives on the east "bank," a language, and the salmon that every year follow the currents on their way to the Fraser River.

Of all the salmon species, the most abundant and first to arrive has always been *teki*, "sockeye." The People of the Straits knew the songs to bring the salmon, the songs to thank them for coming. They made a hole or "vulva" in their nets, to ensure there would be fish in the year to come, and set them at shallow reefs where the fish migrated closest to shore. It was an ingenious technology, designed just for the straits. Using weights, camouflage, and the

tides, they simulated an extension of the reef. Year after year, for millennia, the fishermen returned to within inches of the same sites. Off Becher Bay, just north of Victoria, archaeologists counted 61,000 of the heavy beach stones used to anchor their nets. The twine used to lash the stones to the reef nets came from the inner bark of the Pacific willow. A favoured source was the place now occupied by downtown Victoria—Kuo-sing-el-as, "place of the strong fibre."

The English name, Victoria, comes in a roundabout way from the second most important straits staple: the onion-shape bulbs of the wildflower, camas. They were a sweet-tasting source of starch, as important as potatoes or pasta today, and exported up and down the coast. To ensure a reliable crop, the Lekwammen people carefully tended the sun-baked slopes overlooking the straits—clearing away underbrush, turning the soil, sometimes planting seeds. Their fields so enraptured Hudson's Bay Company chief factor James Douglas when he first glimpsed them in 1842 that

Wsanec Chief David La Tasse, centre, who lived to be well over 100 years old, was 14 when he saw the first Europeans land on Lekwammen shores in 1842. He stands with Tommy Paul and Edward Jim, in official robes woven from goat hair.
CREDIT: RBCM 11743

he presumed them God's creation. A "perfect Eden" is how he described what would become the headquarters of the Hudson's Bay Company and, eventually, the capital of Canada's Pacific province.

The Lekwammen people, though at first suspicious of Douglas and his small company of men, cleared a place for them in the inner harbour, built their fort, provided them with salmon. As payment, they received the prized blankets that would come to replace their own, made from goat hair, as chief currency in a complex economy. The Lekwammen saw in the traders an opportunity to increase their own wealth; and, in a sense, they considered them their property. Some 2,000 people moved from their villages and made a new one outside the walls of the fort they helped build. This quickly became a trading centre for thousands more—peoples who travelled from as far south as Puget Sound in Washington and as far north as Alaska to trade and potlatch with the Lekwammen.

Britain in 1849 declared Vancouver Island a crown colony and leased it to the Hudson's Bay Company on the condition it be opened up for settlement. As soon as newcomers began to expand beyond the fort, however, they came face to face with the authorities of the Lekwammen and Wsanec peoples. In 1850, Wsanec *siem,* "respected leaders," forced a stop to loggers cutting trees for masts at Cadboro Bay. Then, when a fourteen-year-old messenger was shot for trespassing on land claimed by James Douglas, the Wsanec and Lewammen prepared for war. Douglas called a meeting.

Many questions are being asked today about the eleven treaties "signed" by leaders from Metchosin to Saanich. About the tidy row of X's that appear to have been made by the same hand, conceding that "the land itself [with the small exception of village sites and enclosed fields] becomes the entire property of white people forever." Wsanec and Lekwammen histories say the *siem* had come to meet with Douglas to prevent a war. Colonial history says they sold their title to their land for 371 blankets and a cap.

The treaty, as it reads today, also stated the People of the Straits would be "at liberty to hunt over the unoccupied lands, and to carry on [their] fisheries as formerly." But nothing would ever be as formerly. In this same decade, venereal diseases, flus, colds, and alcohol killed three-quarters of the people here. The gold rush, in 1858, brought an invasion of as many as 30,000 gold seekers en route to the mainland. And in 1862 one among them carried smallpox. The Lekwammen, vaccinated and quarantined on Discovery Island, actually fared better than their First Nations trading partners. When they were dispersed from Victoria, smallpox went with them to every village that welcomed their canoes.

Along the straits, unoccupied lands—camas beds, willow groves, duck marshes—became occupied lands. And, one by one, laws were written to restrict First Nations hunting and fishing on whatever was left. The federal fisheries, in 1916, outlawed First Nations' use of the reef net, categorizing it a fish trap. Meanwhile, non-native fishermen continued using the borrowed technique.

As the twenty-first century approaches, development continues to devour the alluring shores of southern Vancouver Island. The People of the Straits are torn between repudiating the Douglas treaties as false and relying on them as their only protection of a very few traditional hunting and fishing rights.

HIGHLIGHTS AND EVENTS

INFORMATION AND PROTOCOL

The Lekwammen, Beecher Bay, T'Sou-ke, and Wsanec peoples each have their own traditional territories along Juan de Fuca Strait and the Strait of Georgia. The Lekwammen people today live primarily in two communities near downtown Victoria. Beecher Bay and

T'Sou-ke each comprise one community. The Wsanec (Saanich) people live in four villages on the Saanich Peninsula.

The lands and resources of the Straits Peoples were owned by extended families and managed by their hereditary leaders, respectfully called *siem*. Their important reef-net sites and camas beds could only be inherited, not bought or sold. And proper management was acknowledged during feasts, where wealth was redistributed. Visitors to their territories, in the past as today, arrived by water.

In this urban setting, it is as important as ever to respect the privacy of communities. Appropriate venues for learning more about the history and culture of the Straits Peoples are listed below.

The language spoken by the people here is Northern Straits Salish, from the Coast Salish language family. Traditionally, each of the four peoples described here spoke their own dialects.

Along Lekwammen Shores: Greater Victoria

Lekwammen territories and the boundaries of **Greater Victoria** (Pop. 300,000/2,000 Ab) are almost the same—taking up the shores of southern Vancouver Island from Albert Head to Cordova Bay, but also including the western shores of San Juan Island. A century and a half ago, about ten independent major villages belonging to seven major families looked out to the straits. In 1843, those from the fortified settlement at Cadboro Bay, along with residents of Oak Bay and McNeill Bay, settled in around the new fort at the foot of today's Johnson Street. They came to be known as the Songhees Nation. Soon afterward, families from the more western villages established themselves where the Parliament Buildings are today. Their descendants are the Esquimalt Nation.

The British newcomers initially adopted a Lekwammen name for their Pacific outpost:

Camousun, a rock in the nearby gorge, once a girl, turned to stone by the Transformers, Hayles (Xals or Xexa:ls), to watch over the resources of her people. The fort was soon renamed, however, for the Queen of England. Within two years, its occupants persuaded the Songhees to give them a little breathing space. The Songhees moved, just across the harbour. There, in 1853, they hosted what may have been their biggest potlatch ever. Thousands converged to acknowledge, through the receipt of gifts, that the *siem* were living up to their responsibilities as managers of wealth. Thousands more—Haida, Kwakwa̱ka'wakw, Tlingit, Tsimshian—set up their own subsidiary trading communities around Ogden Point and along Dallas Road, honouring Lekwammen protocol and joining with them in such spirited games as canoe races on the Gorge waterway.

As the European population grew, their sphere once again overlapped too uncomfortably with that of the Songhees. In 1911, under pressure from the provincial government and Victoria's business community, and with $10,000 in cash paid to each family—the Songhees moved to their present location, across the road from the village where their Esquimalt cousins had long been settled.

V Songhees: (Pop. 315/194). West of downtown Victoria at 1500A Admirals Rd. The Songhees people are descendants of many Lekwammen-speaking extended families who came together when Fort Victoria was established. They moved to what is now known as the Old Songhees Village shortly thereafter (see below), and in 1911 moved here to Eyellnuk, "open or clear land." The name Songhees, applied to them by the British, is derived from the name of one of those original local groups.

The Commonwealth Games, in 1994, was the occasion for another historic gathering on Songhees lands around Victoria. Nations of the world looked on as First Nations from up and down this coast entered the harbour in canoes and awaited permission to come ashore from *siem* Norman George—a demonstration of how it is properly done. At their Big House, the Songhees hosted their first potlatch since 1899. They commemorated the event with the erection of the *Spirit of Lekwammen,* currently the world's tallest totem pole (see below). In August 1997, traditional Songhees territories will be the venue for the fifth North American Indigenous Native Games, drawing 6,000 athletes for 14 events, including archery and canoeing. The annual **Songhees Pow-wow**, in August, brings 500 dancers, singers, and drummers from all over North America. Visitors are welcome to stay at **Maple Bank Campground**, 384-0441.

? **Songhees Administration:** 1500A Admirals Rd., Victoria, B.C., V9A 2R1. Tel: 386-1043.

V Esquimalt First Nation: (Pop. 135/63). On Thomas Rd., west of Downtown Victoria. Overlooks Esquimalt Harbour at Kalla, "spring water gushing down the beach," one of several original village sites occupied by the people known as the Kosapsom. They also once lived in villages along Victoria's harbour and the Gorge waterway. The historic Craigflower Schoolhouse, built in 1855, sits at one of these. When Fort Victoria was established, the Kosapsom built a village at a traditional site where the Parliament Buildings now stand, and this site was later recorded on maps as a reserve. But, like their Songhees relatives, the Kosapsom were soon urged to vacate what was becoming a European centre, and to return here to Kalla.

? **Esquimalt First Nation Administration:** 1000 Thomas Rd., Victoria, B.C., V9A 7K7. Tel: 381-7861.

? **Victoria Native Friendship Centre:** 533 Yates St., Victoria, B.C., V8W 1K7. Tel: 384-3211. Information, programs on First Nations issues.

The Old Songhees Village sat opposite the city of Victoria until 1911. The site is now occupied by condominiums, the Ocean Pointe Resort, and the world's tallest totem pole.
CREDIT: RBCM 6804

Camas Fields: The gentle south-facing slopes of Victoria are, in early May, a sea of purple-blue. A most remarkable profusion is in Beacon Hill Park above Dallas Rd. This is Meeqan, "warmed by the sun," where the Lekwammen gathered to enjoy summer games and "warm their bellies in the sun." Below the hill was a defensive site and burial ground. At Anderson Park in Oak Bay, right at its entrance off Island Rd., are several circular depressions dug long ago—roasting pits for the tasty camas bulbs. The hill may have been a lookout for the people who lived at McNeill Bay.

Old Songhees Village: Across Johnson St. Bridge from downtown Victoria. Pallatsis, "place of cradle," is now Songhees Point. After babies had learned to walk, their cradles were left here as offerings toward a long life. The Songhees village was here from 1844 to 1911. Longhouses stretched from the Ocean Pointe Hotel to the north side of the blue bridge.

Some Names to Note: Whosaykum, "clay, or muddy place," in the James Bay area, includes the Empress Hotel; the area around St. Anne's Academy was a camping place for people gathering camas bulbs on Beacon Hill. Heel-ng-lkun, "falling away bank," is the eroding bluff along Dallas Rd. Tiqenen, "place of peas," was a reef-net site, now called Cattle Point. Sungayka, "snow patches," was a very

important village where Gyro Park now overlooks Cadboro Bay. Colquitz is a river, the watershed, and salmon-bearing stream, for what is now Victoria. It rises near Bear Hill and drains Elk and Beaver lakes, reached via Hwy 17, into Portage Inlet. Its Straits name is Hulu-knee-cun, "stream tumbling down."

Fort Victoria: At the heart of downtown Victoria. The fort's pallisades enclosed the area now encompassed by Wharf, Broughton, and Government streets, and Bastion Square. At the Government St. entrance to the square, on the sidewalk, is the octagonal outline of the fort's northeast bastion. At its centre are bricks bearing the names of many connected with the fort's history. Among those less often acknowledged are Victoria's founding women. Amelia Connoly, of Cree and British ancestry, was married to chief factor/governor James Douglas. Isabella Ross of Ojibwa and French descent was married to fort founder Charles Ross; Josette Work's mother was a native of Spokane, Washington. These women exerted considerable influence on the early relationships between the fort's inhabitants and the surrounding First Nations peoples. The last of the fort was pulled down in 1864.

Parliament Buildings: On Belleville St. above Victoria Harbour. Tours daily June to September. The British Columbia Provincial

Legislature opened March 1, 1860, and moved into its new buildings here in 1897 on a former reserve of the Kosapsom people. Within these stony walls is a story of cold relations between the colonial government and First Nations. Early on, the federal government in Ottawa took the job of administering treaties and reserves, while the province dealt with crown lands, law, and order. Both levels of government—via the Joint Indian Reserve Commission in 1876—were involved in the initial establishment of reserves, and with subsequent amendments to them. Every aspect of the lives of First Nations peoples was scrutinized and regulated—where they lived; where they attended school; where and when they fished and hunted. In all of this, the people being governed had no voice. Delegation after delegation journeyed here seeking fair solutions to questions of sovereignty and self-government. Not until 1947 could First Nations people vote in provincial elections (see Introduction, "Voices Yesterday and Today").

⑥ **Royal British Columbia Museum:** 675 Belleville St. Tel: 387-3014. Poles ancient and new greet visitors to the head of Victoria's Inner Harbour, point of intersection for First Nations and Europeans for over 150 years. The sights and sounds of peoples from around the province are presented in elaborate displays that tell their stories from the beginning of time to the present. Visitors enter this world through the doorway of a Kwakiutl longhouse warmed by a fire. Raven calls out. There is a scale-model of the Haida village, K'una, and one of a Ktunaxa encampment. There is a life-size model of a Gilford Island cave where the animal spirits held their winter ceremonies, and another of the man who fell from heaven, leaving his imprint on a rock along the Tsimshian coast. There are canoes, masks, baskets, spindle whorls, whale harpoons, Athapaskan bear snares, and elders on tape, telling of the flood. This museum is in the vanguard, encouraging living, continuing traditions.

Programs feature First Nations historians, storytellers, and artists; there are also educational tours to more distant sites of cultural and historic interest. Three new galleries, focussing on archaeology and aboriginal history, have been created in consultation with First Nations representatives. Excellent gift and book shop. The Guided Spirit concession, outside the museum, offers smoked salmon, bannock, and wild-berry jams during summer months.

⑥ **First People's Festival:** In early August, the museum is the setting for one of the only exclusively native-run arts and cultural events in Canada. It features 350 performers and artists, traditional dance and music, salmon barbecues, storytelling, and arts and crafts for children.

⑥ **Poles:** The ancient poles, from villages throughout the northwest coast, are inside the **Royal British Columbia Museum**. Newer poles, many carved by renowned Kwakwa̱ka̱'-wakw artist Mungo Martin in the early 1950s, are just outside the museum in **Thunderbird Park**. One of his poles, looming 38 m high in **Beacon Hill Park** and telling the story of his family, is the first World's Tallest Totem Pole. It was outdistanced in 1973 by the 52.7-m pole erected at Alert Bay in Kwakwa̱ka̱'wakw territories. In 1994, the 54.8-m *Spirit of Lekwammen* took its place at **Songhees Point** in Victoria. Alert Bay is planning a taller one.

⑥ **Saanich Commonwealth Place:** 4636 Elk Lake Rd. Renowned artist Roy Vickers, of Tsimshian ancestry, grew up in the territories of the Wsanec peoples. Here, he brings together themes of earth and aboriginal peoples at one of the world's most modern swimming/sports complexes. Welcome figures and a nine-panel frieze depicting elders and chiefs draw visitors into the longhouse-style main entrance. History is told on murals, and in the traditional way, on poles.

☯ **Galleries and Shops:** Many feature well-known First Nations artists from the coast and interior. Among those owned and operated by First Nations people are Komokwa Native Arts and Jewelry, 1-602 Broughton St.; Ancestral Journey Gallery, 1141 Fort St.; and Roy Henry Vickers' Eagle's Moon Gallery, 1010 Government St. Cowichan sweaters are a regional specialty (see chapter 2).

Along Beecher Bay and T'Sou-ke Shores: Northwest of Victoria on Highway 14

Some of the most important reef-net sites were along these shores, at Otter Point, Beechey Head, and Macaulay Point, occupied traditionally by the T'Sou-ke people. In the late 1840s, they were joined by Clallum people who came from across Juan de Fuca Strait to make shingles and plant potatoes at the new fort.

∎ **Witty's Lagoon Regional Park:** 2 km west of Colwood Corners, onto Metchosin Rd.; 7 km to park. This area was once occupied by a people called Qeqa'yeqen, and then by the Clallum, who later moved to Becher Bay.

▼ **Beecher Bay:** (Pop. 173/73). 29 km from Victoria on Hwy 14, Gillespie Rd. leads south 6 km to East Sooke Rd. Administration office is 4 km east. After the T'Sou-ke people (see below) left this area in about 1860, some Clallum people, originally from across the straits, moved in from Witty's Lagoon. Cheanuh ("salmon") Development Ltd. here offers excellent marina, moorage, and campground at 4901 East Sooke Rd.; Tel: 478-4880.

❓ **Beecher Bay Administration:** 3843 East Sooke Rd., Box 4, RR 1, Sooke, B.C., V0S 1N0. Tel: 478-3535.

▼ **T'Sou-ke Nation:** (Pop. 148/75). 35.5 km north of Victoria via Hwy 14. Approaching Sooke, at Edward Milne Community School, turn left onto Lazzar Rd. A copper box fell from heaven into the Sooke Basin. In it were ancestors of the T'Sou-ke, Malahat, and Cowichan peoples we know today. Hereditary chief Frank Planes once said that "Sooke was heaven on earth, a sought-after place. . . . For hundreds of years we've fought wars over this place; we don't intend to quit now." The wars he referred to are said to have begun about 200 years ago, and drew in people from as far away as Neah Bay, across the straits. In the end, the original inhabitants of this bay, a people called the Skwanungus, were wiped out, and the T'Sou-ke moved here from their former headquarters at Pedder Bay, just south. Then the T'Sou-ke themselves were attacked by the Clallum people from across the straits, and few survived. Some accounts say the Cowichan and Ditidaht peoples were also involved. They took captives who later returned to re-establish the T'Sou-ke Nation. By the time of the Douglas Treaties, there were about 60 people living here.

Visitors are welcome to visit the carving shed behind the administration office. There are several canoes on display, and artists can be found working. Some T'Sou-ke history is told at the Sooke Region Museum, 2070 Phillips Rd., off Hwy 14 just past the Sooke Bridge. T'Sou-ke and other First Nations artists are often featured at the Sooke Fine Arts Festival in early August, one of B.C.'s largest juried shows.

❓ **T'Sou-ke Nation Administration:** RR 3, Lazzar Rd., Sooke, B.C., V0S 1N0. Tel: 642-3957.

Along Wsanec (Saanich) Shores: Northeast of Victoria on Highway 17

"When other native people spoke of us, they called us the Wsanec people. They knew Saanich Inlet was the saltwater of the Wsanec people," says elder Gabriol Bartleman. The

Wsanec people have always been here, but the name they are known by came later, with the flood. "That was when our people went to the mountain, Lauwelnew," he says. This is Mt. Newton on today's maps. Its Wsanec name means "the place of refuge."

"From there, looking out over the water, it was noticed after a time, that a little mountain to the south [where the Dominion Astrophysical Observatory sits now] was getting higher. One person pointed to it, and said: *Ni Qennet Tte Wsanec*, 'look at what is emerging.'" Since that time they have been known as "the emerging people."

The Wsanec people today live in four communities on the Saanich Peninsula. They are Wjolelp (Tsartlip), Tsawout, Pauquachin, and Tseycum.

"Our people in the early days fought hard to keep the Saanich Inlet and Saanich Peninsula," says Bartleman. "That's why we have such a wonderful and strong bond with our homeland." He believes the time has come for visitors, and for those who now live here with the Wsanec people, to know more about Wsanec place names and history.

"Who were Newton, Douglas, Sidney?" he says. "They had no connection with this land." The mountain now named Newton is Lauwelnew. Mt. Douglas, prevailing over the southern reaches of Wsanec territories, is really Pkols, "white head." The spit jutting out from the town of Sidney is Set,tines, "chest sticking out." The Swartz Bay ferry terminal, where thousands of visitors daily disembark into traditional Wsanec lands, is S,jelkes, "hand sling."

In former times, their many villages extended beyond Saanich Inlet to the neighbouring Gulf Islands—Salt Spring, Pender, Mayne, Saturna—and the San Juan Islands. Gleaming white shell beaches back onto dark, rich cutbanks, then green open spaces: these are middens, suggesting there is probably not a single beach that was not a village or a campsite. The Wsanec peoples used the south

and eastern shores of Salt Spring Island; the Cowichan people (chapter 2) hunted and fished mostly along its north and west shores, almost touching their Vancouver Island territories across Sansum Narrows. Sometime before the middle of the last century, many Wsanec peoples left the islands, seeking safety from northern warriors, and gathered at Tsawout on Saanichton Bay.

Today, place names and a few unoccupied reserves remind us of their relationship to these islands. Mt. Tuam—forming southern Salt Spring Island—takes its name from cu-an, the mountains at "each end." On Saturna Island, tekteksen, "long nose," is the favoured stone and sand spit, East Point. S,ktak, "pass" or "narrows" is the Active Pass of B.C. Ferries' traffic, between Galiano and Mayne Island. Otter Bay on Pender Island is skaetem, "place of otters."

? Saanich Native Heritage Society: Box 28, Brentwood Bay, B.C., V0S 1A0. Tel: 652-5980. Established to protect and promote Wsanec heritage and culture.

V Wjolelp (Tsartlip): (Pop. 660/400). Just beyond Stelly's Cross Rd., Hwy 17A cuts through "place of maple leaves" overlooking Brentwood Bay. About two centuries ago the Jesesinset, "people that are growing themselves up," chose this as a safe haven from northern raiders.

Just south of their community is the J-shaped inlet, Snitcel, or Tod Inlet. In times past, "place of the blue grouse" was important to Wjolelp food harvesting and spirituality. The steep, sun-warmed slopes at the head of the inlet were nesting grounds for the blue grouse. Spring salmon spawned in the creeks here too; deer flourished. After the turn of the century, blasting at nearby quarries—including the one now occupied by Butchart Gardens—drove the grouse and deer from their idyllic habitat.

In 1994, the B.C. government incorporated Tod Inlet and some adjacent lands into the Commonwealth Nature Legacy—1,000 hectares of parkland along most of the east side of Saanich Inlet. Lands adjacent the park are being eyed by developers for a high-density subdivision, and the Tsartlip people are strongly opposed.

Another important Wsanec landmark is the Lauwelnew Tribal School, at 7449 West Saanich Rd., taking its name from their sacred mountain. The school, teaching nursery to grade eight, was built in 1989 on the site of its predecessor operated by Catholic sisters. The tribal school, run by the four Wsanec communities, emphasizes Wsanec language and culture. The pole in front depicts Thunderbird, Killer Whale, Raven, and Black Wolf of the Wsanec crest; the frog and wolf cubs are symbols of new life. Excellent books on Saanich culture are available here; 652-2313. See Further Reading.

Tsartlip Band Campsite, store, and boat ramp, at 800A Stelly's Cross Rd.; 642-4979.

? Tsartlip Administration: Box 70, Brentwood Bay, B.C., V0S 1A0. Tel: 652-3988.

V Tsawout: (Pop. 459/380). Two km north on Hwy 17A to Mt. Newton Cross Rd., then east to Hwy 17; or 15 km north of downtown Victoria. Billboards are a sign. Hwy 17 cuts through the busy west quarter of prime Tsawout land leased to hotels, restaurants, and mobile home parks. Half of the community's 1,500 residents are non-First Nations. In 1994 the Tsawout received authority to collect taxes from those who live within their boundaries.

Mt. Newton Cross Rd. cuts east, leading into the heart of Tsawout lands and the pleasant shores of Saanichton Bay. Here was the original approach to Tsawout, "houses raised up," one of three villages that have stood here in recent centuries. Traditional fishing and sealing grounds extended to Pender, Saturna, D'Arcy, Chatham, and Discovery islands. Nearby Bare Island is where Tsawout women kept the specially bred dogs that provided

wool for the blankets they wove (see "The Cowichan Sweater," chapter 2). **Little Saanich Mountain Store** at 2704 KOA Rd. has arts and crafts and groceries for sale.

? Tsawout Administration: Box 121, Saanichton, B.C., V0S 1M0. Tel: 652-9101.

I Lauwelnew: West off East Saanich Rd. onto Dean Park Rd. This gentle mountain, now known to many as Mt. Newton, is sacred to the Wsanec peoples as "place of refuge." The beautifully illustrated children's book *Lauwelnew*, available from the Saanich Indian School Board, describes how the people tied their canoes to an arbutus tree on top of this mountain during the flood. Later, during the time of frequent raids from the north, this was a place of refuge for women and children.

V Pauquachin: (Pop. 259/161). 3 km north of Wjolelp (Tsartlip) on West Saanich Rd. "Land of many slopes" or "earth bluff" takes in the long stretch of Coles Bay and faces directly across Saanich Inlet to the Malahat First Nation community. Many here trace their origins to there. No visitor services; please drive carefully along this stretch of highway.

? Pauquachin Administration: Box 517, Brentwood Bay, B.C., V0R 1K0. Tel: 656-0191.

V Tseycum: (Pop. 116/84). 3 km beyond Pauquachin on West Saanich Rd., overlooking Pat Bay. They brought their name "clay people" with them from their more ancient home on the peninsula's east side at Tsehum Harbour, too much in the path of northern warriors. Here, the people of Tseycum find themselves too much in the path of highway traffic. West Saanich Rd. slices through their burial grounds. No visitor services.

? Tseycum Administration: Box 2596, Sidney, B.C., V8L 4C1. Tel: 656-0858.

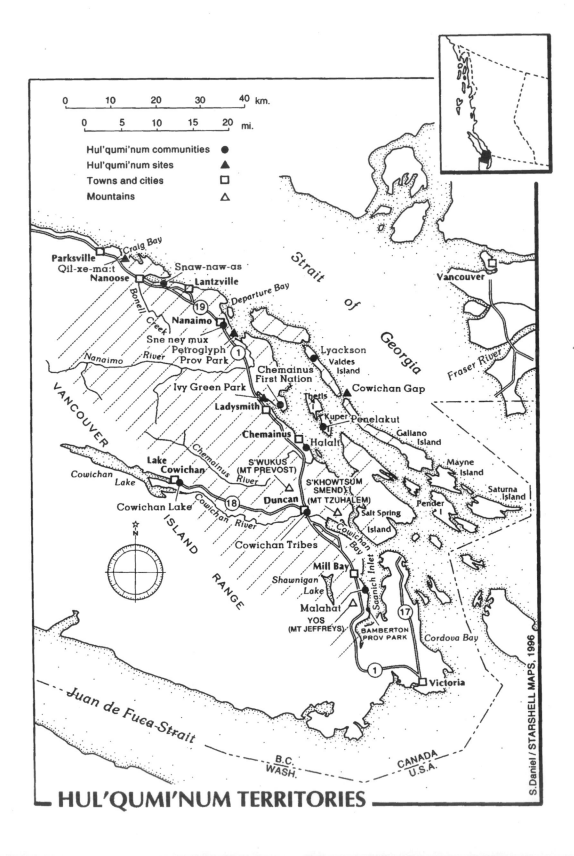

HUL'QUMI'NUM TERRITORIES

Legend

Hul'qumi'num communities ●
Hul'qumi'num sites ▲
Towns and cities □
Mountains △

Scale:
0 10 20 30 40 km.
0 5 10 15 20 mi.

Strait of Georgia

Parksville
Qil-xe-ma:t
Nanoose
Snaw-naw-as
Lantzville
Craig Bay
Departure Bay
Nanaimo
Sne ney mux
Petroglyph Prov Park
Bonell Creek
Nanaimo River
VANCOUVER
ISLAND
RANGE
Lyackson
Valdes Island
Chemainus First Nation
Ivy Green Park
Ladysmith
Chemainus
Halalt
Thetis
Kuper
Penelakut
Cowichan Gap
Galiano Island
Lake Cowichan
Cowichan Lake
Chemainus River
S'WUKUS (MT PREVOST)
S'KHOWTSUM SMEND (MT TZUHALEM)
Mayne Island
Saturna Island
Cowichan River
Duncan
Salt Spring Island
Pender I.
Cowichan Tribes
Cowichan Bay
Mill Bay
Shawnigan Lake
Saanich Inlet
Malahat
YOS (MT JEFFREYS)
BAMBERTON PROV PARK
Cordova Bay
Victoria
Vancouver
Fraser River
Juan de Fuca Strait
B.C. / WASH.
CANADA / U.S.A.

19
1
18
17

S.Daniel / STARSHELL MAPS, 1996

CHAPTER 2

Hul'qumi'num

Names are very important to our people. When relatives hear your name, they know where you are from.
—Abner Thorne, elder, Cowichan Tribes

*H*ul'qumi'num, in the language spoken here, refers to "those who speak the same language." The Malahat people, the Cowichan Tribes, the Chemainus, Halalt, Penelakut and Lyackson peoples, the Sne ney mux (Nanaimo) and Snaw-naw-as (Nanoose) First Nations can be divided up into many peoples, but they also see themselves as one.

Theirs are the sheltered bays of Vancouver Island's southeast coast, basking in the rainshadow of the Vancouver Island Mountains. Here are balmy lowlands, fed by gentle rivers named by newcomers for the people who have always lived here. The Cowichan, Chemainus, and Nanaimo are relatively shallow rivers, narrow, and not too fast. Fish weirs once stretched bank to bank, and women came at night to pull out coho, spring, and chum salmon. Between river mouths, pebbled beaches were gathering places for fat and succulent clams. On the sun-drenched Gulf Islands just offshore, there were more shellfish, deer, and camas bulbs for sweet-tasting starch. Gigantic Steller's sea lions entered the warm inter-island channels through the Cowichan Gap between Galiano and Valdes islands. Hunting them was the specialty of the Chemainus peoples.

Each Hul'qumi'num village existed unto itself, but was also connected to the others in an intricate web of multi-citizenship. These family ties gave more people access to a wider range of resources. So far-reaching was its span, it crossed the Strait of Georgia and embraced the Fraser River all the way to Hope. In a sense, this was the eastern flank of one great country, for here also were "those who speak the same language," or a dialect of it, called Halq'emeylem. The gentle rivers of the island Hul'qumi'num were too shallow for the sockeye salmon that swarmed into the Fraser's wide embrace. And so it was that until early in this century, whole villages canoed across the choppy straits to join parents, sisters, cousins there. They wove themselves into villages, or formed their own along the Fraser's lower reaches for two months of the year or more, picking blueberries, cutting the bulrushes used for making mats. And at the height of the

This salmon weir spanned the Cowichan River in the late 1860s. Fish crowded into the enclosures, to the right, and were scooped or speared.

CREDIT: RBCM 1380

season, these Vancouver Islanders stood among thousands on ancient, family-owned fishing sites, dip-netting for sockeye.

This was also the time for "great deeds," what we now loosely call the potlatch. Hereditary *siem*, "respected leaders," made long speeches documenting their ties to the land and their relatives, reaching back to the flood and before, to the first man who fell "fully formed from the heavens." A feast and goat-hair blankets were payment to those who witnessed this testimony, and simply another expression of sharing.

Homebound in the fall, island canoes linked by planks became salmon barges. Mainlanders were also known to make the crossing over to island beaches, filling their holds with dried clams, joining in "great deeds" there, and in winter ceremonies. Longhouses echoed with the songs of dancers infused with the power of animal and other guardian spirits—wind, thunder, sun—who helped them on their yearly rounds.

Crossings were disrupted, but not interrupted by the Lekwiltok warriors from the northeast coast of Vancouver Island. In the early 1800s they churned the straits from Comox to Puget Sound, and up the Fraser River too. In these dangerous times the island Hul'qumi'num took precautions—travelling in flotillas. They would gather at Lyackson on Valdes Island near the Cowichan Gap, until the canoes of the powerful Cowichan chief, Th'ossieten, joined them. After the new fur-trade post, Fort Langley, was established on the Fraser in 1822, Th'ossieten and other islanders were noted among the traders there.

Strength in numbers was an important feature of the island-mainland bond. In the 1850s, warriors from both sides of the straits, led by Th'ossieten, lay in wait at Maple Bay, just above Cowichan Bay, for the Lekwiltok headed north from Puget Sound. In an epic battle, the Lekwiltok's rule of these seas came to an end.

What finally thwarted their crossings was a new web stretched over the old—smallpox, the gold rush, settlement, the proliferation of commercial salmon canneries, and the *Indian Act* with its suffocating policies determining the location and membership of communities, limiting each individual's citizenship to one self-contained band.

But the Hul'qumi'num web—invisible to

those who live outside it—is as resilient as it is old. Says Abner Thorne, descendant of Chief Th'ossieten, "My Indian name, Tsetkumpen, comes from Cordova Bay. My brother's name comes from the Qwontl'en at Fort Langley on the mainland. My grandmother was from Katzie, down from there on the Fraser. My dad's name is from Komiakin, on Cowichan Bay." The membership of today's island Hul'qumi'num communities in three tribal councils reflects, if anything, a strengthening of relationships throughout southeastern Vancouver Island and the Lower Mainland. And at the display of "great deeds," hosts still address them all: *Huychqu siem na sieya ya,* "Thank you, friend-family."

HIGHLIGHTS AND EVENTS

INFORMATION AND PROTOCOL

Traditionally, hereditary *siem* owned and managed resource sites, and were considered "keepers of the culture." Says Anita Page, of Cowichan, who created the Duncan Heritage Centre's exhibit on hereditary chiefs: "They were our strength, they had a lot of respect." She has been inspired by her great-great-grandfather, Tsahilton, and may be a *siem* herself one day. Today's leadership is elected, though many are descendants of hereditary leaders.

The two main dialects of the Hul'qumi'num language spoken here are Cowichan and Nanaimo.

The "frontier" villages—the Malahat people to the south and Cowichan Lake to the northwest—share ties with their Hul'qumi'num-speaking neighbours and also with adja-

cent speakers of the Wsanec, Ditidaht, and Kwakwala languages.

Appropriate venues for exploration are listed below.

❓ **Mid-Island Tribal Council:** Box 720, Chemainus, B.C., V0R 1K0. Tel: 246-2665. Fax: 246-2347. Members: Chemainus, Lyackson, Penelakut.

❓ **Alliance Tribal Council:** 130 N. Tsawwassen Dr., Delta, B.C., V4K 3N2. Tel: 943-6712. Fax: 943-5367. Lower Mainland and Vancouver Island members include Halalt, Nanaimo, and Chemainus.

❓ **First Nations of South Island Tribal Council:** 2677 Mt. Newton Cross Rd., Saanichton, B.C., V0S 1M0. Tel: 652-2032. Fax: 544-2325. Members include Malahat and Cowichan Lake.

North from Victoria on Highway 1

▌ **Goldstream River:** 20 km north of downtown Victoria on Hwy 1, in **Goldstream Provincial Park**. Now, as long ago, its banks draw throngs of people coming to celebrate the journey of spawning chum salmon. Eagles and seagulls also come to feast. Malahat and Wsanec families together formed a village here in the fall; they also planted potatoes and grew fruit trees where the nature house sits now.

▌ **Yos:** Just past Goldstream Park, the four-lane Trans-Canada Highway begins its ascent of the mountain we know today as the Malahat. To the Malahat people, this is "caution," their Mount Sinai. Creeks cascading into the Saanich Inlet formed sacred bathing pools; caves were used for spiritual enhancement. There are also stories here of large people-like beings called *zamekwes,* who could not bend their knees. In spite of the highway, the Malahat people consider this the last intact sacred site on Vancouver Island south of Nanaimo, and wish to spare it from further development. It is 15 km to the summit and sweeping views of Saanich Inlet and Salt Spring Island.

I   Bamberton: 36 km north of Victoria. In 1912, a delegation of Malahat people addressed a Royal Commission in London, England, in their effort to keep the Bamberton Cement plant from gouging out the base of their sacred mountain, Yos. The community today is at the forefront among opponents of a new scheme to turn this 630-hectare former industrial site into a town of 12,000 people.

V   Malahat First Nation: (Pop. 215/88). 37 km north of Victoria, right onto Mill Bay Rd. (at Bamberton Provincial Park exit), 2.5 km to community overlooking Saanich Inlet. The people here share strong traditional ties with the Wsanec peoples across the water. The name Malahat actually refers to the vicinity of the Mill Bay ferry dock at the south end of their reserve, and is derived from a word describing a previous infestation of caterpillars here.

?   Malahat Administration: Box 111, Mill Bay, B.C., V0R 2P0. Tel: 743-3231.

To Tlul Palus (Cowichan Bay): On Cowichan Bay Road

I   Tlul Palus (Cowichan Bay): 45.5 km north of Victoria turn right off Hwy 1 onto Cowichan Bay Rd. Look out from the government dock to Tlul Palus, "deep sea." Just offshore, Deaf Rock is a reminder that the Transformers, Xals or Xexa:ls, once came and went across these straits, turning people on both sides of the straits into salmon or rocks, teaching them to share. To the north, Sansum Narrows separates Vancouver Island from Salt Spring Island. The Gulf Islands form a continuous chain all the way to Nanaimo. The narrows widen to form the channels that were once the island freeways. On this side of the narrows is Separation (or Octopus) Point,

where the supernatural Shuh-shu-cum, "open mouth," lay waiting to swallow travellers, canoe and all. He was finally subdued, but is said still to be responsible for churning up the waters and creating dangerous whirlpools and eddies.

Rising up from the north side of Cowichan Bay are the cliffs of Mt. Tzuhalem, or, as the people here know it, S'khowtzun Smend, "warmed by the sun." Travellers approaching by canoe saw it resembled a man, or some say a frog, basking in the sun. From this came the name Khowtzun (Cowichan), for the land and its people, sheltered from wind and storms. The name Tzuhalem, as the mountain is commonly known today, was that of a real man, with a troubled spirit, who lived for some time with his many wives in a longhouse at the foot of S'khowtzun Smend.

Flowing into the estuary at the head of the bay is the Cowichan River: focal point for most of the 13 Cowichan Tribes that once lived along the bay and the length of the river to Cowichan Lake. Tzouhalem Rd. leads north from here through two reserves, where two of these tribes were centred.

I   The Butter Church: About 1 km beyond the intersection of Cowichan Bay and Tzouhalem roads, on Comiaken hilltop overlooking the bay. St. Ann's Catholic Church, built in 1868, is the butter church because butter sold by the congregation of five Cowichan tribes and their priest paid for the masonry work. It is also known as the stone church for its half-metre-thick stone walls.

To Cowichan Heartland: North from Cowichan Bay on Highway 1

V   Cowichan Tribes: (Pop. 2,500). Just south of Duncan (pop. 4,055/55 Ab) billboards mark the route into Cowichan headquarters on lands straddled by the Silver Bridge. The Cowichan people are, as they always have been, concentrated along the

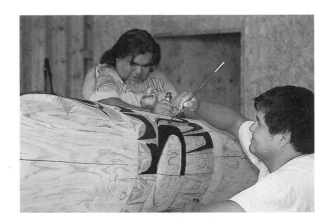

Carvers at the Native Heritage Centre in Duncan invite visitors to watch them work, and may ask them to try their own hand on the "tourist pole."
CREDIT: NATIVE HERITAGE CENTRE

banks of the river that bears their name. Here arc many of the descendants of those who, just over a century ago, occupied 13 villages from the "deep sea" of Cowichan Bay to Kaatze at Cowichan Lake. A few families remain at old sites, Theik and Kilpaulas on the south banks of Cowichan Bay, and at Skutz, Kakalotza, and Tzartlan, upriver. The **Native Heritage Centre**, on the riverbank between two Cowichan residential areas, is the best place to stop and get one's bearings. To the east is the mountain that gives them their name: "warmed by the sun." To the north is S'wukus, also known these days at Mt. Prevost, where the first Cowichan people dropped fully formed from the heavens. The story of the Cowichan Tribes, from these beginnings, to when glaciers became mountain goats, to the flood, the arrival of Europeans, and the present, is part of the Native Heritage Centre's excellent presentation.

The southern quarter of Duncan, calling itself "the city of totems," sits on the reserve, on land leased from the Cowichan Tribes. The city acknowledges those who came first with poles situated throughout the downtown core and along the route of Hwy 1.

? **Cowichan Tribes Administration:** 5760 Allenby Rd., Duncan, B.C., V9L 5J1. Tel: 748-3196.

⑥ **Native Heritage Centre:** 200 Cowichan Way; turn left immediately after the Silver Bridge. Tel: 746-8119. This heritage centre is as much a reflection of who the Cowichan people are today as who they were. Their communities are next door; the footpath along the river's edge is a thoroughfare for Cowichan people going about their daily business; they fish just downriver when the salmon are running. Young artists apprentice in the carving shed; elders pass on traditional teachings. The Big House is a venue for important meetings, Cowichan weddings, and other private and public functions.

During the summer's **Feasts and Legends** program, the *siem* shares with visitors oral histories, the First Salmon Ceremony, and after a feast of salmon, clams, and venison, even the Talking Stick, with any moved to speak. The **Khowutzun Tzinqwaw (Thunder God) Dancers** inspire guests to join them. There are tours, midday salmon barbecues, audiovisual presentations, exhibits, the largest native arts and crafts shop on Vancouver Island, an excellent selection of First Nations books, the **Riverside Cafe**. And the river, flowing by, takes your troubles away.

⑥ **Poles:** At the Native Heritage Centre, in downtown Duncan, and along Hwy 1 are about 70 of over 300 poles in the Cowichan Valley area. They represent a carving renaissance that began in the 1970s and culminated in an international carvers exchange that brought Maori craftsman Tupari Te Whata to Cowichan territories in 1986. His *Te Awhio Whio,* "King of the Cedar Forest," stands next to city hall. Many carvings, such as the *Rick Hansen Man-in-Motion* pole, reflect the evolving nature of this ancient Coast Salish art form. The most contemporary piece is the giant mural on the Superstore opposite the Heritage Centre. For free tours, from the May long weekend to September, call 748-2133, or ask at the Travel Infocentre on Hwy 1 in Duncan. Guidebooks are also available.

🐚 **The Cowichan Sweater:** These sweaters are decendants of the goat-hair blanket, woven from tufts of hair picked off bushes on the mountainsides. Some women also bred small pomeranian-like dogs, shearing their thick, white coats in spring. These precious fibres were woven into currency—"five blankets, a deerskin shirt and a fathom of [dentalium] shells" once bought an ocean-going canoe. In the 1860s, through contact with Scottish settlers, Cowichan women began to knit as well as weave and took advantage of newly introduced sheep's wool. They made sweaters—no two families' designs alike—adorned with eagles, thunderbirds, and whales, in natural whites, greys, and browns.

Cowichan sweaters are made from raw wool hand spun on a treadle spinner.
CREDIT: TOM KERR

Gifts for queens and prime ministers, practical, water-resistant outerwear for fishermen and loggers, they became, at times, a local economic mainstay. Today, there are 2,000 knitters on Vancouver Island and the Lower Mainland. Cowichan sweaters average about $200 in price, no reflection of the time, skill, and quality of materials that go into them. There are machine-knitted imitations: for an authentic Cowichan sweater, look for seams at the shoulders only, natural colours, or a tag bearing the knitter's name.

🐚 **Arts and Crafts:** Arts of the Swaqwun Gallery, 80 Trunk Rd., Duncan; Modeste Indian Sweaters and Crafts Ltd, 2615 Modeste Rd., Duncan; Native Heritage Centre, described above, at 200 Cowichan Way.

🐚 **Annual Art Show and Sale:** Remembrance Day Weekend, early November, is when more than a dozen leading B.C. native artists exhibit their paintings, jewellery, carvings, sculpture, weaving, and clothing at the Native Heritage Centre (above). Admission to show and centre is free on this weekend.

🐚 **Freshwater Eco-centre:** 1080 Wharncliffe Rd. East off Hwy 1 onto Trunk Rd., then follow signs. Tel: 746-6722. The adjacent Vancouver Island Trout Hatchery, on the banks of the Cowichan River, stocks 150 lakes and streams. Here are interactive exhibits on fisheries and traditional fishing equipment used by the Cowichan people, a theatre, and an aquarium of local fish species.

J **Highway 18:** 5 km north of Duncan. Leads west through the heartland of the Cowichan Tribes to Cowichan Lake, the eastern frontier of the Nuu-chah-nulth peoples.

I **S'wukus:** 1.5 km west of Hwy 1, north onto Somenos Rd., then 1 km to Mt. Prevost Rd. About 8 km on rough road to parking lot below the 786-m summit of S'wukus with its sweeping views of the Cowichan and Chemainus valleys. One version of the story describes how the first man, Seahlatsa, dropped from the sky to this peak, and then, with his brother and the One-horned Dog, S'wukus, founded the first Cowichan villages. After the flood, this mountain was again the starting point for the Cowichan Tribes, as its sole survivor took refuge here. This is Mt. Prevost on today's maps.

V Cowichan Lake First Nation: (Pop. 12/10). 28 km west of Duncan, via Hwy 18, at east end of Cowichan Lake. Now a predominantly Ditidaht community (see chapter 3). There are no visitor services.

? Cowichan Lake Administration: Box 1376, Lake Cowichan, B.C., V0R 2G7. Tel: 745-3548.

North of Highway 18 on Highway 1

V Halalt: (Pop. 181/110). 12 km north of Duncan, right onto Hwy 1A (Mt. Sicker Rd.), then left onto Old Chemainus Rd. The original village was on nearby Willy's Island. Today Halalt, "painted designs," sits along the banks of the Chemainus River, and its tributary, the Bonell. The people here are working with neighbouring townsfolk at **Chemainus** to revitalize their coho, chum, and chinook fisheries. A century of cooperation between the two communities is commemorated in one of the 32 murals that makes Chemainus a stopping place for international travellers. Among those featured on the **Native Heritage Mural** in Heritage Square is Mary Rice, great-grandmother of today's Halalt chief, Joe Norris. Also portrayed here is Ce-who-latza, former chief of Lyackson, on Valdes Island; Clay-sa-luke was Chemainus chief.

Halalt has no visitor services at this time, but a salmon hatchery and nature trails are planned. In Chemainus, **Sa-Cinn Native Enterprises** is at 9756 Willows St.

? Halalt Administration: RR 1, 8017 Chemainus Rd., Chemainus, B.C., V0R 1K0. Tel: 246-4736.

V Penelakut: (Pop. 650/400). "Two logs buried in the sand" is a quiet, private community on the south shores of Kuper Island, reached by ferry from Chemainus. It sits just southwest of the Cowichan Gap, between Valdes and Galiano islands, a rare opening in the long wall of Gulf Islands facing out to the Strait of Georgia. Here, the Penelakut, along with their Lyackson and Chemainus neighbours, were the only Hul'qumi'num to hunt the massive Steller's sea lions that entered the quieter, shallower inside channels here in the spring. The Penelakut, like Nuu-chah-nulth whale hunters to the north, built around their hunt a sophisticated marine technology and spiritual practices that included meditation, fasting, and ritual bathing. Certain individuals developed the ability to call the sea lions in and to calm them after the harpoon had struck.

A Roman Catholic residential school established here in 1890 was known by "inmates" from up and down Vancouver Island as Alcatraz. Some children died trying to escape home to families. The school was torn down in 1975, and a new adult learning centre now occupies its site, offering Hul'qumi'num language and cultural programs.

There are no visitor services: kayakers and boaters who wish to camp on reserve land at adjacent Tent Island are requested to contact the Penelakut administration office first. Fires are not permitted.

? Penelakut Administration: Box 360, Chemainus, B.C., V0R 1K0. Tel: 246-2321.

V Lyackson: (Pop. 165/10). North of Kuper Island, on Valdes Island. No public access, wharfs, or dock facilities. Forming the north side of the Cowichan Gap, the community's name is "hole in the wall," for a somewhat smaller gap in a rock bluff on the island's west side—and a safe landing place. The Lyackson, like the Penelakut, were sea-lion hunters. They share with them many stories, as well as an ancient hunting rivalry. One story tells how the Lyackson carved a mock sea lion from arbutus wood and set it on a rock, to fool the Penelakut. The Penelakut harpooned it, and were swept away on a long journey. They escaped dwarfs and giants and finally were led home by three killer whales.

Kayakers wishing to camp on Lyackson reserve land are asked to contact the administration office.

? Lyackson Administration: 9137 Chemainus Rd., Chemainus B.C., V0R 1K0. Tel: 746-0780.

V Chemainus First Nation: (Pop. 817/636). About 12 km north of Chemainus. Their traditional territories embrace Ladysmith Harbour, with the largest of three population centres today being situated on the forested point of land across the harbour from the town of **Ladysmith** (pop. 4,865/50 Ab), adjacent to Yellow Point. At the head of the harbour, 3 km north of Ladysmith, is the Chemainus First Nation–run **Ivy Green Park and Campground**. Visitors are welcome here, to camp or enjoy the day-use area, swim in Ladysmith Harbour's warm waters, and walk among first-growth Douglas firs. This park is made up of a portion of reserve taken away by the government earlier in the century and then returned in 1984, after a claim was launched. Gas bar, convenience store.

? Chemainus Administration: RR 1, Silverstrand Rd., Ladysmith, B.C., V0R 2E0. Tel: 245-7155.

█ Petroglyph Provincial Park: 20 km north of Ladysmith, approaching Nanaimo, within the traditional territories of the Sne ney mux, or Nanaimo First Nation. Here, an arm of the Nanaimo River reaches the sea, and human-

like, birdlike, wolflike, and lizardlike beings, sea monsters, and other supernatural creatures are carved into sandstone rock. An account that suggests they were created at the "beginnings of time" also suggests the artist is here too, turned to stone, perhaps by the Transformers, Xexa:ls. There are many other such petroglyphs in the area, especially along the Nanaimo River, but the park here provides an easily accessible and appropriate venue for appreciating ancient writings often destroyed by vandalism or development.

V Sne ney mux (Nanaimo First Nation): (Pop. 1,000/446). At south entrance to Nanaimo. Six villages once thrived along the river, harbour, and bays where the city of **Nanaimo** (pop. 59,615/950) now sprawls. The people have been here so long the elders say there is no known translation for their name, Sne ney mux, which we pronounce Nanaimo. The largest village was at Departure Bay near the B.C. Ferries terminal where thousands of cars embark and disembark daily coming to and from the mainland. Passengers entering the bay can see just where the ancient Nanaimo capital was, at the south end of the bay, now suburban housing and a children's park. The other villages were at Nanaimo Harbour, now buzzing with float planes, lined with walkways and hotels. Still here is the Hudson's Bay Company Bastion; its cannons protected the interests of the first new residents. There were Sne ney mux villages along the Nanaimo River at its mouth, where the pulp mill is, and there was one on Gabriola Island overlooking what is now known as False Narrows. The origins of today's Nanaimo began in 1850. A Sne ney mux man canoed south to Fort Victoria to present Hudson's Bay Company traders with the black rock he knew they valued. They followed him to rich coal seams around Departure Bay and on adjacent Newcastle Island. To secure perpetual access to the high-quality fuel, the company created the Douglas Treaty of 1854.

By the 1860s, Nanaimo, with a white population of about 700, was among the largest non-native settlements in the new British colony. The Hudson's Bay Company depended upon the Sne ney mux and their neighbours from Chemainus and across the straits at Sechelt to mine the coal, transport it to ships in the harbour, and provide the new industrial hub with food. Wages early on were one blanket for eight barrels of coal. Eventually Scottish miners were imported to work underground; horses were brought in to haul, and a wharf was constructed so ships could be loaded directly, without trans-shipment by canoe. By 1872, wages were $1 a day for First Nations and Chinese workers, and $4 each day for whites. Still, the Sney ney mux continued to work in the industry through to the early 1900s.

By the mid-1900s, the coal-mining era was over, but the city of Nanaimo continued to expand over the traditional lands—the fishing and hunting grounds—of the Sney ney mux people. Also, contrary to the text of the Douglas Treaty, village sites were occupied. Harbour Park shopping mall occupies one of these: it wasn't until the 1990s that maps found buried in the Hudson's Bay Company's Winnipeg archives brought back into the public eye century-old Sney ney mux claims to what is now expensive real estate in the heart of downtown Nanaimo.

Today, most of the Sney ney mux First Nation lives just south of the city centre and in three smaller communities along the Nanaimo River. They are a large community with a small land base, and are now focussed on the current treaty negotiation process.

❓ Nanaimo First Nation Administration: 1145 Totem Rd., Nanaimo, B.C., V9R 1H1. Tel: 753-3481.

Ⓖ Nanaimo Centennial Museum: 100 Cameron St. A major exhibit of the history of the Sne ney mux people. In front of the muse-

um is a petroglyph displaying carved figures of salmon. It sat originally at Jack Point by the Nanaimo River, and was part of rituals designed to bring chum salmon when runs were small or late.

▼ Snaw-naw-as (Nanoose First Nation): (Pop. 177/82). 17.5 km north of Nanaimo on Hwy 19, watch for billboards. Turn right onto Capilano Rd. Today, the main village of the Nanoose or Snaw-naw-as people is at the entrance to the warm, shallow harbour that bears their name. Snaw-naw-as, however, means "way in the harbour," at the head of the bay, where they lived in former times. Creeks flowing there provided them with chum, coho, and steelhead salmon. In summer, they crossed the straits, joining their X'muzk'i'um (Musqueam) relatives for the sockeye salmon season. Development of their balmy shores has diminished these creeks in recent decades, and has also threatened the 4,000-year-old site of the former village, Qil-xe'ma:t, just north of here at Craig Bay. In 1994, elders tried to stop a major townhouse development after the bones of 400 ancestors were unearthed during construction. Their case is now before the Supreme Court of Canada.

On the harbour: **Snaw-naw-as Campsite**, 390-3661; and marina and cafe, 390-2616.

❓ Nanoose First Nation Administration: Box 124, Nanoose Reserve, Lantzville, B.C., V0R 2H0. Tel: 390-3661.

Ⓙ Highway 4: 29 km north of Nanaimo. This is the contemporary overland route from Hul'qumi'num to Nuu-chah-nulth territories. The original route was via the Horne Lake trail (see chapter 4, Qualicum First Nation). For the route north into former Pentlatch and Kwakwaka'wakw territories, continue on Hwy 19 (see chapter 4). In Parksville, **Helin Fine Arts**, 468 West Island Highway, displays jewellery and paintings of Tsimshian artist Bill Helin.

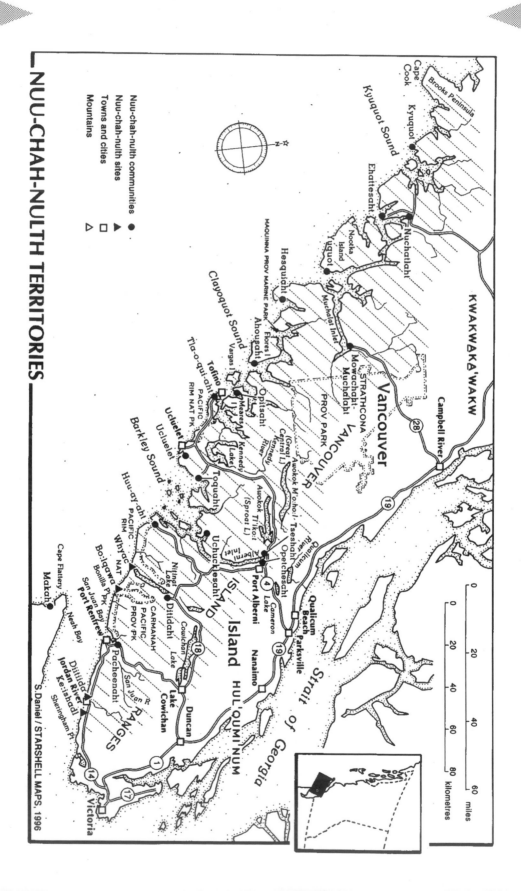

NUU-CHAH-NULTH TERRITORIES

Legend:
- ● Nuu-chah-nulth communities
- ▶ Nuu-chah-nulth sites
- □ Towns and cities
- △ Mountains

KWAKWA̱KA̱'WAKW

Vancouver

Island

ISLAND

HUL'QUMI'NUM

Strait of Georgia

Brooks Peninsula

Cape Cook

Kyuquot Sound

Kyuquot

Ehattesacht

Nuchatlaht

Nootka Island

Yuquot

Muchalat Inlet

Campbell River

28

STRATHCONA PROV. PARK

Mowachaht-Muchalaht

Hesquiaht

Ahousaht

Flores I.

Vargas

Clayoquot Sound

MAQUINNA PROV. MARINE PARK

Opitsaht

Meares I.

Kennedy River

Kennedy Lake

(Great Central L.)

Auokok Mo:ho:i.

(Sproat L.)

STRATHCONA PROV. PARK

Quolicum River

Tseshaht

Qualicum Beach

Parksville

19

Tofino

Tla-o-qui-aht

PACIFIC RIM NAT. PK.

Ucluelet

Toquaht

Barkley Sound

Uchucklesaht

Alberni Inlet

Opetchesaht

Cameron Lake

4

Port Alberni

Nanaimo

Huu-ay-aht

PACIFIC RIM NAT. PK.

Whyac

Bo:iqawa

Bonilla P'k

San Juan Bay

Port Renfrew

Ditidaht

Nitinat Lake

CARMANAH PACIFIC PROV. PK.

Cowichan Lake

San Juan R.

18

Lake Cowichan

Duncan

Cape Flattery

Makah

Neah Bay

Pacheenaht

Ditidaht

Jordan River

Ke:ishadl

Sheringham Pt.

RANGES

1

14

17

Victoria

0 — 20 — 40 — 60 — 80 kilometres
0 — 20 — 40 — 60 miles

S. Daniel / STARSHELL MAPS, 1996

CHAPTER 3

Nuu-chah-nulth, Pacheenaht, and Makah

Tourism gives value to what a lot of us know best— the culture of our area, the geography of our area, the botany of our area. Everything we know, the things we were taught, happens to be what everyone else wants to know.

—Katherine Robinson, Nuu-chah-nulth Tribal Council

Nuu-chah-nulth, in the language spoken here, means "all along the mountains." This is the name for the contemporary alliance of fourteen tribes that share the west coast of Vancouver Island from Sheringham Point to Brooks Peninsula. Behind them, to the east, the mountain spine of Vancouver Island is impermeable and constant compared to what lies before them—the tides and weather of the open Pacific.

The Nuu-chah-nulth tribes each have their own well-defined territories and resources. Yet, on our maps, they appear either as small communities—dots tracing a fragmented coast—or not at all. Some sit at the head of long inlets; others are on islands, isthmuses, peninsulas. Many are reached only by boat or plane. But despite their existence at the edge of a continent, Nuu-chah-nulth histories bustle with visitors.

"There was a Beachkeeper, responsible on behalf of the chiefs for welcoming visitors," explains chief Francis Frank, Tla-o-qui-aht First Nation. "He would patrol the shores,

watching to see who was coming." Maybe it was Quauutz, the Creator, returning, in the form of a great copper canoe. Or Ankoak, "snot boy," born on these shores from the tears and mucous of the very first woman. Ankoak and Kwatyet, the Transformer who travelled through Nuu-chah-nulth territories in the earliest times, were responsible for much that seems familiar now: the specific features of the land, the transformation of the *kyaimimit*— Raven, Deer, and others possessing human qualities—into the "real people" of the complex society that came to be.

Other visitors included Thunderbird, who announced his presence with a thunderous clapping of wings. He was often accompanied by the fire-spitting serpent Hiyitliik. Whales and seals travelled great distances from their own worlds, where they lived in houses and took human form. *Ma'ak,* grey whale, travelled the coast from Mexico to the Bering Sea and back again every year. After a storm, the Beachkeeper might have the fortune to find one on his beach.

Looking out from the edge of a continent, the people of Nuu-chah-nulth villages expect visitors. Here at Ahousaht, guests are welcome to "Walk the Wild Side," on cultural tours to long, sandy beaches and rainforests.
CREDIT: DOROTHY HAEGERT

With a highly sophisticated marine technology, the Nuu-chah-nulth, Pacheenaht, and their Makah cousins on the Olympic Peninsula were the only people on the northwest coast to hunt whales in the open sea. Preparations for the whales' arrival were woven into every aspect of daily life. For the hunters, who were chiefs, there was *osemitch*—meditation, prayer, fasting, abstinence, swimming in icy seas, ritual diving to underwater caves—spiritual and practical training for those who would face many dangers. Two or three whales in any year brought thousands of litres of rich oil, prestige, and many guests at potlatches.

Like the whales, human visitors were either invited to Nuu-chah-nulth territories or drifted in on the tides. Buddhists from China and other fair-skinned races were probably absorbed into hundreds and thousands of generations. It has been only eight generations since *mamalthi*, "people who live on a ship," emerged through the fog.

A storm kept the Spanish from landing on Hesquiaht shores in 1774. Four years later, the Mowachaht found the British Captain Cook drifting too close to a reef and guided him into their harbour at Yuquot. Cook was greeted by hails of "*nootka*": the Mowachaht were counselling him to "circle round" the rocks. He mistook *nootka* as their name and gave it also to other Nuu-chah-nulth peoples. A far more profound misunderstanding led him to claim for his king the sovereign territories of some thirty hereditary chiefs. Even more absurd were the Spanish claims made on the basis of having passed within sight of this country. At Yuquot, the two European nations signed the famous Nootka Convention, averting a world war over the misty isle. The Spanish withdrew, and the flag was planted for a future *British* Columbia.

Meanwhile, Chief Maquinna of the Mowachaht found his friendly cove full of European vessels clamouring to buy his sea-otter pelts. What did he know of the European agreement? He continued to insist upon, and receive, payment for wood, water, even grass. Visitors ignoring his jurisdiction were dealt with according to the law of the land. Every once in a while, somewhere on the coast, a ship was sunk.

But visitors and Nuu-chah-nulth alike were swept up in a lust for resources so insatiable that by the early 1800s, the sea otters were nearly extinct. A century later, the fur seals followed, then the whales, thousands upon thousands taken by gigantic commercial ships. The ancient whale hunters, too, looked out over the same dark precipice, as the complex forces of colonialism pushed from behind. Nations disappeared. In 1904, salvage anthropologists made their way to a strangely quiet Yuquot and managed to remove each and every piece of a sacred whaler's shrine. It is so large and complex, the American Museum of Natural History in New York, now possessing it, has never put it on display.

Since the 1980s, the west-coast nations united under the Nuu-chah-nulth tribal council banner, and the Pacheenaht independently, have been striving for more control over, and protection of, what's left—of their salmon fisheries, their forests, their culture. Now that the grey whales are returning, they want the right to hunt again, for food and ceremony, for who they are. And the Mowachaht are negotiating for a return of their whaler's shrine, with the dream of building their own cultural centre around it.

HIGHLIGHTS AND EVENTS

✆ Tofino	p. 49
✆ Meares Island Tours	p. 49
✆ Hot Springs Adventures	p. 50
✆ Yuquot National Historic Site	p. 51

INFORMATION AND PROTOCOL

Each one of today's Nuu-chah-nulth communities represents a people, reflected in the suffix *aht* or "people"—as in Mowachaht, "people of the deer," or Ahousaht, "people facing away from the ocean." These form the core of what were in former times many villages. Each has its own territory—extending inland as far as

salmon go up the streams, as far up the mountains as the people go for cedar; and out to sea, as far as it is possible to go and still be able to see those mountains. Responsibility lies with the *Howiih*, leaders from birth, who work in consultation with elders, speakers, historians. Their proprietary right to lands and resources —their economic privilege—is referred to as *hahuulhi*.

The peoples from Cape Cook south to Pachena Point speak the "Westcoast" language. The language of the Ditidaht and Pacheenaht peoples is unintelligible to Westcoast speakers, but is closely related to that of their Makah relatives on Washington's Olympic Peninsula.

The Pacheenaht and Makah are not members of the Nuu-chah-nulth alliance at this time.

Appropriate venues for exploration are given below. Please respect the privacy of communities.

❓ **The Nuu-chah-nulth Business Association:** 300 Main St., Box 453, Tofino, B.C., V0R 2Z0. Tel: 1-800-665-9425, or 725-2888. For information and bookings see Tofino, below.

❓ **Nuu-chah-nulth Tribal Council:** Box 1384, Port Alberni, B.C., V9Y 7M2. Tel: 724-5757. Fax: 723-0463. A negotiation and administrative body of elected and hereditary chiefs-in-council.

Southern Gateway to Pacheenaht and Ditidaht Territories: Highway 14

Sheringham Point, about 65 km northwest of Victoria, marks the boundary between those who occupy the protected leeward shores of Coast Salish territories, and the Pacheenaht, "people of the sea foam." Pacheenaht territory extends north to Bo:lqawa, "tide comes right up against the rocks," at Bonilla Point, well beyond the end of the highway, and part way along the West Coast Trail. From here the West

Coast Trail extends into Ditidaht and finally Huu-ay-aht (Ohiaht) territories. The Quu'as West Coast Trail Group—wardens from each of the three tribes—manages the trail, and ancient village, fishing, and whaling sites.

▮ Diitiida: At Jordan River, 57 km from Hwy 1A/14 junction (Colwood Corners). After the flood, the Ditidaht settled here. Most now live at Balaats'adt (see below).

▼ Pacheenaht: (Pop. 205/75). 2 km beyond **Port Renfrew**, on the San Juan River. Here, where the straits first open up to Pacific swells, are the "people of the sea foam." A hundred years ago, they were the first coast guard along an area so treacherous it was dubbed "graveyard of the Pacific" by European sea captains. Many a shipwreck survivor was plucked from the icy swells, and delivered to safety in their seaworthy canoes.

The Pacheenaht today see their future in non-traditional aspects of forestry—silviculture, cedar salvage—and in tourism. The **Pacheenaht Campground**, overlooking 2 km of surf and sand, offers showers and towels to hikers stepping off the West Coast Trail. Bus service links hikers to the north and south end of the trail; there is also a ferry across the Gordon River to the trailhead.

❓ Pacheenaht Administration: Port Renfrew, B.C., V0S 1K0. Tel: 647-5521.

To Ditidaht Village and Carmanah Provincial Park via Logging Roads

❑ Deering Rd: 97 km west of Hwy 1A/14 junction. Turn north off Hwy 14. It is 54.5 km to the village of Lake Cowichan. From here, go past Gordon Bay Provincial Park to Nitinat Main Rd. Take Nitinat Main to Junction South, then turn left onto South Main leading to the Ditidaht village.

▼ Ditidaht: (Pop. 472/184). At **Balaats'adt,** on the northeast shore of Nitinat Lake, above the mouth of the Caycuse River, 70 km west of Lake Cowichan.

The Ditidaht are an amalgamation of formerly autonomous groups. Some trace their origins to Nitinat Lake; some to the Olympic Peninsula across Juan de Fuca Strait. Others say their homeland is Diitiida, near Jordan River. When the great flood came, they moved inland and lashed their canoes to the mountain peak, Kaakaapiyaa (Mt. Rosander), just east of Nitinat Lake. A generation passed before they returned to the coast and made their home at Whyac, "high place," where the sea narrows to become the briney Nitinat Lake. Here they flourished, until recent times, as whalers. Whyac, along the **West Coast Trail**, is distinguished by a big rock with a hole in it, where hunters tied their catch.

The Ditidaht established themselves at Balaats'adt, a former camping and fishing place, in the 1960s, after freight service to their coastal villages ceased, and the road here was complete. This community is now on its way to becoming the service centre for a booming wilderness recreation area: Nitinat Lake brings international windsurfers seeking thermal winds. Cultural and wilderness tours into the area are planned. There is also Parks Canada information and access from here to the West Coast Trail. A new campground has been established on the trail at the old village site, Cheewaht, near Clo-oose. **Carmanah Pacific Provincial Park**, recently set aside to preserve the largest Sitka spruce in the world, is also reached from here. Carmanah, "canoe landing in front," was a Ditidaht village at the mouth of Carmanah Creek. The **Ditidaht Nation Visitor Centre** includes a motel, cafe, laundromat, store, and gas station.

❓ Ditidaht Administration: Box 340, Port Alberni, B.C., V9Y 7M8. Tel: 745-3333.

Gateway to Central Nuu-chah-nulth Territories: West of Parksville on Highway 4

Just before Parksville, Hwy 4 veers west from Coast Salish territories through the Vancouver Island ranges. For the more ancient route linking east-coast and Nuu-chah-nulth peoples at the head of Alberni Inlet, see chapter 4, "Qualicum First Nation."

To Opetchesaht and Tseshaht Lands in the Alberni Valley

ⵀ Alberni Inlet: 84 km west of Nanaimo; 40 km east of the open sea. Charcoal and tool fragments are testimony campfires have been burning here for at least 4,500 years. Into this inlet flows the river, Tis-oma-as, Somass, "washing or cleansing," a salmon-spawning stream rivalling any on Vancouver Island and the primary reason why the people inhabited this place. Today, the industrial complex of **Port Alberni** (pop. 8,265/1,100 Ab) sprawls over a dozen ancient village, ritual, and fishing sites. The two original peoples, the Opetchesaht and Tseshaht, now reside on the city's western outskirts.

Port Alberni today is administrative headquarters for Nuu-chah-nulth tribes. Nuu-chah-nulth Tribal Council offices are at the main Tseshaht village on the west bank of the Somass River (5000 Mission Rd.).

ⓖ Alberni Valley Museum: 4255 Wallace St. Tel: 723-2181. Displays basketry and maps of old village sites and Shoemaker Bay (Toxways) archaeological project.

ⓖ Tlukwatkuuwis: Harbour Quay, at the bottom of Argylle St., was the site of the former Tseshaht village cited below. Salmon jump, and occasionally a sea lion bursts to the surface celebrating its catch. From here, the passenger/cargo ship *Lady Rose* sails down to Barkley Sound, home to one of the largest

concentrations of people on Vancouver Island's west coast. It stops at the Nuu-chah-nulth communities of Uchucklesaht and Huu-ay-aht (Ohiaht) (see below).

ⓖ Sa:ahi (Papermill Dam Municipal Park): From Hwy 4, west of downtown Port Alberni, turn right at River Bend Bridge onto Falls Rd. The sudden narrowing of the Somass River is the traditional fishing site, "to go upriver." Pleasant shores immediately across the river are Tseshaht reserve; fishermen use aluminum gas-powered boats and gillnets. On the park side, there is excellent swimming at the bottom of rapids and inner-tubing through the rapids.

ⵦ Opetchesaht: (Pop. 194/89). On River Rd., on the western outskirts of Port Alberni. Elders past have suggested east-coast links were once stronger here than west-coast links. The Alberni Inlet route to the west coast was blocked at Hell's Gate by a sea monster who devoured people, canoes and all. It was not until after the Transformer, Kwatyet, let himself be swallowed by the monster and chopped up its intestines that hunters of seal and salmon ventured through from the west, and in time merged with the Opetchesaht. These people moved from their main village site at Tl'ikwuut, where the Sproat and Somass rivers meet, shortly after the first Europeans arrived in 1860 to set up their sawmill. Today, this very private community, served by an all-woman council, is concentrating on developing its commercial fisheries. There are no tourist facilities at this time.

❓ Opetchesaht Administration: Box 211, Port Alberni, B.C., V9Y 7M7. Tel: 724-4041.

ⵦ Tseshaht: (Pop. 900/700). On western outskirts of Port Alberni, on Mission Rd. overlooking the Somass River, and 3 km west, on Hwy 4. About two centuries ago this second powerful Barkley Sound tribe emerged to share the head of the inlet with the Opetchesaht. Their name, "where the whale bones on the beach smell," refers to their former home in the Broken Group Islands, and their traditional occupation as whalers. The first people encountered by the Tseshaht were at the village Nuupts'ikapis, "one tree on the beach." They were all women, who turned into swans and flew away.

The Tseshaht established their main village and winter ceremony area at Tlukwatkuuwis. When spring came, they went back down the inlet to Barkley Sound, returning again in the fall. When the Anderson Company arrived in 1861, looking to build B.C.'s first export sawmill, they coveted the Tseshaht's chosen site, and purchased it for the sum of 50 blankets, some muskets and molasses. The Tseshaht moved their salmon weirs and seal traps up to Nuupts'ikapis, the place from which the swans had earlier fled.

Near their village overlooking the Somass River was the Alberni residential school established in 1892. Over the next three-quarters of a century it exacted its toll on five generations of children forbidden to speak their own language or grow up with their traditions. Tseshaht member George Clutesi (1905–1988) lived and later worked here. At the very time his culture was being repressed, he emerged as an artist, author, actor, and teacher of songs and dances nearly lost. Among his many awards are an honorary doctorate from the University of Victoria in 1971; the Order of Canada in 1973; and an ACTRA award in 1975 for his role in the evocative film *Dreamspeaker*. The one remnant of the residential school today houses the elementary school, IIa-hopayuk, focussing on Nuu-chah-nulth language and culture. On this site are also the Nuu-chah-nulth Tribal Council offices, and Tseshaht and Uchucklesaht offices.

The **Tseshaht Market** and gas station is on Hwy 4 about 3 km beyond River Bend Bridge. **Clinta's Indian Crafts** is open May to September and before Christmas. Also here is a new branch of the Bank of Montreal, in a longhouse-style building designed with the help of elders and artists.

? **Tseshaht Administration:** Box 1218, Port Alberni, B.C., V9Y 7M1. Tel: 724-1225.

To Uchucklesaht and Huu-ay-aht Territories: West from Port Alberni by Ferry

The passenger and cargo ship *Lady Rose*, cited above, departs from Port Alberni.

V **Uchucklesaht:** (Pop. 118/20). At the head of Uchuckleset Inlet is Elhlateese, "farther down the beach." This rare, level place along a steep-sided fjord is not far from the place that gives them their name, "people who live in there on the beach." The Uchucklesaht were once a dominant force in eastern Barkley Sound, with an estimated population of several thousand. Today, they are a few families guarding their privacy. Visitors are welcome at nearby Cowishil, "salmonberry place." Here, where Uchuckleset Inlet joins the Alberni Inlet, are log cabin rentals and marine sales.

? **Uchucklesaht Administration:** Box 157, Port Alberni, B.C., V9Y 7M7. Tel: 724-1832.

V **Huu-ay-aht (Ohiaht) First Nations:** (Pop. 438/123). At Pachena Bay, 3 km by logging road from Bamfield; at the western terminus of the **West Coast Trail**. Much confusion has arisen since government surveyors named the Huu-ay-aht's bay Pachena, after their Pacheenaht neighbours to the south. The Huu-ay-aht have long known it as Anacla.

Pachena Bay Campground has daily fees for camping by the sea and sand dunes, and yearly passes for access to nearby islands and beaches on Huu-ay-aht reserve land. Ask campground manager or administration office for details, and about art for sale, whale-watching, sports fishing, and sightseeing charters.

The pictograph, K'ak'awin, at Sproat Lake Provincial Park near Port Alberni, is said to be the work of the Transformer, Kwatyet.
CREDIT: RBCM 11733

? Huu-ay-aht First Nation Administration: Box 70, Bamfield, B.C., V0R 1B0. Tel: 728-3414.

To the Peoples of Clayoquot Sound: West from Port Alberni on Highway 4

From Port Alberni, Hwy 4 cuts through traditional Opetchesaht deer-hunting grounds, and between the vast lakes, Awokok M'o:ho:l and Awokok Tl'iko:t, we know as Great Central and Sproat. This is the realm of Thunderbird. Tota, "thunder mountain," lies beyond Great Central Lake.

◼ K'ak'awin (Petroglyphs at Sproat Lake Provincial Park): 10 km from Port Alberni. A trail leads from the main parking lot to a rock face lapped by the lake during high waters. It is called K'ak'awin, "something stuck on the middle of the back," perhaps for the fin on one of the nine mythical marine creatures, and is said to be the work of the Transformer, Kwatyet. A similar petroglyph at Great Central Lake was drowned when a dam was built there. Gilbert Malcolm Sproat was Indian Reserve Commissioner between 1877 and 1880.

Beyond Awokok M'o:ho:l (Sproat Lake), Hwy 4 enters the territories of five Clayoquot Sound peoples: the Toquaht, Tla-o-qui-aht, Ucluelet, Hesquiaht, and Ahousaht. The tourism and fishing-based village of Tofino provides access to their 350,000 hectares of islands, inlets, sea, and forest, the focus of considerable international attention since the 1980s. First Nations and environmentalists have struggled together and separately to influence the future of these old-growth rainforests. Francis Frank, Tla-o-qui-aht First Nations chief, reminds us the first peoples of Clayoquot Sound, who make up 42 percent of

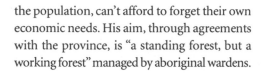

the population, can't afford to forget their own economic needs. His aim, through agreements with the province, is "a standing forest, but a working forest" managed by aboriginal wardens.

V   **Toquaht:** (Pop. 101/34). 76 km west of Port Alberni, a road leads to the village at Macoah. The Toquaht take their name, "people of the narrow, rocky beach," from an ancient summer village at Stuart Bay. The river flowing into it is said to be where Kwatyet lived while on earth, and the Toquaht are the tribe from which all other Barkley Sound peoples come. By 1874, only 47 people remained of the tribe that once controlled the strategically important sites at the mouth of Ucluelet Inlet. Since the Toquaht moved to Macoah a decade ago, they have recovered much ground and now operate a logging company (ask about sawmill tours) and the **Du-quah Gallery**, in the non-native town of Ucluelet (see below).

?   **Toquaht Administration:** Box 759, Ucluelet, B.C., V0R 3A0. Tel: 726-4230.

J   **Ucluelet-Tofino Junction:** 96 km west of Port Alberni.

V   **Ucluelet:** (Pop. 479/310). 2 km beyond junction, Port Albion Rd. leads 12 km to Ittattsoo, at the head of Ucluelet Inlet. In the last century, the people of Ucluth, "wind blowing into the bay," were a dominant force in Barkley Sound. Here are **Dawn's Market** and laundromat; whale-watching charters out of Tofino.

?   **Ucluelet Administration:** Box 699, Ucluelet, B.C., V0R 3A0.

T   **Ucluelet:** (Pop. 1,595/55 Ab). At the tip of the Ucluth Peninsula. This is a logging and fishing community which also serves as a base for sports fishing and whale-watching. **Du-quah Gallery**, 1971 Peninsula Rd., is owned and operated by the Toquaht.

I   **Pacific Rim National Park (at Long Beach):** 1 km beyond junction. Within what is celebrated as 8,100 hectares of undisturbed west-coast wilderness, is Hisaawista (Esowista), the largest of two contemporary Tla-o-qui-aht villages and the only First Nations village in a Canadian national park. There are also at least 6 more major village sites, 22 camps, 2 defensive sites, and 4 lookouts no longer occupied within this section of Pacific Rim Park. Among them are Tl'atl'athis, "sand dunes," just north of the Wickaninnish Centre, where plentiful red kinnikinnick berries were picked and mixed with fermented salmon eggs to make "Indian cheese." At today's Green Point is Muyap'alhh: from here comes the story of a beached whale that was cut in half to accommodate the boundary between the Tla-o-qui-aht and "long beach people," since merged with the Ucluelet. Beyond that, T'ashii, the "trail," where canoes were portaged from the inland waters of Grice Bay to the open sea. There was a village called T'ayis, "anchorage," at today's Schooner Cove. Just outside the park's boundaries was Ch'ahayis, "sound of ocean on the beach," where women gathered cedar bark and men trolled for spring salmon—now the favoured sands of Chesterman Beach.

V   **Hisaawista (Esowista):** (Pop. 130). 16 km beyond the junction. In times past "clubbed to death" was the home of a powerful and aggressive people. Eventually, they were defeated by the Tla-o-qui-aht, "people different from who they were." Once peaceful, known for their proficiency as canoe builders, the Tla-o-qui-aht embarked upon a period of war and southward expansion just before Europeans arrived. They swept up or over as many as 10 other west-coast tribes. In 1890, when reserves were established on this coast, there were a few houses here at what was primarily a halibut fishing station. During World War Two, the military constructed its own village at Esowista. After 1959, the Tla-o-qui-aht began establishing it as their primary home; and national park boundaries were drawn around it in the decades to come. The wide bay to the east is named for Wickaninnish, "having no one in front of him in the canoe," leading chief at Clayoquot Sound in the late 1700s. His wealth and power, like Chief Maquinna's, was enhanced in the early days of the sea-otter trade through his role as intermediary between white and First Nations traders. Today, Tla-o-qui-aht are full participants in a burgeoning tourist industry, operating **Tin Wis Resort Lodge,** whale-watching tours, fishing charters, and water taxis. **First Nations Visions and Images arts and crafts** is located at Esowista.

? **Tla-o-qui-aht First Nations Administration:** Box 18, Tofino, B.C., V0R 2Z0. Tel: 725-3233.

T **Tofino:** (Pop. 1,085/110 Ab). 34 km beyond the junction, on the tip of Esowista Peninsula near the entrance to Clayoquot Sound. For most of this century this has been downtown for the surrounding Nuu-chah-nulth communities, fishing port, and debarkation point for those with family or business in larger centres to the south. It now serves as a centre for explorations of Nuu-chah-nulth culture.

? **Nuu-chah-nulth Booking and Information Centre:** 300 Main St., Box 453, Tofino, B.C., V0R 2Z0. Tel: 1-800-665-9425 or 725-2888. One-stop First Nations tourism resource centre, for restaurants, lodging, sightseeing, sports fishing, whale watching, hiking and exploring, eco-tours, arts and crafts. Included are trips to Meares Island, hot springs, and remote island drop-offs.

⑥ **Tin-Wis Resort Lodge:** 1119 Pacific Rim Hwy. Tel: 725-3402. Tla-o-qui-aht First Nations offer traditional food, entertainment, arts, guided tours, whale watching, and a marina. Tin-wis, "calm beach," is on the ocean

front at Mackenzie Beach, where people stayed during halibut fishing season, and whales were sometimes anchored before being towed to processing sites.

⑥ **Himwitsa Lodge:** Box 453, Tofino, B.C., V0R 2Z0. Tel: 1-800-665-9425. Offering views of forests, mountains, inlets, and islands; art gallery and adventure bookings.

⑥ **House of Himwitsa Gallery:** 300 Main St. Nuu-chah-nulth and other First Nations arts.

⑥ **Sea Shanty Restaurant:** 300 Main St.

⑥ **Eagle Aerie Gallery:** Campbell St. Renowned artist Roy Henry Vickers is a Tsimshian guest in Nuu-cha-nulth territories. His longhouse-style gallery, with carved and painted house front and interior totem poles, provides the ambience of his home village of Kitkatla to the north.

⑥ **West Coast Maritime Museum/Whale Centre:** Town centre. Displays include some history of Nuu-chah-nulth whaling traditions.

To Meares Island

V **Opitsaht:** (Pop. 125). A tranquil scene, this Tla-o-qui-aht village is visible from Tofino's government dock. Its name is "rising or falling sun's rays reflected on village." For two centuries, however, Meares Island has seen some of the most intense encounters with *mamalthi.* In 1791, Captain Gray of the American vessel *Columbia* established the short-lived Fort Defiance here. A few months later, he attacked Opitsaht and obliterated 200 homes in retaliation for a foiled plot to attack his crew, led by Chief Wickaninnish. From 1900 to 1971, Christie Residential School at nearby Kakawis left its painful imprints on some 8,000 coastal First Nations children. Then in the 1980s the Tla-o-qui-aht and environmentalists brought international attention to the island's ancient cedar forests scheduled for the chainsaw. On the east coast alone are thousands of culturally modified trees—from which a strip of bark, even a plank, was removed centuries ago, leaving the tree healthy and intact. The Nuu-chah-nulth declared the island a tribal park in 1984; a temporary court injunction against logging announced the following year is still in effect. Island tours depart from Tofino.

? Tla-o-qui-aht Administration: Box 18, Tofino, B.C., V0R 2Z0. Tel: 725-3233.

Nuu-chah-nulth Territories of the Central Coast: By Sea and Air from Tofino

V Ahousaht: (Pop. 1,411/678). North from Tofino by air or water taxi leads to a grey-green confusion: straits become inlets; peninsulas become islands or, maybe, whales. On an isthmus, on a small handle of land attached to the southeast coast of Flores Island, sits the largest Nuu-chah-nulth community. The Ahousaht, "people facing away from the ocean," were whalers who until 150 years ago lived on the smaller, more exposed Vargas Island to the south. Here, on Flores, at the village of Marktosis, were the Otsosaht: they gave the Ahousaht the whaling ceremonies which had come to them from the Ye-ii, a race of fair-skinned supernatural beings. The Otsosaht also possessed a dozen salmon-bearing rivers which the Ahousaht coveted, and won, after a long war beginning in the early 1800s. Its battles were fought on the beaches of many islands—Flores, Vargas, Bartlett—and ultimately drew in most of the peoples of Clayoquot Sound. Few Otsosaht survived. Stories are still told of the deeds of Qamiina, the Ahousaht war chief. To prepare for war, he practised ritual diving into an underwater cave, and is said to have bitten a piece from the fin of a basking shark.

Today, the Ahousaht are fighting to keep their salmon rivers and forests from the devastation of clearcut logging. They are also strong singers, dancers, and weavers; the elders here are often consulted on matters of language and history. Here also is B.C.'s first all-native RCMP detachment.

A twice-daily seabus, *Spirit of Marktosis,* links Tofino to Marktosis. Once there, **Walk the Wild Side** offers guided cultural tours through rainforests to beaches. A boardwalk trail is being built to protect the trail from erosion, and plans are in store for an above-ground passage, supported by trees, similar to those in South American forests. The **Ahousat Guest House** has accommodation and information on boat trips to nearby sites, whale-watching/seafood-feasts; 670-9511.

? Ahousaht Administration: General Delivery, Ahousaht, B.C., V0R 1A0. Tel: 670-9563.

V Hesquiaht: (Pop. 514/141). 40 km north of Tofino, at Refuge Cove in Sydney Inlet, reached by float plane or water taxi from Tofino. Their name, pronounced "haish-quee-at," comes from *hiishiisa,* the sound of people eating herring spawn deposited on surf-grass or sea grass. Once, five separate groups of Hesquiaht lived around Hesquiat Harbour, Hesquiat Peninsula, and Hesquiat Lake.

Just off Hesquiat Peninsula is where the first recorded contact between Europeans and Nuu-chah-nulth peoples occurred. In 1774 Juan Perez of Spain, seeking sovereignty over an unseen coast, spotted land. Three canoes from a village, Paata'ista, paddled out to his ship. But before the Spanish set foot on land, a storm came up and blew them away. A century later to the year, the first Catholic priest on this coast chose the Hesquiaht to host his mission. Father Brabant stayed 33 years.

Hot Springs Adventures offers lodging at misty water's edge, across the cove from the only known hot springs on this coast. The *Matlahaw Pride*—named for the 19th-century chief who rescued the crew of an American ship that sank in Hesquiat Harbour—delivers lodge guests to **Maquinna Provincial Park** and the start of a 2-km boardwalk through lush forest to the hot springs. Dinghies are also available. Hot water bubbles from the springs, then cascades over falls into natural rock pools cooled by incoming waves from the Pacific Ocean. There are also chances to see grey whales, sea lions, eagles; salmon fishing, hiking, exploring. Info and bookings: 1-800-665-9425 or 725-2888.

? **Hesquiaht Administration:** Box 2000, Tofino, B.C., V0R 2Z0. Radio Phone: Boat Basin 98077, Hesquiaht Band.

Northern Nuu-chah-nulth Territories: Highway 28 from Campbell River

Northern Nuu-chah-nulth territories are reached by travelling along Vancouver Island's east coast as far as Campbell River—well into Kwakwaka'wakw territories—then winding west, via Hwy 28, between the vertebrae of Vancouver Island's mountain spine. Approximately at the eastern entrance to Strathcona Provincial Park, 40 km west of Campbell River, is the eastern frontier of Muchalaht territories. The Muchalaht, who lived in many villages along Gold River and Muchalat Inlet, were once warring neighbours of the Mowachaht. The Mowachaht, "people of the deer," prevailed in villages throughout northern Nootka Sound. Today, the two tribes (pop. 373) are family.

V **Ahaminaquus:** 126 km west of Campbell River, Hwy 28 ends at Gold River, the instant town built providentially, in 1965, a comfortable distance from the pulp mill which is its raison d'être. Pulp Mill Rd. leads 12 km farther downriver to the industrial complex at the edge of Muchalat Inlet, on Muchalaht reserve land, and right across the road from this Mowachaht-Muchalaht village. The 40-km

inlet is closed to shellfishing because of dioxins and furans. And, after three decades of toxic air emissions, truck traffic and noise, the village has closed too. In 1996 its residents moved into new houses at Ts'xanah, a traditional site 3 km north of Gold River. Ahaminaquus is now a marina and commercial centre.

? **Ahaminaquus Tourist Infocentre:** Box 459, Gold River, B.C., V0P 1G0. Tel: 283-7464. Bookings for water taxis, cabins, and camping at **Yuquot National Historic Site** (see below); gift shop.

The freight and passenger ship MV *Uchuck III* departs from the wharf at the end of Pulp Mill Rd. In summer there are once-weekly excursions to Yuquot National Historic Site for one-hour tour. It is possible to stay overnight and return to Ahaminaquus by water taxi. The *Uchuck* also offers 10-day excursions taking in Yuquot, Tahsis, and Kyuquot Sound. Tel: 1-800-663-1915 or 283-2515.

V **Yuquot (Friendly Cove):** On the south tip of Nootka Island, at the entrance to Muchalat Inlet. First contact, first European settlement, first industry, and first ghost town: Yuquot is now a national historic site because British Columbia's history began here, in 1778.

Sitting on the crescent beach here, Marsha Maquinna explains why Yuquot, "where the wind blows from all directions," is so important to the Mowachaht. "This is our true home," she says. "This is where *our* history begins." Long, long before Captain Cook, a woman lived alone in these forests by the sea, until one day, the tears and mucous of her loneliness gave rise to the tiny male form of Ankoak, or Snot Boy. He grew up quickly, and from their union came the ancestors of those who in time populated dozens of Mowachaht villages.

A foghorn bellows today where the Mowachaht guided *mamalthi* around the rocks. Their leader, Maquinna, guided his own people through fears—molasses and biscuits . . .

Objects from this whaling shrine were collected by ethnographers in 1904, and are currently in storage at the American Museum of Natural History in New York. The Mowachaht are hoping to repatriate the shrine and build their own cultural centre around it.
CREDIT: NO. 104474. GEORGE HUNT, COURTESY DEPARTMENT OF LIBRARY SERVICES, AMERICAN MUSEUM OF NATURAL HISTORY

blood and bones? What if the newcomers were cannibals? The fur trade was soon underway, and Maquinna, "possessor of pebbles," became an even greater chief than he already was.

Ambrose Maquinna, his descendent, says "a chief should never break his roots." But in the mid-1970s he too succumbed to the forces pulling the Mowachaht, family by family, from their ancestral home at Yuquot. The cannery that employed them, then the school, closed. Things looked more promising in Gold River, Victoria, Vancouver.

In 1978, the B.C. government set out to celebrate the 200th anniversary of Captain Cook's landing. They invited the world to Friendly Cove. But, say the Mowachaht, the politicians forgot whose land they were inviting the world to. The Mowachaht gently asserted their jurisdiction, wearing T-shirts that read "Cook the Captain."

Visitors are heartily welcomed. The Mowachaht only ask that Yuquot be respected as their place of origin, the place where their families still gather every summer—where one family has stayed on, and others talk of returning.

In July and August, Mowachaht tour guides lead visitors by the seaside cemeteries where their grandparents rest and to poles, old and new. There is camping or accommodation in new rustic cabins tucked into the old-growth forest by the lake where generations of Maquinnas bathed. Ray Williams, who continues to live here, conducts fishing charters. The **Yuquot Summer Festival** in August features traditional drumming and singing, arts and crafts, and a salmon barbecue.

▼ **Nuchatlaht:** (Pop. 121/62). By road from the logging town of Zeballos. In the early 1990s, the "people of the mountain" moved here to Oclucje, overlooking Espinoza Inlet, from the northwest coast of Nootka Island.

❓ **Nuchatlaht Administration:** Box 40, Zeballos, B.C., V0P 2A0.

▼ **Ehattesaht:** (Pop. 185/94). Chenahkint, in Kyuquot Sound, is a stop-off point for the *Uchuck III.* It is not accessible by road. In the waters of the "people of the big beach area" thrive tiny bottom-feeding mollusks, their shells about the size and shape of a little finger. These are the rare and beautiful *haiqua,* or dentalium, once worn as an ornament. During the fur trade they became currency, increasing in value the farther they were traded throughout western North America. *Haiqua* were gradually replaced by blankets, beads, dollars.

Today, the Ehattesaht earn their wealth from fishing, logging, and aquaculture.

❓ **Ehattesaht Administration:** Box 716, Campbell River, B.C., V9W 6J3. (201-938 Island Hwy). Tel: 287-4353.

▼ **Ka:'yu:'K't'h'/Che:K̲'tles7et'h̲'** (Kyuquot) First Nation: (Pop. 378/331). The villages at Houpsitas, in Kyuquot Sound, and at Actis, on Village Island, are only accessible by boat. This is the Nuu-chah-nulth/Kwakwa̲ka̲'-wakw frontier, more in the middle of things than on the fringes. United here are the Che: K̲'tles7et'h̲ of Brooks Peninsula, who once spoke both languages, and the "people of the needle-sharp bush." All the forces that decimated other shores also entered these mussel-rich inlets. And in 1902, the "cream of Kyuquot manhood" went down with the sealing schooner *Hatzie.* The Kyuquot people enjoy sharing their land and stories with visitors. Here are bed and breakfast, boat charters, motel and restaurant, and water taxi.

❓ **Kyuquot Administration:** General Delivery, Kyuquot, B.C., V0P 1J0. Tel: 332-5259.

Makah Territories: On the Olympic Peninsula, across Juan de Fuca Strait

▼ **Makah:** (Pop. 1,900/800). At Cape Flattery, on the northwest tip of the Olympic Peninsula. It's an accident of geography and international politics that the Makah and the Nuu-chah-nulth live in two different countries. They call themselves kwih-dich-chuh-ahtx, "people who live by the rocks and seagulls," referring to the ruggedness of their cape. They occupied at least five permanent villages here. It was their Clallam neighbours that called them Makah, sometimes translated as "generous with food."

Today, most live at Diah, on Neah Bay. The **Makah Museum** here was built to house artifacts recovered in the 1970s from Ozette village, partially buried by mud three centuries ago. Like Pompei, this tragedy preserved a day in the life of these whale hunters and fishermen, and sparked a rebirth of art, language, and spirituality, buried by a century of repression. Among the 55,000 items found, and now on display, is the delicate 2.5-cm carving of Snot Boy, in a real mussel shell. But it's the trickster q'(w)e.ti, the size of a 10-year-old boy, who is better known here. One of his stories is told as part of one-hour PBS video presentation, *A Gift From the Past,* shown twice daily at the museum. Makah artists are featured in the craft shop. Makah Days are late August, in Neah Bay. A trail leads to Cape Flattery, a good place for watching whales. Tel: 360-645-2711.

❓ **Makah Tribal Council:** Box 115, Neah Bay, WA, U.S.A., 98357. Tel: 360-645-2201.

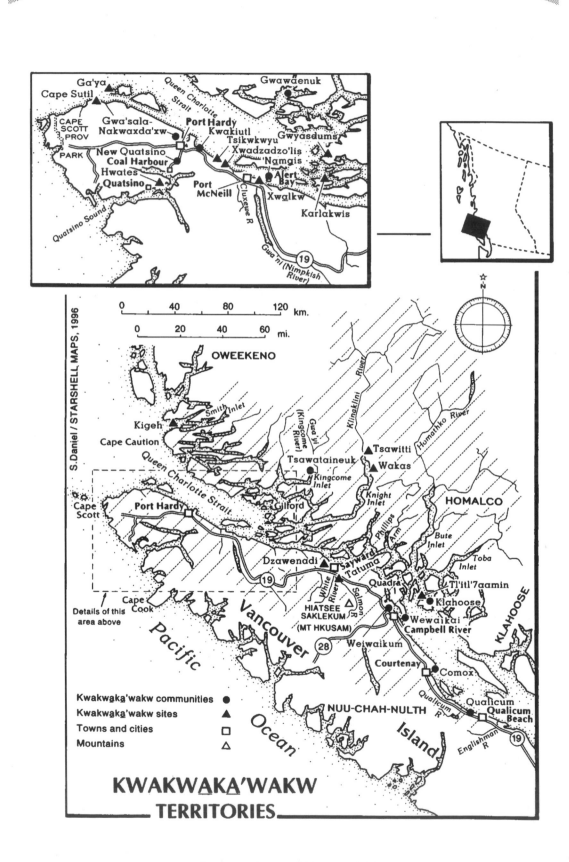

KWAKWA̱KA'WAKW TERRITORIES

S. Daniel / STARSHELL MAPS, 1996

Inset map (top):

Ga'ya
Cape Sutil
CAPE SCOTT PROV PARK
Gwa'sala-Nakwaxda'xw
New Quatsino
Coal Harbour
Hwates
Quatsino
Quatsino Sound
Queen Charlotte Strait
Port Hardy
Kwakiutl
Tsikkwyu
Xwadzadzo'lis
'Namgis
Alert Bay
Port McNeill
Cluxewe R
Xwalkw
Karlakwis
Gwawaenuk
Gwyasdums
19
Gwa 'ni (Nimpkish River)

Main map:

OWEEKENO
Smith Inlet
Kigeh
Cape Caution
Queen Charlotte Strait
Cape Scott
Port Hardy
Cape Cook
Details of this area above
Cape Cook
Pacific Ocean
Vancouver Island
NUU-CHAH-NULTH
Gwa yi (Kingcome River)
Tsawataineuk
Kingcome Inlet
Klinaklini River
Tsawitti
Wakas
Homathko River
Knight Inlet
Gilford
Dzawenadi
Sayward
Tatuma
White River
Salmon R
HIATSEE SAKLEKUM (MT HKUSAM)
28
Weiwaikum
Phillips Arm
Bute Inlet
Toba Inlet
Quadra I
HOMALCO
Tl'itl'7aamin
Klahoose
Wewaikai
Campbell River
Courtenay
Comox
KLAHOOSE
Qualicum R
Qualicum
Qualicum Beach
Englishman R
19
Weiwaikum

0   40   80   120   km.
0   20   40   60   mi.

Legend:

Kwakwa̱ka'wakw communities ●
Kwakwa̱ka'wakw sites ▲
Towns and cities □
Mountains △

CHAPTER 4

Kwakwa̱ka̱'wakw

We want to know whether you have come to stop our dances and feasts, as the missionaries and agents who live among our neighbours try to do . . . if you come to forbid us to dance, begone. If not, you will be welcome to us.

—*Kwagul chief to anthropologist Franz Boas, 1886*

*K*wakwa̱ka̱'wakw means "speakers of Kwak- wala," and refers to the 15 modern-day tribes sharing the northeast coast of Vancou- ver Island and the adjacent mainland coast. Theirs is a landscape better understood when we imagine our entry into it from the north by sea, between Cape Caution and Cape Scott. Queen Charlotte Strait becomes a world unto itself, narrowing almost to a close at Quadra Island, which marks the southern reaches of Kwakwa̱ka̱'wakw territories.

That the Kwakwa̱ka̱'wakw would hold the greatest potlatch ever is only fitting. Up and down the coast they were, and still are, admired as masters of art and drama. In 1994, at the opening ceremonies of the Common- wealth Games in Victoria, Chief Adam Dick, carrier of the ancient name Kwaxistala—"the smoke of the big house fire reaches around the world"—blurred the boundaries between sleight of hand and real magic. True to the purpose of a potlatch—*max(w)a*, "doing a great thing"—he transformed a sports field into a Big House, filled it with the spirit of his

ancestors, and invited the whole world to bear witness to his history.

Queens and prime ministers were spell- bound. Through his songs and the dances of puppets whose heads touched the sky, Kwax- istala established himself as direct descendant of Kawadelekala—the first man of his tribe. He emerged when the world as we know it was still very young, in the mountains of King- come Inlet, from the supernatural Wolf, Gila la thleed. In this time-honoured way, Kwaxistala confirmed his rights, and also his obligations to the river there, Gwa'yi, and the little fish that have always sustained his tribe, the Tsawa- taineuk, "people with eulachon."

Like the Tsawataineuk, each Kwakwa̱ka̱'- wakw tribe has its own story. Some are descended from the Transformers—Qulus, Killer Whale, Juna. Others are from Sun, Griz- zly Bear, or Thunderbird, who removed their masks to step upon the earth as chiefs.

"It would take such a long time to explain *supernatural*," says Daisy Sewid-Smith, *he lox ta*, or translator, for Kwaxistala. It would take

Kwakwa̲ka'wakw Big House at the Opening Ceremonies of the Commonwealth games in 1994. In
front, left to right, are Dora Sewid-Cook, Kim
Recalma-Clutesi, Daisy Sewid-Smith, and Adam
Dick. They gave people from around the world a
rare opportunity to witness their history.
CREDIT: TIM HOGUE

even longer to unravel the complex social and
economic system that grew up around the first
chiefs and their families, *nu'mima,* or "one
kind," to which all Kwakwa̲ka'wakw still trace
themselves. When Captain Vancouver first
sailed between the capes in 1792, there were
about 100 *nu'mima* threaded into 30 Kwak-
wa̲ka'wakw tribes. Each tribe, each *nu'mima,*
each woman, man, child, was ranked within
the potlatch securities-and-investments system. "You might compare it to a blending of
the federal government and Toronto stock
market," Sewid-Smith says.

Many took quick advantage of new
opportunities to trade with the Europeans,
add to their coppers (see "Since the Beginning
of Time," p. 9), and raise their status within
their own system. When the Hudson's Bay
Company established Fort Rupert in 1849 to
access nearby coal deposits, four tribes immediately incorporated there, becoming B.C.'s
first mining company. They allowed the
British company a small patch of land for their
fort, but employed their own workers to mine

the coal. By the time the fort closed in 1882,
the Kwagul tribe there had achieved high
standing among the Kwakwa̲ka'wakw tribes. It
was also their name—Kwagul or Kwagiulth or
Kwakiutl—that the newcomers gave to all
Kwakwa̲ka'wakw people.

The costs of contact quickly outweighed
its benefits. With depopulation, ranking positions within the system could not be filled.
And in 1884, the dominion government and
missionaries conspired to outlaw the potlatch.
The sentence for such pagan depravity: time
in jail and an eternity in hell. The Kwak-
wa̲ka'wakw saw this clearly as an attempt to
undermine their government. They resisted,
potlatching openly and underground, such as
on remote islands during storms, or after the
rivers froze and villages were inaccessible to
lawmakers. In 1921, the full weight of colonial
law fell upon Village Island and a potlatch
being held there to honour the marriage contract between Emma Bell and Dan Cranmer.
Chiefs who did not surrender ceremonial
masks, drums, carvings, and coppers were
jailed. Those items relinquished went to museums in central Canada.

Thirty years passed; then anti-potlatch
laws were quietly removed from the books.
That same year, 1951, there was what appeared
to outsiders as a sudden revival of Kwak-
wa̲ka'wakw art. Willie Seaweed, James and
Ben Dick, Mungo Martin and his apprentice-
relations were celebrated as a new line of
Kwakwa̲ka'wakw artists, though they were, in
fact, part of an ongoing tradition that never
ceased. Their descendants are now known
worldwide for their flamboyant style, creating
huge masks with moving parts; masks that
open to reveal yet another mask—a wolf, then
suddenly, a supernatural man. Not just art.

By 1979, those who had witnessed the
Cranmer potlatch were now the elders, looking on, many in tears, as the masks and coppers taken in 1921 were returned. To guard
and protect them, and as a condition of their
return, the Kwakwa̲ka'wakw built their own

cultural centres, one on Quadra Island, another on Cormorant, focal points now for young Kwakwa̱ka̱'wakw learning how to potlatch. All who come respectfully to these places are honoured guests. The Kwakwa̱ka̱'wakw say *Gilaks'la*, "Welcome." Or, more precisely: "A most effusive, humble, acquiescent, self-effacing, delicate and graceful celebration of your presence."

HIGHLIGHTS AND EVENTS

- ⑥ Campbell River Museum   p. 58
- ⑥ Kwagiulth Museum   p. 59
- ⑥ U'mista Cultural Centre/Alert Bay   p. 63

INFORMATION AND PROTOCOL

In Kwakwa̱ka̱'wakw territories there are several ways to describe where you come from. There are the newcomers' names, like Kingcome Inlet or Cape Mudge, and traditional names, Gwa'yi or 'Yalis. There are also tribal names, such as Tsawataineuk or Wewaikai. In some cases, several tribes are represented in one place, as at Alert Bay. Sometimes, the people of one tribe live in several communities.

Many can be reached only by boat or plane. Most should be visited by private invitation only. Campbell River, Cape Mudge, Alert Bay, and Fort Rupert offer a range of tourist facilities.

The language here, Kwakwala, is being taught both at the cultural centres and in public schools. Kwakwala is now accepted as a second language for students entering the University of Victoria.

Included in this section are the people of Qualicum, some of whom are descended from the Salish-speaking Pentlatch. They are now closely linked through marriage and custom to the Kwakwa̱ka̱'wakw people.

? **Kwakiutl District Council:** Box 2490, Port Hardy, B.C., V0N 2P0. Tel: 949-9433. Fax: 949-9677. Members: Weiwaikum (Campbell River), Wewaikai (Cape Mudge), Comox, Gwa'-Sala-Nakwaxda'xw, Kwakiutl, Kwiakah, Mamaleleqala-Qwe'Qwa'Sot'Enox, Quatsino, Tanakteuk, and Tlatlasikwala.

? **Musgamagw Tsawataineuk Tribal Council:** Box 90, Alert Bay, B.C., V0N 1A0. Tel: 974-5516. Fax: 974-5466. Members: Kwa-Wa-Aineuk (Gwawaenuk), Kwicksutaineuk-Ah-Kwah-Ah-Mish (Hahuamis), Namgis (Nimpkish), Tsawataineuk.

? **Whe-la-la-u Area Council:** Box 150, Alert Bay, B.C., V0N 1A0. Tel: 974-5220. Fax: 974-5904. Members: Tanakteuk, Tlatlasikwala, Tlowitsis-Mumtagila.

North from Qualicum Beach on Highway 19

V **Qualicum First Nation:** (Pop. 76). Just north of the town of **Qualicum Beach** (pop. 4,420/20 Ab), the Big Qualicum River flows into the Strait of Georgia. The river's name comes from *squal-li*—"chum salmon" in the Coast Salish language of the Pentlatch people who first occupied a winter village here. The Pentlatch language was unintelligible to their southern Hul'qumi'num-speaking neighbours. Their territories extended north from the Englishman River at Parksville, embracing Comox Harbour, Kye Bay, and Denman and Hornby islands. The Qualicum River was a most cherished site. The *squal-li* were low in fat (because of the short river), good for preserving, and thus an important trade commodity. The village here was also at the head of one of the few trails linking west- and east-coast peoples. The Horne Lake trail traced the shores of Horne Lake to the head of the Alberni Inlet.

As a distinct people, however, the Pentlatch are said to exist no longer. They were especially hard hit by smallpox, which swept through in the late 1700s. The Qualicum First Nation is now home to the descendants of a small number of Pentlatch, their spouses, and others who have joined them.

The **Qualicum Campsite** offers river and oceanfront camping at 5850 River Rd.; 757-9337, in summer only. From October to April, their estuary is closed to fishing and recreation to protect and enhance the fragile salmon fishery and wildlife.

Southern Kwakwa̱ka'wakw Territories: The Lekwiltok Tribes

From the Englishman River at Qualicum north to the Salmon River near Sayward is a region of relatively recent Kwakwa̱ka'wakw predominance. Formerly, this was home for Coast Salish-speaking peoples who still occupy the adjacent islands and mainland coast. They shared this northern frontier with a powerful confederation of Kwakwa̱ka'wakw tribes, called the Lekwiltok, dubbed "the Vikings of Vancouver Island" for their prowess as seamen. The Lekwiltok people's first ancestor and patriarch was Wiakay, whose family was chosen by a supernatural being to survive the flood. After the waters receded, two canoes landed at Jackson Bay just across the narrow strait from the Salmon River. Two of the strongest Lekwiltok tribes today, the Wewaikai and Weiwaikum, derive their names from Wiakay. According to Lekwiltok historians, two more of Wiakay's sons drifted away, one north to Kitamaat, and the other south to Neah Bay.

About two centuries ago, the Salmon River Kwakwa̱ka'wakw joined the northernmost Coast Salish-speaking Comox people, and began moving south from Jackson Bay, into strategic sites along the narrow channels, on Quadra Island, and at present-day Campbell River. Sometimes they kept the old Salish names for their new homes, sometimes they gave them their own, in their Kwakwa̱ka'wakw dialect, Likwala. These areas became home base for their many excursions—dreaded by people from Puget Sound to Yale on the Fraser River.

V　**Comox:** (Pop. 237/110). 4 km east of Courtenay, on Comox Rd., overlooking Comox Harbour. Many of the Salish-speaking peoples from the Salmon River area finally coalesced here. But it wasn't long before Lekwiltok culture prevailed, by way of intermarriage. Comox, "abundance" in Kwakwala, has long been treasured for its wealth of resources. There may be artists at work in the new craft building adjacent the Big House; artifacts and work for sale are on display. Also on display is the community's canoe, *I'hos,*—"double-head serpent."

?　**Comox Administration:** 3320 Comox Rd., Courtenay, B.C., V9N 3P8. Tel: 339-4545.

I　**Big Rock:** About 40 km north of Courtenay, near Rotary Beach at the entrance to Campbell River. The Comox people say this was Whale; he swallowed Mink for making fun of him. Mink decided to make a fire and cook up some herring (the whale's undigested supper). Tired of bumping his head on Whale's heart, he sliced it up, causing Whale to beach himself here.

T　**Campbell River:** (Pop. 21,005/610 Ab). Administrative, transportation, and service centre for about 30 Kwakwa̱ka'wakw, Nuu-chah-nulth, and Coast Salish communities of northeast Vancouver Island and the adjacent mainland coast. Some have even moved here from their remote coastal locations. Among them are the **Kwiakah**, whose name, "to club," reminds us they too were warriors once, from Phillips Arm. Also here are members of the **Mamaleleqala** and **Qwe'Qwa'Sot'Enox** tribes from Village and Gilford islands, and **Homalco** people (see below).

☉　**Campbell River Museum/Regional Centre of Culture and History:** 470 Island Hwy, south of city centre; 287-3103. The impressive new structure overlooking Discovery Passage and Cape Mudge is a cultural gateway. Items from collections are used in ceremonies;

visitor programs and tours draw upon First Nations experts. Construction of major exhibits is an ongoing project. Those focussing on First Nations include *The Undersea Realm of the Kwakwaka'wakw,* which features ceremonial items illustrating the dance prerogative of a chiefly family. The exhibit was developed in consultation with the family whose tradition is being depicted. The museum also has archives, a gift shop, and books.

⑥ **Poles:** At public sites throughout Campbell River, and at Weiwaikum community, below. Ask at Travel Infocentre.

▼ **Weiwaikum:** (Pop. 486/195). On the north side of Campbell River, take Weiwaikum Rd. off Hwy 28 to administrative centre. This former Comox village was already abandoned when Lekwiltok chief Kwaksistala, "Captain John," and his Salish wife came here at the end of the last century, to establish Klamata on the rich Campbell River estuary, where Tyee Spit juts into Discovery Passage. The community has flourished, and is now planning one of the largest First Nations' developments in Canada. There will be a big-house-style cultural centre, major marina and cruise-ship facility, hotel, shopping centre, and fish-processing plant. Already bustling, the busy **Discovery Harbour Marina**, 287-2614; **Seabreeze Cafe**; and **Thunderbird RV Park**, 286-3344; these are reached via Spit Rd. off Hwy 28. The Kwakiutl District Council is also based here.

❓ **Weiwaikum Administration:** 1400 Weiwaikum Rd., Campbell River, B.C., V9W 5W8. Tel: 286-6949.

❓ **Mamaleleqala-Qwe'Qwa'Sot'Enox Administration:** 1400 Weiwaikum Rd., Campbell River, B.C., V9W 5W8. Tel: 287-2955. Those wishing to visit Village Island (see below) must obtain permission and pay a small fee here.

❓ **Kwiakah Administration:** 1440 Island Hwy, Campbell River, B.C., V9W 2E3. Tel: 286-1295.

▼ **Homalco:** (Pop. 130). Erickson Rd., then Homathco Dr. The "swift water" people are Coast-Salish speakers from the mainland. They once occupied many villages in their traditional territories, along Bute Inlet and the rivers flowing into it (see chapter 7). By 1900 most had settled at Church House, and are now concentrated in Vancouver, Powell River, and here (see Campbell River, above).

❓ **Homalco Administration:** 1218 Bute Cres., Campbell River, B.C. Tel: 923-4979. Homalco is also a member of the Alliance Tribal Council (see chapter 7).

To Cape Mudge by Ferry from Campbell River

▼ **Wewaikai (Cape Mudge):** (Pop. 705/329). On the south end of Quadra Island, reached by regular ferry from downtown Campbell River. The village, on sandy cliffs overlooking Discovery Passage, is visible from Vancouver Island. In former times, its walls and lookouts augmented the natural fortification and its moat of perilous rip tides. Anyone paddling south to trade at the new fort in Victoria would have to pass through this, the narrowest passage between Vancouver Island and the mainland. Plankton-rich tides support all five salmon species.

⑥ **Kwagiulth Museum:** At Cape Mudge. Tel: 285-3733. Its seasnail-inspired design houses sacred ceremonial objects and regalia used in winter dances. These are some of the items that were confiscated by the federal government in the early 1900s: a portion were returned in 1979. The museum is managed by the Nuyumbalees Society, "the beginning of all legends," to help keep the histories of the *nu'mima,* the original families, alive. It also helps keep the culture alive. "Cedar the Tree of Life" is a demonstration of the many uses of cedar—how the inner bark of the tree was used to make rope and clothing; how bentwood boxes were made from a single piece of wood. When the tide is low enough, there are tours to petroglyphs along the shore. There are also several petroglyphs right at the museum. In summer, a favourite is the Puppet Theatre, featuring Kwakiulth legends. The gift shop features a wide selection of First Nations' book titles, and pieces from such artists as Pam Holloway (paintings and prints) and Cecil Dawson (masks).

⑤ **Tsa-Kwa-Luten Lodge:** Via Lighthouse Rd. beyond Cape Mudge. Box 460, Quathiaski Cove, B.C., V0P 1N0. 285-2042; reservations 1-800-665-7745. This dramatic cedar-and-glass big house looking out over Discovery Passage takes its name, "the gathering place," from the Salish village that once stood here. On the rocky shore below, petroglyphs and the layers of earth and shell that form the very bluffs speak of previous hosts and guests. Modern feasts feature salmon, clams, prawns, mussels, fiddlehead ferns, salmonberry shoots and dulse, followed by traditional dances and stories, and luxurious accommodation.

⑤ **We Wai Kay Campsite:** Follow signs from ferry to beach and forest sites overlooking Rebecca Spit; 285-3111.

❓ **Cape Mudge Administration:** Box 220, Quathiaski Cove, B.C., V0P 1N0. Tel: 285-3316.

To Coast Salish Territories on Cortes Island, by Ferry from Quadra Island

This side trip takes you out of Kwakwaka'-wakw territories, and into the territories of Coast Salish-speaking Klahoose peoples. Cortes Island should be included with the Coast Salish–speaking Shíshálh and Sliammon

peoples (see chapter 7) on the mainland; however, for today's highway and ferry travellers, access is possible only from Vancouver Island.

The Klahoose people once lived in a dozen villages on Cortes Island's north half and along Toba Inlet, on the mainland. Among their ancient island sites was Tl'it-l'7aamin. Young women, shaking clam shell rattles, drove porpoises into the shallow lagoon, where young men wrestled them to demonstrate their strength. Today, the Klahoose people live on Cortes Island at Tu7kw, Squirrel Cove (below), and near Powell River with their Sliammon relatives. There are still impressions in the ground from their fortified village at Smelt Bay. Houses were built in deep trenches; tunnels led to hiding places in the forest.

Tiny **Mitlenatch Island** to the south received its name from the Salish-speaking people who gathered seagull eggs here. "Calm back end" provides safe moorage whichever way the wind blows. The island was once a canoe: Crow and his companions, travelling from the head of Toba Inlet, were fleeing the Transformer. He caught up with them.

▼ **Klahoose:** (Pop. 60). At Tu7kw, **Squirrel Cove**, on Cortes Island. This is the only portion of Klahoose territories reached by car. Other areas are reached by boat or seaplane. Here on Cortes Island, the Klahoose people and the B.C. government jointly manage **Von Donop-Hathayim Provincial Marine Park**, at Von Donop Inlet. The park protects tidal lagoons and old-growth forests of this place long known as Hathayim and traditionally used for clamming, hunting, fishing, and gathering roots and bark. Today, visitors are welcome here for wilderness camping. The park can be reached by boat, but is only accessible overland from Squirrel Cove at low tide.

❓ **Klahoose Administration:** Box 9, Squirrel Cove, Cortes Island, B.C., V0P 1K0. Tel: 935-6536.

North from Campbell River on Highway 19

❚ **Keep Your Eyes Open For:** Dzunukwa is the wild woman of the woods. She steals children. Sisutl, the double-headed serpent, can bring great power—or death—to those who encounter him. Wend (z)isbalis, who has no head at all, was last seen near Cape Mudge about 40 years ago, floating like a drift log. Bagwees, a hairy little man about 1 m tall, lives much as we do, only at the bottom of the sea.

❚ ❏ **Salmon River/Road to Sayward:** 64 km north of Campbell River. These are the northern reaches of territories occupied until recent centuries by the Salmon River people. The highway junction also marks the confluence of the Salmon and White rivers, and the village site of Tatuma. To the north, on the Salmon River's west bank, is the modern town of Sayward, at the former site of D(z)awenadi, "having coho salmon." On the east bank was Hkusam, "greasy, or oily." That village's name endures on the nearby Mt. Hukusam. The mountain's Kwakwala name is Hiatsee Saklekum, "where the breath of the sea lion gathers at the blowhole," for the fog that hovers over its peak.

❏ **Beaver Cove Road:** 122 km north of Sayward junction. Leads 2 km to the non-native village of **Telegraph Cove**.

Gateway to Kwakwaka'wakw Islands and Inlets

Telegraph Cove overlooks the cluster of islands and peninsulas that bring the straits almost to a close. This is the departure point for freight and mail services to small Kwakwaka'wakw communities with long names, long histories. There are few visitor services.

The entrance to Knight Inlet is shared by three tribes: the Mamaleleqala, the Matlipi, and the Tlowitsis. The first ancestor of the

Mamaleleqala was a blind man who lived near here, at Beaver Harbour. He tricked the Transformer into restoring his sight to the point where he could see monsters in the ocean's darkest depths. Much of recent Mamaleleqala history is concentrated on **Village Island**, where Emma Bell and Dan Cranmer held their potlatch in 1921 (see chapter introduction). The last families left here 30 years ago, and today most live at Alert Bay, Port Hardy, and Campbell River. The old longhouse, school, and poles draw cultural tours, kayak excursions, private visits. Within the traditional territories of the Tlowitsis is **Robson Bight**, an ecological reserve protecting killer whales who come to rub their bellies and backs on the gravelly shallows. About 150 years ago, the Tlowitsis took over the former Kwakiutl village, Karlakwis, "bent beach," on Turnour Island, after its occupants moved to Beaver Harbour. The Tlowitsis continue to live on Turnour Island, and also at Alert Bay.

Gilford Island, in relatively recent times, has been shared by four tribes: the Gwawaenuk, Qwe'Qwa'Sot'Enox, Hahuamis (Ah-Kwah-ah-Mish), and Tsawataineuk. Known collectively as the Musgamagw, or the four Tsawataineuk tribes, their territories extended north, west, and east of Gilford. In 1856, a group of northerners attacked the main Qwe'-Qwa'Sot'Enox village of Gwyasdums, killing all but 20 people, many of whom moved to Village Island. The Gwawaenuk, Hahuamis, and Tsawataineuk then began to occupy this choice location. They all potlatched together here until the early 1900s when many Tsawataineuk and Gwawaenuk returned to their ancestral villages (see below), leaving Gwyasdums to the descendants of the surviving Qwe'Qwa'Sot'Enox and the Hahuamis.

Upper Knight Inlet is shared by the Tenaktak and the Awaetlala tribes. Every spring thousands of Kwakwaka'wakw travelled great distances to reach Tsawatti, "having eulachon," at the mouth of the Klinaklini River. *Klinaklini,* in Kwakwala, means "eula-

The U'mista Cultural Centre at Alert Bay, built in 1979, is home for repatriated potlatch treasures. All who come respectfully are honoured guests.
CREDIT: DOROTHY HAEGERT

chon oil." In 1860, after a slide destroyed the Tenaktak's main village, Wakas, they and their Awaetlala friends began a century of migrations that have led them to Alert Bay.

Kingcome Inlet is homeland of the Tsawataineuk, "people with eulachon" (see Gilford Island, above). Their ancient village Gwa'yi, "downriver," sits on the banks of the Kingcome River, a source of sustenance since their first ancestor, Kawadelekela, came from the mountains. In 1993, for the first time in living memory, the eulachon failed to arrive. The Tsawataineuk worry about the logging upriver, filling the Kingcome with silt.

❓ Tsawataineuk Administration: Kingcome Inlet, Kingcome Village, B.C., V0N 2B0. Tel: Kingcome Operator 5255.

Tiny Watson Island, just west of Kingcome Inlet, is original home of the Gwawaenuk, "the downstream people," who moved back here from Gwyasdums (see above) early this century. Their village, Hikums, is also known as Hopetown.

❓ Gwawaenuk: Box 344, Port McNeill, B.C., V0N 2R0. Tel: 949-8732.

North of Beaver Cove/ Telegraph Cove on Highway 19

◼ Nimpkish River: 2 km beyond Beaver Cove junction, Hwy 19 crosses the Nimpkish River just above its wide mouth. This was once the main village of the Nimpkish or 'Namgis people. They call the river Gwa'ni, honouring the supernatural origins of both the river and their ancestors. A complete rendering of the story is given at the U'Mista Cultural Centre in Alert Bay, where the 'Namgis now live. It tells how the Transformer, K̲'anik̲ilakw, came here and impregnated three daughters belonging to Gwa'nalalis. He married the fourth, and turned Gwa'nalalis into a river, "full of salmon so that your descendants may never starve." Their village here, called Xwalkw, "logs placed crosswise," became known to newcomers as Cheslakee—for the chief who met Captain Vancouver in 1792. From here, the Nimpkish controlled the main Kwakwa̲ka'wakw overland route to the west-coast peoples, whom they supplied with eulachon oil. Guns they received in trade were traded again to Lekwiltok warriors. About 125 years ago, the 'Namgis moved their main winter village to Alert Bay, already an important fishing site, to take advantage of new economic opportunities (see below). A right turn off the bridge leads to the **Cheslakee Salmon Hatchery**; 956-4712.

To Alert Bay: By Ferry from Port McNeill

▼ **'Namgis (Nimpkish):** (Pop. 1,336/714). On Cormorant Island, directly across Broughton Strait from the Nimpkish River, is 'Yalis, "spreading leg beach," new home of the 'Namgis. They sometimes refer to this as the "Vancouver" of Kwakwaka'wakw territories, and call the residents of the much larger islands—Gilford, Turnour, and Village—"the islanders."

'Yalis is actually host to three main communities. The non-native community of **Alert Bay** (pop. 630/105 Ab) sits to the right off the ferry. To the left, Bill Cranmer's cafe marks the beginning of the 'Namgis reserve, embracing as well the Whe-la-la-u community—people from Village Island, Knight Inlet, and Cape Sutil.

The 'Namgis and non-native communities have grown up together here: first as trading partners, then with the development of a salmon saltery, cannery, mission, and Indian Agency, all before 1900. Since then, the 'Namgis have grown independently, maintaining one of the province's largest First Nations–owned fishing fleets.

St. Michael's Residential School, built in 1929, now houses Kwakwaka'wakw and 'Namgis administrative offices. And Alert Bay is the venue for many potlatches, including those hosted by smaller communities.

Ⓖ **U'Mista Cultural Centre:** Box 253, Alert Bay, B.C., V0N 1A0. Tel: 974-5403. Left from ferry dock. The word *U'mista* hearkens back to the time people were taken as slaves, then,

through providence, found their way home—like the masks and coppers of untold value, taken after the Cranmer potlatch. Visitors enter from the right—as a dancer does. Potlatch items appear in order of importance. Also to see are a petroglyph from Nimpkish River, baskets and carvings, photographs, and stories from the beginning of time. *Box of Treasures* is a video about Dan Cranmer's potlatch. For groups, there are special performances, tours, and lectures. Kwakwaka'wakw children and adults also come here to learn or teach: there are dancing and singing lessons, language and art classes, courses in making button blankets. This is also a research and resource centre: the staff works closely with tribal and band councils. For visitors, there is a book and gift shop.

Ⓖ **World's Tallest Totem Pole:** Above cultural centre. At its base, a chief holds a copper, the symbol of wealth and all that is temporal. Above him, spirit, law, human will, and the intoxicating powers of this world are represented by figures of Raven, Grizzly Bear, the serpent Sisutl, and the wild woman, Dzunukwa. On the very top is a sun mask; at 52.7 m, it is visible to all approaching 'Yalis. It was carved by Chief Adam Dick (Kwaxistala), his father, James Dick, brother Ben, and Dora Cook. Since 1972, when it was raised, this pole has maintained its title in the *Guinness Book of Records* as the world's tallest. In 1994, the Lekwammen, in Victoria, raised a pole 2.1 m taller. The 'Namgis will not be outdone—there are plans to raise another.

Ⓖ **Alert Bay Indian Day School:** Turn left off ferry dock. Opened in 1900, the school was used as the lock-up during the potlatch trials of 1922. Nearby at **Christ Church**, built in 1892, hymns and prayers are offered in Kwakwala and English.

Ⓖ **Nimpkish Burial Grounds:** Right from ferry dock. There are 10 poles, one raised for

Mungo Martin (see page 26). Please appreciate, respectfully, from outside the fence.

Ⓖ **Gator Gardens Ecological Park:** Trails and boardwalk offer passage through the marsh created by a dam at the turn of the century. Bring Nancy Turner's *Plants in British Columbia Technology*. Trail #2 leads to culturally modified trees, where strips of cedar bark and, in one case, a plank of wood have been taken.

Ⓖ **Events:** Father's Day weekend, during **June Sports**, First Nations soccer teams from up and down Vancouver Island are featured. The **Sea Festival**, mid- to late August, features a salmon barbecue, dancing, and boat races.

❓ **Nimpkish Council:** Box 210, Alert Bay, B.C., V0N 1A0. Tel: 974-5556.

❓ **Tanakteuk Council:** Box 330, Alert Bay, B.C., V0N 1A0. Tel: 974-5489.

❓ **Tlowitsis-Mumtagilia Council:** Box 150, Alert Bay, B.C., V0N 1A0. Tel: 974-5501.

❓ **Tlatlasikwala Council:** Box 270, Alert Bay, B.C., V0N 1A0. Tel: 974-2000.

❓ **Whe-la-la-u Area Council:** Box 150, Alert Bay, B.C., V0N 1A0. Tel: 974-5904.

▮ **Cluxewe:** Just beyond Port McNeill, Hwy 19 crosses the river named for the village formerly on its east bank. The village, Xwadzadzo'lis, sat on the west bank, and Tsikwkwyu was about 2 km upcoast. Represented here were three of the four Kwagul or Kwakiutl tribes that coalesced at Fort Rupert in 1849 (see below). From 1836 they mined coal in this area and sold it to the Hudson's Bay Company.

▼ **Kwakiutl (Fort Rupert):** (Pop. 530/278). 42 km north of Port McNeill, take the airport turnoff onto Beaver Harbour Rd. Then turn onto T'sakis Way. Tsaxis, or "stream running on beach," was known for its fat and plentiful clams long before it became fur-and-coal capital for the four Kwagul tribes whose name, "smoke of the world," came to rise above all others.

In 1849, the Hudson's Bay Company, hoping to gain more control of nearby coal fields, established Fort Rupert here. The Kwagul tribes, aiming to clinch their intermediary role in the fur trade, joined them. They left their main villages along the Cluxewe River and, on either side of the fort's palisaded walls, built new longhouses in rows facing the harbour. Tsaxis became a metropolis of 3,000. The Kwagul set up a treaty, requiring the Hudson's Bay Company to pay for its allotment of land. The coal was the Kwagul's, to mine and sell—a point they were forced to reiterate when the company imported Scottish miners to work underground. Conflicts that arose from this, and the location of better-quality coal at Nanaimo to the south, contributed to the company's departure in 1882.

The fort's last chief factor, Scottish-born Robert Hunt, and his wife, Mary Ebbetts, a Tlingit noblewoman from Alaska, stayed on to run the old company store. They had 11 children—most of whom married into the Kwagul people, who by the turn of the century numbered only 100. Local folklore says anyone who has lived on northern Vancouver Island for more than two generations is related to the Hunts. Among them are some of the best artists and dancers in the world today. George Hunt (born in 1854), worked with German anthropologist Franz Boas, collecting artifacts and documenting the pre-contact ways of the Kwagul people.

Administrative offices look out to the lone chimney that remains of the old fort. From the beach are views of Deer Island, where Edward Curtis filmed *Land of the Headhunters* (renamed *Land of the War Canoe*) with a cast of Kwakwa̱ka'wakw pursuing their love for the arts. (The film can be viewed at

Port Hardy Museum in Port Hardy, below.) Ask for permission and directions to see the petroglyphs. **The Copper Maker**, 114 Copper Way, is a carving studio and gallery owned by Calvin and Marie Hunt. At nearby Port Hardy Airport are poles carved by Charlie James, the chief who taught Mungo Martin how to carve.

? **Kwakiutl Administration:** Box 1440, Port Hardy, B.C., V0N 2P0. Tel: 949-6012.

West off Highway 19 toward Coal Harbour

V **New Quatsino:** (279/183). 2 km north of turnoff to Beaver Harbour Rd., Coal Harbour Rd. leads west, 12 km to New Quatsino. It was just a few strokes of an Indian agent's pen that turned one tribe into another. The people of Quatsino are, actually, mostly Koskimo. In 1929, the Quatsino numbered only 7; the Koskimo, 39. These were the survivors of the six tribes that two centuries before ruled the capes from Scott to Cook. Eventually they coalesced at the heart of the four long inlets of Quatsino Sound, at Hwates, an ancient Koskimo home, just a few kilometres east of the non-native community, Quatsino, only accessible by boat or plane. In the early 1970s they came to New Quatsino, a clearcut 2 km from the sea, closer to hospitals, schools, work; not far, as the spirit flies, from the wind-lashed capes of the northwest tip—their place of origin and the beginning of so many legends featuring the Transformer, <u>K</u>'ani<u>k</u>ilakw.

? **New Quatsino Administration:** Box 100, Coal Harbour, B.C., V0N 1K0. Tel: 949-6245.

V **Gwa'sala-Nakwaxda'xw:** (452/372). A suburb of **Port Hardy** (pop. 5,070/150 Ab), at Tsulquate, "having heat." In the 1800s, the Gwa'sala, "northern people," lived at Kigeh in Smith Inlet, on the frontier bordering the Oweekeno territories. The Nakwaxda'xw,

"people from all around," had villages throughout the maze of inlets just this side of the Gwa'sala. A century ago, they came together at Blunden Harbour, for better access to halibut and deep-sea fisheries, and the new economy. They moved to Port Hardy in 1962.

? **Gwa'sala-Nakwaxda'xw:** Box 998, Port Hardy, B.C., V0N 2P0. Tel: 949-8343.

☉ **Port Hardy Museum and Archives:** 7110 Market St.; 949-8143. Edward Curtis's epic film, *Land of the War Canoe,* is on video, as is the film *Kwakiutl of B.C.* The museum also houses an exhibit on the excavation site at Bear Cove—a midden that now lies beneath the B.C. Ferries parking lot. People lived here 12,000 years ago.

The Windy North Tip of Vancouver Island

On the north tip of Vancouver Island the winds blow ceaselessly. But they're nothing compared to the foul tempests that kept the first Nahwitty people at Ga'ya, known today as Bull Harbour, from fishing for halibut and cod, or even gathering mussels. Slowly starving, they called on their supernatural chief to defeat Malalanukw—from whose anus the great wind came. In setting Malalanukw on fire, the chief got from him a promise there would be, from time to time, four days of good weather in a stretch, so his people could harvest food.

The Nahwitty people are actually three tribes. The largest is the Tlatlasikwala, those "outside . . . on the ocean shore," whose domain is the very north tip on either side of Cape Scott. At contact, the tribes shared a village-fortress on the rocks at Cape Sutil. But, vulnerable to attacks from northern First Nations as well as European ships, they made their way back to Ga'ya. Most of the Nahwitty are now at Alert Bay.

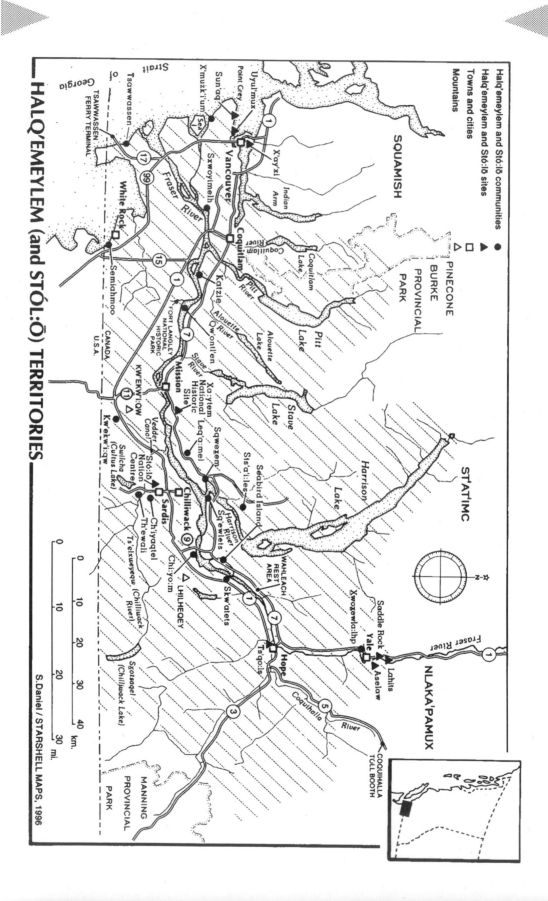

HALQ'EMEYLEM (and STÓL:Ō) TERRITORIES

S. Daniel / STARSHELL MAPS, 1996

Halq'emeylem and Stó:lō communities
Halq'emeylem and Stó:lō sites
Towns and cities
Mountains

SQUAMISH

Strait of Georgia

Tsawwassen
TSAWWASSEN FERRY TERMINAL

X̱'muzk'i'um
Point Grey
Uy'ul'mux
Sun'aq
Sxwoyimelh

Vancouver
Sey
X'ay'xi
Indian Arm

Coquitlam River
Coquitlam Lake

PINECONE BURKE PROVINCIAL PARK

White Rock
Semiahmoo
Semiahmoo

Fraser River

CANADA
U.S.A.

Katzie
Qw'ontl'en
Alouette River
Pitt Lake
Alouette
Alouette Lake

FORT LANGLEY NATIONAL HISTORIC PARK

Mission
Xa:ytem National Historic Site/ Leq'a:mel

KWE'KWE'I:QW

Stave River
Stave Lake

Sawexem

Sumas Canal

Vedder Canal

Sis'a:tles

Seabird Island

Harrison Lake

STAT'IMC

Sucilcha (Cultus Lake)
Kwekwi:qw
Stó:lō Nation Centre
Ch'iyaqtel
The'wali
Sardis
Chilliwack (9)
Chi'yo:m
Ts'elxweyeqw (Chilliwack River)
LHILHEQEY
Skw'atets
Harrison River Squewlets
WAHLEACH REST AREA

Xwoxewla:lhp
Saddle Rock
Lahlts
Aselaw
Yale

NLAKA'PAMUX

Fraser River

Tsqo:ls

Hope

Coquihalla River

COQUIHALLA TOLL BOOTH

Sxotsaqel (Chilliwack Lake)

MANNING PROVINCIAL PARK

N↑

0 10 20 30 40 km.
0 10 20 30 mi.

CHAPTER 5

Halq'emeylem (including Stó:lō)

Our elders tell us we have been here since time immemorial. They also tell us through stories and legends that many of our resources were at one time our ancestors. . . . So when we use a resource, like a sturgeon or a cedar tree, we have to say a prayer to our ancestors who were transformed into these things.

—Albert "Sonny" McHalsie, Yewal Siya:m, Ohamil

Halq'emeylem is the language spoken by the people whose world, Temexw, begins where the Fraser River pours out from the narrow canyon above Yale and extends 180 kilometres to its wide mouth in the Strait of Georgia. Here, the word for all rivers is *stó:lo,* but this is *the stó:lo.* As many as one million salmon, sturgeon, eulachon, and trout may, on any given day, seethe through the murky waters of the Fraser. It is one of the largest food reservoirs on the continent. In earlier times, the river's life-giving energies sustained the thousands of people who lived along its banks, and thousands more who journeyed here from Vancouver Island as part of a re-markable web of families spanning the straits.

Today, many of the 30 communities along the Fraser River's banks and tributaries are joined in a political alliance called the Stó:lo Nation. And all Halq'emeylem people share strong links to one another through their extended family networks, their river, and their resources.

From canyon to sea, their villages trace its banks. Their histories reach back to the beginning of time, when certain people were transformed into the river's first salmon and the first sturgeon. There are many accounts of the Transformers, Xexa:ls—three brothers and a sister—who travelled up and down the river. Across the straits and back again they came, "making things right," teaching people not to be greedy with their resources.

Just below the canyon, at Aselaw, archaeologists have measured at least 9,500 years of human occupation. Excavations farther downriver, at the village now embraced by **Xa:ytem National Historic Site**, tell a similar story. The **Great Fraser Midden**, on the rich lowlands down at the river mouth, is 3,000 years deep—people were living at the nearby village, X'muzk'i'um (Musqueam) before the deltas separating the river's north and south arms were even formed. The *stó:lo* is still depositing silt here; the delta is growing three metres a year.

Whatever touches the river touches its people; what travels by the river finds them.

Sto:lo fisherman at Saddle Rock, the first major rapids on the Fraser River, and one of the most important fishing sites on the river.
CREDIT: RICK BLACKLAWS

Slellacum—supernatural beings—entered a delta bog from the straits by way of an underground channel. Silquey, the double-headed serpent, brought death or power to those who encountered it in the sloughs near Chilliwack. Coastal raiders seeking slaves came as far as the canyon. The river was a route for smallpox in the 1760s and again in the 1800s—it took up to 90 percent of a large population.

Then came the *xwelitem,* "the hungry people." First the Spanish, then the British, sailed into the straits in the 1790s, but somehow missed the *stó:lo.* It wasn't until the spring of 1808 that the explorer Simon Fraser drifted downriver from the canyon, lacking food and relatives to feed him. The Halq'emeylem gave him what he needed. In the early 1820s, British fur traders established Fort Langley on the river's south bank. The abundance of salmon here did not go unnoticed any more than the thousands of people who canoed past them in early August, bound for their canyon fishing sites. They passed by again in September on their return, their vessels joined by planks to form dried-salmon barges. The Europeans, though few in numbers, bought huge quantities of salted salmon from the river people, then exported it to even hungrier posts, as far away as Hawaii and California.

In 1858, some 30,000 *xwelitem* swarmed up the *stó:lo.* Their hunger for gold was soon replaced by a hunger for the land itself. The colony of British Columbia was declared, with the fur- and fish-trading centre of Fort Langley its first capital. In the 1860s, New Westminster, on the site of the former Qw'ontl'en capital, became the "first incorporated Canadian city west of the great lakes." In 1866, the first Fraser River cannery was established right across the river, and by 1888 there were *xwelitem* laws declaring it illegal for the people of the river to sell their salmon. By the turn of the century, 30 canneries clogged the Fraser's lower reaches. Halq'emeylem leaders protested reckless overfishing and the dumping of millions of salmon by dozens of canneries unable to process them all. The province's reply: further restrictions on their access to both commercial and food fisheries.

It has taken nearly a century, but finally in 1990, the Supreme Court of Canada acknowledged aboriginal peoples' right to fish for food, for ceremonial and societal purposes, maintaining this is second in importance only to the conservation of salmon. The Halq'emeylem people are still subject to strict federal fisheries laws; their allowable catch remains a fraction of that given commercial and sports fisheries. But their presence on the river never ebbs: they have been among the first aboriginal peoples to sign agreements in recent years, ackowledging their right, for the first time in a century, to sell a portion of their allowable catch. And they are in the forefront of programs aimed at preserving this resource they still honour as being among their ancestors.

INFORMATION AND PROTOCOL

The Stó:lo Nation is a modern alliance of 24 communities. It comprises the House of Siya:m (leaders elected from each communi-

ty), the House of Elders, and the House of Justice (which oversees culturally specific legal matters). The Katzie, Coquitlam, X'muzk'i'um, Tsawwassen, and Yale communities, though not members of the Stó:lo Nation, maintain strong cultural ties, and participate in joint initiatives.

The language, Halq'emeylem, is composed of an upriver and downriver dialect. The word Halq'emeylem is spelled here according to the upriver dialect. The downriver spelling sometimes appears as Hun'qumi'-num. A third, Vancouver Island, dialect is pronounced and spelled Hul'qumi'num.

The Semiahmoo people, also included in this section because they are on the traveller's route, share cultural and language ties with the Lummi and Samish peoples south of the Canada-U.S. border, and with the Lekwammen and Wsanec peoples across the Strait of Georgia.

Only Stó:lo communities with visitor services are listed in the route description below. Travellers interested in learning more are most welcome to visit the new **Longhouse Interpretive Centre** in Sardis, near Chilliwack. The Stó:lo Nation is also preparing a book on their history and territories.

Please drive slowly, heed signs.

? **Stó:lo Nation:** 7201 Vedder Rd., Box 310, Sardis, B.C., V2R 1A7. Tel: 858-3366. Fax: 858-4790. Members: Aitchelitz, Chawathil, Chi:yo:m (Cheam), Qw'ontl'en, Kwak-wakw-A-pilt, Leq'a:mel (Nicomen), Matsqui, Ohamil, Popkum, Scowlitz, Seabird Island, Ska-wah-look, Skowkale, Skw'atets (Peters), Skway, Soowhalie, Squiala, Kw'ekw'i:qw (Sumas), Ch'iyaqtel (Tzeachten), Union Bar, Yakweak-wioose.

? **Allied Tribal Council:** 130 N. Tsawwassen Dr., Delta, B.C., V4K 3N2. Tel: 943-6712. Fax: 943-5367. Ten Lower Mainland and Vancouver Island members include Tsawwassen, Sliammon, and Katzie.

Gateway to Temexw: Approaching Vancouver

Overlooking the Strait of Georgia, the X'muzk'i'um, Tsawwassen, and Semiahmoo peoples sit strategically at the entrance to the *stó:lo* we now call the Fraser River. Today, their communities are also gateways to the largest city on Canada's west coast, named for the British Captain George Vancouver, one of the first Europeans they met. The X'muzk'i'um look out to the Vancouver International Airport; the people of Tsawwassen look out to the B.C. Ferries Terminal. The Semiahmoo community is just this side of the Canada-U.S. border.

▼ **X'muzk'i'um (Musqueam):** (Pop. 890). Salish Dr., off South West Marine Drive in Vancouver. These marshy lowlands overlooking the north arm of the Fraser River have been their home for 3,000 years—longer than the species of grass that once thrived on the foreshore here and which may be the root of their ancient name, X'muzk'i'um, or Musqueam. This is the central village of many ancestral sites that stretched from the south arm of the Fraser River to the mountains of the North Shore—where they harvested the white wool of the mountain goat for weaving.

Just 3 km south of X'muzk'i'um, at the foot of Granville St., blacktop, sidewalks, and the Fraser Arms Hotel sit atop a plateau of rich earth mixed with clam and mussel shells. The **Great Fraser Midden**, or Marpole site, first examined in the early 1890s, marks not only an ancient village, but a shift in understanding. In the 1950s, the first radiocarbon dating on the Northwest Coast was conducted here, catapulting scientific guesstimates of the age of this sea-and-salmon-based culture to several millennia, from just six or seven hundred years. Results countered the prevailing notion that this society was young and mobile, "proving" its stable nature and verifying what the people here have always said. The village reached its peak 2,500 years ago. It watched

the river giving birth to Sea Island, metre by metre. As the *stó:lo*'s silt moved the west coast farther west, the Marpole people shifted too, gradually joining those already at X'muzk'i'um. Sea Island continued to grow. Two small villages eventually appeared. And in the 1970s, the X'muzk'i'um looked out to see Vancouver's international airport emerging there.

Throughout what is now the city of **Vancouver** (463,385/5,950 Ab) are sites the X'muzk'i'um selected and developed long ago. Still favourite places: S7xi'lix, "standing rock," in **Stanley Park**, where the Transformers commemorated a young man's devotion to tradition by turning him to stone for all to see. X'ay'xi at nearby Lumbermen's Arch was a village named for the mask held sacred to the Halq'emeylem peoples and their Squamish neighbours. Its middens were used in the late 1880s to surface a road around the perimeter of the new park; its houses were burned and people were told to leave after smallpox broke out. False Creek, site of today's trendy Granville Island Market, was much bigger than now, and a favoured place for catching sturgeon and salmon. At Locarno Beach is another ancient midden and archaeological site. Sunaq, at Kitsilano, was a seasonal village —too windy, the elders say, to stay there in the winter. Less than 1 km farther were the two villages, Uyul'mux, and "little" Uyul'mux, at Jericho Beach.

X'muzk'i'um has been home and headquarters since the colonial period, when it was marked out as the reserve. Today, jets land and take off within view of their small community; behind it, traffic hums steadily along Marine Drive, a thoroughfare tracing their ancient trails around the coast. Here are the estates of Point Grey and the sprawling campus of the University of British Columbia. This is real estate so precious that the X'muzk'i'um have leased a portion of their reserve lands for two golf courses and high-priced homes.

Yet the X'muzk'i'um community remains an island unto itself. "It was the X'muzk'i'um

Among the many monumental poles in the Great Hall at the UBC Museum of Anthropology are these red cedar house posts carved by Kwakwa̱ka̱'wakw artists George Nelson and Quatsino Hansen, circa 1906.
CREDIT: UBC MUSEUM OF ANTHROPOLOGY

way to be very private," says Pat Berringer. Fishing is, as always, essential to their livelihood. Carvers and weavers continue to develop their subtle Coast Salish style. Their art has always been more private than many of the other, more flamboyant styles. That is where its power lies. Soon this will be evident to those entering Temexw via the **Vancouver Airport**. When the new terminal is completed, international visitors will be greeted as they disembark by a prominent display of X'muzk'i'um culture. Two 6-metre cedar "welcome figures" and the largest spindle whorl ever carved will be accompanied by gigantic Coast Salish weavings.

The X'muzk'i'um people welcome visitors to their territories; they invite them to stroll the beaches where their villages stood and to view house posts from these villages, now on display at the **University of British Columbia Museum of Anthropology** (see below). The **Vancouver Museum** has artifacts from the Marpole Midden. The Marpole village site itself, never set aside as a reserve, has recently been purchased by the X'muzk'i'um as a protective measure, with hopes that in the future it will become a cultural centre.

? **X'muzk'i'um (Musqueam) Administration:** 6370 Salish Dr., Vancouver, B.C., V6N 2C6. Tel: 263-3261. Fax: 263-4212.

University of British Columbia Museum of Anthropology: 6393 North West Marine Dr. On the bluffs of Point Grey, at the very tip of the broader land mass the X'muzk'i'um called ʔelqsen, "point." Inside a monumental structure overlooking mountains and sea, are poles, feast dishes, masks, and other carved works in silver, gold, argillite, and wood. Some are from X'muzk'i'um villages, some from Haida Gwaii, the Gitxsan's "river of mists," as well as Kwakwaka'wakw, Oweekeno and Nisga'a territories. Some were carved 150 years ago; some very recently. The wind blows, the building hums and whistles; the carvings are saying something and, like the sloping floor of the Great Hall, draw you in to their stories. Renowned Haida artist Bill Reid gives us Raven perched on a giant clamshell, cajoling the First Humans to come out. The rotating exhibits are a constant flow of stories from artists who keep ancient art forms evolving.

This museum is a dynamic centre: even research collections are displayed in "visible storage." There are public programs and performances, and an excellent book and gift shop. Tel: 822-3825 (recorded message for days and hours) or 822-5087.

Vancouver Museum: 1100 Chestnut St., south end of Burrard Bridge. Tel: 736-7736 (recording); 736-4431. On the former site of the village, Sunaq, is a building shaped like a Coast Salish hat, honouring the original inhabitants of these shores.

UBC Continuing Studies: University of British Columbia, 5997 Iona Dr., Vancouver, B.C., V6T 1Z1. Tel: 222-5251. Courses introducing oral traditions, arts, games, and governments of First Nations are often hosted at Sty-Wet-Tan, First Nations Longhouse on the UBC campus, or at First Nations communities.

Simon Fraser University/Museum of Archaeology and Ethnology: 10 km east of Vancouver city centre, via Hwy 7, in Burnaby.

Call ahead: 291-3325. Permanent exhibit features archaeological excavation of Namu, on northwest coast in Heiltsuk territories: the 9,000-year-old site is among the oldest on B.C.'s coast. Also on display are poles, bentwood boxes, musical instruments.

Aboriginal Peoples' Pavilion: At Pacific National Exhibition, late August. Theatre, storytelling, dancers from B.C. and abroad, children's activities, food.

First Nations Cultural Festival: May. Sponsored by Native Indian Urban Education Society. Tel: 873-3761. Traditional games, performances, art, and food.

The Heartland: Central Vancouver, until the 1850s, was a "wilderness" of small lakes, creeks, and thousand-year-old Douglas fir, cedar, and hemlock forests. Where the X'muzk'i'um once harvested beaver, deer, bear, and forest products is today an urban and administrative centre for First Nations from all over North America. The Union of B.C. Indian Chiefs and United Native Nations have offices here, as do a multitude of First Nations' business, trade, fishing, and veterans associations, and education and law programs. Galleries and shops feature artists from the four directions.

Liliget Feast House: 1742 Davie St. Tel: 681-7044. Dolly Watts from Gitxsan territories and her son Wallace offer traditional foods in a longhouse setting. The menu features alder-barbecued salmon, duck, venison, seaweed, and rice, steamed fern shoots, and a rare chance to sample eulachon grease served as a condiment and whipped sopalahlie berries— "Indian ice cream." Dolly Watts also operates Just Like Grandma's Bannock, serving smoked salmon lunches outside the UBC Museum of Anthropology, and caters to banquets.

Chief's Mask Bookstore: 73 Water St. Tel: 687-7512. An excellent selection of First

Nations books and music. **Union of B.C. Indian Chiefs** offices are located on the 7th Floor, 73 Water St., Vancouver, B.C., V7P 3J3. Tel: 990-9939.

V　Tsawwassen First Nation: (Pop. 158/59). 30 km southwest of Vancouver, off Hwy 17, immediately north of B.C. Ferries terminal. It has been said this square-bottomed peninsula upon which the Tsawwassen people live was once an island fastened to the mainland by a cedar rope. The Transformers, Xexa:ls, anchored it to the sea bottom, and it grew to join the mainland. Tsawwassen, "looking towards the sea," emerged as the centre of fishing and clamming stations stretching from Lulu Island in the Fraser River to Point Roberts. The people here were known for their waterproof mats and cloaks, made from the bulrushes that grew in abundance. In 1959, a 2-km causeway was built, linking their peninsula, and the reserve, with the B.C. Ferries Terminal. One of the first two B.C. Ferries was named *Tsawwassen,* after them. Today, their burgeoning community, transected by Hwy 17, looks out to the ongoing development of valuable coastline properties. Some of it is on their own lands, leased for private homes, the Splashdown Waterpark, and extra parking for the ferry terminal. Their most recent project is the Tsa Tsu Shores condominium development on the causeway's south side.

Visitors are welcome to visit the **Yohalla** (eagle) **Cafe**, and view the poles located just past Tsawwassen First Nation administration offices.

At the **Delta Museum**, 4858 Delta St., in nearby Delta, is a pole carved in 1932 by Chief James Wilkes, honouring Tsaatzen, the first man of Tsawwassen, and his helpers, black bear, eagle, and beaver.

?　Tsawwassen First Nation Administration: Building 132, North Tsawwassen Dr., Delta, B.C., V4K 3N2. Tel: 943-2112.

V　Semiahmoo: (Pop. 41). 40 km south of Vancouver; just south of White Rock at the Canada-U.S. border, via Hwy 99, then Beach Rd. The Semiahmoo are more closely related to the Lummi and Samish peoples across the international border, and to the Lekwammen and T'Sou-ke across the Strait of Georgia, than they are to the Halq'emeylem-speaking residents of the *stó:lo.* These people of the strait are united by their Straits Salish language, and by their tradition of using an elaborate reef-net system to catch sockeye salmon as they entered Juan de Fuca Strait and the Strait of Georgia from the south, on their migration to spawning grounds in the Fraser (see chapter 1). **Bayside Campsite**, 16565 Beach Rd., 531-6563, offers quiet, family-oriented camping by the sea, in summer season.

?　Semiahmoo Administration: RR 7, 16006 Beach Rd., White Rock, B.C., V4B 5A8. Tel: 536-3101.

East from Vancouver: Tracing the North Bank of the Stó:lo (Fraser River)

The Stó:lo people traditionally travelled the rougher waters of the "open" Fraser in large cedar canoes, navigating the shallower sloughs and tributaries in smaller dugouts. Today, powerboats provide access to family-owned sites from the river's mouth to the head of navigation, above Yale, at the Stó:lo's ancient fishing boundary with the Nlaka'pamux, "people of the canyon" (chapter 10). Stó:lo Fisheries officers maintain the tradition of "watchmen" committed to the safety of the people and their resource.

I　Sloughs: These shallow, meandering backwaters are the *stó:lo*'s traditional backroads. Inaccessible to island raiders who 150 years ago scoured the main river in large sea-going canoes, they offered slow but reliable passage for downriver travellers in smaller vessels. And for those heading upriver, quicker passage. They were also the setting for many villages that Simon Fraser missed in his informal census—often used in estimates of the Stó:lo's pre-contact population. It is said these sloughs are trails created by the winding movements of Silqhey, the supernatural double-headed serpent.

The warmer sloughs are also breeding places for the giant white sturgeon that live up to 150 years in the Fraser's deepest waters. Stó:lo elders tell of these primeval bottomfish, weighing up to 450 kg, hauling the fisherman away. After a century of overfishing, reclamation projects, and pollution, the sturgeon is endangered. A Stó:lo Fisheries ban on killing sturgeon was recently followed by one imposed by federal authorities.

Sxwoyimelth: 12 km southeast of downtown Vancouver. Former village at present-day **New Westminster** (pop. 42,605/335 Ab) is said by some to take its name from a warrior turned to rock by Xexa:ls. The rock was destroyed prior to construction of the New Westminster Bridge. Like the city now here, Sxwoyimelth too was a capital. The Qw'ontl'en, "tireless runners," had villages at the Brunette River mouth, and just east of the Patullo Bridge, on the Fraser's south bank—now tiny reserves surrounded by gravel pits and log booms. In 1827, to gain control of the new fur trade and salmon industry, they moved their headquarters to be close to Fort Langley (see Fort Langley National Historic Park, below).

Highway 7 East

Coquitlam: (Pop. 82,830/295 Ab). On Hwy 7, east of New Westminster. City and district municipality take their name from the Kwikwetl'em people. Their small community sits near the Coquitlam River mouth. The name translates as "smell like fish." The Coquitlam River was listed third on the Outdoor Recreation Council of B.C.'s list of the

10 most endangered rivers in the province. The Fraser River was listed first.

Katzie: (Pop. 377/194). About 25 km east of downtown Vancouver, south off Hwy 7 on to Harris Rd., through Pitt Meadows. Left on to Fraser Industrial Way and right onto Bonson Rd., to community on the banks of the Fraser River.

Like Xexa:ls, Swaneset was a Transformer. Here, where there were marshes, he put the multi-coloured moss that would be the foundation for a new village. The name Katzie, or *q'eyts'i,* describes the action of a person's foot pressing down on the moss. People from up and down the Pitt and Alouette valleys were drawn by the eulachon and sockeye salmon Swaneset provided, and also by the wild potatoes that grew in abundance.

Their long history, as told by respected Katzie elder Old Pierre, has been transcribed for us in *Katzie Ethnographic Notes/The Faith of a Coast Salish Indian,* published by the B.C. Provincial Museum. It is a rare chance to journey with Swaneset as well as Xexa:ls, to better understand why the flood came, and the devastation of smallpox.

In 1995, 38,000 hectares of the sacred marsh and alpine lands embracing the western shore of Pitt Lake was designated **Pinecone Burke Provincial Park**, to be jointly managed by the Katzie people and the provincial government. Cultural tours will include guided nature walks into parkland. There are also powerboat and war-canoe trips to Pitt Lake. Visitors are welcome, the third week of August, for **Slehal tournaments** featuring the traditional gambling game where goat-hair blankets and baskets were once stakes.

Katzie Administration: 10946 Katzie Rd., Pitt Meadows, B.C., V0K 1Z3. Tel: 465-8961.

Mission: (Pop. 25,565/500 Ab). 65 km east of Vancouver, Mission lies on the boundary between two peoples who no longer exist:

the Whonnock and the Xat'suq' (Hatzic). The main village of the Xat'suq' people, 2 km east of Mission, was emptied by smallpox. It is now **Xa:ytem National Historic Site** (see below). In 1861, the Oblates established St. Mary's Mission atop the hill, and later opened a residential school attended by Stó:lo and St'at'imc children.

⑥ **Toti:lthet Centre:** 34110 Loughheed Hwy, east of downtown Mission. "Learning together for the future," a Stó:lo learning centre and trade school, also trains tribal police cadets from across Canada. Visitors are welcome to enjoy meals prepared by culinary arts students. The centre also houses Monaque Native Crafts; 826-9347; and the offices of In-SHUCK-ch Councils, serving the St'at'imc communities of Anderson Lake, Samahquam, Douglas, and Skookumchuck (see chapter 12).

⑥ **Mission Annual Powwow:** Second weekend in July. At Fraser River Heritage Park, off Hwy 7 on Stave Lake St., right on 5th Ave., to site of former St. Mary's Mission (7494 Mary St.). This major event has been drawing drummers, singers and dancers from all over North America for two decades. Three days of events include blessing of powwow grounds, grand entry, and demonstrations by hoop dancers, fancy dancers, grass dancers, traditional and jingle dancers of all ages. Call the Mission Indian Friendship Centre, on First Avenue in Mission, at 826-1281. The centre provides a range of workshops and programs to people of all backgrounds.

▮ **Xa:ytem National Historic Site and Interpretation Centre:** About 2 km east of Mission Infocentre, on Hwy 7. Tel: 820-9634. "Sudden transformation," or "zapped" is just one of many landforms created by Xexa:ls that are held sacred to the Stó:lo people for the teachings they embody. The move to preserve this rock from development led to the recovery of 7,500 years of history. This site was the

main village of the Xat'suq' (Hatzic), "sacred bulrushes," people. Archaeologists have traced out depressions from an unusual 5,000-year-old "pit-plank" house, along with 180 post holes indicating the village had been renovated over time, and continuously occupied.

V Leq'a:mel (Nicomen): (Pop. 88/55). 18 km east of Mission. Leq'a:mel is the local pronunciation of Halq'emeylem, and is said to be the place where the language originated. The community runs a cafe and video store.

V Sq'ewlets (Scowlitz): (Pop. 198/91). 28 km east of Mission, just past Lake Errock. "Turning the canoe around the corner" describes where the main village used to be, just to the east, where the Harrison River curves sharply to enter the Fraser. Now, most of the people live by the creek at Sqwexem, overlooking the pretty west shore of Harrison Bay.

Pictographs, pit-house villages, and 1,400-year-old burial mounds built of huge, geometrically arranged boulders are some of the history and archaeology explored in **riverboat tours** departing from here. A pleasant campground amidst maple trees has hook-ups.

❓ Scowlitz Administration: Box 76, Lake Errock, B.C., V0M 1N0. Tel: 826-5813.

To the Harrison River via Morris Valley Road

V Sts'a'i:les (Chehalis): (Pop. 785/503). 32 km east of Mission to Morris Valley Rd., then 6.5 km to Chehalis Rd. "Running aground on a sandbar (with the chest of the canoe)" is one translation for the name of this Stó:lo community farthest from the Fraser. Their territory shares boundaries with the St'at'imc to the north. The name may also mean "beating like a heart," for rhythmic pounding of waves against a nearby rock on windy days. General store, cafe, and gas bar.

East of Morris Valley Road on Highway 7

V Seabird Island: (Pop. 576/343). 3 km east of the Hwy 9 junction, the highway weaves through this island reserve. Turn left to community centre at the island's south end. A cedar welcome figure outside the new salmon-shaped school reflects the embracing nature of the newest community here. In 1879, Seabird Island was set aside by the Department of Indian Affairs for all upper Stó:lo communities. Today's orchards and hay fields are the product of efforts to transform fishermen into farmers. At the north end of Seabird Island Rd. is the **Seabird Island Cafe and Truck Stop Inn**, with a store, arts and crafts, and gas bar.

⑥ Events: Seabird Island Indian Festival, late May, canoe races, arts and crafts, barbecues, soccer and baseball tournaments. **The Earth Voice Festival**, late July, grew out of the Voices for the Wilderness Festival calling for a stop to logging in the Stein Valley (see chapter 10). This is one of North America's largest open-air gatherings.

? Seabird Island Administration: Box 650, Agassiz, B.C., V0M 1A0. Tel: 796-2177.

I Wahleach Safety Rest Area: A few kilometres north of Seabird Island Cafe. Just downriver from former village of Xwelich or Wahleach, a lively Ministry of Transportation and Highways kiosk features words of welcome from Stó:lo *siya:m*, an introduction to their territories, map, photos, and art.

I Ts'qo:ls: 15 km beyond the rest area. Where the trees are "bare on one side" is the site of the ancient village superseded by the town of **Hope** (pop. 3,045/180 Ab). Hang-gliders sweeping eastward into the valley between mountains are another clue to the wind that blows incessantly one way. The village stretched along the Fraser's east bank from the mouth of the Coquihalla River to the present location of the **Telte Yet Campsite** (see below).

When the Hudson's Bay company, in 1848, built Fort Hope at the junction of what is now Fort and Water streets, the Tel Tit— "from upriver"—people here concentrated their settlement about 1 km from the fort's palisades and mounted cannon. By the time the fort closed in 1892, most of the Tel Tit had moved downriver to other villages.

Telte-Yet Campsite is at the old Ts'qo:ls village site, by the river, on Hwy 1 just past the Hope Travel Infocentre (600 Water Ave.). Here are convenience store; arts and crafts; 869-9481.

Between Hope and Yale were some of the richest gold-bearing gravel bars. During the gold rush, the Stó:lo panned gold here, alongside *xwelitem* miners.

J Highway 1/Highway 3/Highway 5: Stó:lo territories extend northeast via Hwy 5 to just beyond the toll booth, and east, via Hwy 3, to about the west gate of Manning Provincial Park. These are traditional travel corridors. The Coquihalla Lakes area drew Stó:lo and interior peoples for the blueberries which grew in abundance.

North from Hope on Highway 1

V Xwoxewla:lhp: 24 km north of Hope, on the river at **Yale**. For the past century, this has been barely a whistle stop for two railways and a highway on their way across Canada. For millennia before that, this was *the* debarkation point on the province's major riverway. Canoes, having navigated 200 km of choppy straits and sandbars, could go no farther. Thousands of people, like the salmon they came upriver to net, rested and regrouped at villages on both sides of the Fraser before making their way to the rapids above. Here, on the west bank, was Xwoxewla:lhp, "willow trees," where a small, private Stó:lo community resides today.

As in the past, dip-net fishermen today scoop salmon out of fast-moving waters at family-owned sites along the Fraser River.
CREDIT: RBCM 5876

The village on the east bank was Xelhalh, "injured person," the place Simon Fraser described as "village of the bad rock." The rock we now call Lady Franklin is the first in a chain of impasses to the canyon.

Travellers today must go out of their way for even a glimpse of this, one of B.C.'s most important and least acknowledged historic sites. There are glimpses of the rock from Hwy 1, just north of the Yale Tunnel, but no safe pullouts.

Community members operate two campgrounds just south of Yale: **Yale Campground**, and **Everitt Hope**, on opposite sides of Hwy 1.

The **Yale Museum**, 31179 Douglas St.,

features First Nations' artifacts and historic photos of salmon drying at Hells Gate (chapter 10).

■ **Aselaw:** On the east bank of the Fraser River, a few kilometres north of Yale. Stó:lo tours are being planned for this otherwise inaccessible village site. Archaeologists have estimated at least 9,500 years of continuous occupation.

■ **Saddle Rock:** 5.5 km north of Yale, just outside Saddle Rock Tunnel. There are no safe pullouts to view another of the most important fishing sites on the entire Fraser River. These are the first major rapids, where the greatest number of fish met, and still meet, the greatest number of fishermen. In summer, look for blue and orange tarps covering campsites and drying racks. These replace the fir boughs traditionally, and sometimes still, used for cover.

B   Lahits: 8.5 km from Yale Tunnel, at Sailor Bar, a big rock marks the ancient, and somewhat flexible fishing boundary between Stó:lo and Nlaka'pamux peoples. For Nlaka'pamux territories, see chapter 10.

This route description returns south and west on Hwy 1, following the Fraser's south bank through the territories of the Halq'emeylem people.

V   Skw'atets (Peters): (Pop. 98/43). 20 km west of Hope, via Peters Rd. Here on the flood plain is "water going through the roots of the trees." The community is also known as Peters, for a former *siya:m*. It is also the surname of most of the people who live here. **Peters Arts and Crafts** offers sweaters, beadwork, carvings.

?   Skw'atets (Peters) Administration: RR 2, 16650 Peters Rd., Hope, B.C., V0X 1L0. Tel: 794-7059.

I   Lhilheqey (Cheam Peak) Viewpoint: 24 km west of Hope. For a time she was Mt. Baker's wife. But missing the Stó:lo and their river, she returned home with her three daughters. They were turned into mountains, and Lhilheqey was given the responsibility of looking after the river, salmon, and people. On maps, this is Mt. Cheam, named for the Stó:lo community due west.

V   Chi:yo:m (Cheam): (Pop. 305/156). 35 km west of Hope, administration office just north of Hwy 1 on Hwy 9. Small community sits just upriver. These are descendants of the Mountain Goat People who once lived deep inside the mountain, Lhilheqey. The place called Chi:yo:m, "always wild strawberries," is mostly under pavement now. In summer, there is a fruit stand here, and arts and crafts.

T   Chilliwack: (Pop. 49,030/780 Ab). 52 km west of Hope (100 km east of Vancouver). Named for the Ts'elxwiqw people whose nine villages today form this city's western perime-

ter and the heart of **Sardis** to the south. Their name, "going back upstream" or "backwaters," refers to where they lived until two centuries ago—in the mountains to the east, along the upper reaches of the fast-flowing Chilliwack River.

The complicated intersections and one-way streets of downtown Chilliwack were once the swamps, pools, and sloughs where sturgeon bred, or slept, and the serpent, Silqhey, lurked. On the pole at **Salish Park**, artist Stan Greene has encapsulated the story of "The River People" back to the time of the Transformers, Xexa:ls.

South of Chilliwack on Vedder Road

I   Stó:lo Nation Centre: Just south of Hwy 1, at 7201 Vedder Rd. Tel: 858-3366. Kw'eqwalith'a (Coqualeetza), "beating the blankets" is the Stó:lo name for this traditional site. It was given to the residential school established here in 1888. The school's brick buildings, supplemented by a fleet of trailers, now house **Stó:lo Nation** offices, bustling with treaty negotiations, Stó:lo Fisheries, a resource centre, educational, cultural, and social programs.

The **Coqualeetza Longhouse Interpretive Centre** here offers insight into the culture and history of the Stó:lo people. Gift shop features prized Salish weavings, baskets, limited edition prints, moccasins, and books.

☺   Area Events: Cultus Lake Indian Festival, canoe races, arts and crafts, salmon barbecue, soccer tournament.

V   Ch'iyaqtel (Tzeachten): (Pop. 264/133). About 5 km south of Hwy 1, Vedder Rd. leads through the western edge of a large reserve marked by billboards and hydro lines. "Fish weir" sits beside the now dry bed of the Chilliwack River, redirected by the Vedder Canal scheme in the 1920s. Here are a mini-mall and batting range.

▼ Th'ewa:li (Soowahlie): (Pop. 246/85). About 10 km south of Hwy 1, cross the Vedder River bridge, and take the road immediately to the left. The village is just north of the deep, dark, forest-fringed waters of Cultus Lake, from which the community's name and much of its history originates. "To disappear" or "dissolve" describes the fate of those who descended into the lake seeking its healing powers. Other power-seekers encountered a supernatural bearlike being, a type of *slellacum*, responsible for fierce and sudden winter storms. The lake's Chinook Jargon name, *cultus*, means "bad."

Sweltzer Creek Campground offers tranquillity and pleasant swimming, 160 Sleepy Hollow Rd.; 858-4603.

❓ Soowahlie Administration: Box 696, Vedder Crossing, B.C., V0X 1Z0. Tel: 858-4603.

West of Chilliwack on Highway 1

■ Kw'ekw'i:qw and Sema:th: 17 km west of Chilliwack, Hwy 1 crosses Vedder Canal, then skirts the mountain, Kw'ekw'i:qw, "sticking up." During the flood, canoes drifting from moorings here deposited people as far away as Lummi Island to the south and Bella Coola, up the coast. Kw'ekw'i:qw on today's maps is Sumas Mountain; it is also the name of the people who live beneath it. They are often referred to as the Sumas band. Their main village formerly overlooked Sema:th (Sumas Lake), a vast lowland lake that got even bigger when the Fraser River flooded. Its name describes the thick reeds that once grew there. The warm, shallow waters were full of food for migrating waterfowl, and sturgeon came here to breed. In the 1920s, *xwelitem* transformed what they considered a "mosquito-infested swamp" into fertile farmland. With dikes and pumps, lake became prairie. Even years later, farmers were ploughing up live, hibernating sturgeon waiting for the river to flood. And the Kw'ekw'i:qw people (pop. 218/140), like their giant fish, became land-locked.

■ Fort Langley National Historic Park: 60 km west of Chilliwack, then north onto Hwy 10 to a small community of Fort Langley. Park is at 23433 Mavis St., on an 8,000-year-old site at the gateway to Stó:lo territories. The Qw'ontl'en (Kwontlen) moved here with the fort from its first site, 4 km downstream, in 1838. Milton Gabriel, Qw'ontl'en tour guide since 1974, reminds us of the story, often underplayed. Fort Langley, with all its bastions, palisades, cannon, and adventuring fur traders, "was completely dependent on First Nations people." Fleets of thousands of canoes passed the little fort on their way to and from fishing grounds upriver. The company purchased from the Stó:lo—and hired them to process —up to 2,000 barrels of salted salmon a year, for the fort and for export. They relied on the Stó:lo to transport their goods and grow their potatoes. For its 20 years, the fort had no control over life beyond its walls. Then the 1858 gold rush turned everything upside down. Here, at Fort Langley, the first government of British Columbia was officially proclaimed, and *xwelitem* law broke through the confines of the fort walls. Tel: 888-4424.

▼ Qw'ontl'en (Kwontlen): (Pop. 128/62). On McMillan Island, across bridge from Fort Langley National Historic Park. These are the direct descendants of the people who established British Columbia's first commercial fisheries.

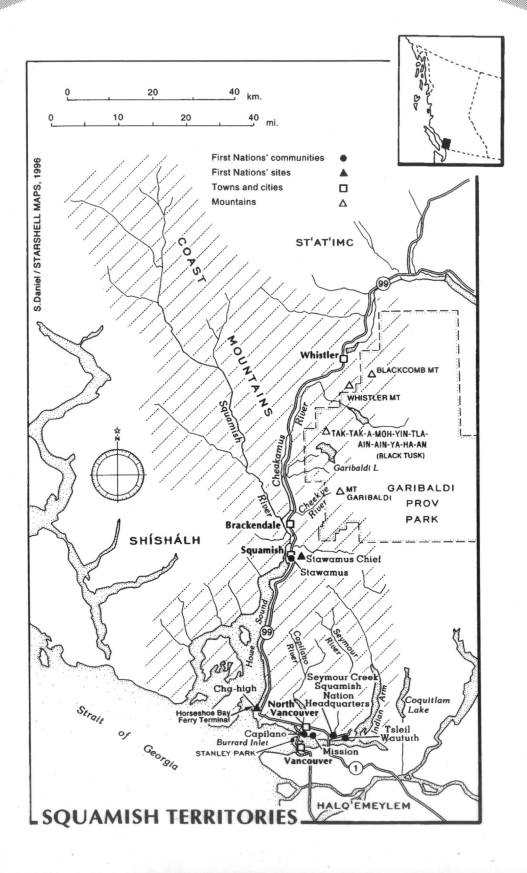

SQUAMISH TERRITORIES

CHAPTER 6

Squamish and Tsleil Waututh

The Squamish Nation has existed and prospered within our traditional territory since time immemorial...Our society is, and always has been, organized and sophisticated, with complex laws and rules governing all forms of social relations, economic rights and relations with other First Nations. We have never ceded or surrendered title to our lands, rights to our resources or the power to make decisions within our territory.

—*The Squamish Nation Assertion of Aboriginal Title*

In 1990, the Squamish Nation wrote this Assertion of Aboriginal Title in an effort to increase public awareness of their view of the land question and the impending treaty process. In introducing themselves and their homeland now, the Squamish Nation wishes to "speak directly" to visitors, offering more of that message.

"Our traditional territory is located in the Lower Mainland region of British Columbia. Prior to and following the arrival of Europeans in the late 1700s, the lands and waters we used and occupied either exclusively, or jointly with our First Nation neighbours, were as follows: from Point Grey on the south to Roberts Creek on the west; then north along the height of land to the Elaho River headwaters including all of the islands in Howe Sound and the entire Squamish Valley and Howe Sound drainages; then southeast to the confluence of the Soo and Green rivers north from Whistler; then south along the height of land to the Port Moody area, including the entire Mamquam River and Indian Arm

drainages; then west along the height of land to Point Grey.

"This territory included some of the present-day cities of Vancouver, Burnaby, and New Westminster, all of the cities of North Vancouver and West Vancouver, Port Moody, and all of the District of Squamish and the Municipality of Whistler. These boundaries embrace all of Howe sound, Burrard Inlet, and English Bay as well as the rivers and creeks that flow into these bodies of water. In addition, we used and occupied the various islands located in Howe Sound.

"Our historical links to these lands and waters are numerous. Squamish place names exist throughout the territory. In many instances, a location has particular meaning to our people because of the existence of oral traditions that served to explain that place in the Squamish universe and in our relationship to the land. In addition, the land bears witness to the settlements, resource sites, and spiritual ritual places of our ancestors, including villages, hunting camps, cedar bark gathering areas, rock quarries, clam processing camps, pictographs, and cemeteries. Some of these village sites date back 8,000 years.

"The Squamish Nation's use and occupation of our land has continued uninterrupted since the arrival of Europeans. Despite the negative impact that European settlement has had on our access to our land and resources, our current relationship to the land is extensive, varied and consistent with the reality of life in the late twentieth century. We continue to occupy our traditional territory as witnessed by the existence of 28 Squamish reserves. We continue to harvest fish and other marine resources from both freshwater and saltwater. We continue to take game from the land. We harvest timber and other resources from the forest. In addition, we have established our place within the modern economic infrastructure by relying on our historic rights. Despite the intense pressure of massive urban development, we have never ceded or surrendered our aboriginal title."

INFORMATION AND PROTOCOL

The Squamish Nation consists of seven main communities and about 2,700 people. They live, primarily, at three North Vancouver reserves—Mission, Capilano, and Seymour (also Squamish Nation headquarters)—and at four of nine reserves in the Squamish Valley to the north. The Squamish villages were formally amalgamated into the Squamish Nation in 1923. The route description below includes those communities offering visitor services or points of historic interest.

Also included below is the Tsleil Wututh First Nation, sometimes referred to as the Burrard Band. The Tsleil Wututh people live immediately east of the Squamish Nation on Burrard Inlet and share close cultural, family, and historic ties with them.

? **Squamish Nation:** 320 Seymour Blvd., North Vancouver, B.C., V7L 2J3. Tel: 980-4553. Fax: 980-4523.

? **Tsleil Wututh First Nation:** 3082 Ghumlye Drive, North Vancouver, B.C., V7H 1B3. Tel: 929-3454. Fax: 929-4714.

North Across Lions Gate Bridge on Highway 99

The south and north shores of Burrard Inlet, from Point Grey east, including Stanley Park, have always been used and occupied by the Squamish people. The Lions Gate and Second Narrows bridges today serve as busy gateways to the heart of Squamish territories. From there, the Sea-to-Sky Highway, Hwy 99, traces what was until the last century a major overland trade route linking the coastal Squamish and interior Lil'wat peoples.

▪ **Stanley Park:** On Hwy 99 linking Vancouver and North Vancouver; at the foot of West Georgia St. This 405-hectare peninsula between English Bay and Burrard Inlet has long been a point of intersection for First Nations peoples on either side of the inlet. The former village of Xwayxway is of cultural significance to the Squamish people. They also have many stories of "standing rock," which

Every year thousands of eagles follow spawning salmon to the confluence of the Squamish and Cheakamus rivers, an ancient and important Squamish fishing site.
CREDIT: TIM HOGUE

newcomers sometimes call Siwash Rock. (Siwash, in the Chinook Jargon trade language, is derived from the French *sauvage,* and was in the last century applied to all aboriginal peoples.) The city of Vancouver took root in the sawmills just east of here, on the south shores of Burrard Inlet. A generation after the park's establishment in 1888, a few Squamish families, considered squatters, hung on at Xwayxway. It was about this time, in the early 1900s, that Tekahionwake, Pauline Johnson, a Mohawk-English poet and performer, met Squamish Chief Joe Capilano. She recorded in her *Legends of Vancouver* his stories of this area. Kwakwaka'wakw, Haida, and Nisga'a poles are represented at the southeast end of the park.

V Capilano: The Lions Gate Bridge delivers travellers to the doorstep of the largest and busiest of today's Squamish communities. Whu-mul-chits-tun, as the Squamish know it, was a prime salmon-fishing site at the mouth of the Capilano River. Capilano was a young leader here when British explorer Captain Vancouver entered Burrard Inlet in 1792. His ancestry was Squamish and Musqueam, and the name Capilano has been passed down through generations of both peoples. The name Capilano has also been given to a community college, a lake, and one of a fleet of B.C. Ferries. It is also a regional park, suspension bridge, and salmon hatchery reached via Capilano Rd.

The Park Royal Shopping Mall is on land leased from the Squamish Nation.

Annual Squamish Nation Powwow: Usually early August (B.C. Day long weekend) at Capilano Park, at the foot of Capilano Rd. This event draws drummers, singers, dancers from across North America. Call Squamish Nation for schedule.

⑥ **Khot-La-Cha Coast Salish Handicrafts:** 270 Whonoak St. In its second generation of business.

⑥ **Capilano RV Park:** 295 Tomahawk Ave. Tel: 987-4722.

⑥ **Capilano Suspension Bridge:** 3735 Capilano Rd. This, one of Greater Vancouver's earliest tourist attractions, was built in 1899 by Scotsman George MacKay and well-known Squamish figures, August Jack and his brother Willie. Mary Capilano, born in the first half of the nineteenth century, often came here to visit the bridge and sell her fish. Her story is presented at the Story Centre, linking the history of the bridge with the history of Vancouver, and a pole raised here in 1993 was dedicated to her. Tsimshian and Tlingit craftsmen work in the carving shed. A large collection of First Nations art is on display.

West via 3rd Street

▼ **Mission:** (Pop. 269). About 3 km east of Hwy 99, at Esplanade and 3rd St. People were drawn to Slah-ahn, "head of the bay," for its fat and plentiful clams. In the 1860s, the Squamish people under Chief Snatt found common ground between their beliefs and the Catholicism presented by the Oblates at New Westminster. They requested their own mission, which drew people here year-round. It is a pleasant drive along narrow streets and past old homes to St. Paul's Church, built in 1886 to replace the 1866 chapel—the first Roman Catholic Church in what is now Greater Vancouver.

⑥ **Nahanee's Arts:** 424 W. 3rd St. Alfreda Nahanee was taught to knit goat's-wool sweaters by her Cowichan relatives in Duncan. Jewellery and carvings are also on display.

⑥ **Native Arts and Crafts:** 445 W. 3rd St. A wide range of creations are offered.

⑥ **Mosquito Creek Marina:** At the foot of Forbes Ave. Tel: 987-4113. This is the largest marina in B.C., with 400 berths, dry dock, laundry, showers.

⑥ **North Shore Indians Lacrosse Club:** North Vancouver Recreation Centre, 23rd and Lonsdale Ave. Lacrosse champions for generations, the Squamish Men's A League won the President's Cup, a national title, in 1985 and 1993. Season games are Wednesday nights. There is also a Junior B team, and field lacrosse.

▼ **Seymour Creek:** (Pop. 64). About 9 km east of Hwy 99 via 3rd St., or via Hwy 1, just east of the north foot of the Second Narrows Bridge, at 320 Seymour Blvd. The Seymour River here was the focus for an ancient Squamish village that has seen people coming and going over the last century. The community is growing now, and Squamish Nation headquarters have also moved here.

⑥ **Seymour Creek Golf Driving Range:** 321 Seymour Boulevard (east side of Hwy 1). Tel: 987-8630.

▼ **Tsleil Waututh:** (Pop. 300). About 3 km east of Second Narrows Bridge, via Dollarton Hwy. The "people of the inlet" live near but not quite on Indian Arm, looking out to oil refineries on the southern reaches of their traditional territories across Burrard Inlet. Their range formerly spanned the entire inlet, reaching north up Indian Arm, and south to Burnaby and Deer lakes. Tsleil Waututh leader, Dan George, in the 1950s was an Academy Award nominee for his performance in the movie *Little Big Man*. He also wrote two popular books, *My Heart Soars* and *My Spirit Soars*.

The Gathering Place Cafe, 3010 Sleil-

Waututh Rd., off Dollarton Hwy, offers Indian River burgers, buffalo chili, and salmon bannock, as well as BLTs. In July, as many as 2,000 visitors gather at Cates Park for the **Whey-ah-wichen Canoe Festival**. War-canoe racers come from all over the Lower Mainland, Vancouver Island, and the U.S. The day offers dancing, singing, drumming, arts and crafts, and salmon barbecue. The community also operates Takaya Golf Centre at 700 Apex Rd., off Mount Seymour Parkway.

? **Tsleil Waututh Administration:** 3082 Ghumlye Dr., North Vancouver, B.C., V7H 1B3. Tel: 929-3454. Fax: 929-4714.

North on Highway 99/ Squamish Highway

▮ **Cha-high:** Horseshoe Bay, site of the B.C. Ferries terminal, was a camping place for people travelling between present-day Squamish and Burrard Inlet.

V **Stawamus:** At the head of Howe Sound, on Hwy 99, 1 km south of the town of **Squamish** (pop. 11,635/160 Ab). Here are a small community, satellite offices of Squamish Nation, and the Sta-wa-mus Native Cultural Centre, which may have some carvings and jewellery on display. Long ago, a giant serpent, of much cultural and historic significance to the Squamish peoples, slithered across Howe Sound, then left its track across the steep face of the rock known today as the **Stawamus Chief.** At 652 m, this is said to be the second-largest piece of granite in the world, attracting expert international climbers unaware of the serpent's passage here.

▮ **Cheakamus River:** From about 8 km north of Squamish, the highway follows this river named "salmon weir place." There were once several Squamish villages near the salmon-rich confluence of the Cheakamus and Squamish rivers, in the vicinity of today's Brackendale. A century ago, many people went to work at a hop farm owned by the well-known Bell-Irving family, and a few still live at nearby Seaichem. Highway viewpoints and events organized at Brackendale offer opportunities to view thousands of eagles that nest here in winter.

▮ **Cheekeye:** A few kilometres north of Brackendale, at the southeast edge of Garibaldi Provincial Park. The name "dirty place" was given to the muddy Cheekeye River, and the mountain now known as Garibaldi, from which it flows. During the Great Flood, the Squamish people lashed their canoes to this 2,678-m-high peak, which is seldom visible from behind its veil of clouds.

▮ **Tak-tak-a-moh-yin-tla-ain-ain-ya-ha-an:** Just north of the Cheekeye is "the landing place of the Thunderbird," now called Black Tusk. Trails within Garibaldi Provincial Park lead to views of the 2,316-m peak.

▮ **The Height of Land:** 56 km north of Squamish, Whistler village marks the divide. Hwy 99, paved over time-worn trails, eases between Coast Mountains. Green Lake feeds the Lillooet River system. Just on this side of the pass is a hidden spot where the Transformers came upon some Squamish people camped too close to Lil'wat territories, and turned them into a pile of rocks.

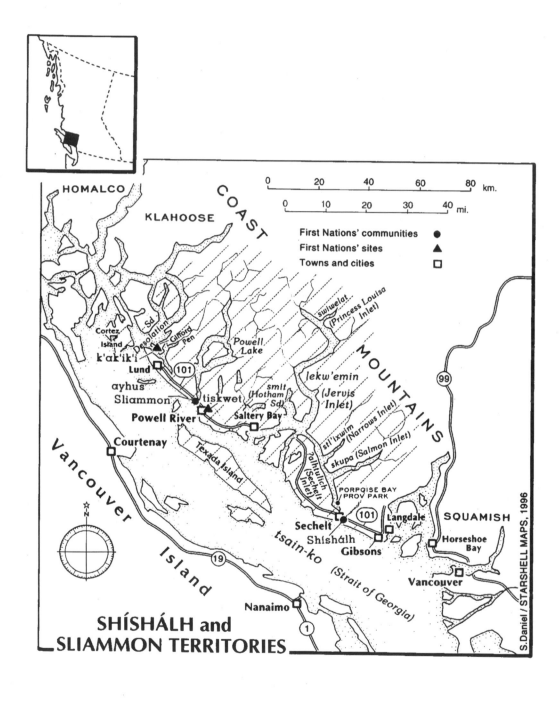

First Nations' communities ●
First Nations' sites ▲
Towns and cities ☐

HOMALCO

KLAHOOSE

COAST

MOUNTAINS

SQUAMISH

swiwelat
(Princess Louisa
Inlet)

lekw'emin
(Jervis
Inlet)

Powell
Lake

Cortez
Island

k'ak'ik'i

ayhus
Sliammon

Sd

Desolation

Gifford Pen.

Lund

tiskwet

smit
(Hotham
Sd)

Powell River

Saltery Bay

101

99

stl'ixwim
(Narrows Inlet)

skupa (Salmon Inlet)

Courtenay

Texada Island

ʔalhtulich
(Sechelt
Inlet)

PORPOISE BAY
PROV PARK

Sechelt

Shíshálh

Gibsons

101

Langdale

Horseshoe
Bay

Vancouver

Vancouver Island

19

tsain-ko

(Strait of Georgia)

Nanaimo

1

N

0   20   40   60   80   km.

0   10   20   30   40   mi.

S.Daniel / STARSHELL MAPS, 1996

SHÍSHÁLH and
SLIAMMON TERRITORIES

CHAPTER 7

Shíshálh and Sliammon

We want people to know that before the Indian Act, we were totally self-sufficient. When people come to our museum they will see how we lived in the past, and where we've come to in the present.

—*Tom Paul, shíshálh people*

The shíshálh are the people whose traditional territories correspond roughly with what is now referred to as the Sunshine Coast. The present-day town of Sechelt, midway along a stretch of coast that gets its share of both sun and rain, takes its name from the shíshálh. This new community shares, with a very old one, an isthmus less than one kilometre wide. Here, facing tsain-ko, the windy straits we now call Georgia, is the ancient winter gathering place the shíshálh call ch'atlich, "outside," and the headquarters of the Sechelt Nation.

Behind them are the calmer, sun-warmed waters of an inland sea known by many as Sechelt Inlet. The shíshálh people call this ʔalhtulich, "inside." This is the gentle way into their great and splintered world of fjords—lekw'emin (Jervis Inlet), lilkw'emin (Agamemnon Channel), smit (Hotham Sound), and stl'ixwim (Narrows Inlet), skupa (Salmon Inlet), swiwelat (Princess Louisa Inlet)—cleaving nearly 100 kilometres into ice-peaked Coast Mountains. The memories of the shí-

shálh people reach that far too: to the time when all this sharp-edged beauty was created by the "rasping action" of heaven-sent Xeyals. These beings were followed by the Spelemulh, the "first people," who formed the first villages, and brought to each a gift: the art of making fires or canoes, trapping salmon, cooking clams.

From the head of Jervis Inlet to what is now Lang Bay, many bands emerged, linked by social, political, cultural, spiritual, and economic ties. The four main divisions were the xenichen, at the head of Jervis Inlet; the ts'unay, at Deserted Bay; the tewankw of Sechelt Inlet, Narrows Inlet, and Salmon Inlet; and the sxixus, from Roberts Creek to Lang Bay. They named places, too many for any map, where they lived in the summer or in winter, harpooned sea lions, hunted deer with the help of dogs, mined pure jade to make adzes, harvested fruit. There were the places where the sea serpent, tchain-ko, left his trail on the rocks; where the people who had seen him left their own marks. Pools where they bathed to cleanse their spirits, and the mountains—

kulse, "anchor mountain," and min'atch, farther north—where they took refuge from the flood.

The arrival of Europeans brought the shíshálh people into contact with much that was detrimental to their independence and survival. Most devastating were the epidemics —smallpox and tuberculosis. Finally, with their numbers reduced, all the tribes, all the villages and histories, came together at this one point on the isthmus, at ch'atlich (or Sechelt). The mission established here by the Catholic Oblates, and the residential school system, further eroded shíshálh society by rejecting traditional values and language.

Two centuries later, the Sechelt Nation is in the avant garde of First Nations seeking self-government. With the Sechelt Act in 1986, they replaced the federal government's *Indian Act* here with their own laws and constitution. For the shíshálh, independence is not separation or isolation. The Sechelt Indian Government District works within existing federal and provincial structures, and it works in partnership with neighbouring communities, planning for everything from water supply to schools.

The irony, says Tom Paul, is "self-government allows the shíshálh people to cooperate more with neighbouring businesses and municipalities." As part of their agreement, the Sechelt Nation owns outright its 1,000-hectare base of reserve land, until now held "in trust," as all Indian reserves have been, by the federal government. This means there is more certainty, and the Sechelt Nation can encourage investors.

Now they say, all systems are in place for a resolution of treaty negotiations with federal and provincial governments. Says Paul, "This will give us the economic base we need to be totally self-sufficient."

HIGHLIGHTS AND EVENTS

INFORMATION AND PROTOCOL

The language spoken here is shashíshálhem, a dialect of Coast Salish.

Visitors are welcome, and encouraged to visit the Sechelt Nation's Tems swiya Museum and administration offices.

☎　**Sechelt Nation:** Box 740, Sechelt, B.C., V0N 3A0. Tel: 885-4589. Fax: 885-3490.

North from Langdale Ferry on Highway 101

Horseshoe Bay, north of Vancouver, at the junction of Hwys 1 and 99, is the terminal for B.C. Ferries to Langdale on the Sunshine Coast.

▼　**Sechelt Nation:** (Pop. 650). 27 km north of Langdale ferry terminal. Here, where inside and outside meet, are the Sechelt Nation and the town of Sechelt. About 30 percent of the reserve population is non-First Nations enjoying long-term leases. Upon entering the town, travellers are greeted by the House of hewhiwus, "House of Chiefs," the offices of the Sechelt Indian Government District, cultural library and museum—right next to the town of Sechelt's Travel Infocentre. In former times, a canoe skid, near the south end of today's Inlet Avenue, linked tsain-ko with ?alhtulich, the outer sea with the inner sea, sparing travellers a 120-km paddle around Sechelt Peninsula.

☎　**Sechelt Nation:** Box 740, Sechelt, B.C., V0N 3A0. Tel: 885-4589.

ⓖ　**Tems swiya Museum:** In the House of hewhiwus. The museum's name means "our

Poles near the House of hewhiwus (chiefs) look to where the shíshálh people have been, and to where they are going.
CREDIT: TEMS SWIYA MUSEUM

world." On display are photographs of elders, a history of fishing and logging, cedar baskets, masks; the replica of a 2,500-year-old stone bowl found nearby, and an equally ancient rock statue—a human figure holding a child. Also here are **Tsain-Ko Arts and Crafts**.

⑥　**Poles:** Near the House of hewhiwus, eight poles, carved in the 1970s, look to where the Sechelt people have been, and where they are going.

⑥　**Sechelt Hatchery:** On East Porpoise Bay Rd. adjacent to Porpoise Bay Provincial Park. Call 885-5562 for tours and times. The Sechelt Nation's comprehensive salmon enhancement program here is already benefiting non-First Nations commercial and sports fishermen. They are planting the seeds for their own—future—commercial fisheries.

⑥　**Charters:** Depart from Sechelt to inlets, pictographs, and Skookumchuck Narrows rapids. Contact Sechelt Travel Infocentre, Box 360, Sechelt, B.C., V0N 3A0. Tel: 885-3100.

Sliammon

The Sliammon people today live in one village roughly at the centre of their territories. They face out to the most exposed waters of the Strait of Georgia between the north tip of Texada Island and Cortes Island. The people have always lived here. The winds have always blown: in the very earliest of times, the people of Sliammon tell us, Raven and some other people journeyed north and killed the tiresome Wind-Maker and his wife, but brought their gusty son home with them.

Sliammon villages were once on southern Cortes Island, and in the small inlets at the entrance to Desolation Sound. To the north, beyond Sliammon lands, are the territories of their friends and relatives, the Klahoose people, whose villages were concentrated on Toba Inlet and Cortes Island, and the Homalco, the "swift water" people of Bute Inlet. Their inlet is fed by the Homalco River. Over the last 150 years, both of these peoples have moved gradually away from their inlet worlds as definitions of remote have changed to mean places reached only by sea, not land. Here, at the entrance to Johnstone Strait, a dozen islands sit like puzzle pieces, suggesting the mainland and Vancouver Island were once joined. Likewise, where the people live today reflects traditional links across the straits, their highways. Many Klahoose and Homalco people now live with the Sliammon people just north of Powell River on Hwy 101. The headquarters of the Klahoose people are now on Cortes Island: it still takes two ferries to get there via Campbell River on Vancouver Island (see chapter 4). And the Homalco people have recently established a new home base on the outskirts of Campbell River.

HIGHLIGHTS AND EVENTS

⑥ Sliammon Creek Salmon Hatchery p. 91

INFORMATION AND PROTOCOL

The Sliammon, Homalco, and Klahoose peoples call their language *ey7a7juuthem,* "talk the language." It is part of the larger Coast Salish language family.

The Homalco people today live mostly at Sliammon, in Vancouver, and at their new home base in Campbell River, an area once occupied by Coast Salish-speaking peoples, and more recently by Kwakwa̱ka̱'wakw peoples (chapter 4). The people of Klahoose are based in their traditional territories on Cortes Island (chapter 2).

?   **Sliammon Native Council:** RR 2, Sliammon Rd., Powell River, B.C., V8A 4Z3. Tel: 483-9646. Fax: 483-9769.

?   **Alliance Tribal Council:** 130 N. Tsawwassen Dr., Delta, B.C., V4K 3N2. Tel: 943-6712. Fax: 943-5367. Members: Sliammon, Homalco, Klahoose, Tsleil-Waututh (Burrard), Halalt, Katzie, Nanaimo, Chemainus, Tsawwassen, and Squamish.

North from Saltery Bay on Highway 101

From Sechelt territories at the north end of the Sechelt Peninsula, B.C. Ferries cross Jervis Inlet to **Saltery Bay** at the frontier of Sliammon lands.

T   **Powell River:** (Pop. 12,790/255 Ab). 31 km north of Saltery Bay. There was a Sliammon village here at tiskwet, "wide river bed," until about 1910. The Powell River, just north of today's townsite, runs 500 metres from Powell Lake. When the dam and pulp mill were built, the Sliammon people here joined those at Sliammon Creek. In former times, a whale once lived in the pool at the base of Powell River Falls. When the weather was about to change for the worse, it made a noise that could be heard all the way to the Sliammon Creek village.

V   **Sliammon:** (Pop. 748/560). 3 km north of Powell River the highway crosses a bridge over Sliammon Creek. The village here, T'eshusm, has always been important to the Sliammon people for its stream: chum salmon were traditionally caught in a tidal rock weir. Among their many other villages was K'ak'ik'i, to the northwest, tucked into Grace Harbour on the Gilford Peninsula. Sliammon, Klahoose, and Homalco peoples all gathered there for winter ceremonies. Some people lived there until the 1960s. The Sliammon people today own and operate Mermaid

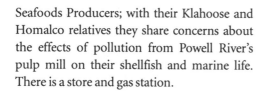

Seafoods Producers; with their Klahoose and Homalco relatives they share concerns about the effects of pollution from Powell River's pulp mill on their shellfish and marine life. There is a store and gas station.

⑥   **Sliammon Creek Salmon Hatchery:** At Sliammon. Follow the life cycle of salmon from eggs to spawning, when they become food for eagles; also chances to see black bear, otter, and mink.

❓   **Sliammon Administration:** RR 2, Sliammon Rd., Powell River, B.C., V8A 4Z3. Tel: 483-9646.

North of Sliammon village, Hwy 101 continues 20 km to its terminus at Lund. Here are views of Ayhus, "double-headed serpent," now known as Savary Island. The Transformer turned the serpent into an island before it could get into his cave.

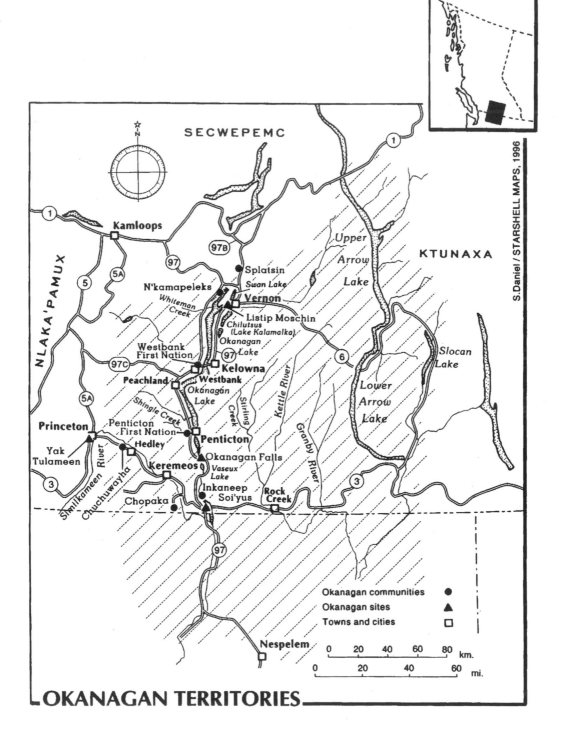

SECWEPEMC

KTUNAXA

NLAKA'PAMUX

Kamloops

1
5
5A
97
97B

● Splatsin

Swan Lake

N'kamapeleks

Whiteman Creek

□ **Vernon**

Listip Moschin

Chilutsus
(Lake Kalamalka)

Okanagan
Lake

Westbank
First Nation

97C

97

□ **Kelowna**

Peachland

Westbank

Okanagan
Lake

Upper
Arrow
Lake

6

Slocan
Lake

Lower
Arrow
Lake

Shingle Creek

Stirling Creek

Kettle River

Granby River

Princeton

5A

▲
Yak
Tulameen

Penticton
First Nation

● Hedley

Smilkameen River

□ **Penticton**

Keremeos

Chuchuwayha

Chopaka ●

▲ Okanagan Falls

Vaseux
Lake

● Inkaneep
Soi'yus

▲

□ Rock
Creek

3

3

97

□ Nespelem

Okanagan communities ●

Okanagan sites ▲

Towns and cities □

| 0 | 20 | 40 | 60 | 80 | km. |

| 0 | 20 | 40 | 60 | mi. |

OKANAGAN TERRITORIES

CHAPTER 8

Okanagan

Okanagan, in the language spoken here, is sometimes translated "head of the river." Not the river's northernmost beginnings above Okanagan Lake, but the falls, south of there, below Penticton. This is the point beyond which the salmon do not travel, and some have said it is the ancestral home of the northern Okanagan peoples. Others believe Okanagan is farther south, across the 49th parallel, where the Similkameen River pours into the Okanagan River and there was once a village fortress. Two centuries of distortion by English tongues has left much room for nuance, and so we have also for the name Okanagan, "people living where you can see the top of Mount Chopaka." Its rocky peak rises above the yellow Okanagan hills just south of the border near Keremeos.

Where their meanings overlap is in their description of wholeness. The Okanagan people and their territories flow north to south, like their rivers, long lakes, and mountain ranges. They do not stop when they reach an international border that puts six communities in Canada and two in the United States. Since the beginning of time, the Okanagan people travelled the full length of their territories, harvesting its fruits and roots. At such vital sites as Okanagan Falls, and Kettle Falls to the south, they harvested salmon.

Their relationships with the first white fur traders were characterized by the same spirit of generosity and mutual advantage the Okanagan people practised among themselves. In 1808, those who lived along the Arrow Lakes shared their food with explorer-trader David Thompson, and led him to the headwaters of the Columbia. Under Chief Nicola, son of the great leader Pelkamu'lox, the Okanagan people allowed subsequent traders passage along their network of highways, shared their grasslands, and provided fresh horses at camps between fur-trade forts. Here the two cultures met, married, exchanged technologies and world views.

The year 1858 marked the end of a way of life. Many thousands of gold seekers en route to the Fraser River and the Cariboo crossed the new international border via Okanagan trails. Oblate missionaries followed them, and, after opening Okanagan Mission near Kelowna, encouraged permanent white settlement of Okanagan territories.

In 1875, weary of violence, disease, and limited access to their own lands, Okanagan leaders joined their Secwepemc allies in a "council of war." The history of the interior of B.C. would have turned out quite differently if not for Chief Nicola's nephew and heir, Tselaxi'tsa. Convinced the Queen of England would see justice served, he opposed a forceful eviction of settlers. The war council dissolved in response to promises the land question would be addressed.

Some of the land cut off from earlier allotments was returned, and three extensive commonages of grazing lands to be shared by the Okanagan people and settlers were established. But these were soon reduced and opened for settlement. Likewise, many other Okanagan reserves were, after 1916, cut back to accommodate a growing influx of immigrants.

The question of reserves and commonages, and the larger one of aboriginal title, are still far from resolved. Dozens of dams up and down the Columbia River have put an end to once vital salmon fisheries. First Nations people at Penticton struggle to reduce the encroachment of development on their traditional lands. After more than a century, the Okanagan struggle has, if anything, become greater.

HIGHLIGHTS AND EVENTS

◉	Cathedral Lakes Powwow, May	p. 95
◉	Chopaka Rodeo, Easter weekend	p. 96
◉	Inkaneep Tours	p. 96
◉	Sen Klip Theatre Company	p. 99

INFORMATION AND PROTOCOL

A number of today's Okanagan communities are centred at ancient and sacred gathering places. Appropriate venues for exploration are listed below. Okanagan peoples are among the Colville Confederated Tribes, Box 150, Nespelem, WA, U.S.A., 99155. Call 509-634-4711 for information about events and recreational opportunities on their lands, set between the confluence of the Okanogan and Columbia rivers. Access is via Hwy 97 from Osoyoos.

The language spoken here is Syilx.

From Princeton East on Highway 3

The story of the Okanagan people of the Upper Similkameen valley, from Princeton to Keremeos, is enriched with an extra and somewhat mysterious dimension. Sometime between long, long ago and about 1700, a people sometimes called "the strangers," and sometimes called the Stuwix, arrived here. They spoke a language all their own, perhaps of Athapaskan origin, and lived in relative harmony with their Okanagan neighbours to the east. Through marriage with them, and a general migration in this direction, the Okanagan language and ways prevailed. Meantime, "the strangers," vulnerable to attack, were themselves diminishing in number. There are places in this valley with names given by those earlier people, but there is no longer anyone left who can tell us what they mean. See also chapter 11.

▮ **Yak Tulameen:** At **Princeton** (pop. 2,770/20 Ab), where the Tulameen River flows into the Similkameen. On the flats occupied today by the RCMP and a ball field was "the place where red earth was sold." This precious ochre, mined in the valley, was used as a base for paint. Black paint was made from charcoal and oil.

▼ **Chuchuwayha:** (Pop. 50). The 40-plus km from Princeton to the far side of Hedley is the "meeting of many creeks" where the Upper Similkameen people once fished for trout. Irrigation and other recent changes here have dried many of them up. About 31 km from Princeton, highway improvements at the Stirling Creek bridge have turned up tools and bones, evidence that people were here 7,000 years ago. In more recent times this was an important trading centre. Standing out on the plateau just before Hedley, the newly restored St. Anne's Catholic Church dates back to the early 1900s. Below it, not visible from the highway, is the original Oblate mission church, built in the 1880s. No visitor services at this time.

? Upper Similkameen Administration: Box 310, Keremeos, B.C., V0X 1N0. 499-2221.

▮ Cathedral Lakes Powwow Grounds: South off Hwy 3, 63 km east of Princeton, onto Ashnola Rd. Cross the Red Bridge, and continue to the new powwow arbour visible from the road. This is the site of a major May long-weekend gathering. Visitors are welcome.

▮ Standing Rock/Native Art Gallery: Entering Keremeos, about 65 km east of Princeton. From his gallery on the south side of the highway overlooking the Similkameen River, Henry Allison tells visitors how the rock, standing across the road, was an important traditional gathering place for the Okanagan people.

Inside the gallery are Allison's own creations in Similkameen gold; he also has a fine selection of pottery, clothes, carvings, drums, and moccasins. Tel: 499-2297.

T Keremeos: (Pop. 935/10 Ab). 67 km east of Princeton. "To cut across the flats, from the creek," is the administrative and cultural centre for Upper and Lower Similkameen peoples today.

? Upper Similkameen Administration: 517-7th Ave., Keremeos, B.C., V0X 1N0. Tel: 499-2221.

Okanagan storyteller Harry Robinson. His life spanned the twentieth century (1900–1990); his stories, told to Wendy Wickwire in *Write it on Your Heart* and *Nature Power,* reach back to the beginning of time.
CREDIT: ROBERT SEMENIUK

? Lower Similkameen Administration: Box 100, Keremeos, B.C., V0X 1N0. Tel: 499-5528. The Lower Similkameen band (pop. 336/300) consists of the people of Chopaka, Blind Creek, north of Cawston on the Old Fairview Rd., and Ashnola. They tend to live spread out, ranching and farming. The **Cathedral Lakes Powwow** is on the May long weekend, and the annual **Native Rodeo** is Easter Sunday, in Chopaka.

V Chopaka (Lower Similkameen): 27 km east of Keremeos, Chopaka Rd. traces the Similkameen River for 9 km to the village. Visible to the south is the peak of Mt. Chopaka. This, suggests Mourning Dove of the Colville Confederated Tribes, is the point of origin for the name Okanagan. She thinks it comes from the name Wickanakane—"seeing the top," an abbreviation of "people living where you can see the top of Mt. Chopaka." A few century-old buildings and Our Lady of Lourde's Roman Catholic Church, 1896, mark this quiet community. The all-native **rodeo** on Easter Sunday has been hosted here for three decades.

∎ **Spotted Lake:** 38 km beyond Keremeos. Spots are from epsom salts rising to the surface. The Okanagan people call it Klilok.

J **Hwy 97/3:** 46 km east of Keremeos, at **Osoyoos** (pop. 3,345/20 Ab). Hwy 3 leads east from here, and at Rock Creek meets the Kettle River for the first time. The river and highway separate, join, separate, until finally at Christina Lake, the Kettle descends into Washington State, where it becomes the "big water" of Kettle Falls, a major Okanagan fishery until construction of the Grand Coulee Dam in the 1930s. The upper Kettle River people hunted in the territories embracing Christina Lakes and the Arrow Lakes.

From Osoyoos North on Highway 97

Hwy 97 traces the long Okanagan lakes and river into the heart of north Okanagan territories.

V **Inkaneep (Osoyoos):** (Pop. 350/260). 8 km north of **Osoyoos,** Number 22 Rd. leads to Black Sage Rd., then McKinney Rd. The ancient headquarters of the people "at the bottom" was just south of here, at the *top* of Osoyoos Lake. Today their reserve stretches north along the east side of Hwy 97, reaching almost to Vaseux Lake. It comes up short, on both ends, of two other meeting places: the vital fisheries at "the falls" to the north, and Soi'yus, "gathered together," below the town of Osoyoos.

In spite of a substantial reduction to their reserve in 1868 favouring white settlers, the people "at the bottom" are faring well. They operate Canada's second-largest vineyard and a golf course here and lease land to Vincore International's winery. A major resort and cultural centre are in the works.

There is still room for the natural yellows and browns that put their land into sharp contrast with the lush orchards across the highway, room for the Saskatoon bushes and bitter root—once the main harvest of Okanagan peoples—with its April blossoms that look like crocuses. Glen Baptiste, who calls himself "head groundskeeper," guides tours and puts things into perspective. There are pit-house depressions, pictographs. "Thousands of them," he says. "You may be standing right beside one and not know it."

Ask at the administration office for a tour. **Inkameep Campground** and **Wolf Creek Trail Rides** are off Hwy 3, east of Hwy 97 junction, and north off 45th St. They offer an oasis on the lake and trail rides into the desert to see underground waterfalls, mountain sheep, bears, rattlesnakes, and coyote. Tel: 495-7279.

? **Inkaneep (Osoyoos) Administration:** RR 3, Site 25, C-1, Oliver, B.C., V0H 1T0. Tel: 498-3444.

∎ **McIntrye Bluff:** Singular among bluffs north of Inkaneep is this ancient camping place and assembly area.

∎ **Okanagan Falls:** 40 km north of Osoyoos. Some say this is Okanagan, ancestral home of the people so named, and "head of the river" in that the falls here were a barrier beyond which the Columbia River salmon could not pass. When a dam was built here to control flooding, the thunderous falls became just another rough spot in the river. Says Glen Baptiste, "There aren't any really big salmon here any more, just a few small ones exhausted from fighting the dam down at Oroville [Washington]."

▼ **Penticton First Nation:** (Pop. 691/437). 60 km north of Osoyoos. West off Hwy 97 to Green Mountain Rd., then onto Westhill Dr. to administration offices. In the past, as still, Penticton lands have supported one of the largest populations in the Okanagan Valley. The Penticton people enjoyed fishing for salmon at the falls, and for trout and kokanee above them; they hunted in the Marron Valley and made their permanent home at the mouth of Shingle Creek, flowing into the Okanagan River just above Green Mountain Rd. Today the river is a manmade channel, and the Penticton people spend much of their time protecting what remains of their land from the effects of adjacent development.

Snow Mountain Market, gas station, convenience store, arts and crafts, are just off Hwy 97, on Green Mountain Rd.

❓ **Penticton Administration:** RR 2, Site 80, Comp. 19, Penticton, B.C., V2A 6J7. Tel: 493-0048.

▼ **Penticton:** (Pop. 26,895/170 Ab). On the east side of the Okanagan River Channel. The **En'owkin Centre** here is a gathering place, learning institute, and writing school attracting First Nations authors, instructors, and students from all over North America. Theytus Books here publishes First Nations fiction, non-fiction, and poetry. Their first science fiction, published in 1995, is *The Black Ship*, by Gerry William. The centre is open for book sales and information. Regular public events feature visiting and local artists and authors. The resource centre, focussing on Okanagan language, history, culture, and environment, is open to all. 257 Brunswick St., Penticton, B.C., V2A 5P9. Tel: 493-7181.

▮ **The Serpent N'xa'xa'etkw:** About 35 km north of Penticton, just south of Peachland, the opposite shores of Okanagan Lake curve round Okanagan Mountain (1,574 m) and Squally Point. Here was the residence of the serpent N'xa'xa'etkw, "spiritually powerful in the water." Anyone passing by in a canoe was careful to make appropriate appeasements. There may be a link between N'xa'xa'etkw and the lake monster known as Ogopogo, now protected by the B.C. *Wildlife Act.*

▼ **Westbank First Nation:** (Pop. 467/260). 48 km north of Penticton, just beyond the Kelowna satellite of **Westbank**, is the Westbank First Nation. Their reserve, Tsinstikeptum, stretches to the bridge across Okanagan Lake. There, at Siwash Point, where the lake is narrowest, was a village, Stekatkolxne'ut, "lake at the side," thriving on the abundance of freshwater mussels, waterfowl, and wild roses. *Siwash* comes from the French *sauvage*, commonly applied during the early fur-trade era to First Nations business partners. Siwash Point was also a favoured canoe crossing; those with horses continued on trails along the west side of the lake. Between 1826 and 1847, the old Okanagan trails were incorporated into the fur-trade route linking Fort St. James to the north with Fort Vancouver to the south. Until 50 years ago, a towering fir stood not far from the present-day Westbank First Nation administration offices. Its great branches gave shelter to Okanagan and Hudson's Bay Company traders. A cairn now honours their relationship.

Westbank First Nation lands continue to bustle: the **Wild N' Wet Water Slide** is 1 km east of Westbank on the Old Okanagan Hwy; 786-7600. Adjacent is the **Waterslide Campground**; 768-7426. Nearby are **Old McDonald's Farm**, petting zoo, amusement park, fruit stand, and heritage gallery; 768-5167. A marina and restaurant are by the bridge. There are also two service stations. The **Trading Post**, offering arts and crafts, is at 107-515 Hwy 97.

❓ **Westbank Administration:** 301-515 Hwy 97 S., Kelowna, B.C., V1Z 3J2. Tel: 769-4999.

J Okanagan Trails: Just before the bridge across Okanagan Lake, Westside Rd. overlaps and parallels an ancient overland route. It is about 40 km to N'kamapeleks, the "head of the lake," home to the Okanagan community known as the Okanagan Band. N'kamapeleks is also accessible from the northeast side, via Vernon.

T Kelowna: (Pop. 74,285/655 Ab). On the east side of Okanagan Lake, opposite West-bank. The city's roots are in the mission estab-lished in 1859 at Mission Creek to the south. The first Oblate priest was Charles Pandosy, who came here after closing his mission to the Yakima people in Washington State. He built this mission around Okanagan people who gathered seasonally at Mission Creek. A school for Okanagan children opened at the mission in 1865. Priests timed their visits to outlying villages according to seasonal cycles. To main-tain their influence, they introduced the Durieu System with its hierarchy of officials that incorporated existing Okanagan leaders and *suxencwiltm,* "the ones who discipline." In 1892, the European settlement moved up to the lakeshore and incorporated as a town. Its name, Kelowna, comes from the Okanagan village that elders past remember as Skela'-un.na, "grizzly bear."

⑥ Father Pandosy Mission: South off Hwy 97 at Benvoulin Ave., drive 4 km. Open daily April–October.

⑥ Kelowna Centennial Museum and Exhibition Centre: 470 Queensway. Tel: 763-2417. A reconstructed pit-house dwelling is among Okanagan displays.

I Lake Kalamalka: 31 km north of Kelow-na. Named for a chief who was son of an Okanagan woman and a fur trader. The local name for these turquoise waters is Chilut-sus. Lands along the lake to the west of the highway were part of the 9,700-hectare com-

monage shared by native and non-native cattle-men until the latter pressed for sole access.

T Listip moschin (Vernon): 46 km north of Kelowna. The city of **Vernon** (pop. 22,905/22 Ab) is set between Kalamalka Lake, Oka-nagan Lake, and Swan Lake, and along an ancient trail linking Secwepemc territories with the Columbia River. The trail was broken by the creek flowing south from Swan Lake. Where it was narrowest, someone built a slight bridge. Still, most people just jumped over the creek, and so the place became known as Lis-tip moschin, "jumping over place." One chief's family established a winter home here, and hosted major sports events, like the Olympics. There were running, jumping, wrestling, shooting, weight-lifting, and rock-put con-tests. The site's value as a transportation nexus soon drew the Hudson's Bay Company, Barnard's Express stagecoach and freight ser-vices, a post office, a hotel: by 1892, the city of Vernon was taking shape. Listip moschin is still here—behind the Safeway store at 35th St. and 30th Ave. A tiny park embraces the gulch. There's the creek—jump over it.

⑥ Greater Vernon Museum and Archives: 3009-32nd Ave. Tel: 542-3142. Displays food gathering and a canoe. (Okanagan people used both dugout canoes and the sturgeon-nosed birch-bark canoes of their Ktunaxa neighbours.) The gift shop features high-qual-ity Okanagan beadwork and hand-tanned leather work.

V N'kamapeleks (Okanagan Band): (Pop. 1,385/693). 12 km northwest of Vernon is N'kamapeleks, the "bottom or root end" of Okanagan Lake—the narrow, marshy begin-nings of the string of lakes flowing south into the Columbia River. Two centuries ago, this became the seat of power for the upper Okanagan people. The renowned chief Pelka-mu'lox presided until then at the village fortress Salilxu, "heaped-up stone," at the con-

Cast from Sen Klip Theatre's "How Food Was Given."
CREDIT: SEN KLIP THEATRE

fluence of the Similkameen and Okanagan rivers. Accepting an invitation from the Secwepemc chief, Kwoli'la, he moved his summer headquarters to the Nicola Valley, where he was granted perpetual use of the abundant fishing and hunting grounds (see chapter 11). He made his winter headquarters at N'kamapeleks, where his descendants continued after him, influential leaders through times of great change.

N'kamapeleks lands today—refreshingly undeveloped—encompass the north and west shores of Okanagan Lake along Westside Rd., all the way to White Man Creek. About 8 km south of the administration offices, the Earth Woman stage and tipis mark the headquarters of the **Sen Klip Theatre Company**, gaining appreciation worldwide for its blending of traditional Okanagan and modern arts. *Sen Klip,* in the Syilx language spoken here, is "the imitator," coyote, important in Okanagan lore; 549-2921. In summers, one of two troupes performs at **Newport Beach Recreational Park** off Westside Rd. Tel: 542-7131. Here is RV camping, marina, crafts, gas.

? **Okanagan Administration:** RR 7, Site 8, Comp. 20, Westside Rd., Vernon, B.C., V0R 1B0. Tel: 728-3414. (On Westside Rd., just south of Hwy 97.)

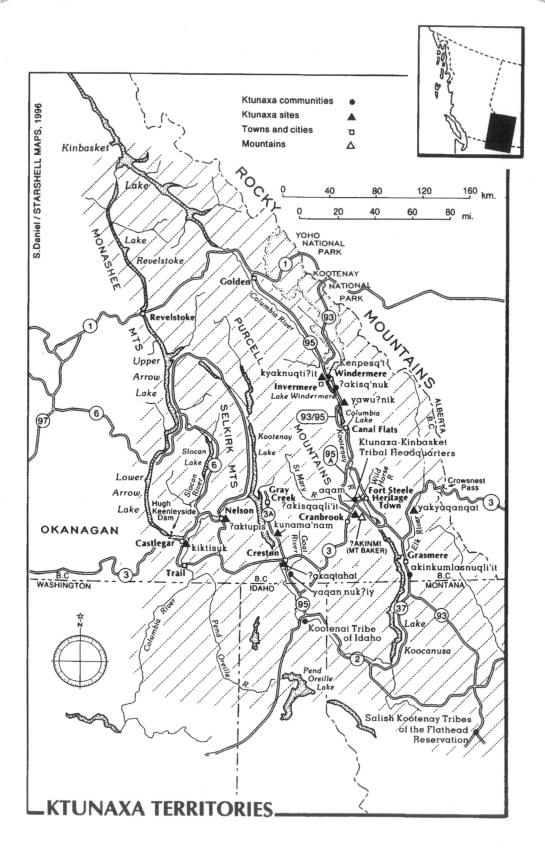

Ktunaxa communities ●
Ktunaxa sites ▲
Towns and cities ⌂
Mountains △

0   40   80   120   160 km.

0   20   40   60   80 mi.

Kinbasket

Lake

ROCKY

Lake

Revelstoke

MONASHEE

MTS

YOHO
NATIONAL
PARK

1

Golden

KOOTENAY

NATIONAL

PARK

93

Revelstoke

PURCELL

Columbia River

95

MOUNTAINS

1

97

6

Upper
Arrow
Lake

SELKIRK MTS

Kenpesq't
kyaknuqti?it   Windermere
Invermere   ?akisq'nuk
Lake Windermere   yawu?nik

93/95   *Columbia*
Lake
Canal Flats

ALBERTA
B.C.

Kootenay
Lake

6

Slocan
Lake

Kootenay

MOUNTAINS

Ktunaxa-Kinbasket
Tribal Headquarters

95
A

Slocan River

Lower
Arrow
Lake

Hugh
Keenleyside
Dam

OKANAGAN

Nelson

3A

?aktupis

Gray
Creek
?akisqaqli'it
kunama'nam

aqam

St. Mary

R.

Wild Horse R.

Fort Steele
Heritage
Town

Crowsnest
Pass

Elk River

yakyaqanqat

3

Castlegar

kiktisuk

Creston

Cranbrook

3

?AKINMI
(MT BAKER)

Grasmere
akinkumlasnuqli'it

Trail

3

B.C
WASHINGTON

B.C
IDAHO

Goat River

95

?akaqtahat
yaqan nuk?iy

B.C
MONTANA

37

93

Columbia River

Pend
Oreille
R.

Kootenai Tribe
of Idaho

2

Lake

Koocanusa

Pend
Oreille
Lake

Salish Kootenay Tribes
of the Flathead
Reservation

KTUNAXA TERRITORIES

CHAPTER 9

Ktunaxa and Kinbasket

*People on the outside don't know very much about us.
We are told our survival is for that reason—others were
exploited, weakened spiritually. Some people don't like
to be reminded of our existence and longevity. Our stories tell us we even survived the ice age here. Our legends describe animals that may have been dinosaurs.*

—Wilfred Jacobs, elder, yaqan nu?kiy

*K*tunaxa is simply what the people here
have always called themselves. But, to
accommodate modern times, the elders recently gathered together and deliberated over
a translation into the language spoken by their
grandchildren. "Lean and fast," the "way we
kept our horses," emerged in English. And so
did "to lick the blood from the spear," a sym-
bolic reference to their marksmanship.

Ktunaxa boundaries are irrefutable. Their
seven communities occupy the wide valley
trenches of southeastern B.C. and the adjacent
American states of Montana and Idaho. The
3,000-metre walls of four parallel ranges—the
Rockies and Purcells, the Selkirks and Mona-
shees—rise suddenly from plains and plateaus,
creating a mountain enclave that flourished
unto itself for thousands upon thousands of
years. The Ktunaxa language is a rare "isolate."
Like that of the Haida on their remote archipelago, it has no links to any other. The culture
that goes with it is steeped in the mists of
the continent's most ancient landforms. And
their history reaches back to account for the

more "recent" developments here, such as the
formation of rivers.

Some elders say the name Kutunai, given
them by their Prairie neighbours, is from their
word, *kulni*, "to travel by water." And they
speak of Natmuqcin, a giant who travelled
about the land giving places names. In the
wide trench between the Rockies and Purcells,
he moulded, with his knees, one of this continent's most remarkable features: the two-kilo-
metre portage that separates the Columbia
River at its very source from the first freshets
of the Kootenay River. From here, these two
great rivers, channelled by the ranges, flow in
opposite directions: the Columbia to the
northern perimeter of the Ktunaxa world, the
Kootenay to its southern reaches. Then, both
rivers, having travelled the same distance, turn
and merge in the heart of Ktunaxa territories.
They continue to the sea as the Columbia, the
fourth-longest river on the continent.

The story of Natmuqcin is echoed by
archaeologists who have followed an unbroken trail of Ktunaxa presence here that dates

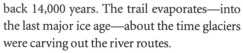

back 14,000 years. The trail evaporates—into the last major ice age—about the time glaciers were carving out the river routes.

In the 7,500 years following the ice age, the Ktunaxa were concentrated in the then dry, open forests of the Purcell Mountains. Then, when the climate changed again, the Purcells became, conversely, a divider. The people on the moister, west side travelled the rivers and lakes in canoes, fishing and pursuing small game. Those on the drier east side hunted bison and large prehistoric animals. Some Ktunaxa people crossed to the far side of the Rockies, hunting for bison, then returning. They thrived as a whole, cooperative civilization, enduring earthquakes, floods, blocked salmon runs, and little ice ages like the one that ended just two centuries ago.

In 1807, the first white fur trader, David Thompson, made his way through the rocky barriers with the help of the Ktunaxa. They even assisted him in setting up the region's first post, Kootenae House, on the west shores of Lake Windermere. But for some, his arrival engendered a deep sense of foreboding. One Ktunaxa prophet travelled ahead of Thompson's party as it continued down the Columbia River to the coast, warning all she met: the end of the world was coming.

Within half a century, smallpox had turned gathering places to ghost towns. Gold seekers, silver, lead, copper, and coal miners blasted their way through the ancient mountain walls. An invisible and arbitrary international boundary in 1846 formed a new wall, dividing north and south. In 1887 Ktunaxa law was challenged at what became Fort Steele by an army of North West Mounted Police. Then the *Indian Act* imposed its more than 200 laws and regulations on a reserve-bound people. Natmuqcin's rivers—the Columbia and Kootenay—were dammed, from head to mouth, their power siphoned to smelters and cities.

Still, the Ktunaxa endure. Together with their closest Secwepemc neighbours, the Kin-

basket people, they continue to address the land question, knowing its resolution may take generations. They resist the invisible boundary, and strive for the preservation and practice of their culture, language, and identity. They have initiated the Canadian Columbia River Intertribal Fisheries Commission, to restore life—salmon—to their rivers. The prophet promised: the end of the world would be followed by a time of plenty.

HIGHLIGHTS AND EVENTS	
ⓖ Ktunaxa Tipi Company	p. 104

INFORMATION AND PROTOCOL
Before reserves were set out in 1887, the Ktunaxa people travelled freely, gathering at several settlements each year. Communications were informal but constant and extensive, enhanced, in recent centuries, by the introduction of horses. Leadership was hereditary —father to son, or adopted son, until 1953, when the federal government imposed its electoral system on First Nations across Canada.

Today, the Ktunaxa/Kinbasket Tribal Council represents four Ktunaxa communities in Canada, and the Kinbasket people, the easternmost community of Secwepemc (Shuswap) peoples. The Ktunaxa people north of the 49th parallel are related to and aligned with the Kootenai Tribe of Idaho, based at Bonners Ferry, and the Kootenai of the Confederated Salish Kootenai Tribes of the Flathead Reservation, Pablo, Montana. Each year since 1979 a general assembly of Ktunaxa peoples has been held as a forum for discussing issues common to all.

The Ktunaxa population within Canada is 1,000 or more; outside, 600.

The language spoken here is Ktunaxa: it is not related to any other, anywhere.

Appropriate venues for exploration are given below.

For at least 5,000 years, Ktunaxa people used these sturgeon-nosed canoes to transport people and goods through the rich marshlands and sloughs of the Kootenay and Columbia rivers system.
CREDIT: RBCM 8679

? **Ktunaxa/Kinbasket Tribal Council:** SS #3, Site 15, Comp. 14, Mission Rd., Cranbrook, B.C., V1C 6H3. Tel: 489-2464. Fax: 489-5760.

East from Castlegar: Where the Rivers Meet

I **kiktisuk (Castlegar):** Where "two rivers meet"—today's **Castlegar** (pop. 6,530/0 Ab) looks out to the Kootenay River flowing into the Columbia, at the end of its long journey around mountain ranges. From here north, Ktunaxa place names trace the east shores of Lower Arrow Lake, now the 232-km reservoir behind the Hugh Keenleyside Dam, completed in 1965.

From kiktisuk (Castlegar) East along the Kootenay River on Highway 3A

I **The Sinixt People:** In earlier times, the Ktunaxa shared their western frontier with the Sinixt, a Salish-speaking people. The Ktunaxa called them catunik, "people of the small lake." When smallpox swept down upon them from both west and east, the Sinixt barely survived, and by the late 1800s they were one small community, with many Ktunaxa among them, on the west shore of the lake opposite Burton. After the last registered Sinixt died in the 1950s, the federal government declared them extinct and closed the book on Sinixt land claims. But recently the Sinixt have emerged, alive and well. Some with origins here have been living with family south of the border, where the Sinixt are still recognized. Others, it seems, have been here all along, in the Columbia and Slocan river valleys, overlooked by census takers.

▮   **ʔaktupis:** 41 km east of kiktisuk (Castlegar) the city of **Nelson** (pop. 8,630/30 Ab) looks out over the west arm of Kootenay Lake, and the traditional Ktunaxa site, "gills."

▮   **Tipi Camp at Pilot Bay:** 34 km beyond ʔaktupis (Nelson), the ferry at Balfour crosses Kootenay Lake to Kootenay Bay. It is 11 km farther to Gray Creek, departure point for Pilot Bay. This 2,500-year-old camping place is the setting for new tipis—accommodation during Family Days, July and August, when the general public is welcome. The non-profit Guiding Hands Recreation Society custom-designs programs for groups seeking to connect with nature, and often draws on elders and healers from Ktunaxa and other First Nations to lead sessions. Tel: 227-9555.

▮   **kunama'nam:** 52 km south of Kootenay Bay, near the Kuskonook Rest Area. The Canadian Pacific Railway line ran west from the Crowsnest Pass and, in the early 1900s, paused here at "road leading down"—a manmade spur to barges that carried rail cars across Kootenay Lake.

T   **ʔakaqtahat (Creston):** (pop. 4,125/15 Ab). 79 km south of Kootenay Bay, at the lower end of Kootenay Lake in the wide valley at the confluence of the Goat and Kootenay rivers. The Ktunaxa name refers to the sloughs or marshlands where they navigated their unusual "sturgeon-nosed" canoes, hunting and harvesting the wild rice that grew as tall as they were. The wetlands challenged trail-blazers David Thompson and Edgar Dewdney, and land developers such as W.A. Baillie Grohman (see below). In the late 1800s, the Ktunaxa who lived here strongly opposed the draining of their slough and the destruction of their cemetery for orchards and alfalfa fields. They left their village, but their history remains: at higher elevations are rock paintings, obsidian quarries, and tools, often turned up during road or house construction. These

indicate that water levels were much higher at one time. The people remained in the area: they are the yaqan nuʔkiy of today (see below). Land reclamation projects continued in earnest through the 1930s.

Ⓖ   **Creston and District Museum:** 219 Devon St. Tel: 428-9262. Ktunaxa tools on display.

V   **yaqan nuʔkiy (Lower Kootenay):** (Pop. 156/87). From Creston, Erickson Rd., then Hwy 21, lead south about 6 km to the administrative centre in a building of tipi-inspired design. It is 1 km farther to the community overlooking the Kootenay River and named for a rock formation to the east which served as a landmark for water-borne travellers. Here, elders Wilfred and Agatha Jacobs operate the **Ktunaxa Tipi Company**. As children, they lived in tipis made traditionally from animal hides and reeds. Today, they are cut from great sheets of canvas to a range of sizes. For tours and sales, call 428-4582. The band office has information about guided trail rides into the mountains north of here. There is also a powwow in May.

?   **yaqan nuʔkiy Administration:** Box 1107, Creston, B.C., V0B 1G0. Tel: 428-4428.

South into Idaho and Montana

From yakan nuʔkiy, the Kootenay River snakes south across the B.C./Idaho border. When government officials first came to discuss this boundary with the Ktunaxa people, they interpreted them to mean the land was literally going to be cut in two. It is 50 km via Hwys 1 and 95 to the Kootenai Reservation at **Bonners Ferry** (pop. 100). Box 1269, Bonners Ferry, Idaho, U.S.A., 83805. Tel: 208-267-3519. There is a powwow here in mid-June. From there, the highway continues to trace the river, then the east shores of the 110-km reservoir, Lake Koocanusa (Kootenay-Canada-U.S.A.), created by the Libby Dam. It is about 280 km from Bonners Ferry to Elmo, Montana, where the confederated Kootenay and Salish Tribes (pop. 6,700) occupy 500,000 hectares of mountain and valley. Box 278, Pablo, Montana, U.S.A., 59855. Tel: 406-675-2700. Here is the **Sqelix'u Aqlcmaknik Cultural Centre**, 406-675-1060, **Camas Hot Springs Spa**, wilderness recreation, camping. The **Standing Arrow Pow Wow** is in late July.

North into British Columbia at Roosville on Highway 93

V akinkumlasnuqli'it (Tobacco Plains): (Pop. 149/89). The reserve stretches 12 km from the Canada-U.S. border at Roosville to the community centre at Grasmere. Its Ktunaxa name means "tobacco plains." Tobacco was cultivated in two locations just south of the border, and on this side too. Some accounts give the plant a local origin, like the rivers, in the vicinity of Canal Flats. It was not smoked for pleasure: the Ktunaxa offered it ceremonially to the spirits, so they would take care of the people. Its cultivation and use fell off after European diseases swept through the land. These plains were also a base camp for bison-hunting expeditions and the setting, until the late 1800s, for religious dance ceremonies.

Many here today are descendants of Ktunaxa from yakyaqanqat, "way through the mountain," 65 km north, now the coal-mining centre of Fernie. It was the Ktunaxa who in the late 1800s led gold commissioner William Fernie to the Elk Valley coal they had long used to keep their fires burning. Elders speak of the time he persuaded a young woman to divulge the source of the coal she wore as a necklace. He later spurned her and invoked her mother's wrath. She called upon the spirits to deliver a curse upon the valley, and the history of the town of Fernie from then on is a litany of disaster after disaster—an explosion, fires, and a flood. In 1964, Tobacco Plains chiefs Red Eagle and Big Crane held a ceremony to lift the curse.

Tobacco Plains today is a strong community with an eye on the future. In the 1960s, the Ktunaxa's first woman chief was elected here. In 1979, this was the site of the first annual General Assembly of all Ktunaxa people. The community runs a **duty-free shop** at the border; **Edwards Lake Campground**, via a road leading right from the General Store in Grasmere, offers basic camping, pleasant swimming.

? **Tobacco Plains Administration:** Box 21, Grasmere, B.C., V0B 1R0. Tel: 887-3461. In log building on Hwy 93.

From Tobacco Plains, Hwy 3 leads north and east along the Elk Valley. Here, somewhere— its location currently guarded—is a bison jump similar to Head-Smashed-In, Alberta's World Heritage Site, where hunters on foot stampeded buffalo over the edge of a cliff. The Elk Valley jump is one of only two known west of the continental divide in Canada. It was last used about 1600, when the little ice age wiped out the bison here. After that, the Ktunaxa, who did survive, made regular journeys through Crowsnest Pass to hunt bison in the warmer "chinook" country.

Along the Kootenay River on Highways 3/93/95

I ʔakisqaqli'it: Where **Cranbrook** (pop. 16,245/220 Ab) sits today, at "two little creeks or channels." The 1860s–1880s was a time of great change even for the adaptable, mobile Ktunaxa people—and things changed here as much as anywhere in their territories. In 1863, just north at Wild Horse Creek, the region's biggest gold strike drew 1,500 miners and a small group of settlers around Galbraith's Ferry. A cable-powered vessel eased miners across the Kootenay River just below its confluence with the St. Mary's River.

About this time, Chief Joseph and his followers, the akamnik, "people of the thick woods," who gathered on Ktunaxa lands south

Residential school at aqam (St. Mary's).

of the 49th parallel, chose "where two ram horns lay," on the east side of Cranbrook's present-day townsite as their winter headquarters. By the 1870s, white settlers were crowding in on "Joseph's Prairie." The akamnik returned to a quieter base at the junction of the St. Mary and Kootenay rivers, the west side of Galbraith's Ferry. In 1874, when Father Fouquet of the Oblates took up permanent residence at St. Eugene's Mission just a few kilometres up St. Mary's River, the akamnik formed its nucleus and later became known as the St. Mary's band. Joseph handed over chieftainship to his adopted son, Isadore.

In 1884, as told by the chief's descendants today, a Ktunaxa man named "Little Isadore" came upon a pair of prospectors who had built a cabin on their land. "They didn't understand white language, they didn't know white law said non-natives could take up land regardless of the Ktunaxa." The misunderstanding led to violence and two miners died.

Meanwhile the Canadian Pacific Railway joined British Columbia to the rest of Canada, cutting into Ktunaxa territories at Golden to the north in 1885, drawing more settlers and speculators into Ktunaxa lands. Among the latter was Colonel Baker, magistrate and member of the provincial legislature—elected by at least 11 of the 22 white people he repre-

sented. From Galbraith, a settler and ferry operator, he bought Joseph's Prairie, and despite Chief Isadore's protests, surveying and fencing was underway. Then, two men, including Little Isadore, were arrested and jailed near Galbraith's Ferry for the murder of the miners. Chief Isadore, declaring that "Indians have been found dead, yet no white man was ever put in jail," freed the accused and ordered Baker's surveyor out of his territory. The North West Mounted Police—75 armed men—were called in to enforce the new government's law and order. Chief Isadore returned the prisoners, and although NWMP Inspector Sam Steele ultimately released them for lack of evidence, colonial law prevailed. The NWMP departed; Chief Isadore agreed to leave Joseph's Prairie to the newcomers. By 1887, Ktunaxa reserves were defined as the small spaces where they still live today, marking the biggest change of all—the Ktunaxa no longer travel freely throughout their land.

To Fort Steele

▪ **Fort Steele Heritage Town:** On Hwy 93, 8 km north of Hwy 3/93 junction, 17 km northeast of Cranbrook. Tel: 489-3351. Grounds open year-round. From 1863, Galbraith's Ferry carried miners across the Kootenay River here.

In 1887, Sam Steele and his division of North West Mounted Police put up a rectangle of buildings for their winter quarters. There were no palisades, as the fort reconstruction suggests, but this was a bastion of white authority nonetheless. Some of that story is told here. The museum, open July and August, displays the unusual Ktunaxa canoe, made from a single piece of white pine bark set in a frame. Archaeologists speculate that these vessels, in use for at least 5,000 years, served as early ore cars, transporting heavy materials up and down the rivers. Outstanding Ktunaxa bead and leather work is also featured.

To Ktunaxa Headquarters

V aqam (St. Mary's): (Pop. 245/203). 2 km north of Cranbrook turn east off Hwy 95A and follow signs to aqam and Ktunaxa-Kinbasket Tribal headquarters. The St. Eugene Mission was founded here by the Oblates in 1855; a resident priest arrived in 1874. The "people of the thick woods," who lived here under Chief Joseph, became known as outstanding farmers and still operate a 240-hectare cattle ranch and Christmas-tree farm.

The elegant St. Eugene Church was built in 1897, and remains a rare example of Ktunaxa benefits from modern-day mining. A Ktunaxa man, Pierre, led Father Coccola and a mining promoter to the galena deposits that became the St. Eugene Mine. Pierre, at the urging of the priest, spent most of his profits on the church which has hand-painted Italian stained and leaded glass, pinnacles, and buttresses. The mine prospered after they sold out, giving Consolidated Mining and Smelting Canada, "Cominco," its start.

The mission residential school, built in 1912 and closed in 1971, is being converted into a major destination resort and meeting facility, with banquet room, craft shops, golf course, and recreation centre. It will also house a **Ktunaxa interpretive centre**, a **Native Womens' Arts and Crafts Cooperative**, and serve as headquarters for the **Kootenay Ecomuseum**, intended to give the Ktunaxa more stewardship of some of the oldest petroglyphs in the world, alpine game-drive sites, bison jumps, prehistoric mine shafts, and village sites that are being lost, daily, to development.

? **St. Eugene Mission Development Project:** Site 15, SS #3-14, Cranbrook, B.C., V1C 6H3. Tel: 489-2372.

I **?akinmi:** Southeast of aqam, this mountain's name, "pile of arrows," refers to a Ktunaxa creation story. On today's maps it is Mt. Baker, for the colonel who fenced in Chief Isadore's land and later named it Cranbrook, for his birthplace in England.

I **Canal Flats:** 68 km north of Fort Steele. Hwy 93/95 traverses the 2-km "portage" of land between the Kootenay River and the Columbia River. In the 1880s, W.A. Baillie Grohman began digging a canal through it, with the stated aim of reducing flooding farther south, and as a thoroughfare for boats. Blocked by strong objections from Columbia Valley residents and the Canadian Pacific Railway, who feared they would be flooded, his fantastic scheme died—until the 1970s, when B.C. Hydro considered diverting the Kootenay River to increase the electrical generating capacity of the Columbia system.

I **Columbia Lake:** Just beyond Canal Flats. Headwaters of the Columbia River. A fishing site for Ktunaxa peoples until the late 1920s.

I **Hoodoos:** At the north end of Columbia Lake. The Ktunaxa say an enormous fish wounded by Coyote tried to make its way along the Rocky Mountain Trench, where it finally gave up and died. As its flesh decomposed, the ribs fell apart and half became the hoodoos here; the other half are hoodoos farther south, near St. Mary's. At a campsite, yawu?nik, just below the hoodoos, people

Encampment near Windermere.
CREDIT: BCARS B03802

came to gather tamarack moss, which was roasted and eaten.

V Columbia Lake: (Pop. 203/141). The reserve, well above Columbia Lake, embraces the shores of the Columbia River and Lake Windermere from just north of Fairmont Hot Springs to the town of Windermere. The administration office is just before Windermere Loop Rd. The Ktunaxa call this area ʔakisq'nuk, "two bodies of water," for the two lakes. This community runs the family-oriented **Lakeside Resort**, 2 km south of the administration office; 342-6352. The Ktunaxa name for Windermere is yaqunaki, mentioned in the story of the giant, Natmuqcin, and also site of a mission village.

? Columbia Lake Administration: Box 130, Windermere, B.C., V0B 2L0. Tel: 342-6301.

I Kootenae House: 6 km north of Windermere, take road leading toward Invermere. Turn right onto Wilmer-Panorama Rd., then right on Westside Rd. A few hundred metres along this road, on the right, a cairn marks the site of the first trading post in these territories, established by David Thompson and the Ktunaxa in 1807.

I kyaknuqtiʔit: "Prairie on top of a hill," the community known as Invermere.

V Kenpesq't (Kinbasket): (Pop. 210/136). On Hwy 93/95 just north of Invermere exit. About 100 years ago, the Secwepemc leader Kenpesq't and followers, most from the Upper Thompson River area, established a new community here. In time, they became allies of the Ktunaxa.

? Kinbasket Administration: Box 790, Invermere, B.C., V0A 1K0. Tel: 342-6361.

I Ktunaxa Travels: From Kenpesq't, Hwy 95 follows the Columbia, the river route of the Ktunaxa people, to Secwepemc frontiers. Hwy 93 traces the Kootenay River to its very beginnings in the Rocky Mountains. After the little ice age which caused the disappearance of bison on this side of the Rockies, and then the timely arrival of horses, the Ktunaxa made regular treks through the mountains to Kootenay Plains, west of Red Deer, Alberta, to hunt bison and to trade. The more northern passes were especially vital after the 1800s, with the Blackfoot people blocking the southern routes. These mountains, designated a World Heritage Site, and embraced by a chain of national parks, were held sacred to the Ktunaxa, as all things are. But Sinclair Pass tracing the Kootenay River (now Hwy 93 from Radium Hot Springs) was particularly so. The hot springs at Radium were a place of spiritual cleansing; the canyon beyond, their cathedral. Here too, was a valuable source of iron oxide, pigment for the paints the Ktunaxa applied to horses, tipis, shields, their faces, clothing, and rock walls, and which they traded for bison products up at Kootenay Plains.

Farther along, their trail traces the turquoise Vermilion River—the glacial headwaters of the Kootenay River—to yet another source of the pigment, the **Vermilion Paint Pots**. The way is marked for us now; 83 km beyond Kootenay National Park's west gate, signs lead off Hwy 93. Here, we can bend to the yellow earth, rub a little of it on our fingers.

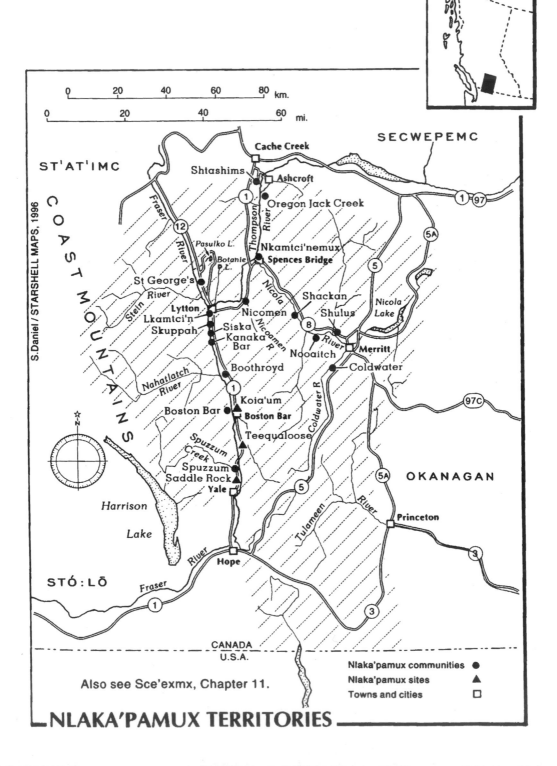

NLAKA'PAMUX TERRITORIES

CHAPTER 10

Nlaka'pamux

The Stein Valley is not just a place to preserve. The rock paintings were put there for future generations—which happen to be today's. Our responsibility is to teach all who wish to learn about the spiritual values we hold. In the history of our people we have never turned anyone away. We welcomed people, taught them, made them into our family, part of our culture. That hasn't changed.

—Darryl Webster, Lytton First Nation

Nlaka'pamux, in the language spoken here, means "people of the canyon." Their world is the Y where the earth-brown Fraser River receives the sky-blue Thompson, then thunders through chasm after narrow chasm. Just a hint of the intensity of life that was here until 150 years ago can be gleaned from today's maps outlining reserves. From above Lytton to the west and Ashcroft to the east, then down to Spuzzum where the canyon opens into Stó:lo territories, are dozens of tiny reserves. Some embrace only as much space as it takes to net a salmon, and together they represent just a fraction of the land long used by these people. This was one of the most densely populated places on earth. The ancient capital of the Nlaka'pamux world was Kumsheen— confluence of the two great rivers. Today, the town of Lytton is still a "centrepost" for 11 contemporary Nlaka'pamux communities.

Food for these thousands was, and still is, the salmon, swarming against the Fraser's current, netted easily where they rested in canyon pools or muscled through eddies. The Nlaka'pa-

mux tell us it was Coyote who broke a dam blocking their passage at the foot of the canyon long ago. Archaeologists say that dam was glacial sediment, undone sometime during the past 10,000 years.

Here also, in the deep valleys of the dozens of rivers and creeks flowing into the Fraser, is an unequalled source of spiritual sustenance. There are places like the valley of the Stein (StI'yen) or "hidden place," a major tributary of the Fraser unknown to the outside world until the 1970s when, to keep it from being logged, the Nlaka'pamux and the St'a-t'imc who shared it began to reveal its secrets. The Stein, say the people who live here, is to them "like Moses' Mountain or Rome to the Catholics." Along its corridor are caves, rock shelters, cliffs, and boulders where shamans and young initiates seeking *xa'xa*—the power of nature—left in red ochre testimony of their dreams and experiences. Recorded here are supernatural beings, historic events, first encounters with white men. Some of the earliest writings are said to be the teachings of the

Rediscovery camp in the Stein Valley, where young initiates still seek the power of nature.
CREDIT: GARY FIEGEHEN

Transformer, Xwekt'xwektl, on the arts of survival and social conduct.

"It's really the history of people's life on this earth," said Annie York, of the Stein Valley. Archaeologists have verified it as one of the largest rock-art sites in Canada. Environmentalists focussed on the ancient trails leading through old-growth forests, and an international call went out to "Save the Stein." The Nlaka'pamux and St'at'imc delivered their own *Stein Declaration*. In 1995 the entire 107,000-hectare valley was permanently protected as the Stein Valley Nlaka'pamux Heritage Provincial Park to be managed cooperatively by the province and the Lytton First Nation.

In times past, the Stein Valley trail was shared by allies and enemies alike—"for dreaming," Annie York said, "you can go to other peoples' country."

It was with this kind of openness that the Nlaka'pamux received the fur-trade explorer Simon Fraser on his 1808 quest down the river now bearing his name. And, while being led down the canyon at Hells Gate, he did come face to face with *xa'xa*: "We had to pass where no human being should venture." Some among the canyon people suspected Fraser was Coyote, and that his accomplices were the mythical Sun, Moon, Morning Star, and Arrow Arm.

Fifty years of fur trade passed before the dreams of the canyon people and those of the newcomers seriously collided. It all began in 1856 with an innocuous sip of water from the Thompson River, the glimmer of gold in the clear waters there, and just a thought, in the mind of the Nlaka'pamux trader, that this might be worth something down at the Hudson's Bay Company's Fort Kamloops. For two years the Nlaka'pamux mined and sold their gold to the company. But by late 1857, American miners at the loose end of the California gold rush began to find their way up the Fraser. They approached from the coast, and also from the south via the Okanagan Valley, across the 12-year-old Canada-U.S. border. The canyon people tried to block them, but many, trained on the American frontier, had learned violence would get them through.

Historians are only beginning to appreciate what was, in fact, a war here in the canyons of the Fraser. The miners strategized, waited for their ranks to grow, formed military-style companies. The Nlaka'pamux prepared to defend their sovereign lands from an invading force. From the beginning, there were casualties on both sides, and a blood-bath was imminent as more miners arrived determined to annihilate the Indians. It was on the eve of this that an American named Snyder addressed a mass meeting at Yale: there would be no winners. He proposed another way. With a company of 180 men, he travelled up the Fraser, brokering peace with Nlaka'pamux chiefs.

At Lytton, Chief Cixpe'ntlam, "a man of great influence within our whole nation," waited for him. His word would determine which way the wind blew in the canyons. Snyder cautioned him that though this time the miners came in hundreds, next time they would come in thousands, and "drive [the canyon people] from the river forever." Cixpe'ntlam declared his sovereignty: "At Lytton is my centrepost. It is the middle of my house and I sit here. . . ." Then he counselled peace, for at this time, Nlaka'pamux and white miners were working side by side on the gravel bars of the river.

November 19, 1858, the colony of British Columbia was declared. From here, the story flows as elsewhere. Nlaka'pamux land was taken up by settlers. Colonial policies designed to turn the canyon people into farmers located reserves on rock or without legal access to water. Salmon-spawning beds were eaten up by placer mines, and the salmon by commercial fisheries at the Fraser's mouth. Laws limited where, when, and how the Nlaka'pamux fished. And their ancient fishing rocks were dynamited to make way for roads and the "national dream"—the transcontinental Canadian Pacific Railway.

In 1913, during construction of the second national railway along the opposite riverbank, the canyon wall just above Hells Gate slid down into the Fraser. An already fast and narrow passage became narrower and faster. Upriver, up the Fraser and all its tributaries as far north as Stuart Lake, people waited in anticipation of that year's major run of sockeye salmon. Meanwhile, at Hells Gate, just a fraction of the long journey from the sea, millions of fish battered themselves to death trying to reach their spawning grounds. In the years to come, only certain species of salmon would—when water levels were low enough—get past the new barrier. It's a law of nature for salmon: what doesn't go up, doesn't come down as the next generation of spawners. Salmon runs have never recovered from this,

B.C.'s biggest environmental disaster. Fish ladders are helping now, but says Debbie Abbott of the Nlaka'pamux Nation Tribal Council, "it has been a constant battle to ensure the resource is there for our grandchildren."

Darryl Webster says he hopes "the Stein Valley can serve as a vehicle, to explain why we believe we should manage our resources in our area. We would like a good, healthy discussion of the treaty process—ask people to open their minds, listen, and really hear what we're saying, without having to be in our shoes and experience what we went through."

HIGHLIGHTS AND EVENTS

◌ Fishing in the Canyon: From June to October, concentrated in August, the canyon rocks below the highway are speckled with the orange and blue tarps of fishing camps and drying racks. While some fishermen and women still use traditional dip-net and spear techniques, most set gill nets into murky waters.

◌ Stein Valley Nlaka'pamux
   Heritage Park   p. 117

INFORMATION AND PROTOCOL

Many of the 11 Nlaka'pamux bands, as they are identified today, consist of several communities. The Lytton First Nation, for example, consists of people living on 21 reserves. In addition to the main Nlaka'pamux nations/communities described below are four that identify themselves collectively as the Sce'exmx, "people of the creek," and occupy the upper reaches of the Nicola River, a tributary of the Thompson River. For these, see chapter 11.

Appropriate venues for exploration of Nlaka'pamux culture and history are listed below.

❓ **Nlaka'pamux Nation Tribal Council:** Box 430, Lytton, B.C., V0K 1Z0. Tel: 455-2711.

Fish drying racks at Hells Gate are testimony to the abundance of salmon here in the late 1860s. Half a century after this photo was taken, a landslide, caused by railway construction, made the gorge impassible to spawning salmon, and stocks have never recovered.
CREDIT: RBCM 1426

Fax: 455-2565. Members: Aschroft, Boston Bar, Lytton, Siska, Boothroyd, Spences Bridge, Oregon Jack Creek.

? Fraser Canyon Tribal Administration: Box 400, Lytton, B.C., V0K 1Z0. Tel: 455-2279. Fax: 455-2772. Members: Kanaka Bar, Skuppah, Nicomen, Spuzzum.

Enter Nlaka'pamux territories North of Yale on Highway 1

Sailor Bar, 8.5 km north of Yale, is identified nowadays as the fishing boundary between the Stó:lo and Nlaka'pamux peoples. Traditionally it was a very fluid line that shifted with relations between families at Yale and Spuzzum.

Between Yale and Lytton are 90 km of chasms and gorges carved by the Fraser on its plunge through the Coast Mountains. The Nlaka'pamux call this portion of their country Uta'mqt, "below." Here, Hwy 1 approximates the route of the old Cariboo Wagon Road, built in 1864 to link Yale with interior gold fields. Nlaka'pamux helped construct the road and advised on its route. Before that, they guided pack trains over the trails they had been travelling for thousands of years. M.B. Begbie, Chief Justice of this new British colony, wrote: "No supplies were taken in [to the gold districts] except by Indians . . . Without them . . . the country could not have been entered or supplied in 1858–1860."

V Spuzzum: (Pop. 161/37). 15 km from Yale Tunnel to administration office just off Hwy 1. "Little flat," a few families living between

Saddle Rock and Spuzzum Creek, has long served as a cultural and economic gateway between the people of the river and the people of the canyon. They shared, as hunting grounds, the watershed of Spuzzum Creek where mountain goats ranged. Both canyon and river peoples were known for their exotic goat-hair blankets. From Spuzzum a trail led west over the mountains to villages at the head of Harrison Lake. These mountains were spiritual training grounds. Spuzzum was also home of Annie York, prominent Nlaka'pamux cultural authority, healer, and teacher until her death in 1991. No visitor services.

? Spuzzum Administration: RR 1, Yale, B.C., V0K 2S0. Tel: 863-2395.

✖ Teequaloose: 21 km north of Yale. Look upriver and down from the old bridge in **Alexandra Bridge Provincial Park** for signs —nets, floats—of Nlaka'pamux still fishing at this ancient site.

✖ Hells Gate Fishways Viewpoint: 30 km north of Yale. Displays here tell of difficult passage for early explorers in 1808, and for salmon, especially after the rock slide in 1913. Guy Dunsten, from the Nlaka'pamux community of Siska, describes the rough passage for his people: "That [slide] was the end of our river and the beginning of government restrictions . . . a lot of us starved." The fisheries and marine department response to the disaster was to curtail First Nations fishing on the Fraser. The fishways, built in 1944, help surviving salmon species over the obstacle.

▼ Boston Bar: (Pop. 190/68). 42 km north of Yale. At the town of Boston Bar cross Cog Harrington Bridge to Kopchitchin, "north bend," site of this Nlaka'pamux community's administrative offices and a residential area. They also operate **Anderson Creek Campground**, at the ancient site, Tuckkwiowhum, about 5 km south of there. A century and a

half ago, these people formed the largest village of the lower Nlaka'pamux, at Koia'um, "to pick berries," site of today's non-native community, Boston Bar. The harvest of berries and roots is still an important part of a traditionally oriented diet. Several other reserves— ancient sites—were small farms in more recent times.

? Boston Bar Administration: SS 1, Green Ranch Rd., Boston Bar, B.C., V0K 1C0. Tel: 867-8844.

▼ Boothroyd: (Pop. 250/108). 55 km north of Yale, band office on Kamuse Rd., at Kahmoose. Logging roads rather than ancient trails provide access to their sacred watershed, the Nahatlatch River, flowing in from the west, and longer than the Stein. It was known to the people here as the "salmon river"—all five species spawn here. Women harvested cedar bark and roots; seekers of *xa'xa* left their stories on rock. The people of Kahmoose today are working on an integrated resource-use plan with the ministry of forests to restore and enhance salmon runs, preserve hunting and harvesting grounds, and develop sustainable tourism and forestry. Access to the Nahatlatch River is via Cog Harrington Bridge at Boston Bar. Chaumox Rd. leads north 15 km to a bridge across the Nahatlatch. It is 10 km to the lakes chain, and Forest Service campsites.

The Boothroyd community operates Fraser Acres Restaurant on Hwy 1 south of the administration office, and is planning a campground at nearby Blue Lake.

✖ Boothroyd Administration: Box 295, Boston Bar, B.C., V0K 1C0. Tel: 867-9211.

▼ Kanaka Bar: (Pop. 150/44). 70 km north of Yale. A sign on the highway indicates the administration office. To the Nlaka'pamux, this is Nlaqla'kitin, "the crossing place." During the gold rush it was named for the Kanakas—Hawaiians who had arrived earlier

Lytton Coyote Dancers: Dempsey Webster, Sam Adams, and David McKay.
CREDIT: GRAHAM EVERETT

in the century as employees on Hudson's Bay Company trading ships. They came here seeking their fortunes as prospectors. Many married into First Nations communities.

? Kanaka Bar Administration: Box 400, Lytton, B.C., V0K 1Z0. Tel: 455-2279 (offices of Fraser Canyon Tribal Administration).

V Siska: (Pop. 235/125). 75 km north of Yale (12 km south of Lytton), left off Hwy 1. Siska, in the Nlaka'pamux language, means "uncle." Today it refers to the people and their creek. Where the Siska flows into the Fraser are the fishing camps where people net salmon and prepare them to be dried or smoked as they have for millenia. They acquired horses over 300 years ago, and their salmon trade burgeoned. As many as 75,000 sticks of dried salmon a year were exchanged for interior goods, including hemp, for making their nets. In 1872, the Siska selected as their reserve lands these traditional fishing camps, intending to continue their lucrative sales to miners and settlers. However, government legislation supported commercial fisheries offshore and this, say the Siska, has caused them much hardship.

Today, the Siska Valley is the last unlogged watershed between here and saltwater. Like the Stein, "dreamers" came here on their spiritual journeys and marked their experiences in ochre, and it is still the place where young Siska artists go to restore their vision. But this valley too is now being threatened. Chief Guy Dunsten and the Siska Halaw Singers-Drummers and Coyote Dancers represent the spirit of the community in their effort to prevent its destruction. Their message travels far. The Europe-based Incomindios, the International Committee for the Indians of America, is among those echoing their plea in letters to local decision-makers.

Fred Sampson is among a number of local artists incorporating Siska Valley pictographs into their soapstone carvings. Their work, along with that of other First Nations artists, is on display in the **Siska Art Gallery**, located in the new log administration centre just off the highway. Guided trail rides can be arranged here. Gas bar, for native status-card-holders only; small convenience store.

? **Siska Administration:** Box 358, Lytton, B.C., V0K 1Z0. Tel: 455-2219.

V **Skuppah:** (Pop. 60/45). Left off Hwy 1, just north of Kanaka Bar, about 5 km south of Lytton. At Inklyuhkinatko. Says Doug McIntyre, "Blink your eyes when you go by and you'll miss us." People are employed in forestry and in the town of Lytton. Here are administration offices of the Fraser Tribal Administration complex; visitors are welcome.

? **Skuppah Administration:** Box 400, Lytton, B.C., V0K 1Z0. Tel: 455-2279.

V **Lytton First Nation:** (Pop. 1,500/835). 108 km north of Yale at the junction of Hwys 1 and 12. The town of **Lytton** (pop. 335) is Kumsheen or Lkamtci'n, "confluence," the ancient and contemporary centre of the Nlaka'pamux world. This is where Coyote's son landed after returning from the upper world. A flat rock, considered sacred, at nearby Lytton Creek marked the spot. It was destroyed to make way for the railroad. Kumsheen is also where Simon Fraser, in 1808, shook 1,000 hands; and where some took him to be Coyote. During the period of great transition that followed, Chief Cixpe'ntlam declared in 1858 that Lytton was the centrepost of his vast territories. For his role in ending the Fraser River war, a commemoration plaque has been erected, on church grounds, at the corner of Fraser and 7th.

The Lytton First Nation today consists of 21 communities ranging in population from 1 to 111, occupying the banks of the Fraser and Thompson rivers on either side of the town of Lytton. Administration offices are at St. George's, 5 km up the Fraser via Hwy 12 (see below). In Lytton itself, the people of the canyon are a strong presence. Nlaka'pamux Tribal Council offices are on the main street, just upstream from the Lytton First Nation's **Lytton Hotel**. At the northeast edge of town by the bridge, they fish for salmon, as always.

The name Lytton honours Sir Edward Bulwer Lytton, British colonial secretary during the gold rush, who said of First Nations peoples: "It might be feasible to settle them permanently in villages; with such settlement civilization at once begins. Law and Religion would become naturally introduced . . ." Always in view from his namesake town is the deep gorge of the Stein River, where the prophets and teachers developed and taught their religion and law; it was a university, says Annie York. "All those rock writings—they are there to remind the young people that there was a person with knowledge on this earth for thousands of years before people came from Europe."

Across the Fraser to the Stein Valley

I **Stein Valley Nlaka'pamux Heritage Park:** Cross the Fraser at Lytton via the reaction ferry. It is 4.5 km to the parking lot marked by a cairn, and the start of the Stein Heritage Trail; about 2 km beyond the parking lot are the clear, energizing river, walking trails, and pictographs. This is Lytton First Nation reserve land. Watchmen charge a small registration fee to hikers who must enter here. The 75-km heritage trail tracing the Stein to its headwaters in the Coast Mountains is for hardy people who appreciate that "great strength and power can be derived from rocky places where water moves down through the mountains and hills . . ." Watchmen will eventually offer guided tours, to share their knowledge of cultural and spiritual values and to show how the trail itself is a guide. Maps and guidebooks have also been published.

Among the pictographs here are records of the recent 70-year war between the St'at'imc and Nlaka'pamux. It ended about 1850. The next 135 years of peace culminated in the unified struggle of the Mount Currie and Lytton peoples to preserve the valley. In 1985, their first Voices for the Wilderness Festival, to raise awareness of the heritage about to be destroyed, drew thousands of First Nations and supporters from around the world. It is now called the **Earth Voice Festival**, held in late July on Seabird Island, in Stó:lo territories (see chapter 5).

North from Lytton along the Fraser River

I   **Road to Botanie Valley:** 2 km north of Lytton, a gravel road leads northeast off Hwy 12, tracing Botanie Creek. "The Stein is only one component of the area we use and live in," says Darryl Webster. It is 17 km to Lytton First Nation reserve, Botanie and Pasulko lakes, and the meadows and slopes where Nlaka'pamux have long come in great numbers to harvest berries and such favoured roots as avalanche lily and spring beauty. The valley's name, Botanie, is actually of Nlaka'pamux origin, rather than an English description of its garden qualities. Its story is of a woman from Lytton, taken away by a great chief who some say was the Sun. She dropped an abundance of roots and berries here to keep her people fed.

Pasulko Lake is the setting for an annual summer healing gathering (see below). Ask at Lytton First Nation offices for permission and directions to camp on their land; there are also Forest Service campsites just before the reserve. There may be a small fee for berry pickers. Cattle wander freely: lakes are not suitable for swimming; bring water.

V   **Lytton First Nation at St. George's:** 5 km north of Lytton, on Hwy 12. This is the largest of the Lytton First Nation communities. St. George's Residential School opened here in 1939, closed in the 1970s, and though it burned down shortly thereafter, the name still sticks. Three generations of children attended. Ask here about the Stein Trail, Botanie Valley, and annual summer Healing Gathering, to which visitors are welcome. Says Darryl Webster: "We are in the healing mode —for us to be able to heal, others have to be able to heal too, and open their minds."

?   **Lytton First Nation Administration:** Box 20, Lytton, B.C., V0K 1Z0. Tel: 455-2304.

I   **Lytton Heritage Park:** 8 km north of Lytton. Being developed by local Lions Club. Nlaka'pamux pit houses, gold rush and ranching history. Ask at Lytton Infocentre, 400 Fraser St. Tel: 455-2523.

B   **St'at'imc Territory:** About 48 km north of Lytton on Hwy 12, approximately where Texas Creek flows into the Fraser River.

Tracing the Thompson River: East of Lytton on Highway 1

V   **Nicomen:** (Pop. 88/55). About 14.5 km east of Lytton, Hwy 1 curves with the Thompson River, passes by "Frog Rock," shoots under the Canadian Pacific Railway bridge, then crosses the Nicoamen River. Here a road leads right off the highway, then immediately left to an informal pullout on Nicomen reserve land for a glimpse of long and wispy Nicoamen Falls. It was nearby that the four-headed cannibal, Opia'skay'uuxw, made Ndjimkaa's wife crack open human bones, take out for him the marrow he loved to eat, and cache the remains. He was finally defeated by the young boy, Ngliksentem, who tossed pieces of the cannibal to such faraway places as Honolulu and Mexico, where they now form volcanoes;

Jesse Webster of Ahousaht, in 1984, with granddaughter Jesse modelling Maquinna-style hat her grandmother was renowned for weaving.

CREDIT: DOROTHY HAEGERT

Kwaxistala of Gwa'yi establishes himself as direct descendant of Kawadelekala. He emerged when the world was young from the supernatural Wolf, Gila la thleed, in the mountains of Kingcome Inlet.

The Commonwealth Games opening ceremonies in Victoria, 1994, presents the artistry and magic of Kwakwa̱ka'wakw leaders and designer, Mary Kerr.

Gwa'yi, Kingcome Inlet.
CREDIT: DOROTHY HAEGERT

On the sun-baked slopes overlooking their straits, the Lekwammen people carefully tended the camas crops which the first Europeans presumed to be God's creation.

Camas flowers at Meeqan, in Victoria.
CREDIT: JOHN LUTZ

First Nations from up and down the coast request permission to land in Lekwammen territories for 1994 Commonwealth Games in Victoria.

CREDIT: CITY OF VICTORIA PR74

Dancer at Songhees Powwow.

CREDIT: CITY OF VICTORIA PR74

Nisga'a law holds them stewards of their territories. Their history and the land itself offer stark reminders of times when they forgot this.

Nisga'a Lava Bed Memorial Park.
CREDIT: JOHN LUTZ

**Nisga'a artist Alver
Tait, carving a pole.**
CREDIT: GARY FIEGEHEN

The link between the First Nations and salmon continues to be expressed in where people live, where they work, what they eat; in their art, stories, and struggles.

Spawning salmon, Adams River.

Tahltan smokehouse.

CREDIT: GARY FIEGEHEN

A foghorn bellows today where the Mowa-chaht guided the first European ships around the rocks. Yuquot, "where the wind blows from all directions," is where Mowachaht history began, long, long before Captain Cook arrived.

View of Yuquot from lighthouse.
CREDIT: JOHN LUTZ

Fallen pole at Yuquot.

Tahltan guide Willie Williams.

CREDIT: GARY FIEGEHEN

The story of the name Tahltan has its origins just upriver from here, where the Stikine canyons are steepest and narrowest.

Telegraph Creek, overlooking the Stikine River, with today's Tahltan village on the highest terrace.
CREDIT: GARY FIEGEHEN

"To me, this valley is my cathedral; I come here to worship. I strongly say what my people want, which is to share this valley with the people of the universe, to come and see what the creator has left."

Henaaksiala elder Cecil Paul, at Kitlope Lake.
CREDIT: GRAHAM OSBORNE, COURTESY OF B.C. GOVERNMENT

The Kitlope valley.
CREDIT: GRAHAM OSBORNE, COURTESY OF B.C. GOVERNMENT

Fallen pole at Gitwangak, Gitxsan territories.
CREDIT: DOROTHY HAEGERT

the white of his eye became White Rock near Vancouver. The Nicoamen watershed was a favoured place for spiritual development: the Lytton prophet who foresaw the coming of Europeans and their technology trained above the falls and near the lake, Neqa'umin, "wolf water."

The road continues right a short distance to Nicomen community. No visitor services.

?   Nicomen Administration: Box 400, Lytton, B.C., V0K 1Z0. Tel: 455-2279.

J   Hwy 8: 37 km northeast of Lytton, at Spences Bridge. This route traces the Nicola River, home of the Sce'exmx, "people of the creek" (see chapter 11).

V   Spences Bridge: (Pop. 273/115). At the confluence of the Thompson and Nicola rivers, on the perimeters of present-day Spences Bridge, are three small communities of Nkamtci'nemux, "people of the confluence." Their many villages of former times stretched up to the frontiers of Secwepemc country.

It was here in May 1911 that 450 people representing First Nations from Tahltan to Stó:lo gathered. Some came by train, most on horseback, to respond to statements made by Premier McBride at a prior meeting in Victoria: that First Nations had no title to unsurrendered lands, that he would not allow the question into the courts, that reserves were already too large. The B.C. government's position was that undeveloped reserve lands hindered settlement and the development of resources, roads, and railways. New laws had been passed to allow for the expropriation of reserves, and already, railway construction along the Fraser was mangling their tiny allotments.

"We call on the dominion government in Ottawa . . . to have the question of title to our lands of this country brought into court and settled," the leaders reiterated in one of a series of ongoing memorials and declarations. Their open meetings continued until 1927, when the

Indian Act was amended, making fund-raising by First Nations political organizations a criminal offence.

At the west entrance to Spences Bridge, a small Anglican Church looks out over the Thompson River. The original Nkamtci'nemux village here, and the original church, were down closer to the river. On August 13, 1905, the mountain on the opposite bank came crumbling down, burying several people and damming the Thompson, which then swept over the village and drowned about 13 more people. Its force was so strong salmon were flung onto the railway tracks in the path of an oncoming train.

?   Spences Bridge Administration: Box 1000, Spences Bridge, B.C., V0K 2L0. Tel: 458-2224.

V   Oregon Jack Creek: (Pop. one family). 63 km from Lytton via Basque Rd. One family operates a ranch at Nte'qem, "muddy creek," overlooking the Thompson. No visitor services.

?   Oregon Jack Creek Administration: Box 490, Ashcroft, B.C., V0K 1A0. Tel: 453-9098.

V   Shtashims (Ashcroft): (Pop. 184/47). 75 km northeast of Lytton, take south turnoff to Ashcroft. The people of Shtashims moved to this site in the early 1860s to take advantage of work opportunities at the new Ashcroft Ranch, operated by the British Cornwall brothers. In a land exchange with the brothers, they lost water rights.

St. John's Anglican Church, built in 1890, still has services. Across the road is a **campground** (if no one is there, check at the administration office) and the **Nl'akapxm Motorplex**, 453-9131, featuring a quarter-mile race track.

?   Ashcroft Administration: Box 440, Ashcroft, B.C., V0K 1A0. Tel: 453-9194.

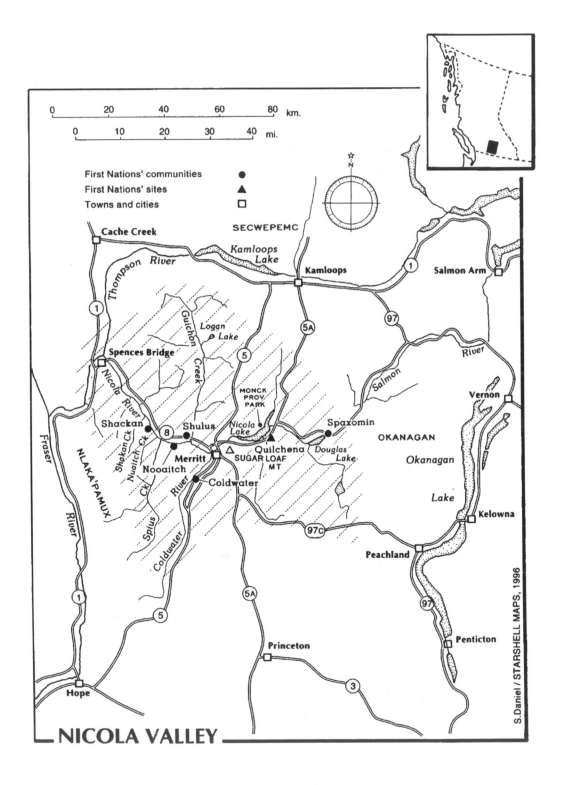

First Nations' communities ●
First Nations' sites ▲
Towns and cities □

SECWEPEMC

Cache Creek

Kamloops Lake

Thompson River

Kamloops

Salmon Arm

1

97

5A

Salmon River

Guichon Creek

Logan Lake

Spences Bridge

Nicola River

MONCK PROV. PARK

Vernon

Shackan

8

Shulus

Nicola Lake

Quilchena

Spaxomin

OKANAGAN

NLAKA'PAMUX

Shakan Ck

Nualtch Ck

Merritt

SUGAR LOAF MT

Douglas Lake

Okanagan Lake

Nooaitch

Spius Ck

Coldwater

Coldwater River

97C

Kelowna

Fraser River

Peachland

97

1

5

5A

Princeton

Penticton

3

Hope

S.Daniel / STARSHELL MAPS, 1996

NICOLA VALLEY

CHAPTER 11

The Nicola Valley:
Sce'exmx and Okanagan

The provincial government wants us to draw solid lines, solid boundaries, for the treaty process. But the reality is we overlap.

—*Harold Aljam, Nicola Valley Tribal Council*

The Nicola Valley, or Nicola's country, as it was earlier known, is shared today by two peoples and the memory of a third. The Sce'exmx, "people of the creeks," live along the tributaries of the lower Nicola River, closest to its meeting with the deep blue Thompson. They share their language, history, families with the Nlaka'pamux, the "people of the canyon" who prevail there.

Farther east are their Okanagan confederates, the Spaxomin people, fishing in and ranching around the lakes that form the Nicola River's headwaters. The lakes came to them two centuries ago, through the friendship between their leader, Pelkamu'lox, and Kwoli'la of the Secwepemc to the north who then controlled this frontier. Pelkamu'lox's son and successor was Hwistesmetxe'qen, "Walking Grizzly Bear." French-speaking fur traders in the early 1800s chose to call him Nicola. They referred to this as Nicola's country; the river running through it as Nicola's river. His own people pronounced his new name Nkwala. Nicola's legacy reaches far beyond names,

however. His 15 to 17 wives and more than 50 children embodied the alliances he forged with the surrounding nations and his skills as a peacemaker. Nicola became the nexus, also, between his people and the newcomers. Through the fur trade, the gold rush, and early settlement, Nicola was the most influential man of his very turbulent times.

The third people of Nicola Valley are the enigmatic Stuwix, sometimes called "the strangers." As a tangible, distinct people, they no longer exist, and are more of a mystery now than at the time of their appearance here. Athapaskan roots—a possible link with the Tsilhqot'in to the north—have been suggested. It is agreed they came here from somewhere else sometime between long, long ago and the 1700s. The most vivid account comes from the Okanagan Mourning Dove. In her biography she suggests the strange people were Chinookan speakers from the lower Columbia River. This is as she heard it from an aged Okanogan woman, Modesta: "They were a people from the south who left their home-

Nicola Valley sweat lodge in the early 1900s. Similar lodges are still being built, and private rituals held, drawing together the elements of fire, water, earth and stone, for physical and spiritual purification.

CREDIT: RBCM 999

land on account of a quarrel that started when two men argued over what caused the soft, whistling, whisperlike sound made by a flock of geese in flight . . . They [went up] the Columbia, travelling slowly, stopping for a year at one place after another . . . At the mouth of the Okanogan River, they turned upstream and turned again into the Similkameen Valley under the grandeur of Mount Chopaka. There Okanogan people treated them well, better than any other tribe they met . . ."

The Stuwix, squeezed between the Nla-ka'pamux and Okanagan (see also chapter 8), and vulnerable to attacks from more distant peoples, were either killed or absorbed through marriage. By the early 1800s, the only predominantly Stuwix community was at Guichon, on Nicola Lake. A few decades later, they were attacked from the north. It was Nicola who came in afterwards and buried the dead.

Today, the peoples of Nicola's valley cherish their far-reaching ties and their common ground. More than 20 percent of the population is First Nations, and the city of Merritt, at an intersection of highways paved over long-travelled routes, is the hub. Here are Tribal Council offices and offices for four of the five communities. Much of their focus is on the watershed they all share, its fisheries, and the impact upon it from logging and mining.

Harold Aljam borrows the local sports-fishing motto: " 'A lake a day as long as you stay.' A lot of native people depend on fish for food. We are out educating our own people not to fish out the salmon. Our lifestyle is to live in harmony, never extinguish what you need."

INFORMATION AND PROTOCOL
The main languages spoken here are Nlaka'pamux and Okanagan, but there are elders here who speak up to seven languages.

Appropriate venues for exploration are listed below.

❓ Nicola Valley Tribal Council: Box 188, Merritt, B.C., V0K 2B0. Tel: 378-4235. Fax: 378-9119. Members: Coldwater, Shulus (Lower Nicola), Nooaitch, Shackan, and Spaxomin (Douglas Lake).

East from Spences Bridge on Highway 8

Hwy 8 from Spences Bridge leaves behind the relatively cool mountains of the Thompson Valley for the gentler but hotter hills, the rangelands of today's Sce'exmx and Spaxomin cowboys.

▼ Shackan: (Pop. 112/76). 22.5 km east of Spences Bridge. The community's name, "little rock," comes from the large stones that constitute much of the land around the village. Most of the people here are ranchers. Their creek, Skakan, is known for its steelhead, and they operate a fish hatchery. A small unserviced campground looks out over the cool, peaceful Nicola River. Local crafts, concession.

❓ Shackan Administration: Bag 6000, Merritt, B.C., V0K 2B0. Tel: 378-6141.

▼ Nooaitch: (Pop. 172/129). 44 km beyond Spences Bridge. Their creek is the Nuaitch. "It has the clearest water for miles," says chief Kowaintco Shackelly, working to keep it that way. Spring is when the spring salmon come —people use traditional-style hooks, catch them when the water's high and the meat is still fresh. Along the creek are their sweat lodges—the men's farther up, the women's, below. People here are working on the Nicola watershed protection program, construction, and administration. No visitor services at this time.

❓ Nooaitch Administration: Bag 6000, Merritt, B.C., V0K 2B0. Tel: 378-6141.

▼ Shulus (Lower Nicola): (Pop. 776/494). 61 km east of Spences Bridge. The largest Sce'exmx community is where Guichon Creek flows into the Nicola River. They run some 1,800 head of cattle just west of here. In 1975 the government took land to widen the road that traces Guichon Creek north to Mamette Lake—now part of Hwy 97C between Merritt and Logan Lake. The people here were not consulted: after 18 years of litigation and negotiation, they finally received a cash settlement, some land, and a contract for roadwork. The community bustles with a new health centre, powwow arbour, and a number of businesses, including artists and craftspeople, and **Johnny's Golf Range**.

❓ Lower Nicola Administration: RR 1, Site 17, Comp. 18, Merritt, B.C., V0K 2B0. Tel: 378-5157.

▼ Merritt: (Pop. 6,220/555 Ab). 65 km east of Spences Bridge, at the confluence of the Nicola and Coldwater rivers. Offices of Nicola Valley Tribal Council and Sce'exmx band offices are at 2090 Coutlee Ave.

Camp of the Nicola chief Noxwiskans, at west end of Nicola Lake, about 1910.
CREDIT: NICOLA VALLEY MUSEUM/ARCHIVES, MERRITT, B.C.

The five Nicola Valley communities jointly own and operate the full-facility **Grasslands Hotel**, 3350 Voght St.; 1-800-665-7117. The art gallery there features prints by Opie Openheim, from Coldwater (see below). He is also becoming widely known by the stage name "the cool warrior," as a stand-up comic. At the street mall on Labour Day weekend, early September, the arts-and-crafts community displays its best work—native-style "ribbon" shirts, buckskins, blankets, dream-catchers.

The **Nicola Valley Museum and Archives** (2202 Jackson Ave.) displays Sce'exmx artifacts. (Write Box 1262, Merritt, B.C., V0K 2B0. Tel: 378-4145.) Also here are materials belonging to James Teit (1864–1922), now regarded as the foremost ethnographer of B.C.'s interior First Nations. He came from the Shetland Islands to Spences Bridge at the age of 19, to join an uncle who had settled there, and later made his home with the family of his Nlaka'pamux wife, Lucy Antko. His life's work is a record of the history, sciences, arts, and spiritual practices of peoples from Okanagan to Tahltan territories. The museum archives holds the complete and highly valued collection.

South from Merritt, along the Coldwater River

Turn right on Coldwater Rd., 2 km south of Merritt.

V Coldwater: (Pop. 605/377). 10 km south of Merritt on Coldwater Rd. The name originates from the Nlaka'pamux word Ntsla'tko, "cold water." This is a quiet community, where people work in forestry and ranching.

? Coldwater Administration: Bag 4600, Merritt, B.C., V0K 2B0. Tel: 378-6174.

East from Merritt on Highway 5A

■   **Sugarloaf Mountain:** South of the south end of Nicola Lake. The Sce'exmx call it "tree milk" for the Douglas firs there, which produce wild sugar, or Douglas fir sugar.

■   **Quilchena Trading Post:** 23 km east of Merritt. Across from golf course. Traditional bone jewellery, handmade mandelas, dreamcatchers are for sale. Quilchena is Nlaka'pamux for "red bluffs," the name of a former nearby village.

J   **Douglas Lake Road:** 27.5 km east of Merritt. Unpaved road leads through ranchland to Spaxomin.

V   **Spaxomin (Douglas Lake):** (Pop. 727/463). At the west end of Douglas Lake is Spaxomin, "bare" or "smooth." The village is named for the open, rolling landscape where the Okanagan chief Pelkamu'lox brought his people 300 years ago at the invitation of his Secwepemc neighbour, Kwoli'la. It was at Komkena'tko, "headwaters," now called Fish Lake or Salmon Lake, where they made their lasting agreement, and Pelkamu'lox was granted "perpetual use" of the rich lands embracing Douglas and Fish lakes and reaching west and south to meet those held by the Sce'exmx and Stuwix.

In 1884, the Douglas Lake Cattle Company was established in this area, ranging thousands of head of cattle over 200,000 hectares. From then until now the Spaxomin people continue to cross the company's cattle guards and fences, both to fish their traditional lakes for kokanee and lake trout, and as ranch employees. They also manage their own herds. At round-up time in spring and fall, Spaxomin cowboys come sweeping down the mountain behind the village, cajoling some 400 horses to corrals for counting and branding. Rodeos are held regularly at their Quilchena reserve on Nicola Lake.

?   **Douglas Lake Administration:** Bag 3700, Merritt, B.C., V0K 2B0. Tel: 350-3311.

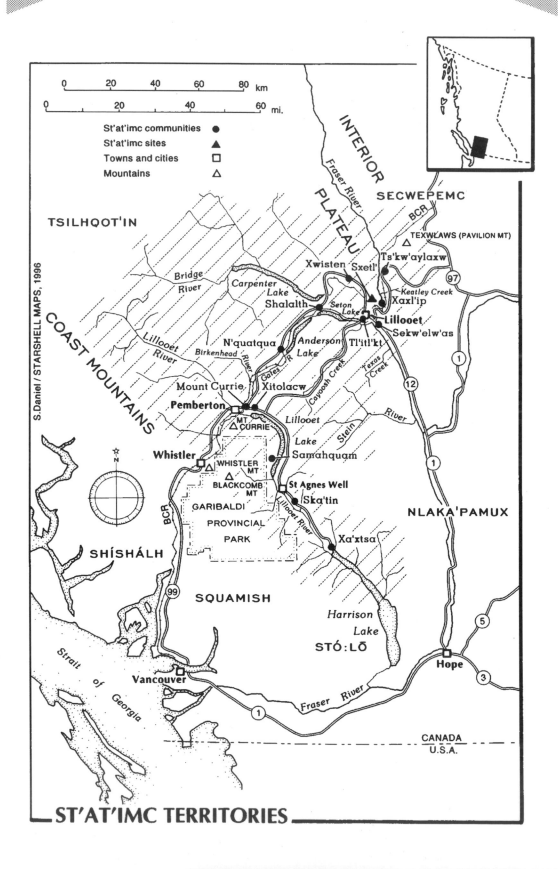

Scale:
0 20 40 60 80 km
0 20 40 60 mi.

St'at'imc communities ●
St'at'imc sites ▲
Towns and cities ☐
Mountains △

S.Daniel / STARSHELL MAPS, 1996

TSILHQOT'IN

INTERIOR PLATEAU

SECWEPEMC

BCR

TEXWŁAWS (PAVILION MT) △

Bridge River

Carpenter Lake

Xwisten 'Sxetl'

Ts'kw'aylaxw

97

Keatley Creek

Xaxl'ip

Shalalth

Seton Lake

Lillooet

COAST MOUNTAINS

Lillooet River

N'quatqua

Birkenhead River

Gates R.

Anderson Lake

Tl'itl'kt

Sekw'elw'as

1

Mount Currie

Xitolacw

Cayoosh Creek

Texas Creek

12

Pemberton

MT CURRIE △

Lillooet

Stein River

Whistler △

WHISTLER MT △

Lake Samahquam

1

BCR

BLACKCOMB MT △

St Agnes Well

Ska'tin

NLAKA'PAMUX

GARIBALDI

PROVINCIAL

PARK

Lillooet River

Xa'xtsa

SHÍSHÁLH

99

SQUAMISH

Harrison Lake

STÓ:LÕ

5

Strait of Georgia

Hope

3

Vancouver

1

Fraser River

CANADA
U.S.A.

ST'AT'IMC TERRITORIES

CHAPTER 12

St'at'imc

Everywhere we look, we see trails, places where people used to live, our relationship with the neighbouring tribes. For non-native people, once they learn about our past, maybe they will be more comfortable with our land claims.

—Larry Casper, natural resources development coordinator

*S*t'at'imc, in the language spoken here, links the people and their rivers. It refers today to 11 communities that share a language, but occupy two distinct landscapes on either side of the high and rugged Coast Mountains. One is the canyon world of the earth-brown Fraser River, looking east to the dry expanses of the interior plateau. The other is the emerald-green world of the Lillooet River, descending between glaciers and fir-forested mountains.

The valleys of the Lillooet River and its tributaries are rich with tales of Atsemal, the Transformers—four brothers and their sister travelling by canoe. (Actually, the sister *was* the canoe.) They came in from the Fraser by way of Harrison Lake, "setting things right" for the people they met along the way. They veered east off the Lillooet, along the Birken River, and descended to the mouth of Cayoosh Creek—but only briefly, before returning to the coast.

The canyons themselves, say the St'at-'imc, were for the most part Coyote's realm. He often travelled with Sun, Moon, and Arrow-

armed person, and brought the salmon, having undone the gigantic weir blocking the Fraser's mouth. "Fix your fish weirs and your drying racks!" he barked, "The salmon are coming up the river." Above the town of Lillooet, where the Fraser curves in a dramatic U, then chutes through a narrow gap, he made the fishing sites. Dry winds blowing from the plateau, combined with the quality of salmon here—just the right amount of fat this far on their journey made this one of the most productive fishing places on the entire 1,370-kilometre Fraser River. There were enough to meet the St'at'imc needs and then some. This surplus, traded and invested, allowed for the growth of large villages, such as the one that stood at Keatley Creek 7,000 years ago.

Hard times—brought by the landslide at Texas Creek 2,000 years ago, blocking the passage of salmon below Lillooet, and periods of famine—didn't break the continuity of the complex civilization that emerged here. When the fur-trade explorer Simon Fraser arrived at the St'at'imc's fortified city near the rapids,

Bridge River Rapids.
CREDIT: RICK BLACKLAWS

June 15, 1808, he was met by 1,000 people "who never saw the face of a white man." Elders of today repeat accounts given by their great-great-grandparents who were there. They tell how "the drifters," led by a man with a tattooed image of the Sun on his forehead and the moon on his chest, asked for help in getting their canoes around the rapids, and for directions beyond, to the sea. There were some among the St'at'imc who entertained the possibility that Simon Fraser was Coyote.

Coyote had brought them salmon, but the fur traders, gold seekers, settlers, and fishermen who followed the drifters soon depleted their livelihood. The occupants of Fort Kamloops sought in the St'at'imc a major supplier of fish, and at least one account describes how the smallpox vaccine was withheld until the traders got the quantities they demanded. Miners, hungry for gold, raked and gouged the fragile spawning beds of Bridge River and Cayoosh Creek, pulled down mountainsides, blocked salmon runs. By 1900 there were 76 canneries at the mouth of the Fraser being fed with salmon that would have swarmed to the rapids here. All this, plus the theft of their root crops, livestock, and land, led the St'at'imc chiefs, in 1911, to draft their *Declaration of the Lillooet Tribe*, a reiteration of their jurisdiction over the land, the rivers, and their resources.

Eighty years have passed. Some things never change: the St'at'imc still stand by their declaration, just as they still congregate at the rapids to catch and dry their salmon.

INFORMATION AND PROTOCOL

The St'at'imc story is written on the land. Time-worn trails link village sites, where depressions from pit houses and plank houses are still apparent. In the mountains are signs of deer corrals and cache pits, and of other hunting and spiritual endeavours. It is important not to disturb any archaeological site you might come upon; instead contact the Lillooet Tribal Council. Gill nets and drying racks left at fishing sites also must not be disturbed.

Traditionally, each village had a hereditary chief who worked in consultation with a council of elders. There were also leaders for hunting, war, and speaking. Today's reserve-based communities elect councils and still consult the elders. Tribal Police provide culturally sensitive law enforcement within communities.

The language spoken here is St'at'imcets, a branch of the Interior Salish language family.

Despite this territory's relative proximity to the freeways of the Lower Mainland, several transportation corridors are either newly developed, or for the adventurous only and best reached by four-wheel-drive or in summer. BC Rail, running from North Vancouver via Whistler, remains a practical way to reach St'at'imc villages from Mount Currie, along Anderson and Seton Lakes, to Lillooet. Accessibility by road is outlined in the route descriptions below. Refer to your map. The St'at'imc communities of the Fraser River are described first.

? **Lillooet Tribal Council:** Box 1420, Lillooet, B.C., V0K 1V0. Tel: 256-7523. Fax: 256-7119. Members: Bridge River, Cayoose Creek, Lillooet, Mount Currie, Pavilion, Seton Lake.

? **In-SHUCK-ch Councils Administration:** Toti:lthet Centre, 34110 Lougheed Hwy, Bag 80, Mission B.C., V2V 4L8. Tel: 820-2680. Members: Anderson Lake, Samahquam, Douglas, and Skookumchuck.

Enter St'at'imc Territories North of Lytton, via Highway 12

Because the canyon waters were so turbulent, the St'at'imc travelled mostly on land to reach their dozens of major Fraser River fishing sites. At eddies, still-net fishermen waited for resting salmon to swim into their nets; dip-netters scooped their catch from faster-moving rapids. In some places scaffolds were hung from the rock and lowered as river levels dropped. Each site had a name—"long point of land," "splash on back," "sitting in water" —and a history. Some were family-owned; others, open to all.

I **Texas Creek:** About 48 km north of Lytton. Two thousand years ago a landslide here backed up the river, flooded villages on the lower banks, inhibited the passage of salmon, and brought famine upriver. While archaeologists suggest this marked a turning point for the society here, the St'at'imc say the landslide was just one of a series of events in their long history.

V **Tl'itl'kt (Lillooet):** (Pop. 277/168). 66 km north of Lytton. On Mountain Rd., above the town of **Lillooet** (pop. 1,720/155 Ab). The people here were named Lillooet by the Department of Indian Affairs for the new town that in 1860 took over their village, burial ground, and gathering place on the lower terraces, at the meeting of the Fraser, Cayoosh, and Bridge rivers. This new town took its name from the people who live at what is now known as Mount Currie, on the Lillooet River. As the nexus between the Douglas Trail (see below) and the Cariboo wagon road to interior gold fields, the town of Lillooet by 1863 was a base for some 15,000 newcomers, well served by saloons. The St'at'imc made their new village here at Tl'itl'kt, "white," named for lime deposits in the rocky mountains. Today, this is headquarters for the Lillooet Tribal Council and Lillooet (band) administration offices. There are pit-house replicas beside the Lillooet Nation Tribal Police office. The town below is service centre for six surrounding St'at'imc communities. After the wild rose blooms in August, the riverbanks below are busy too, as people gather to catch and dry their salmon.

☎ Lillooet Administration: Box 615, Lillooet, B.C., V0K 1V0. Tel: 256-4118.

☺ Old Bridge Across Fraser: North on Main St. in Lillooet, right on Old Bridge Rd. Walk onto bridge for views of river, salmon drying in the wind, the sound of crickets.

☺ Lillooet Museum: 790 Main St. Tel: 256-4308. Cedar root baskets, projectile points, and other artifacts are on display.

☺ Lillooet Friendship Centre: 357 Main St. Tel: 256-4146. May have art for sale.

V Sekw'elw'as (Cayoose Creek): (Pop. 155/98). 1.5 km south of downtown Lillooet via Hwy 99, near the mouth of Cayoosh Creek. *Cayoose* is Chinook Jargon for "horse." The village's traditional name, Sekw'elw'as, "split rock," dates back to the Transformers' visit. The rock has been destroyed by development. September is the time to see pink salmon at the community-run **Seton River Lower Spawning Channel** and hatcheries, established 2 km upriver in 1966 after a B.C. Hydro dam altered the waterways. Light-

foot gas station is on Hwy 99. The community is also planning a cultural centre.

☎ Cayoose Creek Administration: Box 484, Lillooet, B.C., V0K 1V0. Tel: 256-4136.

North from Lillooet on Moha Road

V Ⅰ Xwisten (Bridge River) and the Bridge River Rapids: (Pop. 313/159). Moha Rd. leads 6 km north of Lillooet to the most important fishery of the middle and upper Fraser. Just above the meeting of the sparkling blue Bridge and muddy Fraser rivers, is Sxetl', "the drop off," where the Fraser surges through a 30-m gap. Coyote is said to have created the falls by "stepping to and fro across the river three times." From July through August, St'at'imc fishermen gather at community- and family-owned sites to catch and prepare salmon for freezing, salting, smoking and, most importantly, drying in racks set, as they have been for thousands of years, at just the right angle to catch the wind. The St'at'imc know the time is right for making *tswan*, "wind-dried salmon" when the air is filled with the sound of the grasshopper, *tl'ekatl'ek'a*. They say the pronunciation of its name resembles the sound of people cutting fish.

The people of Bridge River, or Xwisten, "place of foam," now invite visitors to join them in mid-August for a weekend salmon bake by the river. They are welcome to watch and ask questions about traditional dip-netting techniques. Contact the Bridge River band office, 11 km west along narrow canyons of the Bridge River.

☎ Bridge River Administration: Box 190, Lillooet B.C., V0K 1V0. Tel: 256-7423.

From Xwisten, a gravel road traces Bridge River west then south to the Terzaghi Dam. This is the western rim of a 60-km reservoir known as Carpenter Lake. Waters are fun-

Fishing for salmon on the Fraser River.
CREDIT: RBCM 6263

nelled from here down two tunnels drilled through Mission Mountain. On the other side, at Shalalth, they are forced through electric generators, then emptied into Seton Lake. This massive project, completed in 1959, flooded St'at'imc hunting and fishing sites and diminished the Bridge River and its fisheries.

A very rough road continues over the mountain to the St'at'imc village of Shalalth on Seton Lake. A summer-only road continues beyond Shalalth to Anderson Lake (see below).

V   Shalalth (Seton Lake): (Pop. 529/274). 62 km west of Bridge River by all-weather road; 30 km (one long hour) east of Anderson Lake by summer road. This quiet community knows itself as Shalalth, "lake." The administration office is just off Shalalth Dr., at the base of steep Mission Pass to Bridge River. People here work for BC Rail, the Seton Lake Band, the ministry of forests, B.C. Hydro, the store and restaurant.

?   Seton Lake Administration: Site 3, Box 76, Shalalth, B.C., V0N 3C0. Tel: 259-8227.

North from Lillooet: Across Fraser River on Highway 99

I   Fort Berens: Opposite Lillooet, on Hwy 99. The Hudson's Bay Company fishing depot was closed in 1860, soon after it opened, after the route via Lytton, Ashcroft, and Clinton became the major route to the gold fields.

▮ Rapid Views: Find a safe place to pull off the highway. North of Lillooet are vistas of fishing tarps, the falls, the Bridge-Fraser confluence.

▼ Xaxl'ip (Fountain): (Pop. 715/521). Via Fountain Valley Rd., 13.5 km north of Lillooet on Hwy 99. "Brow of the hill" sits on a bench high above the river. Gold miners in 1858 made it a watering stop on their way to the interior, so the hill people moved up higher. Xaxl'ip was later pre-empted, then returned, as a reserve. The people here fish down at the Bridge River rapids, approaching by the steep east bank. Some people take horses down, some just carry their dividend of fish up. **Fountain Fabrication** here makes fibreglass canoes, boats, and dip nets.

? Xaxl'ip Administration: Box 1330, Lillooet, B.C., V0K 1V0. Tel: 256-4227.

▮ Ancient Village: About 23 km north of Lillooet, the highway crosses Sallus Creek bridge. Road construction here ran into materials dating back 7,000 years. Just beyond, along Keatley Creek, a major archaeological study uncovered a village site inhabited by some 500 people.

▼ Ts'kw'aylaxw (Pavilion): (Pop. 392/261). 20 km north of Fountain, at the gateway to Secwepemc territories where Hwy 99 cuts east away from the Fraser River. Ts'kw'aylaxw, "frosty ground," is a Secwepemc term: the people here have roots in both Secwepemc and St'at'imc traditions. The community is working to reintegrate those traditions into their daily lives. The surrounding landscape is rich in their history, and although there are no visitor services here at this time, arrangements can be made, by calling the administration office, for visits to pictographs and sites of ancient pit-house dwellings.

Pavilion Rd. leads north from here 31 km to Clinton, traversing 2,089-m Texwlaws, or Pavilion Mountain. This was the place to gather spring beauty, tiger lily, and wild onion, and there is still evidence here of deer runs used to herd the animals toward hunters. After the land was pre-empted, the people of Ts'kw'aylaxw worked there as ranch hands.

? Pavilion Administration: Box 609, Cache Creek, B.C., V0K 1H0. Tel: 256-4204.

From Pavilion, Hwy 99 northeast continues deeper into the heart of Secwepemc territories. Just before Pavilion Lake, look to the right of the highway for a glimpse of K'lpalekw, "Coyote's Penis."

West from Lillooet across the Mountain Ranges via Highway 99 (Duffey Lake Road)

▼ Mount Currie: (Pop. 1,500/1,060). 100 km southwest of Lillooet via Duffey Lake Rd. Highway is gravel where it transects reserve. Although their name has been applied to people on both sides of the Coast Mountains, these are the "real" Lillooet, or Lil'wat people. Their traditional territories embrace the Lillooet River, and its long, cold green lake. To the southeast are the headwaters of the Stein River, its valley corridor long shared by the Lil'wat and their Nlaka'pamux neighbours into whose territories it flows. Together, in the 1980s, they led the vigorous battle to save its natural and human heritage from the chainsaw (see chapter 10).

West of the Stein are the ice-clad peaks of Garibaldi Provincial Park, and Whistler and Blackcomb mountains, hunting grounds of former times, shared with the Squamish people to the south. The sky due south of the village is darkened by the sharp peak of Mount Currie, named for the Scottish gold seeker who married a Lil'wat woman and took up ranching here in the late 1800s.

Three recent phases in the history of the Lil'wat people are apparent. Entering the community from the east, the road passes a turnoff to the newest subdivision, Xitolacw, "skunk cabbage," referring to a small lake at the foot of the hill where the large, water-repellent leaves from this plant were harvested for use as basket liners and drinking cups, or to dry berries on. The new school and cultural centre here are a reflection of the community's burgeoning growth. About 7 km farther west along Lillooet Lake Rd. is the post-1947 community, where many of the services listed below are located, as well as the tribal police station. Those planning to explore the reserve outside the downtown core are asked to drop in to the administration offices, also here. The community's oldest quadrant, with buildings from the late 1800s, sits on the north bank of Lillooet River along Old Pemberton Rd.

⑥ **Native Cultural Learning Centre/WD Bar Ranch Lil'wat Adventures:** 2.5 km east of turnoff to Xitolacw. Box 239, Mount Currie, B.C., V0N 2K0. Messages: 894-5669. North America's First Nations bronco-riding champion introduces visitors from around the world to Lil'wat history, landscape, food, and current issues. Overnight horse-pack trips, day trips, canoe trips to old village sites.

⑥ **Lillooet Lake Rodeo:** Long weekends May and September; 1.5 km east of turnoff to Xitolacw.

⑥ **Lilwat Place Rustic Campground:** Near rodeo grounds, very pleasant, very rustic.

⑥ **The Spirit Circle Art, Craft and Tea Company:** Downtown Mount Currie. A pleasant ambience, First Nations food, books, art, clothing, and cappuccino.

⑥ **Gathered from the Earth Market:** Across from tea house.

⑥ **Other stopping places:** Coffee shop and corner store in village; gas station on Lillooet Lake Rd. heading east; arts and crafts store with some Lil'wat work represented at Pika's Restaurant, on top of Whistler Mountain.

? **Mount Currie Administration:** Box 165, Mount Currie, B.C., V0N 2K0. Tel: 894-6115.

J **B** **Highway 99:** From Mount Currie, Hwy 99 leads southwest into Squamish territories.

North from Mount Currie via All-weather Road to Anderson Lake

This paved road climbs 38 km over the Coast Mountains to Anderson Lake. It traces the Birkenhead River flowing down the west side, then the Gates River flowing down the east side. In 1860, this ancient route linking Lil'wat and Fraser River St'at'imc peoples became part of the Douglas Trail to the interior gold fields, consisting of a series of portages between Harrison, Lillooet, Anderson, and Seton lakes.

V **N'quatqua (Anderson Lake):** (Pop. 221/ 151). 38 km north of Mount Currie. The Gates River salmon migrate up the Fraser River to Lillooet, turn left at Seton Lake, and travel to the very end of Anderson Lake to reach their place of rebirth. They have survived the 1913 blockage of the Fraser at Hells Gate, logging, and flood control projects. But to give them a fighting chance in this modern world of obstacles, the **Gates River Spawning Channel** has been built to provide them with a clean, reliable flow of water. In Anderson Lake, at 100 Lakeshore Dr., August visitors will see salmon winding 2 km through a manmade labyrinth to spawn. Fry spend their first year in Seton Lake before heading out to sea. Twenty percent of returning adults contribute to native food fisheries and spawning for the next gen-

The Church of the Holy Cross, built 1905–1906, at Ska'tin (Skookumchuck).
CREDIT: JOHN LUTZ

eration; 80 percent are taken by commercial fisheries.

Late January to early February, when the south wind comes up, people here know it's time to fish for the land-locked sockeye, kokanee. They call them "floaters," because at the end of their lives their bellies distend with gas and they rise to the surface of Anderson and Seton lakes, attracting eagles.

Red Barn Campground on the lake across from the spawning channels has a boat launch and fast-food restaurant; 452-3406. Administration offices are next to Holy Rosary Church, built circa 1900.

? Anderson Lake Administration: Box 88, D'Arcy, B.C., V0N 1L0. Tel: 452-3221.

From here the road leads 30 km to Shalalth (see above). Travel this route in summer only, and even then, at your own risk.

From Mount Currie South along Lillooet River via the Old Douglas Trail

Just east of Mount Currie a gravel road forks off Hwy 99 to skirt the northeast shores of Lillooet Lake. It soon becomes washboard, then worse. Distances between recreational properties grow, and the glacial-green lake narrows to river—calm on the surface, rife with undercurrents. This is home to three small Lillooet communities. **Samahquam** consists of about a dozen homes along the river, with most of its population dispersed throughout the Fraser Valley; there are a few people at **Xa'xtsa** (Douglas) at the head of Harrison Lake. The village of **Ska'tin** (Skookumchuck) is described below.

This is a portion of the route travelled by the Transformers in millennia past. It also overlaps with the first road to the Cariboo gold fields. St'at'imc and Stó:lo peoples here guided surveyors in 1860, and later worked as packers along the 160-km trail strewn with thousands of miners trudging by wagon, ox, horse, and canoe. When smallpox struck in 1862, many St'at'imc took refuge at Mission, on the Fraser River, leaving the Lillooet River to the saloons and the burgeoning villages of newcomers. But in 1864, an alternate road opened from Yale, and soon things were quiet again. By the 1870s, only one white settler remained at the boom town of Port Douglas adjacent to the St'at'imc village of Xa'xtsa.

At the southeast end of Lillooet Lake is the mountain In-shuck-ch, "it's split." Long ago, a Mount Currie chief, advised by the Great Chief In-Chee-nim-kan, made a great rope from cedar bark and willow, gathered salmon eggs, and when the rains became a flood, anchored his canoe to this peak.

◆ St. Agnes Well Hot Springs: 48 km south of Mount Currie. Busy hot springs, now complete with rustic shelter and pool, were created by the Transformers. They used them for boiling food. Lil'wat people used them for bathing and cleansing, and still do, if ever there is solitude.

▼ Ska'tin (Skookumchuck): (Pop. 300/24 on; 275 off). 52 km south of Mount Currie. The village's name, Ska'tin, means "swift waters." The nearby rapids made this an important fishing site for people up and down the river. Says Leslie Sam who lives here, "There was an Irish priest who couldn't pronounce that name, he called this place Skookumchuck"—"swift waters" in Chinook Jargon. The Skookumchuck Church of the Holy Cross, blending Lil'wat and Gothic Revival styles, is one of the most significant mission churches in B.C. Built in 1905–1906, it was the third church here since the mission was established in 1861. Now at the end of the road, surrounded by a dozen simple homes, its three tall spires outside and ornate altar inside inspire a belief in miracles.

? Skookumchuck Administration: Box 523, Pemberton, B.C., V0N 2L0. No phone.

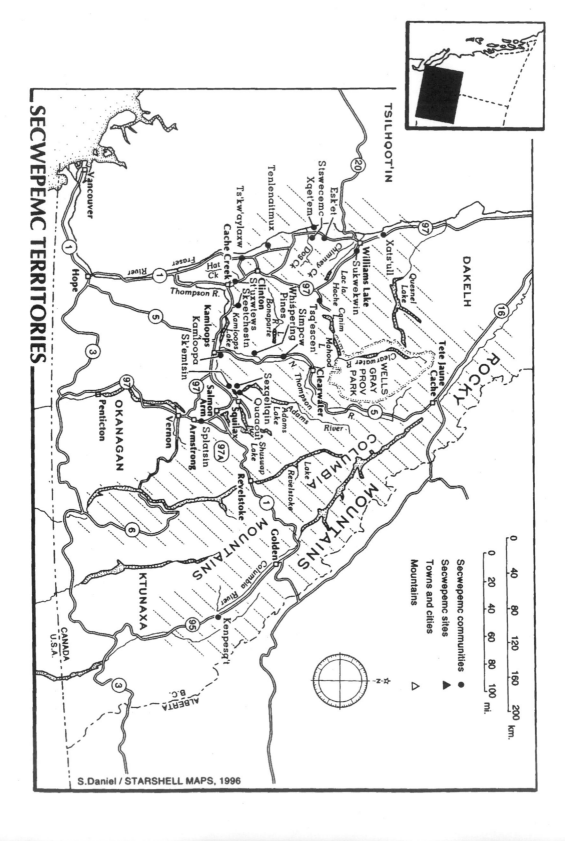

SECWEPEMC TERRITORIES

S.Daniel / STARSHELL MAPS, 1996

CHAPTER 13

Secwepemc

We are not presenting here a culture under glass. We want people to understand we are very much alive.

—*Leona Thomas, Secwepemc Heritage Park*

Secwepemc is an ancient name expressing, in its three short syllables, the relationship between the people here and their complex waterways. Secwepemc territories are a vast 180,000 square kilometres of gently rolling highlands reaching their limits in the Rocky Mountains. In that rugged northeastern frontier, three of this continent's most important rivers are born. The Fraser, Thompson, and Columbia, on their remarkable journeys through this and other lands, drain a full 70 percent of British Columbia. In their middle reaches they loop around to form, in an intricate mesh of tributaries and lakes, the southwestern frontier of Secwepemc territories. Here are situated most of today's 17 Secwepemc communities.

The Secwepemc tell us their sacred boundaries were marked out by Coyote. There are "Coyote rocks" at Yexyex near Yellowhead Pass, at Three Valley Lake near Revelstoke, at Tececoytsen (Chaperon Lake), and at Q'wyucenk (Ball Mountain). Coyote's Sweat House and another marker at Cwelcestcen tell us how

far west—across the Fraser—Secwepemc territories extended until smallpox killed most of the people there. Now other—Tsilhqot'in—peoples fish those rivers.

It was Coyote who put the salmon in the rivers. He even made the fishing sites. But there were also "the ancients" before and after him, wandering this land known as Secwepemc Ellex, adding to its features. The Secwepemc people honour Spelkamu'lax as the Old One who first taught them the basics of survival.

The first white men found wandering through this country in the early 1800s brought to mind, for some, Coyote's caprice. One prophet told the Secwepemc that the white men in black robes were, in fact, descendants of Coyote. Like him, they were powerful, but they were also "very foolish, and told many lies." The prophet cautioned that if the Secwepemc followed these new ways, they would soon be poor, foolish, and helpless. The Secwepemc's first relationships with French-speaking fur traders were nevertheless quite in keeping with the custom of the land. The new-

Sign in Secwepemctsin language at Skeetchestn: "Watch out, children at play."

comers "acknowledged our ownership of the country, and treated our chiefs as men." They exchanged what they had lots of for furs and salmon, plentiful here. And they stayed, married, learned the language—a process of integration prevailing since the beginning of time.

The Secwepemc called them *Seme7uwi*, "real whites," to distinguish them in later years from the "other whites" who followed. An increasing lust for Secwepemc resources culminated in the gold rush, but was sustained inexorably, in the building, here, of an "empire of grass." Sweet, and tall as a horse's belly, reaching as far as the eye could see, in all its golden splendour—and for the taking, as stated by new colonial laws. Ranchers were granted 320 acres (130 hectares), and could buy that much again at a very reasonable price. The Secwepemc got their reserves—eight hectares per family—with no option even to buy more of the lands that had always been their range.

And so it was that Secwepemc horsemen, hunters, and harvesters became cowboys— often working for the big ranch owners, but sometimes for themselves, winning rodeo competitions, raising cattle stock prized world-

wide. This was not a sign of their surrender, but of their ability to survive.

Secwepemc leaders meanwhile sought just, but peaceful solutions to the occupation of the lands bound by Coyote's rocks. Nevertheless, in 1875 they found themselves in alliance with Okanagan and Nez Perce peoples to the south, on the brink of war. A rare and evocative testimony of the events of this time, the roots of their frustration, and the basis of their decision not to fight is contained in their *Memorial to Sir Wilfred Laurier*, addressed to Canada's prime minister 35 years later. "Something we did not understand," they wrote, "retards [white people] from keeping their promise."

We can look back now on a century of government-to-government appeals. Chief Louis of Kamloops, in 1906 and again in 1909, travelled all the way to England to meet directly with the Queen. In the 1960s, George Manuel from Neskonlith rose up to become a world leader among aboriginal peoples seeking self-government. He was founding president of the World Council of Indigenous Peoples based in Geneva. In this period, too, Len Marchand, of Okanagan descent, living in Kamloops, became the first aboriginal member of the Canadian parliament. This spirit of nationhood is reflected today in Secwepemc communities from Kinbasket on the Columbia River to Soda Creek on the Fraser, where each takes a turn at hosting annual gatherings.

HIGHLIGHTS AND EVENTS

◐ Secwepemc Native Heritage
  Park/Museum   p. 140
◐ Adams River Salmon Run,
  October   p. 144

INFORMATION AND PROTOCOL

Secwepemc Ellex, or "territories," were owned cooperatively by the Secwepemc peoples, who travelled great distances from one season to the next. Traditionally, everyone had a voice in decision-making—that hasn't changed.

Pavilion, the westernmost of today's Secwepemc communities, is described in chapter 12 along with the St'at'imc people with whom they are intermixed.

The language spoken here is Secwepemc-tsin.

Weytk is a Secwepemc greeting, like "hello."

? **Shuswap Nation Tribal Council:** 345 Yellowhead Hwy, Kamloops, B.C., V2H 1H1. Tel: 828-9789. Fax: 374-6331. Members: Adams Lake, Canoe Creek, Kamloops, North Thompson, Spallumcheen, Bonaparte, High Bar, Neskonlith, Skeetchestn, Whispering Pines.

? **Cariboo Tribal Council:** Box 4333, Williams Lake, B.C., V2G 2V4. Tel: 392-7361. Fax: 392-6158. Members include the four northern Secwepemc communities of Alkali Lake, Canim Lake, Soda Creek, Williams Lake.

East of Cache Creek on Highway 1

V **Skeetchestn:** (Pop. 366/143). 30.5 km east of Cache Creek, north onto Deadman-Vidette Rd., 7 km to village site. Skeetchestn, "the meeting place," sits at the heart of the Deadman Valley where Secwepemc peoples from Pavilion to Kamloops once gathered for fishing, meetings, and celebrations. The dead man was a Northwest Company clerk, killed in a squabble in 1817. For settlers, that name held its power: ghostly barns, fence posts, and parched fields are signs of their failed attempts to survive here. The river, too, one of the most important habitats on earth for spawning steelhead, has suffered erosion and blockages from irrigation and logging. From runs of thousands, the steelhead are down to only a few hundred, and declining. The people of Skeetchestn today operate a hatchery as part of a larger project to revive the Deadman River.

Visitors are welcome to join in their ongoing celebration of this land as they know it. Skeetchestn ethnobotanists and guides lead **First Nations Cultural Adventure** weekends: trail rides through pine forests and sagebrush, folklore, drumming and singing, a chance to play the bone game, camping in *c7istken*—traditional Secwepemc winter homes sometimes called pit houses or *kekulis.*

In the village, a convenience store offers a gas bar, local crafts, and western wear. Ask about hatchery tours. Also view historic St. Mary's Church.

? **Skeetchestn Administration:** Box 178, Savona, B.C., V0K 2J0. Tel: 373-2493.

V **Kamloopa (Kamloops):** (Pop. 805/514). 80 km east of Cache Creek. "Where the rivers meet" spreads over the fertile veld where the North and South Thompson rivers merge, drawing waters from the entire Secwepemc heartland. A 2,300-year-old village sits by the riverbank, in front of contemporary Secwepemc cultural and political headquarters. On the opposite bank is the city of **Kamloops** (pop. 66,220/1,345 Ab), founded on the centrality and vitality of the people here. In 1812, the Pacific Fur Company established itself on one side of the river, the North West Company on the other. The two soon merged, and in 1821 fell under the Hudson's Bay Company. Since then, Kamloopa has been a centre for the expression of Secwepemc jurisdiction. Chief Louis, in the early 1900s, was among delegates who travelled to British Columbian, Canadian, and British capitals seeking recognition of his government.

Today, the Chief Louis Centre occupies the old residential school, where strapping, head-shaving, and bread and water diets were accepted methods of disciplining Secwepemc children who spoke their own language, or missed their parents too much. It is one of Canada's busiest centres of First Nations government, culture, and business. The Union of

Before this century, circular subterranean houses comprised the winter villages of Secwepemc and other interior B.C. peoples.
CREDIT: NO. 43101. HARLAN I. SMITH, COURTESY DEPARTMENT OF LIBRARY SERVICES, AMERICAN MUSEUM OF NATURAL HISTORY

B.C. Indian Chiefs and B.C. Native Women's Society are among the many organizations based here. The Secwepemc Cultural Education Society develops curriculum and museum programs, maintains an archives, publishes books. University-affiliated courses in language, archaeology, ethnology, and sociology attract First Nations students from across Canada.

The Kamloopa reserve extends 11 km along the shores of the North Thompson River, 11 km up the shores of the South Thompson: 170 non-native businesses lease land from and pay taxes to the Kamloops First Nation.

⑥ **Secwepemc Native Heritage Park/Museum:** 355 Yellowhead Hwy. Tel: 828-9801

or 828-9781. This is "not just for tourists, my people wouldn't go for that," says cultural historian Mary Thomas in the 20-minute video presentation that begins this Secwepemc experience. Guided tours of a reconstructed winter village, traditional food plant gardens, and a salmon-fishing station are followed by an exploration of the museum, book store, and gift shop. There is also song, dance, story-telling, and salmon barbecues in the traditional summer lodge. The adjacent Kamloopa Powwow Stadium is a dramatic venue—visible from the Trans-Canada Yellowhead Highway—where thousands of dancers, drummers, and singers gather from all over North America for annual events.

⑥ **St. Joseph's Historic Church:** A focal point of Kamloops village in historic times. The first church was built in 1846; this one has been restored to its 1900 incarnation.

❓ **Kamloops Indian Band Administration:** 315 Yellowhead Hwy, Kamloops, B.C., V2H 1H1. Tel: 828-9700.

Across Yellowhead Bridge to Kamloops

Ⓖ **Kamloops Museum:** 207 Seymour St. Tel: 828-3576. Tells of links between Secwepemc and newcomers. An important link was St. Paul, otherwise known as Jean Baptise Lolo, for whom Mt. Paul and Paul Lake are named. His cabin was the original museum and is still an important part of the new one. St. Paul was a Metis from the east, serving as Hudson's Bay Company interpreter in Kamloops after 1828. He retired in 1843, just before the fort closed, but stayed on.

Ⓖ **Kamloops Art Gallery:** 207 Seymour St. Tel: 828-3543. Includes major and innovative exhibitions of Secwepemc artists.

Ⓖ **Four Corners Art Gallery:** 119 Palm St., Kamloops. Tel: 376-0550. Operated by the Interior Indian Friendship Centre.

North of Kamloops, along the North Thompson River via Westsyde Road, Highway 5

V Whispering Pines: (Pop. 100/48). From west Kamloops, Westsyde Rd. leads 30 km north to this relatively new village site. In 1972, the "people of the white earth place" left their home at Pelltiq't near Clinton, because of ongoing B.C. Hydro developments, and moved to the cool banks of the North Thompson River. Part of the ranch that was Whispering Pines has been converted into a recreation and convention centre with rodeo grounds hosting regular rodeo and children's events, and a campground. Packages feature traditional Secwepemc equestrian events and cuisine, including venison and salmon, or even grouse, rabbit, and moose. There are plans for a major destination resort.

? Whispering Pines Administration: RR 1, Box 4, Site 8, Kamloops, B.C., V2C 1Z3. Tel: 579-5772.

About 65 km north of Kamloops, Westsyde Rd. joins Yellowhead Hwy 5 as it continues tracing the North Thompson River to its headwaters.

I Fishtrap Canyon: At highway rest area 48.5 km from Kamloops. The rapids where the people of the upper reaches set their salmon weir are not visible from the rest area.

V Chu Chua (Simpcw): (Pop. 498/231). Just north of the town of Barriere, Dunn Lake Rd. leads to Chu Chua, today's home base for the "people of the North Thompson River." Traditionally, their winter villages and food cache sites extended from McLure to the North Thompson's headwaters, and around the headwaters of the Fraser River. This quiet community is focussing on its sawmill and logging, the Dunn Lake Salmonid Enhancement Program, and language and cultural programs for children and adults. Ask at the administration office for permission to see the small museum.

? North Thompson Administration: Box 220, Barriere, B.C., V0E 1E0. Tel: 672-9995.

I North Thompson River Provincial Park: 117 km north of Kamloops. At the confluence of the North Thompson and Clearwater rivers. Pit-house depressions by the river's edge, near the picnic area, are the first and most accessible of many signs of long Simpcw history in the Clearwater area.

T Clearwater: 122 km north of Kamloops. Eastern gateway to **Wells Gray Provincial Park**. At the park's infocentre, Hwy 5 and Clearwater Valley Rd., 674-2646, see display on Simpcw people. Also ask about the pit-house depressions at the base of White Horse Bluffs, pictographs on north shore of Mahood Lake, and cache pits on "Cache Pit Island" in the Clearwater River Recreation Area. In the Stephens Lakes area are remains of rock fences built by Simpcw hunters to drive caribou into the lake.

T **Tete Jaune Cache:** 388 km north of Kamloops. In the early 1800s, there was a village here of Iroquois people who travelled occasionally to Kamloops to trade their furs. That village, this town, and the mountain pass to the east are all named after a dark-skinned, fair-haired Metis—Pierre Hatsinaton or Pierre Bostonais—nicknamed in French "yellow head." He came through the pass with a group of Hudson's Bay Company traders in 1820. A version of his story is Howard O'Hagan's 1939 Canadian classic, *Tay John*.

East of Kamloops on Highway 1

This route traces the South Thompson River to the rich fishing grounds of the Shuswap Lakes, named for the Secwepemc peoples.

V **Sk'emtsin (Neskonlith):** (Pop. 481/250). About 45 km east of Kamloops. The ancient village Sk'emtsin, "rock near the shore," overlooks the placid blue Thompson River. It is marked for today's travellers by billboards, an Esso station, and administration offices on the right just off the highway. Niskonlith was chief here in the mid-1800s, a voice against reserve reductions and subsequent infringements. Post–World War One, chief William Pierrish arranged for a horn to be sounded, to call people "from the hills" when organizers for Allied Tribes of British Columbia held meetings.

This was the atmosphere into which George Manuel was born in 1921. Crippled by osteomyelitis, yet an agile boom man renowned for his log-jam-busting skills, he was impassioned by his community's lack of access to health care, and became a world leader for aboriginal peoples seeking self-government. "At this point in our struggle for survival, the Indian people of North America are entitled to declare a victory." He said, "We have survived." In 1989 Manuel was buried

just above this village, a few hundred metres from where he was born.

? **Neskonlith Administration:** Box 608, Chase, B.C., V0E 1M0. Tel: 679-3295.

V **Sexqeltqin (Adams Lake):** (Pop. 557/ 369). 58 km beyond Kamloops to the town of **Chase**, then across the bridge over the South Thompson River. These are the people of Sexqeltqin, named for their ancient headquarters on Adams Lake. They also had a major fishing and trading centre along the banks of the "little river" between the Shuswap and Little Shuswap lakes. There, the Sexqeltqin gathered in early October with their Quaaout relatives (see below), for the famous Adam's River run of sockeye salmon. The creeks and rivers were once so full of salmon the water would not cover them. The people of Sexqeltqin could tell when the fish were coming by the warm west wind they called "breath of the salmon." It also helped dry the salmon on the racks. The trading centre that grew up here attracted Okanagan and Ktunaxa peoples well into this century, coming to trade their meat for fish and for the ochre from pyrite found in nearby caves.

Adam was the name given the powerful chief, Sehowtken, when he was baptized in 1849. He died during the smallpox epidemic of 1862. There are no visitor services in the village at this time.

Many of the people of **Chase** (pop. 2,085/ 25 Ab) living across the bridge from the Adams Lake band are themselves Secwepemc descendants: the early settler Whitfield Chase married a local woman, Per-Soons, and together they had 10 children. The **Chase Museum**, 1042 Shuswap Ave., has a small Secwepemc display.

? **Adams Lake Administration:** Box 588, Chase, B.C., V0E 1M0. Tel: 679-8841.

Salmon drying on racks reflects abundance of former times.
CREDIT: BCARS 22936 A-8313

▌ **Squilax General Store and Travellers Hostel:** 7 km east of Chase, north side of Hwy 1. This is a good source of directions to Secwepemc sites, and local information about powwows and performances and the Adams River salmon run. *Squilax* means "black bear."

North off Hwy 1 at Squilax, to Little Shuswap Lake and the Adams River

▼ **Squilax/Little Shuswap Lake:** (Pop. 256/180). 7 km east of Chase, take a turnoff to the Squilax Bridge and cross the "little river."

From here, Little Shuswap Lake Rd. leads 1 km to administration office and Quaaout, "the first place the sun's rays hit when the sun is coming up." It is **Quaaout Lodge** today that catches much of that light. Overlooking the east shores of Little Shuswap Lake, this $4.5-million architectural wonder, inspired by the pit house, draws its guests out into the surroundings as much as it does into its cozy inner sanctums. Trails lead through pine forests; sailboats and canoes are available to explore the land by water—there are pictographs on Copper Island. Guides lead fishing trips to the Adams River. The lodge has hot tubs, fireplaces, pools, and fine dining; but there are tipis too, for balance. Quaaout Lodge: Box 1215, Chase, B.C., V0E 1M0. Tel: 1-800-663-4303.

Also here at Quaaout is a rare congregation, as many as 3,000 small brown Yuma bats.

A maternity colony of females lived from April until October in the attic of the old church here, until 1993, when the church burned down while the bats were away. The people of Quaaout have tried to accommodate them with new lodgings—bat houses on poles, down by the administration offices.

?   **Little Shuswap Administration:** Box 1100, Chase, B.C., V0E 1M0. Tel: 679-3203.

☉   **Squilax International Powwow:** In mid-July, fancy dancers, singers and drummers gather from all over North America. Arts and crafts, and traditional food.

✘   **Adams River Salmon Run:** At Roderick Haig-Brown Provincial Park and Conservation Area, 5 km east of Squilax Bridge on Squilax-Anglemont Rd. To see the salmon surging, resting, spawning, dying here, touches something primal. Their battered silvery skins now pea green mixed with crimson, it has taken them only 17 days to journey 485 km up the Fraser's canyons from the sea, to this 11-km river, their birthplace four years before. Now they become food for gulls, eagles, bears, people, and their spirit passes on. The poignancy is intensified knowing their utter determination has, in recent times, come up against the apathetic hand of human industry—insatiable commercial fishing and the 1913 landslide at Hells Gate on the Fraser. There is a four-year cycle that produces a "dominant" run, a kind of baby boom. In the fall of 1989, only 79 sockeye were counted. In 1990, some 3 million swarmed through this channel; many million more were taken in nets before they had a chance to spawn.

✘   **Shuswap Lake Provincial Park:** 19 km east of Squilax Bridge on Squilax-Anglemont Rd. Here are depressions from a 3,000-year-old village, and a reconstructed pit house.

East of Squilax on Highway 1

T   **Salmon Arm:** (Pop. 11,950/110 Ab). 111 km east of Kamloops, at the mouth of the Salmon River. The salmon once ran so thick they sounded like a storm coming; they overflowed onto the banks and even those in the river gasped for oxygen. After 1913, when their Fraser River route from the sea was blocked, they, unlike their Adams River kin, never returned. The Secwepemc peoples are among the Friends of the Salmon River who are working to make these waters habitable again, for colonizing salmon of a different race.

South of Salmon Arm, on Hwy 97B, to southern frontiers of Secwepemc territories

V   **Splatsin (Spallumcheen):** (Pop. 565/319). 6 km north of Armstrong, on Fortune Rd. "When you get on top of the hill on the highway to Armstrong, you can see it's kind of flat," says Virginia Basil. Hence the name "a little prairie" for this southernmost of Secwepemc communities, where both Secwepemc and Okanagan languages were traditionally spoken. Gas bar, convenience store, arts and crafts.

?   **Spallumcheen Administration:** Box 430, Enderby, B.C., V0E 1V0. Tel: 838-6496.

North from Cache Creek on Highway 97

V   **St'uxwtews (Bonaparte):** (Pop. 644/200 on three reserves). 5 km north of Cache Creek, just off Hwy 97. St'uxwtews is headquarters today for the "people of the valley," whose many villages once occupied the banks of the Bonaparte River. During the gold rush, the Cariboo Wagon Road brought miners and settlers in along their river. Just north of here, at its confluence with the Hat Creek River, the Hat Creek Ranch roadhouse became an important stopping place. Its proprietor, Donald McLean, earned fame in 1864 as the leader of a posse tracking the Tsilhqot'in warriors in the wake of the Chilcotin War (chapter 14). His ranch employed many St'uxwtews people in its time. Now the roadhouse has been revived as a stopover: tour guides tell its history, and "the people of the valley" work here again too, explaining how things were before the gold rush, guiding visitors to a pit-house site. They also tell of their relationship to the ranch and how it changed their lives. In 1910, Chief Basil, of Bonaparte, was among those who signed the *Memorial to Sir Wilfred Laurier,* a call for recognition of title in the face of increasing settlement of their lands. At Bonaparte, there's a convenience store.

? **Bonaparte Administration:** Box 669, Cache Creek, B.C., V0K 1H0. Tel: 457-9624.

V **Tsq'escen' (Canim Lake):** (Pop. 483/ 379). 103 km north of Cache Creek to 100 Mile House, 4 km to Canim Lake Rd., then 36 km to the main village at Tsq'escen', "broken rock"—probably referring to the ancient quarry nearby, where quartz was mined for tool-making. On the east shores of Canim Lake, a ranch occupies the site of the former Secwepemc village, Pesqmimc, "little swan." In the area, at least 60 more names tell the story of the Canim Lake people on this land, places where they camped, fished, hunted, trapped. This is the kind of information being compiled, checked, and cross-checked for treaty negotiations. But, says Elizabeth Pete, "We would like to create more understanding around this issue, to alleviate people's fears about the treaties." The community hosts a major regional art show featuring First Nations and other artists, late August–early September. Handiwork is for sale at the administration office.

? **Canim Lake Administration:** Box 1030, 100 Mile House, B.C., V0K 2E0. Tel: 397-2227.

V **Sukwekwin (Williams Lake):** (Pop.370/ 220). 203 km north of Cache Creek; 11 km south of the town of Williams Lake. William was the chief who shifted his base here from Chimney Creek in the early 1860s. In the decades to follow, as hunting and fishing lands were occupied and his people faced starvation, he sought a just solution to the land question. The Oblates of Mary Immaculate established a mission farm/ranch here in 1867, as a base for maximizing overlaps between their religion and beliefs held by the people here. St. Joseph's Mission residential school opened in 1891, but in its bid to instill obedience through bells and punishment, year after year children ran away, at times abetted by their parents.

The community today runs its own Secwepemctsin language and cultural programs. It also manages logging and wood-remanufacturing companies, and is supporting salmon enhancement efforts. **Chief Will-Yum Campsite**, 296-4544, is south on Hwy 97.

? **Williams Lake Administration:** RR 3, Box 4, Williams Lake, B.C., V2G 1M3. Tel: 296-3507.

T **Williams Lake:** (Pop. 10,265/495 Ab). A meeting place of four peoples: the Secwepemc; the Dakelh of the vast expanse to the north and east (see chapter 15), the Tsilhqot'in who prevail to the east on Hwy 20 (chapter 14); and the newcomers who coalesced here in the 1920s around Pacific Great Eastern Railway tracks.

The Cariboo Tribal Council, at 17 South 1st Ave., represents the northern Secwepemc communities. The Carrier-Chilcotin Tribal Council, a few doors away, at 59 1st Ave., works on behalf of the four southern Dakelh communities, as well as the easternmost Tsilhqot'in community, Toosey. The Tsilhqot'in Tribal Council is at 102-383 Oliver St.

⑥ **Cariboo Friendship Society:** 99 S. 3rd Ave. Tel: 398-6831. **Hearth Restaurant**, and arts and crafts.

The new Xats'ull Heritage Village is a gathering place for elders, young Secwepemc people, and visitors who can participate in activities from hide tanning to drumming and singing.
CREDIT: SODA CREEK BAND

J **Highway 20:** Leads west from Williams Lake into Tsilhqot'in territories (see chapter 14). Just outside of town, the highway crosses Chimney Creek, once an important Secwepemc fishing and village site, now a trailer court.

V **Xats'ull (Soda Creek):** (Pop. 277/149). 36 km north of Williams Lake, via McAllister Rd., then 2 km along Indian Reserve Rd. to a low terrace overlooking the Fraser at the point in its southward journey where it squeezes into unnavigable canyons. Here travellers by water become travellers overland. Xats'ull has been "gathering place by the river" for at least 2,000 years. Archaeologists have barely begun their work: they're digging right in the village —drawing elders and children who peer down at the tools and bones that are their history. Generations are being reunited after a century or more of separation by residential schools

and the public education system. They are asking questions, then answering them, remembering who they are. And there is a spirit of expansiveness, a desire to share with the world. The people of Xats'ull are building here a pit-house village, welcoming groups who wish to experience, as closely as possible, the ambience of river life as their ancestors did two millennia ago. Food is prepared over open fires; salmon and meat dry on racks. Elders lead cultural workshops. (Hot showers and sauna are there, but hidden.) Individual travellers are welcome for day visits. Traditional and modern Xats'ull fare is offered at the community-operated **Soda Creek Emporium**, up on Hwy 97.

Great-great-grandparents of the people here offered guidance to fur-trade explorer Simon Fraser on his way downriver in 1808. During the gold rush, their terraces became the gathering place for thousands who travelled from the south by ancient trails widened into the Cariboo Wagon Road. Sternwheelers, built here, swept them north to goldfields in Dakelh territories. The people of Xats'ull provided them with the necessities of life.

As protectors of the northern Shuswap traditional territories, the people here feel the weight of their responsibility. They are currently working with the provincial government to clarify their role in the management of resources here. They say, "In our discussions, we acknowledge and respect all who live here with us."

? **Soda Creek Administration:** RR 4, Site 15, Comp. 2, Williams Lake, B.C., V2G 4M8. Tel: 297-6323.

Those Forgotten by the Highway: Secwepemc Territories between Soda Creek and Clinton

Gravel roads lead in from Clinton, 100 Mile House, and Williams Lake—so steep in spots that you would back up, or turn around, if you could. To sweep your fears away there are river vistas, mountain sheep, and gratitude that such a place can still exist. In spite of the apparent absence of civilization, there's a lot of history here—pit-house depressions, pictographs on cliff faces, fishing sites. Still, for this part of your Secwepemc journey, it would be best to focus on the road and the landscape. The three communities here are very small and private; their land is sacred.

Make sure you have spare tires, water for your radiator, a good map, and lots of time. All-terrain vehicles are not welcome.

Both sides of the Fraser River, from Pavilion north to Soda Creek, were home of the canyon division of the Secwepemc peoples until the late 1800s. They were struck especially hard by smallpox, and Tsilhqot'in peoples moved in to take their place along the western chasms.

V Tenlenaitmux (High Bar): (Pop. 8, mostly living in Clinton). From Clinton, the road leads 40 km over mountains. Its grade is 27 percent entering the territory of the Tenlenaitmux, "people of the place where the trail goes down." A notice, signed by the chief, clarifies this as her jurisdiction: no hunting, no fishing. It is 9 km to the Big Bar ferry junction. Big and High bars were mined for gold by Chinese.

? High Bar Administration: c/o Fraser Canyon Administration, Box 252, Lytton, B.C., V0K 1K0. Tel: 459-2628.

V Xqet'em (Dog Creek) and Sexqeltqin (Canoe Creek): (Pop. 598/222). On Dog Creek Rd., 75 km north of Big Bar by way of steep and treacherous roads; 70 km west of 100 Mile House; 87.5 km south of Williams Lake. Xqet'em, "deep canyon," is where Dog Creek tumbles to the Fraser. The canyon people are administratively linked with the "people of the creek," the Sexqeltqin, or **Canoe Creek** band, situated a short distance south by Canoe Creek. Dog Creek was one of the worst hit by smallpox—its population was 17 in 1903. Today, these two communities face another precipice: they are unsure whether to step forward into the unknowns of development, or stay where they are, ranching, logging, harvesting berries. High school and university courses already come in via the Internet. Tourism development flickers on and off the agenda, but that doesn't stop the tour-bus operators on "surprise tours" asking for directions to the restaurant. Right now, there's a good general store, some local craftwork, and the gas station. A restaurant may be in the works. There is a very pleasant Forest Service campsite about 10 km down Dog Creek Rd.

? Canoe Creek Administration: General Delivery, Dog Creek, B.C., V0L 1J0. Tel: 440-5645.

V Esk'et (Alkali Lake): (Pop. 584/378). 50 km south of Williams Lake on Dog Creek Rd. A century ago, independent families from the Taseko Lakes to Lac la Hache gathered here, roughly in the centre of their disparate territories, by a small alkali lake. They came at the behest of missionaries, their work hindered by the distances. Today, the descendants of the old families refer to themselves collectively as Esk'et, "the people of the alkali lake." In the heart of ranch country, and a full hour from Williams Lake, Alkali Lake is a modern gathering place, with an annual powwow, store, and cafe. The Esk'et also host cross-cultural weekend workshops in the summer, guiding circle talks, sweat-lodge ceremonies, drumming, dancing.

? Alkali Lake Administration: Box 4479, Williams Lake, B.C., V2G 2V5. Tel: 440-5611.

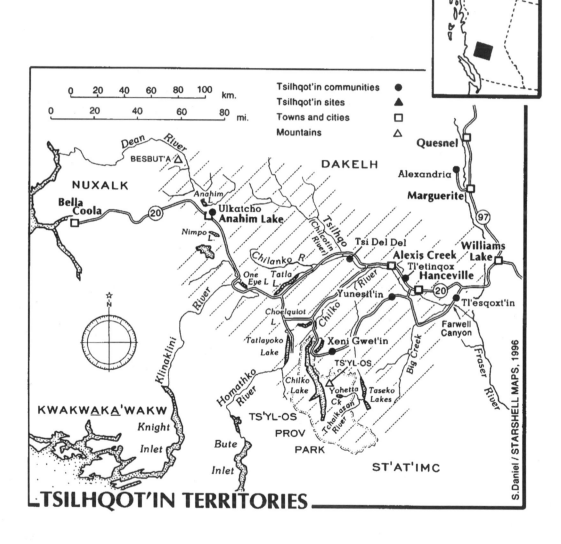

TSILHQOT'IN TERRITORIES

Legend:
- Tsilhqot'in communities ●
- Tsilhqot'in sites ▲
- Towns and cities □
- Mountains △

Scale:
- 0 20 40 60 80 100 km.
- 0 20 40 60 80 mi.

NUXALK

DAKELH

Quesnel

Alexandria

Marguerite

Bella Coola

BESBUT'A △

Dean River

Anahim

Ulkatcho
Anahim Lake

Nimpo L.

Chilanko R.

Tsilhqo (Chilcotin River)

Tsi Del Del

Williams Lake

Alexis Creek

Tl'etinqox
Hanceville

One Eye L. Tatla L.

Choelquiot L.

Yunesit'in

Tl'esqoxt'in

River

Chilko River

Farwell Canyon

Fraser River

Tatlayoko Lake

Xeni Gwet'in

TS'YL-OS

Big Creek

Klinaklini River

KWAKWAKA'WAKW

Knight

Inlet

Homathko River

Chilko Lake

Yohetta Ck.

Taseko Lakes

Bute

Inlet

TS'YL-OS PROV PARK

Tchaikazan River

ST'AT'IMC

S. Daniel / STARSHELL MAPS, 1996

CHAPTER 14

Tsilhqot'in

*Our people stand on the proclamation of 1763. We feel
a precedent has been set. It says lands have to be lost in
war, we have to trade it, or we have to sell it. When we
talk about the Tsilhqot'in War, we are not talking about
only the past. We are talking about the future.*
                    —*Ray Hance, Tsilhqot'in National Government*

*T*silhqo, in the language spoken here, means "young man's river." *T'in,* or *t'ine,* means "people"—the six communities sharing the high plateau stretching 300 kilometres from the Fraser River to the Coast Mountains. Linking them, feeding them, giving character to the land, is the river we call Chilcotin. Its long tributaries and long lakes still bear Tsilhqot'in names. Highway 20 snakes with them across the plateau, following an ancient Tsilhqot'in road. The modern version was completed only in 1953. It is steep and rough, and change must enter slowly. The only *midugh*—"non-native"—settlements here are the tiny, unincorporated villages—Alexis Creek and Anahim Lake—named for Tsilhqot'in leaders of the previous century.

That this remains so ardently Tsilhqot'in country is no accident. It's not because these grasslands were less cherished than others for ranching, or the geography more impossible than, say, the canyons of the Fraser River. The routes that history took through the rest of what became British Columbia would have

been taken here, if not for the Tsilhqot'in themselves, and some inspired help. Ever since this land and its inhabitants were given their form by the Transformers, Lendixtcux and Raven, guardian spirits have maintained their presence. Owl, Beaver, Golden Eagle, and others, link people, land, and resources. From them, the Tsilhqot'in take their names, and receive insight and the power to protect their homeland.

The Tsilhqot'in were not deceived by the small numbers, bared souls, and offers of a better life when the first Jesuit priests arrived in 1822. They kept their feet braced against the doorway to their country. And while they allowed the Hudson's Bay Company to build a fort by the forks of the Chilko and Chilanko rivers in 1829, they limited their access to water and salmon. By 1844 these *midugh* had left in search of more accommodating hosts.

The gold rush was a lust that travelled through the lands of many peoples in tandem with smallpox. It swept away illusions about some of the newcomers' motives; it also swept away the power to stop them. Somehow, the Tsilhqot'in were forewarned. They could not keep the deadly virus out, but in what has become known as the Tsilhqot'in War—said to be the only war west of the Rockies and north of the 49th parallel—they held its carriers at bay. It isn't something the Tsilhqot'in people like to brag about, cautions Annie Williams, former chief of the Xeni Gwet'in community. Anyway, their perspective of the tragedy was never asked for, not then or in the volumes of histories to follow. "To this day, we feel very uncomfortable speaking about it," she says. "We only talk about it late at night, our voices hushed."

"One of the leaders had a dream," said Chief Thomas Billyboy in 1994, before a Vancouver symposium of journalists and historians studying the war. "Something bad in the air." Everything coming from the west. In 1861, Victoria speculator Alfred Waddington schemed to build a toll road to "open up" the interior, to get at the gold fields there. His chosen route: from the head of Bute Inlet, up the Homathko River Valley, into Tsilhqot'in territories, then across to the Fraser River. In 1862, two members of a survey crew fell sick. At the western Tsilhqot'in village of Nagwuntl'oo, they were taken in. They and their hosts died of smallpox. Sickness, fear, confusion, and hunger spread.

Early the next year a few pox-scarred Tsilhqot'in sought work at the road-builders' base camp on the western periphery of their territories. They looked hungry and were accused of stealing flour that had been stored there for the winter. Their names were recorded, and they were told that for their crime they would die of smallpox. To the northeast, a similar threat was made; Tsilhqot'in food was stolen; women were mistreated.

Tsilhqot'in warriors were known for their efficiency, for their two-metre bows, arrows that never missed. The power they possessed, says Annie, was like atom bombs today. In the spring of 1864, a series of attacks left dead 18

road-builders and packers, and the only settler in Tsilhqot'in territories—a man who had reputedly threatened smallpox to protect his tenuous position. Afterwards, Lha tses'in, "nobody knows who he is," who led the warriors, volunteered with seven compatriots to meet with colonial authorities calling for peace talks. They were immediately clamped in leg irons: five were executed.

The war was over, colonial law in place, but for at least two decades to come, the Tsilhqot'in controlled their country's immigration policy. After that there was some settlement, but until the 1950s there was no "road," and horse travel prevailed. In some places, it still does. The Tsilhqot'in continue to live as close to the old ways as possible: fishing, hunting, trapping, and in this past century, tending cattle and horses. In the early 1990s, there was a faint echo of the old war, as the Tsilhqot'in at Nemiah faced unchecked logging on their lands. But this decade has brought them new strategies—and allies among their *midugh* neighbours. In 1993, the Chilcotin Survival Coalition fought to preserve the Nemiah Valley, now embraced by Ts'yl-os Provincial Park, for the Tsilhqot'in to use as they always have, and for the enjoyment of all visitors.

The same year—129 years after 1864—a justice inquiry revisited the Tsilhqot'in War. Its verdict: the execution of Lha tses'in and his men was more an example for the Tsilhqot'in and the colonists than an honest search for truth. Judge Sarich recommended the Tsilhqot'in who were executed in 1864 be granted a posthumous pardon and be honoured with a memorial.

HIGHLIGHTS AND EVENTS

Harvesting spring beauties—wild potatoes—in
the Nemiah Valley.
CREDIT: RICK BLACKLAWS

INFORMATION AND PROTOCOL

All five Tsilhqot'in communities except Alexandria (covered in chapter 15), are reached by way of Hwy 20 west of Williams Lake. Appropriate venues for exploration are given below. If venturing off Hwy 20, be well prepared with Forest Service or 1:250,000-scale maps, water, food, spare tires, and blankets.

The language spoken here is Tsilhqot'in.

Hwy 20 covers a total of 350 km from Williams Lake to Tweedsmuir Park, where it leaves Tsilhqot'in territories for Nuxalk territories (see chapter 20). From there is is another 100 km to Bella Coola, and the end of the road.

❓ Tsilhqot'in Tribal Council: 102-383 Oliver St., Williams Lake, B.C., V2G 1M4. Tel: 392-3918. Fax: 398-5798. Members: Alexandria, Alexis Creek, Anaham, Nemiah, and Stone.

❓ Carrier-Chilcotin Tribal Council: 1460 6th Ave., Prince George, B.C., V2L 3N2. Tel: 562-6279. Fax: 562-8206. The Tsilhqot'in community of Toosey is a member along with the four southern Dakelh communities (chapter 15).

❓ Cariboo Tourist Association: 190 Yorkston Ave., Box 4900, Williams Lake, B.C., V2G 2V8. Tel: 392-2226; 1-800-663-5885. Can provide list of First Nations hunting guides, trail rides, guest ranches, and mountain climbing guides.

Tsilhqot'in Territories begin west of Williams Lake, on Highway 20

T Williams Lake: "Downtown" for Tsilhqot'in and Secwepemc communities. See chapter 13.

B   Chilcotin (Sheep Creek) Bridge: 25 km from Williams Lake, Hwy 20 crosses the Fraser River. While this is now irrefutably Tsilhqo'tin territory, before smallpox it was also home to Secwepemc canyon peoples.

V   Tl'esqoxt'in (Toosey): (Pop. 200/101). 2 km along Farwell Canyon Rd. The Tl'esqoxt'in, "people of mud creek," guard the eastern frontiers of Tsilhqot'in territories. Depressions from old pit-house villages mark their earlier presence up here, on the sky-high plateau, and down along the Chilcotin River, right to its confluence with the Fraser. Their major fishery is at Farwell Canyon, focal point today for people the full length of the "young man's river," and for visitors too, who come to watch them dip-netting. "This is our heartbeat, our livelihood," says chief Francis Laceese, ardent defender of both the river and its land. He is concerned about dioxins and sewage in the Fraser River by which his salmon come: "Our people, when they put the fish out to dry, say they glow in the dark at night." A proposed gold mine east of Taseko Lake now threatens the relatively pristine Chilcotin River. But, says Laceese, "Our nation will not let that happen." Even closer to home, the Department of National Defence has been conducting military exercises just a kilometre from where some of his people live. Laceese has already been arrested once in his ongoing efforts to bring this to a stop. Toosey was an earlier chief here.

?   Toosey Administration: General Delivery, Riske Creek, B.C., V0L 1T0. Tel: 659-5655.

J I   Farwell Canyon: 50 km from Williams Lake, then south, 19 km to bridge. Here are the first glimpses of the "young man's river," just above its confluence with the Fraser. Pictographs south of the bridge are testimony to this canyon's significance as an ancient fishing site. The Tsilhqot'in come down in the early spring to dip-net for steelhead salmon;

July is the time for spring salmon; August brings the sockeye.

J   Road to Nemiah: About 90 km southwest of Williams Lake, at **Hanceville** (Lees Corner). Leads south to two Tsihlqot'in communities, and more than 100 km to Ts'yl-os Provincial Park. This route, just opened in 1973, is not well marked. For a secondary route into Ts'yl-os Park see Tatla Lake, below.

South from Hanceville on Road to Nemiah

V   Yunesit'in (Stone): (Pop. 350). A short distance south of Hanceville via logging road. The Yunesit'in, "people south of the river," had the Forest Service build a bypass to buffer their community from logging trucks. People here used to trade furs and shop at the "post" up at Lees Corner. Today, the Yunesit'in are mostly ranchers; some are loggers.

?   Stone Administration: General Delivery, Hanceville, B.C., V0L 1K0. Tel: 394-4295.

V   Xeni Gwet'in (Nemiah): (Pop. 355/281). 100 km south of Hwy 20 via Nemiah Rd. The Xeni Gwet'in, people of Xeni (or Konni) Lake, live spread out along its north shores and all the way to Chilko Lake. Their connection with the land is as long as it is broad. They remember when Ts'yl-os (Mt. Tatlow, 3066 metres, the highest point in the Chilcotin range) was a man, with a wife named Eniyud, and six children. One day, after an argument, Eniyud stuck the baby in his lap, left him two of the older kids and went away. That's when he turned to rock. Ts'yl-os now watches over the Xeni Gwet'in and, when necessary, intervenes, most noticeably by influencing the weather. Nemiah was the leader who first met with white chiefs 10 generations ago.

It was these roots, and 250 fully loaded logging trucks passing by each day, that led today's generation of chiefs to issue their

Nemiah Valley Declaration: no clearcuts in traditional territories, no mining, no commercial roads, no dams. Allied with environmentalists and local groups, they persuaded the B.C. government to set aside Ts'yl-os Provincial Park, an area the size of Prince Edward Island (see below). The Xeni Gwet'in still consider this land theirs. A management committee—Gwanajegwaten, "running Ts'yl-os Park" —consisting of Xeni Gwet'in, provincial, and local representatives ensures there'll be something left of it when the land question is resolved. Meanwhile, says Chief Roger William, the Xeni Gwet'in are vigilant in their protection of lands, forests, and traplines outside the new park, such as the Brittany Triangle, at the confluence of the Chilko and Taseko rivers, also affected by logging schemes.

? **Xeni Gwet'in Administration:** General Delivery, Nemiah Valley, B.C., V0L 1X0. Tel: 481-1149, ext. 333.

✗ **Ts'yl-os Provincial Park:** Southwest from Nemiah. This is a vast undeveloped wilderness, 233,240 hectares embracing two glacial lakes—the Chilko and Taseko—interior and coastal climatic zones, rivers bearing one-quarter of the Fraser River's salmon. This is the home of grizzlies, bighorn sheep, wild horses, and the Xeni Gwet'in. Their trails are tendrils, and the deal is they will continue to use this land as they always have, trapping, grazing cattle, fishing on the Chilko River. Visitors are welcome to enjoy the land and its scenery. There are a few small campsites and a major new campground on Chilko Lake. A four- to six-day hiking trail leads through Yohetta Valley, Spectrum Pass, and Tchaikazan Valley. The Xeni Gwet'in offer round-trip boat shuttles to one of the trail's main access points.

? **B.C. Parks:** Cariboo District, B.C. Parks, 301-640 Borland St., Williams Lake, B.C., V2G 4T1. Tel: 398-4414.

Route option: from Nemiah Valley a very rough road leads about 50 km around the north shores of Chilko Lake to rejoin Hwy 20 at **Tatla Lake.** Four-wheel drive with good clearance is recommended.

West From Hanceville on Highway 20

V **Tl'etinqox (Anaham):** (Pop. 1,100/about 750 living in this area). 98 km west of Williams Lake. In the 1860s, Chief Anaham moved with his people from Anahim Lake (see below) to the rich grasslands of Tl'etinqox, "field by the river." Many are ranchers today, grazing cattle, cutting hay from fields spreading down to the Chilcotin River. For local guide-outfitters, call administration office.

? **Anaham Administration:** General Delivery, Alexis Creek, B.C., V0L 1A0. Tel: 394-4212.

V **Tsi Del Del (Alexis Creek):** (Pop. 356/ 221 on reserve and surrounding area). 190 km west of Williams Lake. (The Redstone or Alexis Creek people are not to be confused with the non-native community of Alexis Creek.) Until about 40 years ago, most of these people lived to the north at Redbrush and Chezacut. For better access to schools and services, they gradually moved here, to Tsi Del Del, "red stone," named for the rust-red cliff that marks the village entrance. Like Anaham, Alexis was chief during the time of the Chilcotin War. It was he who persuaded the warrior Lha tses'in to meet with white authorities for what he believed would be peace talks. Gas station.

? **Alexis Creek Administration:** Box 69, Chilanko Forks, B.C., V0L 1H0. Tel: 481-3335.

J **Tatlayoko/Chilko Lake Road:** 221 km from Williams Lake. Western access to **Ts'yl-os Park**; to Tatlayoko, Chilko, Choelquiot, and Tsuniah lakes. In other times, Tsilhqot'in took

On the western frontiers of Tsilhqot'in territories, in 1923.
CREDIT: RBCM 3338

this route to the Homathko River to fish, or to trade farther down at Bute Inlet. It was there they sometimes encountered the powerful, birdlike Nentselgha?etsish, who sneaked up behind travellers and tore through their buttocks to get at their entrails.

Klinaklini River: 230 km beyond Williams Lake, Hwy 20 traces the river to One Eye Lake. From its headwaters here, the Klinaklini flows south into Kwakwa̱ka'wakw territories. Its name means "eulachon oil" in the Kwakwala language.

Chilcotin War: 302 km west of Williams Lake (about 5 km beyond Nimpo Lake), a sign marks the site of the final event. After Lha

tses'in and his warriors descended on two work camps on the Homathko River, he travelled here, to stop a pack train—40 horses, eight white men and a Tsilhqot'in woman —headed east. When it was over, three men and the woman were dead.

V   Ulkatcho: (Pop. 659/522). 316 km from Williams Lake, at **Anahim Lake.** On the western frontiers of Tsilhqot'in territories is the southernmost community of Dakelh peoples. The Tsilhqot'in village here was Nagwuntl'oo, on the western shores of Little Anahim Lake. In its day it was an international trading centre situated at the juncture of Tsilhqot'in, Nuxalk, and Dakelh lands, close to important Dean River salmon fisheries. It was also within sight of the mountain Besbut'a, "obsidian hill" (Anahim Peak). This was an important source of the glasslike mineral obsidian, used for making tools and traded both inland and along the coast (also see Mount Edziza, chapter 22).

The Dakelh with the strongest ties to this place were from Ulkatcho, "fat of the land," 90 km north via grease trail.

Anaham, chief here in the 1860s, was of Nuxalk descent. One of his wives was a Tsilhqot'in woman who persuaded him to move to Nagwuntl'oo, from dreary coastal climes to open skies. It was Anaham who in 1862 took in several members of a party of white road surveyors who had fallen ill. Soon, at least one-third of his people were dead of smallpox. A story told here is that a trader, Angus McLeod, later took blankets from some of the dead and sold them to survivors.

Not long afterwards, Chief Anaham and his people moved again, to richer grasslands to the east. Most of Anaham's people resettled at the Anaham Rancheree, others went to Toosey and Alexandria.

This land was left to become home to the Ulkatchot'en who began to move here permanently during the 1940s and 1950s. See Further Reading for a list of books describing their history.

? **Ulkatcho Administration:** General Delivery, Anahim Lake, B.C., V0L 1C0. Tel: 742-3260.

B **Nuxalk Territories:** Just west of Ulkatcho, the Coast Mountain Range rises up from the Chilcotin Plateau, and Hwy 20 climbs into Nuxalk territories. See chapter 20.

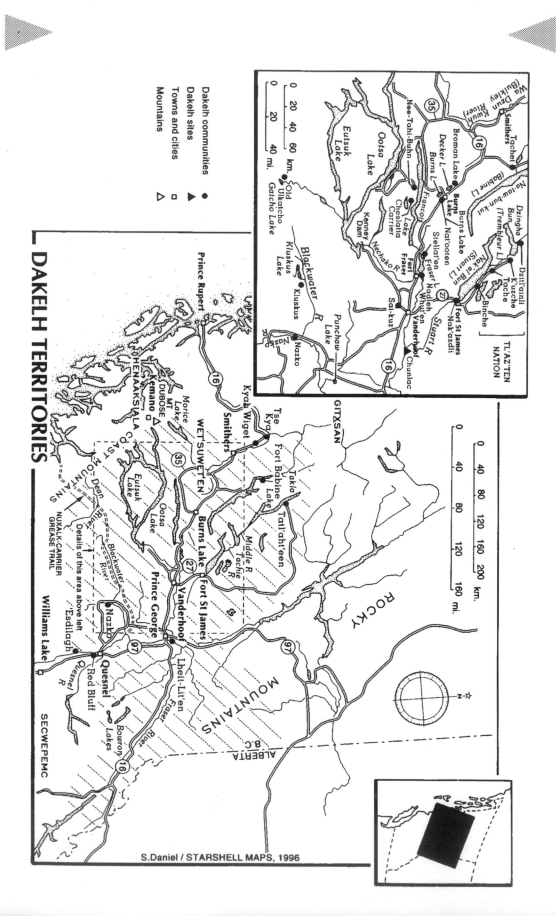

DAKELH TERRITORIES

Dakelh communities ●
Dakelh sites ▶
Towns and cities □
Mountains △

0 20 40 60 km.
0 20 40 mi.

TL'AZ'TEN NATION

Wa Dzun Kwun (Bulkley River)
Na-tow-bun-kut (Babine L.)
Smithers
Tachet
35
16
Nee-Tahi-Buhn
Eutsuk Lake
Ootsa Lake
Broman Lake
Decker L.
Burns L.
Burns Lake
Burns Lake
Natooten
Francois Lake
Cheslatta Carrier
Kenney Dam
Nak'al Bun (Stuart L.)
Na-tow-bun-kut (Trembleur L.)
Dzingha Bun
K'uzche Tache
Dzitl'ainli Bun
Binche
Stellat'en Fraser
Fraser Nadleh
Whut'en
Nautley
Fort St James Nak'azdli
Nak'azdli
Fort Fraser
Nechako R.
Sai-kuz
27
Stuart R.
Vanderhoof
Chunlac
16
Old Ulkatcho Gatcho Lake
Blackwater R.
Kluskus Lake
Kluskus
Nazko R.
Nazko
Punchaw Lake

Prince Rupert

DAKELH TERRITORIES

COAST MOUNTAINS
HENAAKSIALA
Kemano
MT DUBOSE
Morice Lake
WET'SUWET'EN
Kyah Wiget
Smithers
35
Eutsuk Lake
Ootsa Lake
GITXSAN
Tse Kya
Fort Babine
Takla Lake
Tatl'ah'ten
Middle R.
Tachie R.
Burns Lake
27
Vanderhoof
Fort St James
Prince George
ROCKY
Deon River
Blackwater River
Details of this area above above left
NUXALK-CARRIER GREASE TRAIL
Nazko
'Esdilagh
97
97
Lheit-Lit'en
Fraser River
MOUNTAINS
ALBERTA
B.C.
Williams Lake
Quesnel
Red Bluff
Quesnel Lakes
Bowron R.
16
SECWEPEMC

0 40 80 120 160 200 km.
0 40 80 120 160 mi.

N

S.Daniel / STARSHELL MAPS, 1996

CHAPTER 15

Dakelh:
South, Central, and Wet'suwet'en

*Travelling is what got me started. I was with my aunt,
who was quite elderly. She was pointing out landmarks
as we went along, even patches of trees, and telling me
stories about them. It gave me a whole different way of
looking at things.*

—Marlene Erickson, from Nak'azdli, cultural anthropologist

*D*akelh, in the language spoken here,
means "people who travel on the water."
Dakelh Keyoh is their homeland in the heart
of British Columbia—a vast country of a thousand lakes extending from the Coast Mountains to the Rockies.

The people here also go by the name Carrier. Their Sekani neighbours are said to have
been among the first to call them "the ones
who pack." Many here say this refers to earlier
times, when they carried everything on their
backs, or in boats. Others say the name is from
an old custom, where, if a respected leader
died, his widow would carry his cremated
remains with her in a small pouch for a year.
When she returned to her main summer village, her husband's title and territories would
be formally passed on.

These are also the Yinka Dene, "people of
the land." Attaching a single name, or drawing
a boundary, offers only a crude definition of a
people known for their fluidity. There are 18
communities here: peoples unto themselves,
they go by specific names, Tl'atzt'en, "people

of the edge of the bay," Stellat'en, "people of
the confluence." The Wet'suwet'en are the four
villages of the "people of the lower drainage."
But where one begins and the other ends can
be confusing to visitors used to solid lines.
"My grandfather on my mother's side is from
the west, from Hagwilget. My grandmother
was Tsilhqot'in Cree," says Patrick Michell
of the Carrier-Sekani Tribal Council. "There's
a lot of people like that here. Things are
blended. The fine lines you see on maps
today are political boundaries, formed to deal
with the land question."

One common denominator is language.
Yinka Dene is one language of the larger family of Athapaskan languages. But even here,
there are some 11 dialects being spoken.
Then there is the land itself—a great basin of
plateaus, bone dry until the trickster, Utas,
stole water from the old man and his daughter,
spilling the lakes and rivers as he fled.

In time, a metropolis, Dzilke, emerged on
the south bank of the Bulkley River. It was just
west of Kyah Wiget (Moricetown) and only

Dakelh birchbark basket. The arts of interior B.C. reflect the resources and traditional lifestyle of people who travelled with the seasons.
CREDIT: PATRICK MICHELL

about 30 kilometres east of its contemporary —the Gitxsan capital Tam Lax Aamid (chapter 17). Dzilke was a mecca for western Carrier, Sekani, and Gitxsan peoples. Here, all together, they built a huge salmon weir, using stone axes to cut cedar logs, dragging them down to the river's edge with ropes of cedar bark and moose and caribou hide. Then, one day at the peak of the summer salmon run, while many people stood on the weir catching the fish swarming upriver, two squirrels scampered onto the structure. It was taken to be a sign of a terrible upheaval to come, and the people scattered to the many villages where they live today.

Dakelh territories are presented below in three sections—south, central, and Wet'suwet'en—reflecting some of the differences in landscape, histories, and alliances with neighbours.

Southern Dakelh: People of the Great Road

The city of Quesnel, on the Fraser River, is the urban centre today for three of the five peoples who once spanned the Great Road west to the sea. The Lhtakot'en, Nazkot'en and Lhoosk'uzt'en have administrative offices

here, and many also live here or nearby. The Ulkatchot'en, farthest west and traditionally the closest link with the coastal Nuxalk people, have moved south in recent decades: they are now at home on the Tsilqhot'in road, Highway 20 from Williams Lake. A fifth people, centred east of here, around the Bowron Lakes, were swept away by smallpox in the 1860s.

These are peoples who travelled by boat, but depended even more upon their network of overland trails for access to resources and trading partners in all directions. The Great Road was a central corridor from the Fraser River across interior plateaus to the sea. From the "long ago people" comes the knowledge of the meanings and uses of sites all along the road, born of events that occurred as far back as the beginning of time. Some of these stories are related by the southern Dakelh in such rich accounts as *Dakelh Keyoh, The Southern Carrier of Earlier Times,* by Elizabeth Furniss, and *Ulkatcho: Stories of the Grease Trail,* by Sage Birchwater (see Further Reading).

The Great Road, or Nuxalk-Carrier Grease Trail, was a freight route for west-bound obsidian, furs, and caribou meat. East-bound went dentalium shells, salmon, and *tl'enaghe,* "eulachon grease," the Dakelh's most dependable source of fat for surviving cold interior winters. They carried the strong-tasting oil in cedar boxes over steep and rocky trails from the coast, inland, some 500 kilometres. Inevitably, the boxes leaked, leaving behind a grease trail.

It was along this road that the local Dakelh led North West Company fur trader Alexander Mackenzie in 1793. He would become celebrated by outsiders as the "first man west"—the first white man to cross North America, north of Mexico, overland, from sea to sea. The emphasis on Mackenzie's single round trip through this region, and the naming of this portion of his route the "Alexander Mackenzie Heritage Trail," has long irritated descendants of the Nazkot'en, Lhoosk'uzt'en, and Ulkatchot'en who delivered him safely to their saltwater neighbours, the Nuxalk people. On the two-hundredth anniversary of his journey, the peoples of the Grease Trail stood back from Canada-wide festivities. "We cannot blame Alexander Mackenzie for all the problems," they said. "But we seek recognition of the disease, death and destruction that has accompanied the colonialism that followed—and continues today."

Renaming of the trail is a small beginning. The Carrier-Chilcotin Tribal Council, concerned about logging, is also seeking a greater role in the management of the Grease Trail, being recognized now as a resource in itself. While many other ancient trails have been logged, flooded by reservoirs for hydroelectric projects, turned into roads, or overgrown, the Great Road is remarkably as it was: a trek on foot or by horse along the dark, trout-rich shallows of the Blackwater River to the virgin forests of the Coast Mountains; days spent without seeing a soul, and then only the few inhabitants of cattle ranches, fish camps, or old villages.

HIGHLIGHTS AND EVENTS

INFORMATION AND PROTOCOL

Although Dakelh territories were not always marked by precise lines, boundaries existed in the form of place names and the traditional use of resources by each extended family.

To accommodate geography, the predominantly Tsilhqot'in community of 'Esdilagh (Alexandria) is included in this chapter. Conversely, the Dakelh community of Ulkatcho is listed with the Tsilhqot'in communities in chapter 14.

? **Carrier-Chilcotin Tribal Council:** 59 South 1st Ave, Williams Lake, B.C., V2G 1H4. Tel: 398-7033. Fax: 398-6329. Members: Dakelh peoples of Kluskus, Nazko, Red Bluff, and Ulkatcho, and the Tsilhqot'in people of Toosey.

North from Williams Lake on Highway 97

T **Williams Lake:** (Pop. 10,265/495 Ab). This is "downtown" for three nations—the Secwepemc, Tsilhqot'in, and southern Dakelh, particularly the Ulkatchot'en, now at Anahim Lake, due west. The Carrier-Chilcotin Tribal Council, the Tsilhqot'in Tribal Council, and the Cariboo Tribal Council maintain offices here.

V **'Estilagh (Alexandria):** (Pop. 135/58). 62.5 km north of Williams Lake, most of the community lives on the west side of the Fraser River. From about April to September, the Marguerite Ferry shimmies back and forth from the east to west bank of the Fraser River. When the river freezes over, the service is replaced by a passenger-only tram. West Fraser Rd. leads north through ranchland to the village administration office.

The people of 'Estilagh are mostly ranchers, and live spread out along this Dakelh-Tsilhqot'in frontier. Here are descendants of the southern Dakelh who traditionally fished along the Fraser River between here and the

Quesnel River, and the Tsilhqot'in who joined them here in the last century.

? 'Estilagh (Alexandria) Administration: Box 4, RR 2, Rancherie Group, Quesnel, B.C., V2J 3H6. Tel: 747-8324.

⌶ Fort Alexandria: 66.5 km north of Williams Lake. A cairn marks the southern limit of Alexander Mackenzie's Fraser River descent in 1793. Dakelh peoples warned him not to go any farther and shuttled him north, then west along the Great Road from present-day Quesnel. In 1821, the North West Company built a fur-trading post at this long-established gathering place for southern Dakelh, Tsilhqot'in, and Secwepemc peoples. It was also, strategically, near an important Dakelh fishing site. The newcomers, not permitted to fish for themselves, relied heavily on salmon sold to them. Trade was competitive and extensive: furs of every kind, from beaver and bear to wolf, dried fish, meat, and berry cakes were exchanged for guns, gunpowder, axes, tobacco. The southern Dakelh also sold their services as interpreters, couriers, and labourers. Some married traders. In 1836, the fort was moved to the opposite bank of the Fraser; in 1867, in the wake of the gold rush, it closed.

▼ Red Bluff: (Pop. 109/57). Just south of **Quesnel** (pop. 8,090/135 Ab). At the terminus of grease trails, where the Quesnel River meets the Fraser, the easternmost families of the Nazkot'en made their headquarters and fished for salmon. In 1793, Alexander Mackenzie stopped here on his way south to the sea. These were the first Dakelh he had ever met. They counselled him to go west by land, rather than continue his journey downriver. He stuck to his plan, but soon turned around and set out upon their time-worn trails. Simon Fraser, in 1808, stopped here too, hell-bent on the river route. One of his Metis voyageurs later settled in the area and left his progeny. Another gave his name to the gold-rush town

now sitting on their meeting place and burial grounds. The Nazkot'en, joined by people from the east hard struck by smallpox, moved farther down the Fraser. They became known as the people of Red Bluff. This community has no visitor services, but the **Dreamcatcher Gallery**, at the Quesnel Recreation Centre on North Star Rd., features locally made bead and leather work.

? Red Bluff Administration: 1515 Arbutus Rd., Box 4693, Quesnel, B.C., V2H 5H8. Tel: 747-2900.

The Nazko Loop

From Quesnel the paved Nazko Road leads west past fenced pastures and old corrals to the Nazkot'en village. From there, an unpaved road traces their river, the Nazko, north 47 km to Blackwater Road which parallels the ancient Nuxalk-Carrier Grease Trail. It is about 25 km east to the eastern termimus of the Grease Trail, and 60 km farther to return to Quesnel. B.C. Ministry of Forests recreation maps detail roads and campsites.

▼ Nazko: (Pop. 259/235). 100 km west of Quesnel via Nazko Rd. The Nazkot'en are the people of the Nazko, "the river flowing from the south." They live primarily along its middle reaches at the ancient village, Chuntezni'ai, near "stump lake," a sea of submerged trees. The Nazkhot'en today operate a wood remanufacturing plant on the northern outskirts of Quesnel. Their story is told by author Laura Boyd in publications listed under Further Reading.

? Nazko Administration: Tel: 992-9810.

Return to Quesnel

⌶ Nuxalk-Carrier Grease Trail: About 60 km northwest of Quesnel. Take Nazko Rd. to Bouchie Lake; turn right on Blackwater Rd.,

Church at Old Ulkatcho, along Nuxalk-Carrier Grease Trail.
CREDIT: JOHN LUTZ

and continue to the Blackwater Bridge. Park here, at the contemporary start of the 420-km-or-so trail across the plateau and over Coast Mountains to the sea. For weekenders, there is a Forest Service campsite just north at Punchaw Lake. For those walking to the sea, the Grease Trail continues west, "an unmaintained bush track," used by four-wheel-drive vehicles and horse parties, parallelling or overlapping the original Grease Trail. The Dakelh, assisting Alexander Mackenzie, took 15 days to reach Bella Coola from here. Most hikers should plan for two to three weeks one way, with a food drop halfway. This route crosses through or near 22 southern Dakelh reserves and hundreds of archaeological sites, and is the main artery of these territories. Before starting out, call the administration offices of the respective

Dakelh communities: km 0–82, Nazko; km 82–201.5, Kluskus; km 201.5–347, Ulkatcho.

Along the Great Road from Nazko

V Kluskus: (Pop. 147/98). 50 km beyond Nazko by foot, horse, and wagon on Kluskus Rd., or by air. The people of Kluskus live by the edge of "half-of-a-white-fish lake." Nearby is the former village site, Tezdli, where archaeologists have unearthed evidence of 2,000 years of occupation. In 1844, after the Hudson's Bay Company abandoned Fort Chilcotin, they opened Fort Kluskus in this area with little more success. No visitor services.

? Kluskus Administration: Tel: 992-8186.

V Old Ulkatcho: About 100 km west of Kluskus by trail. "Fat of the land" sits on Gatcho Lake, at the headwaters of the Entiako, Blackwater, and Dean rivers. It is usually reached nowadays from the new Ulkatcho village at Anahim Lake, in traditional Tsilhqot'in territories (see chapter 14).

The Central Dakelh

Southern Dakelh trails flow north to meet the trails and waterways of the Nechako River peoples. "The river in the distance" cuts west across the interior from the Coast Mountains, pouring into the Fraser River at Prince George. Some people lived along its banks, but for most it was a travel corridor and destination for annual fishing trips and gatherings. The Nechako is deemed by some the most important tributary to the most important salmon-bearing river in the world. As much as 25 percent of the Fraser's chinook and sockeye salmon spawn here. Still dependent on these salmon are the Dakelh communities situated along the Nechako and the great lakes feeding into it.

Their very survival, tied to the fish, has been tried and tried again. In 1906 the federal fisheries department banned their use of traditional fishing weirs; in 1913, fishermen waited in vain for the "big run"—while hundreds of thousands of salmon tried desperately to get past the rock slide caused by railway construction at Hells Gate on the Fraser River.

In 1952, as the runs were slowly beginning to recover, the most brazen scheme in the history of B.C. was set directly upon "the river in the distance." In the canyons at its middle reaches south of Vanderhoof, the Kenney Dam was built. In front of it, the riverbed was for a time completely dry: millions of salmon eggs never hatched. Behind it, a chain of seven lakes rose up to form a 92,000-hectare O-shaped reservoir. Beneath it lay forests, grease trails, traplines, and the homeland of the Cheslatta people. One day they were simply told to leave.

Meantime, at the river's headwaters to the far west in the Coast Mountains, engineers drilled a 16-kilometre tunnel through Mount Dubose. From the O-shaped reservoir they siphoned west the Nechako River's east-flowing waters. All to spin turbines at Kemano, to make electricity for an aluminum smelter at Kitimat (the surplus being sold to B.C.

Hydro). One-third of the Nechako River—in later periods, significantly more—drained into the saltwater of the Gardner Canal instead of the Fraser.

During the 1950s, the salmon returning to the Nechako wouldn't have fed a family for a season. Even the small game—beaver and muskrats—that once flourished along the riverbank disappeared. Over the next four decades, salmon populations revived, though never to their original levels. Then, in the early 1990s, plans for the Kemano "completion project" were stepped up: a second, parallel tunnel would be drilled through the mountain, another 40 percent of the Nechako's waters siphoned west. One of the province's hottest environmental controversies echoed throughout the province, and among the loudest opponents were the Dakelh. In 1994, the provincial government cancelled the scheme.

Today, through the Carrier-Sekani Fisheries Commission, central Dakelh communities are working together, seeking ways to ensure the survival of their fish.

INFORMATION AND PROTOCOL

Central Dakelh First Nations are gradually integrating aspects of traditional government systems into the structure imposed by the *Indian Act*. Each "people," often denoted by the suffix *t'en*, as in Lheit-Lit'en or Stellat'en, was comprised of four or five clans. Each clan was represented by a hereditary *Dune za* (male) or *Tse-kay-za* (female), who managed the resources of specific territories. From among them, an overall leader was chosen to speak on their behalf. The elders were the "wisdom keepers," consulted in all matters of land use, tradition, and justice. Today, there are Elders Societies. The Yinka Dene Language Institute in Vanderhoof is working to bring the language, culture, and traditions of Dakelh into school curriculums. Yinka Dene is also being taught at the University of Northern B.C. in Prince George.

The Wet'suwet'en communities of Nee-Tahi-Buhn and Broman Lake are included here.

? Carrier-Sekani Tribal Council: 1460-6th Ave., Prince George, B.C., V2L 3N2. Tel: 562-6279. Fax: 562-8206. Members: Broman Lake, Cheslatta, Nadleh Whut'en, Nak'azdli, Stellat'en, Stoney Creek, Takla Lake, the Tl'azt'en Nation, and the Sekani people of Tsay Keh Dene.

? Yinka Dene Language Institute: 179 W. Stuart St., Bag 7000, Vanderhoof, B.C., V0J 3A0. Tel: 567-9236. Fax: 567-3851.

West from the Confluence at Prince George

V Lheit-Lit'en Nation: (Pop. 215/41). 10 km west of downtown **Prince George** on Hwy 16, then 11 km north on Shelley Rd. For as many as 8,000 summers, the "people from where the rivers meet" made their headquarters at the northeast rim of what is now the city of Prince George, B.C.'s geographic centre. Today, their village sits on an awkward patch of land bisected by the Fraser River, well above its confluence with the Nechako.

This reconfiguration marks the beginning of what the Lheit-Lit'en call the winter of their history. It began in 1911, relatively late, at this junction of natural corridors leading in all four directions, and the earliest gateway to the Pacific for newcomers. Alexander Mackenzie missed the Nechako altogether in 1793—though it might have offered him a route to the sea. Fort George, established here in 1807 by Simon Fraser, never became as central to

the fur trade as Fort St. James to the west. And the gold rush, with its Cariboo Trail to the south and the Chilkoot to the north, deflected the throngs of potential settlers away, rather than drawing them to this centre.

The third railway through the Rocky Mountains finally slid into the Lheit-Lit'en's time-worn groove from their eastern hunting grounds, along the Fraser to the Nechako. Its promoters saw the Nechako Valley as a route to the coast, and they saw the value of the Lheit-Lit'en reserve at the rivers' junction. "It's still unclear whether our men signed the document or whether their signatures were forged," say the Lheit-Lit'en today. Whatever happened, they were not prepared to see their village burned, graves dug up, and bones thrown into the river.

On their new reserve 11 km upriver, poverty, sickness, and despair took hold: nearly everybody left. It has been just one short decade now since the Lheit-Lit'en say winter has turned to spring, and they have made remarkable strides toward healing and self-government.

☻ Lheit-Lit'en Elders Salmon Camp: From Hudson's Bay Slough, near Fort George Park, a jet boat carries visitors 29 km down the Fraser to a traditional camp where elders guide them in catching and cooking salmon, and tell stories while they dine on salmon, moose meat, beaver, bear, fiddleheads, and wild rhubarb. Five-hour return trip; July–September; 563-9909.

☻ Dakelh Powwow: Annual event on the banks of the Nechako River adjacent to Prince George, early August.

? Lheit-Lit'en Nation Administration: RR 1, Site 27, Comp. 60, Prince George, B.C., V2L 3J5. Tel: 963-8451.

T Prince George: (Pop. 69,215/ 2,105 Ab). At the junction of Hwys 16 and 97—today a crossroads for Dakelh and other First Nations peoples. "This was our favourite town," said Mary John in *Stoney Creek Woman,* speaking of the 1920s. "Everyone knew that. . . . in Prince George a Native could go into any restaurant or dining room without the Mounties being called to throw him out." Today, the Prince George Native Friendship Centre has over 50 full-time staff helping a constant stream of First Nations newcomers to the city adapt to urban life. The Carrier-Sekani Tribal Council, and distant Tsay Keh Dene and Fort Ware peoples, have their offices here. And the new University of Northern B.C. is emerging as a centre for First Nations studies.

⑥ **Fort George Park/Lheit-Lit'en Cemetery:** At the end of 20th Ave., overlooking the Fraser River. This is the site of the small fort established by the North West Company in 1807, named after King George III of England. Nearly one hectare of the park is Lheit-Lit'en burial ground. The adjacent museum offers limited exploration of Dakelh culture.

⑥ **Native Art Gallery:** 144 George St. Bead work, leather work, wood carvings, and jewellery, prints, books, cards, and examples of birch-bark biting, an ancient art form once commonly practised by northern Woodlands women.

⑥ **University of Northern B.C.:** 3333 University Way, Prince George, B.C., V2N 4Z9. Tel: 960-5555. Languages offered at local or satellite campuses include Yinka Dene, Nisga'a, Haisla, and Sm'algyax (Tsimshian). Undergraduate and graduate programs offer students from across Canada a chance to work with northern First Nations, exploring history, sociology, botany, forestry. Other programs focus on the delivery of services to First Nations communities. Visitors are welcome to drop by the First Nations Centre, home away from home for First Nations students. Plans are underway for an aboriginal museum.

⑥ **Annual Powwow:** Usually held in July, sponsored by Native Friendship Centre; 564-3568.

▮ **Chunlac:** North of the highway about 55 km west of Prince George, where the Stuart and Nechako rivers meet, was Chunlac— from about 2,000 years ago until about 300 years ago, an important Dakelh centre. Some 2,200 food caches and 13 longhouse sites have been counted here; 2,000 artifacts gathered in 1949 are currently housed at the UBC Museum of Anthropology in Vancouver. Elders and historians tell us Chunlac was abandoned after a war with the Tsilhqot'in, and that in the intervening centuries, nothing has grown on the village site. It is not yet accessible to visitors.

▼ **Vanderhoof:** (Pop. 3,965/140 Ab). 97 km west of Prince George, at the junction of roads to First Nations north, south, east, and west. The Yinka Dene Language Institute, 179 West Stuart St., is a partnership between the Carrier-Sekani Tribal Council, school districts and centres of higher education, training language teachers and developing curriculum materials, including books in English and three Yinka Dene dialects. The institute works closely with elders in the surrounding communities. Books and videos on Dakelh culture and language are available. Tel: 567-9236.

From Vanderhoof South to Stoney Creek (Sai-kuz)

▼ **Sai-kuz (Stoney Creek):** (Pop. 875). 11.5 km south of Vanderhoof on Stoney Creek Rd. Mary John is 82 or 83 now. Sai-kuz, "stoney creek," is just a little older. People started moving here from other villages on Nulki Lake about the 1890s. *Stoney Creek Woman: The Story of Mary John,* is the story of her village. It is a rare view of the day-to-day life of people who, in this century, travelled with the seasons. Summers at Sai-kuz, fishing for trout; fall, hunting moose around Cluculz Lake; and in winter, trapping along the banks of the Nechako River, selling furs in Vanderhoof. Mary John recalls being sent to the residential school at Fort St. James when she was seven, and the births of her own 12 children, some of them on the traplines. Later she taught the Carrier language, and worked to bring two solitudes—Stoney Creek and Vanderhoof—together, co-founding the Elders Society in 1978, for the benefit of the young people.

The **Potlatch House** born from that vision welcomes visitors today: arts and crafts include Madelaine Johnny's exquisite birch-bark baskets; *Stoney Creek Woman* is available. The Potlatch House also caters group feasts: offering regular or traditional fare—salmon, bear, moose meat, Indian ice cream, and entertainment by the Stoney Creek Dancers. Vanderhoof's annual Rich Hobson Cattle Drive in late August stops here for a day. **Saikuz Campground** has RV hook-ups, cabins, boat rentals, and a fishing derby on the May long weekend. Bingo fund-raisers are held every Wednesday; giant bingos on Saturdays.

? **Stoney Creek Administration:** RR 1, Site 12, Comp. 26, Vanderhoof, B.C., V0J 3A0. Tel: 567-9293.

I **Kenney Dam/Cheslatta Falls:** 96 km southwest of Vanderhoof. In 1952 a new road was ploughed through Stoney Creek, still without electricity, to the site of the Kenney Dam. The 96,000-hectare reservoir behind it generates power for the aluminum smelter at Kitimat.

North from Vanderhoof on Highway 27

V **Nak'azdli:** (Pop. 1,293/669). Just west of Vanderhoof, Hwy 27 leads north. It is 62 km to the village at the southeast end of Stuart Lake. The Nak'azdlit'en live across the street from the oldest continuously inhabited non-First Nations community west of the Rockies. The

story of **Fort St. James** (pop. 1,995/165 Ab) —founded by Simon Fraser in 1806—is told at the Fort St. James National Historic Site. The story of Nak'azdli, "flowing from Nak'al" —the mountain on the east shore of Stuart Lake we now call Pope, is presented by Lizette Hall in her book *The Carrier, My People*. The great-granddaughter of Kwah, chief here two centuries ago, speaks of the time when the first white traders walked into their lives and built a fort next to their village.

During the 1870s, many Nak'azdlit'en moved to the new mission, a short distance from the village here. Our Lady of Good Hope Church, still there, is the oldest Catholic Church in B.C. The residential school took in Dakelh children from 1917 until 1922, when the new brick school was erected at Lejac. Chief Kwah died in the 1840s and was buried near the Necoslie River mouth, so the salmon would never fail to return. He had 16 children, and many people here are his descendents.

⑥ **Fort St. James National Historic Park:** On Chief Kwah Rd.; 996-7191. Open mid-May to late September. The buildings of this fur-trade outpost are restored to their 1896 appearance. When the fur-trade heyday ended, First Nations people began to find work beyond fishing and trapping: working on schooners and on portages between lakes; on pack trains from Hazelton to Babine. The extension of the BC Railway through Fort St. James in the late 1960s brought opportunities in mining and forestry, and also a new influx of non-First Nations residents.

⑥ **Nak'azdli Handicraft Shop:** Across from the park. Elders Society offers locally made moosehide crafts: moccasins, slippers, jewellery.

⑥ **Fort St. James Hatchery:** Nak'azdlit'en enterprise at northern outskirts of Fort St. James. Tel: 996-8575.

☾ **Annual Stuart Lake Traditional Pow-wow:** Late August.

☏ **Nak'azdli Administration:** Box 1329, Fort St. James, B.C., V0J 1P0. Tel: 996-7171.

✔ **Tl'azt'en Nation:** (Pop. 1,500). Northwest of Fort St. James the "people at the edge of the bay" live in four villages looking out to the oceanlike vastness, the treed islands, gulls, and whitecaps of the lakes Nak'al Bun (Stuart) and Dzingha Bun (Trembleur). The lakes, and the smaller lakes and rivers that feed them, are habitat for the salmon, trout, moose, bear, and beaver that sustain the Tl'azt'en. In the forests here they still set their *keyoh*, "traplines," for marten, lynx, and wolverine. Binche, on the east shore of Nak'al Bun, is 52 km northwest of Fort St. James by gravel road. The Holy Cross Church, a simple, evocative log house, has stood since 1871. It is 19 km farther to Tache, the main village, with an impressively designed new school, administration offices, and the Church of St. Cecilia, built in 1872, rebuilt in 1913. The bell came from France, by steamship, riverboat, and finally by canoe. To the north is K'uzche (Grand Rapids), on the Tachie River. Dzitl'ainli sits at the mouth of the Middle River on Trembleur Lake.

Well-known Tl'azt'en guides, such as Henry C. Joseph, Walter Joseph Sr., and Francis Williams, take visitors to traditional camps and fishing sites. For a free subscription to the *Tl'azt'en Free Press*, write Tl'azt'en Communications Office c/o Tl'azt'en Nation, address below.

☏ **Tl'azt'en Nation Administration:** Box 670, Fort St. James, B.C., V0J 1P0. Tel: 648-3266. Research and Development Office is 648-3212.

✔ **Takla Lake:** (Pop. 488/250). Northwest of Fort St. James. This village on the east shore of Takla Lake sits at the meeting of Dakelh, Nat'oot'en, Sekani, and Gitxsan frontiers. In the 1800s, Fort Connelly, on Bear Lake just northwest, drew all four peoples together, and they form the basis of today's "people of Takla Lake."

☏ **Takla Lake Administration:** General Delivery, Takla Landing, via Fort St. James, B.C., V0J 2T0. Tel: 564-3704.

West from Vanderhoof on Highway 16

◼ **Fort Fraser:** 40 km west of Vanderhoof or 4 km west of the town of Fort Fraser, Nautley Rd. leads to Beaumont Provincial Park at the edge of Fraser Lake. This is where Simon Fraser established a fort in 1806. In the summer, the Nadleh Whut'en (below) operate **Sunset Take-out** here.

✔ **Nadleh Whut'en:** (Pop. 331/195). Via Nautley Rd., through Beaumont Park and across Nautley River bridge to village on slope overlooking Fraser Lake. One doesn't measure a river by its length, but by its salmon. The Nautley, 1 km in length, is said by some to be the shortest river in the world. But from it the people derive their name, Nadleh, "annual run," and traditionally, their livelihood. Stories of earlier runs describe the river, so red with salmon it appeared to be bleeding; in the years of the largest runs, people could walk across the river on the backs of the sockeye. It was these salmon too that kept Fort Fraser running. The Nadleh Whut'en today also make their living through forestry and leasing lakeshore lots.

☏ **Nadleh Whut'en Administration:** Box 36, Fort Fraser, B.C., V0J 1N0. Tel: 690-7211.

◼ **Lejac:** 50 km west of Vanderhoof, an unpaved road leads to the gutted remains of the Catholic residential school, now Nadleh Whut'en reserve. The school was named for Father Lejac, O.M.I. and opened in 1922, sweeping up children all the way to Lower Post. For Mary John from Stoney Creek, there was, each year she returned, "the same porridge to be eaten, the same whippings to be witnessed . . . the same silence at bedtime . . . the same longing to be at home with my family." The cemetery here holds five tidy rows of children who never left, and also their principal, Father Nicholas Coccola, who died in 1943.

? **Fraser Lake Museum:** At Travel Infocentre 5 km west of Lejac. Informative display of Dakelh culture.

V **Stellat'en:** (Pop. 290/201). 3 km beyond Fraser Lake Infocentre. The Stellat'en are the "people of the confluence of two rivers." Flowing into Fraser Lake here are the Endako River and the Stellako, a small river, but vital to the salmon and the people. Just below here, on the banks of the Stellako, is the site of an ancient village where more than 1,000 people lived up until 150 years ago. Smallpox and other epidemics brought that number down to 50 by the 1930s. By that time the Stellat'en—fishermen becoming farmers—were already moving here for the flat and fertile ground.

Tselkin, "red rock," is an extinct volcano about 3 km west of here, where Stellat'en men once undertook vision quests. Its last eruption is thought to have been some 50,000 years ago, but there are still small quakes occasionally. Visitors may go to Tselkin if they stop at the administration office for permission and directions. Women went to Tsekoo Shunk'et, "women gaining spiritual power through music," a nearby mountain cave, no longer accessible. Dennis Patrick tells the story, told to children at bedtime, of the "super woman" Toolah'nan. "One of the greatest women ever to live in modern times," he says.

"This was Tommy George's great-great-grandmother. Two elders—Angeline Patrick and the late Louise Casimel of keyah wejut [the old village]—confirm her existence. They say when Toolah'nan was a young girl she spent some time with the Sasquatch people. The Stellat'en name for Sasquatch is *dune'a-yee*, "man-eater." She would go into a frenzy and scare the kids, and her daughter would try to stop her. Toolah'nan would chase the children and try to bite them. One day she had bitten her daughter's arm but quickly healed it by putting her hands on the injury. We believe Toolah'nan is a real person, with extraordinary powers to heal, and see the future. Her songs would echo into the mountain ranges as she transported herself from mountain peak to mountain peak."

Handicrafts are sold at the village store, Slenya, "food cache."

? **Stellat'en Administration:** Box 760, Fraser Lake, B.C., V0J 1S0. Tel: 699-8747. White building next to playground, access via Stella Rd.

V **Burns Lake:** (Pop. 72/26). 65 km west of Stellat'en village. In southeast **Burns Lake** (pop. 1,585/185 Ab) on Tibbetts Crescent, adjacent Westland Helicopters. Of the six Dakelh/Wet'suwet'en Nations that have offices in the town of Burns Lake, these are the people who have always called these lakeshores their home and spiritual gathering place. The community operates **Rainbow Motel** on Hwy 16 west toward Smithers; 692-7717.

? **Burns Lake Administration:** Bag 9000, Burns Lake, B.C., V0J 1E0. Tel: 692-7717.

V **Nat'oot'en:** (Pop. 900). 819 Centre St., Burns Lake. Here is the newest subdivision and the administrative centre for two other Nat'oot'en communities on the isolated shores of Babine Lake to the north. From the ancient metropolis of Dzilke on the Bulkley River, their ancestors went to Na-taw-bun-kut, "long lake," the largest natural lake in B.C. The Wet'-suwet'en who remained below them on the Bulkley River called them Nat'oot'en, "the people next door." French-speaking fur traders called them *babine* for their custom of wearing labrets. The Nat'oot'en built their society around their salmon-fishing weirs, a complex technology of dams and baskets that allowed them to select specific salmon, letting others pass. Their leaders coordinated a collective labour force, distribution of the catch, and preservation of the resource. In 1822, fur traders established Fort Kilmaur on the south end of Babine Lake's north arm, and later replaced it with one farther up the lake, closer to the main fishery. The purchase of dried salmon for export, not furs, was the mainstay of their business here.

By the early 1900s, the Nat'oot'en were considered obstacles to commercial fisheries. Canneries were proliferating at the Skeena River mouth, salmon disappearing. In 1905, fisheries officials swept into Fort Babine, dismantled the weirs, and left in their place a heap of old gill nets. The Babine Barricade Dispute which followed saw the new law challenged, then reinforced by militia. Nat'oot'en leaders were jailed, and a way of life dating back to Dzilke came to an end.

Today the Nat'oot'en and federal fisheries are working together to preserve and enhance salmon stocks. The Babine River fish-counting fence and salmon enhancement project, 120 km northeast of Smithers, is open to visitors. There is fishing for steelhead in fall, and camping nearby. Call Prince George Radio, Mt. Dixon Ch. N693569, or ask at Nat'oot'en offices in Burns Lake.

Fort Babine, home for about 250 Nat'oot'en, is reached via Babine Lake Rd. from Smithers. Tachet at the mouth of the Fulton River is home for 150 Nat'oot'en. Artists in these communities are known for their fine leather work—moccasins, jackets, and snowshoes—sold from their homes or in Burns Lake.

? **Nat'oot'en Administration:** Box 879, Burns Lake, B.C., V0J 1E0. Tel: 692-7555.

South from Burns Lake on Highway 35

V **Cheslatta Carrier Nation:** (Pop. 200/ 79). 23 km from Burns Lake to Francois Lake ferry, then across lake, and left along Uncha Lake Rd. to administration offices. Their families have always travelled with the seasons, fishing, hunting, trapping, ranching. But ever since the flooding of Cheslatta lakeshores in 1952 for Alcan's Kemano power project, they have been in a state of flux. After their old houses, barns, and gravemarkers were burned, they received new land. But the rhythm, the completeness they knew and depended on, was not so easily replaced. Slowly, the people of Cheslatta began to clear away debris, find some solid ground, plan for the future on their series of tiny scattered reserves.

Forty years later, when Alcan moved forward with plans to complete the project with Kemano II, to back up yet more of the Nechako waterway, flood more land, the Cheslatta were at centre stage among those who—successfully—opposed it. Says Chief Marvin Charlie, "I wouldn't be surprised if Kemano III came along."

? **Cheslatta Carrier Administration:** Bag 909, Burns Lake, B.C., V0J 1E0. Tel: 694-3334.

V **Nee-Tahi-Buhn:** (Pop. 200). South about 12 km from Francois Lake ferry dock, to Olsen Rd. Past the cattle guard, second road on the left leads to office, three houses, gas station. This is the administrative centre for the people of "a body of water," Nee-Tahi-Buhn, also known as Francois Lake. This is an important one of many lakes—Uncha, Isaac, Skins, Omineca—where they live spread out on seven small reserves. They are Wet'suwet'en (see below), and their summer gathering place remains the canyon of the Wa Dzun Kwuh, the Bulkley River, at Moricetown. Plans are in the works for a fishing camp for tourists at Isaac Lake.

? **Nee-Tahi-Buhn Administration:** RR 2, Box 28, Burns Lake, B.C., V0J 1E0. Tel: 694-3494.

Return to Highway 16 at Burns Lake

V **Broman Lake:** (Pop. 138/67). 20 km west of Burns Lake, at Palling, on Decker Lake. South off Hwy 16 onto Defoe Rd. This is also a Wet'suwet'en community, focussing on development of their new subdivision here.

? **Broman Lake Administration:** Box 760, Burns Lake, B.C., V0J 1E0. Tel: 698-7309.

Wet'suwet'en Territories

Just beyond Burns Lake, Hwy 16 crosses the short pass separating the headwaters of the eastbound Nechako, and the westbound Wa Dzun Kwuh, the Bulkley River, which finds its way to the sea by way of the Skeena River. This is the heartland of the Wet'suwet'en, "people of the lower drainage."

Today's four Wet'suwet'en communities —Nee-Tahi-Buhn, Broman Lake, Moricetown, and Tse Kya—are closest to the ancient capital, Dzilke, on the Wa Dzun Kwuh. They are also closest to the Gitxsan, the people of the Skeena, into which their rivers flow. Wet'-suwet'en territories form the western membrane of a body of Athapaskan-speaking peoples extending east as far as northern Quebec. That membrane is porous: the coastal traditions of the Gitxsan, their clans, houses, and the precise boundaries of territories held by each house are understood here. The eastern-most house of Gitxsan territories lies north of Porphyry Creek; the westernmost house of the Wet'suwet'en is on the south side.

Conversely, though, something of Wet'-suwet'en fluidity has been absorbed by the Gitxsan. In 1820, after a rock blocked the Bulkley River and kept salmon from reaching the vital Wetsu'wet'en fishery up at Morice-

town, the Gitxsan made room for them downriver, inside their boundaries, so that they would continue to fish and, therefore, thrive (see Tse Kya, chapter 17). This tradition of cooperation and exchange, reaching back to the time of Dzilke, culminated in 1981, when the two peoples jointly delivered to the Supreme Court of Canada their respective histories and boundaries, testimony in their quest for control of their homelands.

HIGHLIGHTS AND EVENTS	
⑥ Traditional fishing at Moricetown Canyon	p. 170
⑥ Cultural Awareness Week, June	p. 171

INFORMATION AND PROTOCOL

Wet'suwet'en land comprises more than 20 precisely defined House Territories represented by hereditary *deniize'yu*. Nowadays, to survey their boundaries, they fly over them in helicopters. At the feast, they reiterate their laws and re-enact their role of providing for their people. Summer is the traditional time to gather for these important formal events, and to fish at the ancient sites, Tse Kya (Hagwilget) and Kyah Wiget (Moricetown).

The Wet'suwet'en communities of Broman Lake and Nee-Tahi-Buhn have been described in the previous section on the central Dakelh. Tse Kya is described in chapter 17 on the Gitxsan.

? **Office of Wet'suwet'en Hereditary Chiefs:** RR 1, Box 25, Site 15, Moricetown, B.C., V0J 2N0. Tel: 847-3630. Fax: 847-5381.

West from Burns Lake on Highway 16

T **Smithers:** (Pop. 4,975/125 Ab). 145 km west of Burns Lake. **The Wet'suwet'en Arts and Crafts Gallery**, at 1237 Main St., has

Fishing for salmon at
Moricetown Canyon.
CREDIT: JOHN LUTZ

masks, drums, prints, jewellery, moccasins and beadwork. **Interior Stationery and Books**, 1156 Main St., may also have books of interest.

▼ **Kyah Wiget (Moricetown):** (Pop. 1,405/ 651). 32 km west of Smithers, the Wa Dzun Kwuh chutes through a 15-m chasm: the sound of rushing water drowns out all distractions, including the hundreds of visitors who come to watch, as fishermen with gaffs brace themselves on either side, or watch over eddies with dip nets.

Some say Kyah Wiget, the "old village," is almost as old as Dzilke. The archaeological record stands at 4,000 years. A bridge here, like the one once there, spans the river. There was a weir here too. In the early 1900s, federal fisheries officers, declaring "no other way to remedy the evil in that narrow place," went so far as to outlaw fishing in this canyon, except by dry fly. It was just the first in a series of extreme measures—blasting the falls, setting up fish ladders—to save the spawning salmon. Meanwhile, down the Skeena, canneries proliferated.

Cultural Awareness Week, in June, is a major event giving visitors an opportunity to learn from the chiefs about Wet'suwet'en social and government structures, experience performances by dancers from many nations, and enjoy traditional foods. Call the adminis-

Until the early 1900s, elaborate fishing structures such as this were in use on the Bulkley River canyons.
CREDIT: RBCM 3495

tration office for exact dates. **Moricetown Falls Campground** offers pleasant sites and permits for fly-fishing just below the canyon; 847-2133. **Moricetown Handicrafts**, grocery store, and cafe are nearby.

Dzilke: About 30 km west of Kyah Wiget (Moricetown) on the Bulkley River. Thousands of years ago, the first Wet'suwet'en village, "driftwood piled up," occupied both banks of the river. A gigantic fish weir linked the two sides. On one side was a very large house, where the first recorded Wet'suwet'en chief, Goohlaht of the Thin House Clan, resided. All of the Wet'suwet'en creeks and forests west of Kyah Wiget remain to this day the House Territory of the chiefs bearing the name Goohlaht.

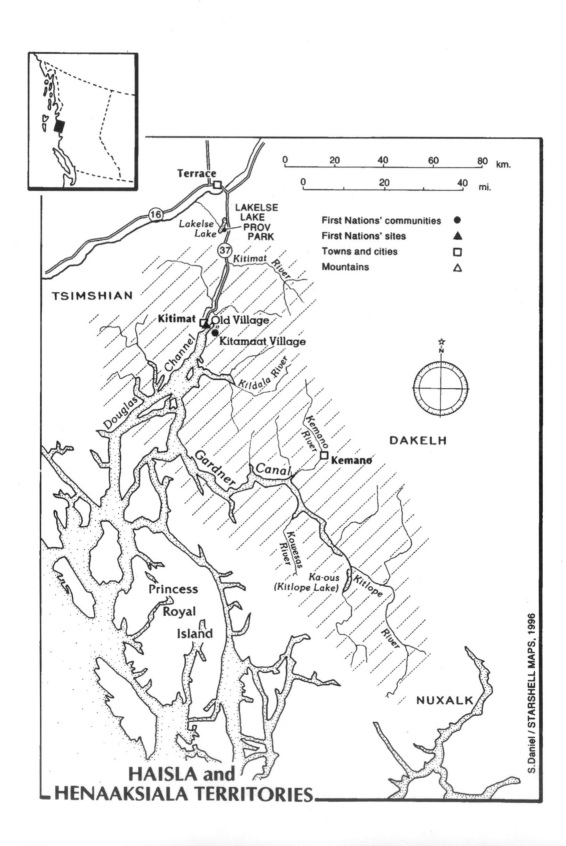

0   20   40   60   80   km.

0   20   40   mi.

First Nations' communities   ●
First Nations' sites   ▲
Towns and cities   □
Mountains   △

Terrace

LAKELSE
LAKE
PROV
PARK

(16)

Lakelse Lake

(37)

Kitimat River

TSIMSHIAN

Kitimat □ ○ Old Village
● Kitamaat Village

Kildala River

N

Douglas Channel

Kemano River

DAKELH

Gardner Canal □ Kemano

Kowesas River

Princess
Royal
Island

Ka-ous
(Kitlope Lake)

Kitlope River

NUXALK

S.Daniel / STARSHELL MAPS, 1996

HAISLA and
HENAAKSIALA TERRITORIES

CHAPTER 16

Haisla and Henaaksiala

*I would like to commission an anthropological study on
the mind set of non-native people—to look at how they
process information that comes from us. What does
sacred land mean to non-native people? I'd like an
anthropologist to look at this.*

—*Morris Amos, Kitamaat Council*

*H*aisla, in the language spoken here,
means "people who live at the river
mouth," and refers to the union of peoples—
Haisla and Henaaksiala—whose traditional
territories embrace 5 of B.C.'s 15 eulachon-
bearing rivers: the Kitimat, Kildala, Kemano,
Kowesas, and Kitlope. Their community and
headquarters, Kitamaat Village, is reached by
Highway 37, part of an ancient network of
grease trails linking them with peoples to the
north, west, and east. Douglas Channel, a busy
shipping route, was their link to the south.

Haisla historians say the first to be drawn
to the great numbers of eulachon here were
seagulls. The flock feeding upon them was
so vast that when it rose up to the sky and then
settled again on the sandbar, it looked from
the distance like a giant mouth—opening very
slowly, then closing. Stories of this monster
kept people away for a long time. Then, a
young Oweekeno man, Waa-mis, after acciden-
tally killing his wife, took refuge in the monster's domain. His small group was the beginning of a village at the Kitimat River mouth.

In time, others—Tsimshian, Tlingit from
Alaska, and Haida—joined Waa-mis. Catching eulachon, making grease, exchanging
stories—a powerful culture emerged, and
endured. But for three decades the heart of
Haisla life nearly ceased to pulse.

The people of Kitamaat Village today
look across Kitimat Arm to the reasons why:
smokestacks, freighters, docks; the model
town of Kitimat, built in the 1950s to serve
Alcan's aluminum smelter. Its powerhouse at
Kemano, to the south, draws its water from
the Fraser River system, 75 kilometres east,
through a giant hole in the mountains. Also
here is Methanex Chemical Corporation, and
Eurocan's pulp and paper mill.

"The oily fish," says Morris Amos, "have
picked up the pulp mill taste . . . All the
resources that should be going into housing
and education are going into our fight to
maintain a healthy environment, and against a
constant stream of new industrial proposals."

To the south, the Greater Kitlope Valley is
ancestral home of the Henaaksiala, "people

In 1967, at one of the last eulachon harvests on the Kitimat River, fish are boiled, and the grease is skimmed into a pail.

CREDIT: JACK FOSSUM AND KITIMAT CENTENNIAL MUSEUM

who live to be old." Much has gone into the battle to save one of the last large stretches—317,000 hectares—of pristine coastal temperate rainforest remaining on earth. The Kitlope and Kemano rivers here are cherished more than ever for their eulachon. The valley is a "power spot," metaphysically significant like the Stein Valley, say the Henaaksiala and Haisla peoples. It vibrates at a higher resonance. Masks, regalia, poles, events came from visions experienced in the Kitlope Valley. Mor-

ris Amos says it's no accident Alcan's power station at Kemano is adjacent to the Kitlope: "What better place to get power than from a power spot." A power spot that was slated for the chainsaw. But in late 1994, after a relatively short campaign and no blockades, the Haisla received the B.C. government's word: the Kitlope would not be logged.

A co-management system for the Kitlope Heritage Conservancy Protected Area, or Huchsduwachsdu Nuyem Jees, is being developed by the Haisla and Henaaksiala people and the provincial government. The nonprofit Nanakila Institute (from the Haisla "to watch over") oversees activities here, with the trained Haisla Watchmen as conservation officers.

INFORMATION AND PROTOCOL

Haisla territories embrace the northern reaches of Douglas Channel and the Kitimat River. Henaaksiala territories include Gardner Canal, and the Kemano and Kitlope rivers that flow into it. Traditional alliances are reflected on the Haisla Tribal Council, where hereditary and elected leaders sit together.

The Haisla and Henaaksiala population here is about 650; an equal number live outside traditional boundaries. The language spoken here is called Haisla; it is closely related to the Wakashan language of the Oweekeno Nation (see chapter 20).

A growing interest in adventure travel has accompanied the recent international focus on the Kitlope Valley. Most access into the region is by boat or air, with Kitamaat Village serving as launching point. The Henaaksiala and Haisla people ask that visitors contact the Nanakila Institute to advise them of their plans and to receive information on routes, safety, guided eco-tours, and protocol. They ask that visitors respect this as their sacred territory: tread lightly. If you come upon a heritage site or object, just leave it as you found it. If you encounter a Rediscovery Camp of elders working with young people, please do not interrupt.

?   Nanakila Institute: 260 Kitlope St., Box 1101, Kitamaat Village, B.C., V0T 2B0. Tel: 632-3308.

?   Haisla Tribal Council: Box 1101, Kitamaat Village, B.C., V0T 2B0. Tel: 639-9382. Fax: 632-2840.

South from Terrace on Highway 37

Haisla territories begin 27 km from the Hwy 16 junction, where the orange bridge crosses the Kitimat River.

▮   Lakelse Lake (Provincial Park): 14 km south of Hwy 16 junction; still within Tsimshian territories. This lake and its river flow north into the Skeena. At their confluence was the village Giluts'aaw. The "people of the way inside" had particularly strong connections with the Haisla. Lakelse, in the Tsimshian language, means freshwater mussels. It was these that attracted the Tlingit traveller Tsasee on his long journey from Alaska in ancient times. He was searching for a new home after his parents' death. His brothers and sisters, travelling with him, had already married into tribes along the way. As he paused here, many supernatural beings—a giant beaver, a huge halibut, and a manlike being—rose up out of the waters before him one by one. Tsasee departed quickly, making his way to the village of the Haisla people. There he stayed, and took on the name Legaik, "overland traveller." Lakelse Hot Springs, a few kilometres beyond park headquarters, was also a stopping-place on this road.

J   Kitamaat Village Road: Turn left off Hwy 37 just past Travel Infocentre (first inter-section on highway). Paved road winds around Kitimat Arm of Douglas Channel.

▼   Kitamaat Village: (Pop. 1,300/600). 11 km from Hwy 37. The original village, founded by Waa-mis, was Kak-la-lee-sala, "gravel banks," at the mouth of the Kitimat River. The river has since changed course several times, the forests have grown up, and the Haisla expanded into several villages. Their main village, like the river, has shifted its position over the generations. The current village site, home for some 200 years, is known to the Haisla as Cheemotza, "snag beach," for the uprooted trees delivered here by tides and storms. The Henaaksiala moved here gradually after the 1930s. Another site, now referred to as the "old village," sits just below the present-day town of Kitimat on the river's east bank. Even before the arrival of Europeans, this was one of the northwest coast's busiest industrial centres, where all stages of eulachon production—storing, drying, boiling, and refining—were carried out. That was before the eulachon began to taste of pulp mill effluent.

The name Kitamaat, "people of the snow," was bestowed upon the Haisla by their Tsimshian neighbours, who joined them here for winter ceremonies. The community is working toward the development of a cultural centre.

☺   Cultural Tours and Charters: Arrangements are made through the Nanakila Institute. Transportation into the Kitlope is provided by individuals well versed in Haisla and Henaaksiala history and traditions. Gerald Amos, **Haisla Charters**; 632-4173. Russell Ross, aboard *Mystic Dream*; 632-7794.

☺   Poles: Haisla poles speak of the past and the future. Presently there are five poles in Haisla tribal territories reflecting the recent re-emergence of this method of recording events. Four of these, carved by Haisla artists, are located in Kitamaat Village; one is at Kemano Village.

? **Kitamaat Village Council:** Haisla Post Office Box 1101, Kitamaat Village, B.C., V0T 2B0. Tel: 639-9361.

South from Kitamaat Village Road on Highway 37

T **Kitimat:** (Pop. 11,275/375 Ab). At southern terminus of Hwy 37. Opposite Kitamaat Village.

⑥ **Kitimat Centennial Museum:** At city centre; 632-7022. The museum has established a tradition of collaboration with the Haisla community. Its first curator in 1972 documented the Kitimat River's last eulachon harvest. Exhibits describe the preparation of eulachon oil and feature Haisla artists.

⑥ **Pole in Centennial Park:** Tells how the first people came to Kitamaat, and how the Haisla nation grew out of that. But, says Morris Amos, "It doesn't really reflect the interests of the Haisla people." It was erected in 1967, as part of Kitimat's celebration of Canada's hundredth birthday.

⑥ **Industrial Tours:** A close-up view of forces deeply affecting the Haisla environment and the culture born from it. Alcan Kitimat Works, one of the world's largest aluminum smelters, produces over 270,000 tonnes of aluminum annually; 639-8259. Methanex Corporation creates ammonia and methanol for petrochemicals and plastics; 639-9292. Eurocan produces pulp and paper; 632-6111.

▮ **Aix-gwa-las:** Sign on Hwy 37 northbound. This is a Haisla word, a way to say good-bye to someone when they're leaving and their future is uncertain.

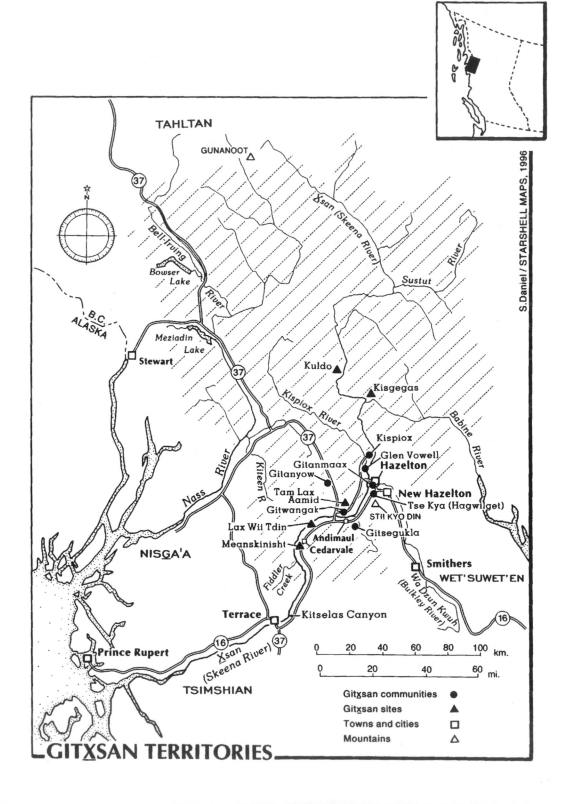

S.Daniel / STARSHELL MAPS, 1996

TAHLTAN

GUNANOOT △

37

Bell-Irving River

Bowser Lake

B.C. ALASKA

Meziadin Lake

□ Stewart

37

Nass River

Kiteen R.

Xsan (Skeena River)

Sustut River

Kispiox River

Kuldo ▲

Kisgegas ▲

Babine River

Kispiox ●

Glen Vowell ●

Gitanmaax ● **Hazelton**

Gitanyow ●

Tam Lax ▲

Aamid ▲

Gitwangak ▲

Lax Wii Tdin ▲

Meanskinisht

Andimaul
Cedarvale ▲

Fiddler Creek

□ **New Hazelton**

Tse Kya (Hagwilget) △

STII KYO DIN

Gitsegukla ●

□ **Smithers**

WET'SUWET'EN

Wa Dzun Kwuh (Bulkley River)

16

NIS**G**A'A

Terrace □ — Kitselas Canyon

16   37

Prince Rupert □

Xsan (Skeena River)

TSIMSHIAN

0	20 40 60 80 100	km.
0	20 40 60	mi.

Gitxsan communities ●

Gitxsan sites ▲

Towns and cities □

Mountains △

GIT**X**SAN TERRITORIES

CHAPTER 17

Gitxsan

You've got to stay here a while to see the nax nok, *the strength of the people, the authority someone like my younger brother carries. He will inherit a very ancient name, Dawamuux, from our uncle. Our grandfathers are walking with him, starting to shape him. You might not recognize it—the magic, emerging. Lately, there have been more magic moments. . . .*

—Gary Patsey, Chief Councillor, Gitanmaax

Gitxsan, in the language spoken here, means "people of the 'Xsan," the river of mists. Their territories begin in the mountains beyond Kispiox, with the first trickles of the river we call the Skeena, and extend to its middle reaches, just above the canyon at Kitselas. Here, under the shadow of the mountain Stii Kyo Din, are six ancient villages. In front of them, the poles that are testimony to a history reaching back not years, but millenia.

The Gitxsan speak of the time before the flood, when some say the ocean, not the 'Xsan, lapped their shores. They remember Tam Lax Aamid—a kind of Eden just southwest of where Hazelton is now—where they came from. It was a metropolis so populous its citizens could shout loud enough to tire and confuse geese passing overhead; so vast that where the exhausted birds fell was still Tam Lax Aamid; so old, archaeologists can't find a shard of it.

Feast halls and avenues, the Street of Chiefs. Here, on the middle reaches of the Skeena, was one of the most sophisticated societies in the world. The *ada'ox* (histories) and *ayok* (laws), through which the Gitxsan today still learn their responsibilities to the land, animals, fish, each other, originated here. Tam Lax Aamid was destroyed or nearly destroyed many times—as lessons. Once, the One-horned Goat lured everyone up to Stii Kyo Din for a feast, and massacred all but the commoner who had spared a young goat from the antics of poorly taught children. Another time, a great Bear tore up streets, trees, and people, avenging the injured spirit of the Trout People.

From Tam Lax Aamid, ideas and things circulated throughout an area larger and more multinational than Europe. The nexus of highways—upon which we now travel—may have in fact linked Tam Lax Aamid to such continents as Europe, where stone artifacts from this valley have been found; and Asia, from whence certain coins, found here, have come. The territory governed by these chiefs is also at a rare juncture of what scientists call biogeoclimatic zones. This is the coast, the interior, and the north.

What made Gitxsan country a nucleus for 10,000 years is also what helped isolate it from contact with colonial Europeans. Buffered by the nations around them, the Gitxsan had been receiving blankets, cast-iron pots, and guns in trade for more than half a century with little need to come face to face with the "ghost men" they had heard so much about. The barriers weakened after 1866, in the wake of an American's dream to link North America with Europe via the Bering Strait by a "talking wire," the Collins Overland Telegraph. Linemen entered Gitxsan territory by trails from the east; their supplies came from the west, up the river of mists, on a steam-powered sternwheeler. They met at "The Forks," near the village of Gitanmaax, where the Wa Dzun Kwuh (Bulkley River) joins the 'Xsan (Skeena), and from there cut deeper into Gitxsan territory, en route to the village of Kispiox, widening the old trails as they went.

Collins' Overland was soon made redundant by a more successful cable under the Atlantic. But it left two legacies counterpoised. One: white settlement; the other: Gitxsan authority. In the short 130 years since Kispiox chiefs warned "they would shoot the first white man that crossed the river who was in any way with the telegraph," the Gitxsan have stood face to face with miners, settlers, missionaries, legislators, road-builders, fisheries officers, loggers. Once in a while, a tale of pluck and savvy like the Skeena Rebellion of 1872, in which the Gitsegukla chiefs blockaded the Skeena River after miners set fire to their village, or the 13-year manhunt for alleged murderer Simon Gunanoot, echoes through histories written beyond the river canyons.

But for those who would hear more, Gitxsan memory is long, and heart-warming. The *ada'ox*, poles, even prints and T-shirts, tell how Gitwangak's Gwiis Gyen stood in front of the train; how, in 1927, Kitwancool chiefs went to Okalla prison for ripping out survey-

ors' stakes; how an Eagle chief hot-wired and seized a front-end loader to slow logging on a Frog chief's land; and about the Marshmallow Wars of 1986, when armed fisheries officers retreated before a hail of marshmallows.

In 1987, the Gitxsan with their old friends and neighbours, the Wet'suwet'en, launched the boldest trial in Canada's history. Fifty-four chiefs seeking outright control of an area spanning 22,000 square kilometres took their case to B.C.'s Supreme Court. Cautiously opening their *ada'ox*, "treasure boxes," they described, in their own languages, territories governed long before written history. Then came the paradoxical judgement of a 100-year-old colonial society, which, in denying their claim, summarized Gitxsan and Wet'-suwet'en life as having been at best, "nasty, brutish and short." An appeal has brought a limited recognition of their rights. It's not ownership or self-government. But the Gitxsan are, in their own words, patient.

Highlights and Events	
⑥ 'Ksan Model Village	p. 183
⑥ The poles	see Gitxsan villages
⑥ Tam Lax Aamid	p. 187
⑥ Fort Kitwanga National Historic Site	p. 187

INFORMATION AND PROTOCOL

Gitxsan territories comprise 63 House Territories, each precisely defined by streams and rivers, or sometimes markers, such as debarked trees; each represented by hereditary *simgiget*, "leaders," trained from childhood to care for the land. Today, the Gitxsan Treaty Office reflects the hereditary system where Speakers are appointed by the *simgiget* to represent them. Decision-making is by consensus.

Hwy 16, Hwy 37, and the Hazelton High Road cut through the houses of many *simgiget*. According to Gitxsan law, one does not go into another's house unless invited. The land, even verbal references to it and disputes about it, are exclusive property. The Gitxsan and close neighbours are kept up to date about boundaries through the Feast. In times past, travellers like ourselves checked in with *simgiget* at lookouts along Gitxsan frontiers. However, taking *recognized* trails across house territories is not considered a trespass, and certain sites, such as villages, though within houses, are common property, and visitors are welcome.

The six Gitxsan villages—Gitwangak, Gitanyow, Gitsegukla, Gitanmaax, Glen Vowell, and Kispiox—are all accessible by road. (There are other ancient village sites not presently occupied.) Visitors are welcome to view poles and visit galleries in communities, as indicated below. Please drive slowly, obey signs, and respect privacy.

Gitxsan population in the territory is about 6,000; outside (mostly in Prince Rupert, Prince George, and the Lower Mainland) it is 2,500.

The language spoken here is Gitxsanmx.

? **Gitxsan Treaty Office:** Box 229, Hazelton, B.C., V0J 1Y0. Tel: 842-6511. Fax: 842-6828.

Enter Gitxsan Territories West of Moricetown on Highway 16

On Hwy 16, about 15 km west of Moricetown, Porphyry Creek flows into the Bulkley River. This marks the entry into the easternmost Gitxsan House Territory, Sagat. From here, Gitxsan territories stretch north for 290 km as the crow flies, to the headwaters of the Skeena and Nass rivers; and west, nearly 190 km beyond Bowser Lake, taking in an area about the size of Nova Scotia.

I **Who's There?** Anything connected with the extraordinary, with power, supernatural gifts, or helpers seen or heard in places of concentrated spiritual energy is called a *nax nok.* A

nax nok might reveal itself as a whistling sound, a salmon or a snail, a quality in a person. But, says Skanu'u, a Gitxsan Speaker, "How, or when they manifest themselves is private and individual. Some people feel it, others don't." Walk softly. One contacted by a *nax nok,* or endowed with its qualities, is a *halait.*

J **Hazelton High Road (Hwy 62):** North off Hwy 16 at Travel Infocentre on outskirts of New Hazelton.

To Gitxsan Territories North

V **Tse Kya (Hagwilget):** (Pop. 562/227). 1 km beyond Hwy 16, on the south banks of the Wa Dzun Kwuh (Bulkley River) canyon. This is said to be an ancient Gitxsan village site, now the home of a Wet'suwet'en community. About 1820 a big rock fell into the Wa Dzun Kwuh, preventing great numbers of salmon from travelling beyond this point to the vital Wet'suwet'en fishing canyon up at Kyah Wiget (Moricetown). Gifts were exchanged. And the people from the canyon moved their summer fishing village from there to a bench here on the river's east side. Their Gitanmaax hosts called this Hagwilget, "place of the quiet people." The "quiet people" called it Tse Kya, "base of rock." The Gitanmaax continued to fish from the opposite shore.

Such diplomatic subtleties were lost on the Department of Indian Affairs, who in 1924 declared this the Hagwilget Band Reserve, locking them into Gitxsan territories, and out of Wet'suwet'en territories. The subtleties were also lost on the Federal Fisheries Department, who in 1958 blasted the rock away, blaming it for the river's shrinking fish stocks (the fish had been doing just fine for over a century). With the rock—a natural weir—now gone, the distressed Tse Kya became fish poor and had to depend on other sites and their kin.

Hagwilget today is just up from its original bench. St. Mary Magdalene Catholic

An earlier model of the Hagwilget Bridge spanning the Wa Dzun Kwuh at Tse Kya.
CREDIT: RBCM 4253

Church is prominent. Ask at the band office
about joining a bingo game (to help finance
the community hall). Ron Sebastian (Gwin
Butsxw) displays his carving, jewellery, silk-
screen prints at **RAS Fine Arts**. Turn right past
the band office, and look for Log House #3.

? **Tse Kya (Hagwilget) Administration:**
Box 460, New Hazelton, B.C., V0J 2J0. Tel:
842-6258.

I **Hagwilget Bridge:** Just beyond Hagwilget. This 75-m steel suspension bridge built in
1931 is the most recent in a series of architec-
tural wonders spanning the Bulkley Canyon.
Its Gitxsan predecessors were more dramatic,
wispier. When the river washed them away,
canoes bridged the gap. The most recent Tse
Kya–Gitanmaax overpass (late 1890s to 1917)
was fortified by telegraph wire. It stretched
44 m across the canyon, 30 m above the water.

J **Kispiox Valley Road:** 4.5 km beyond
Hagwilget, north 13 km to **Kispiox** (see
below). Hazelton High Rd. continues to the
Gitxsan community of **Gitanmaax**, .5 km to
model village **'Ksan**; 1 km to **Hazelton**.

V **Gitanmaax:** (Pop. 1,600/709). The largest
and most central Gitxsan village is the least
visible to outsiders. The "people who fish by
torchlight" live where the Wa Dzun Kwuh
(Bulkley River) pours into the Skeena, and
where three peoples—Gitxsan, Wet'suwet'en,
and European—come together. Gitanmaax
"surrounds" **Hazelton** (pop. 339/90 Ab), the
region's only permanent non-native community for a long time after its establishment in
1871. Dividing lines have never been clear. In
the early days, the Gitanmaax, along with their
other Gitxsan and Wet'suwet'en neighbours,
far outnumbered the newcomers as employers
and employees in North America's largest
packing industry, and in mining, sawmilling,
and railway construction.

In 1889, the Department of Indian Affairs
established its regional government over the
Gitxsan in Hazelton. Today, the Gitxsan Treaty
Office occupies a pioneer-vintage building on

Omineca St. The Education Society prepares students for self-government. Territory Management Training focusses on natural resource management, geographic information systems, culture and language; the School of Journalism, the only one of its kind in Canada, addresses the need for media coverage of First Nations issues.

The Gitanmaax administration office is on Field St. in Hazelton. Outside the Gitanmaax community hall on the way into the village, one old pole still stands, others lie nearby.

? **Gitanmaax Administration:** Box 440, Hazelton, B.C., V0J 1Y0. Tel: 842-5297.

▮ **Skeena River:** In Gitxsan territories, the river of mists is moody and turbulent, occasionally eroding banks, uprooting trees, flooding villages. The people's relationship with their river has varied over time, and place. Though living by its edge, and from its salmon, the Gitxsan, unlike their Tsimshian neighbours, travelled mostly by land. Those from Gitxsan West tended to combine trail and canoe travel. It was not until 500 years ago, when the powerful Tsimshian leader, Legaic, dominated the region's trade, that the river became a major transportation corridor, and the big canoes, some 18 m long, navigated its middle reaches.

▮ **'Ksan Model Village:** Turn off Hazelton High Rd. 500 m before Hazelton. Box 326, Hazelton, B.C., V0J 1Y0. Tel: 842-5544 or 567-4916. Operated by joint Gitxsan and non-Gitxsan non-profit society. Grounds open daily. At the site of the original Gitanmaax village, guides lead visitors through the Frog House of the Distant Past, the Wolf House of

'Ksan model village, at the confluence of the Skeena and Bulkley rivers, where the original Gitanmaax village stood.

At Anspayaxw, Weeping Woman clutches a grouse caught too late to save her brother from starvation.
CREDIT: JOHN LUTZ

Our Great-Great-Grandfathers, and the Fireweed House of Masks and Robes. On Friday evenings throughout the summer the 'Ksan Performing Artists Group explains the *yukw,* "feast," and become *nax nok*—Raven, One-horned Goat, and Black Bear barging through the front door.

The adjacent **Northwestern National Exhibition Centre** (daily in summer, Thursday–Monday off-season; Box 333, Hazelton, B.C., V0J 1Y0; 842-5723) features local and international themes and artists. The **Gift House** showcases contemporary artists, writers, rare collections of traditional lore. The **Kitanmaax School of Northwest Coast In-**

dian Art trains ten students a year. Outside are **poles**. *The Meeting Place,* raised for 'Ksan's opening in 1970, features the three local clans—Wolf, Eagle, Mosquito of the Fireweeds. At the top, a white man (*am sii wa*) with a bow tie stands on leaves of B.C.'s dogwood floral emblem. Some say it's former B.C. Premier W.A.C. Bennett. A short trail leads through salmonberry and cottonwoods to the peaceful meeting of two great rivers. The adjacent full-service **'Ksan Campground** offers idyllic riverside tenting and RV parking in Stii Kyo Din's shadow, May–October. Box 440, Hazelton, B.C., V0J 1Y0. Tel: 852-5940.

To Gitxsan Territories North via Kispiox Valley Road

I   **Gitanmaax Cemetery:** North off Hazelton High Rd. onto Kispiox Valley Rd. Turn left just past the junction onto the gravel road to the cemetery. Here are unobscured views of Stii Kyo Din and the rivers meeting.

J   **Kitwanga Back Road:** Just past the Four Mile Bridge which crosses the Skeena 3 km from Hazelton. Leads west to Tam Lax Aamid (described below).

V   **Glen Vowell:** (Pop. 306/163). 5 km from Hazelton. A road through fields, Salvation Army church in the distance—a pastoral serenity belies this village born of religious war. Nearly a century ago, everyone here lived up the river at Anspayaxw (Kispiox).

"The Catholics were the first to acknowledge we had souls, and I guess the race was on after that," says Wii Muugalsxw (Art Wilson), an Anspayaxw chief. Throughout the 1890s a dramatic conversion to Methodism tore up much of the ancient social fabric. The houses, the clothes people wore, the language and how families related to each other, all changed. Meanwhile, villagers who had been away to the coast returned, soldiers of the Salvation Army. Says Wii Muugalsxw, "The leaders here only wanted one church. There was actual bloodshed."

In 1898, Indian Agent Loring invited the dozen Salvation Army families to make a new home here, at Sik'e-dahk, "bright lights behind the mountain," a traditional Kispiox site and, by this time, Kispiox Reserve #2. He named the glen after B.C. Commissioner of Indian Affairs, A.W. Vowell. Relations between the two communities are delicate to this day. There are no old poles in this "new" Git̲xsan village, but visitors are welcome to visit the church, and with permission, may join some village activities, centred very much around the children.

? Glen Vowell Administration: Box 157, Hazelton, B.C., V0J 1Y0. Tel: 842-5241.

▼ Anspayaxw (Kispiox): (Pop. 1,152/556). Just beyond Glen Vowell. Where the Kispiox River enters the Skeena, pavement becomes logging road. In the time of measles and missionaries, the people of Anspayaxw, "the hiding place" were renamed the Kispiox, "loud talkers" by the Department of Indian Affairs. They were, according to the Indian agent, the "head-centre of disaffection," rejecting telegraphs, reserves, wagon roads, fishing restrictions, logging.

"It's not uncommon to see a hundred logging trucks come by our village in a day," says Wii Muugalsxw, a ranking Kispiox Wolf, fisherman, interpreter, artist. "I always say to people at art shows, this is what's going on." His silk-screen prints are modern *ada'ox*, recording deforestation, the Marshmallow Wars, the Bingo Wars, Oka. "I portray the white people as ghosts and skeletons, not to be derogatory; it was a prophecy. Bini, a Wet'-suwet'en prophet, said 'one day, the ghosts will come and live amongst you.' I might show some without eyes and ears because of their different world view. They have to realize the balance must be kept."

The very first immigrants, says Wii Muu-

galsxw, were from Tam Lax Aamid. Most recently, when the Salvation Army followers left for Glen Vowell, others, from Kuldo and Kisgegas to the north, moved in (see below).

Much of this history is recorded in the poles. There are 15, moved from their original locations throughout the village to a well-manicured enclosure by the river. The most evocative depicts Weeping Woman clutching a grouse caught too late to save her brother from starvation; on top, the One-horned Goat who feasted men. Down the road, Pierce Memorial Church honours the Tsimshian-Scottish reverend who spent 15 years here from 1895.

Wii Muugalsxw and his wife, Velma Sutherland, run the **Bent Box Native Arts Gallery** (842-6179) near the poles. Walter Harris displays his work at the **Hidden Place Gallery** (842-5507), in the new part of the village just across the bridge.

At the **Kispiox Fish Hatchery** (842-6384), open daily 8–4, coho and chinook eggs can be viewed in late August. There are always fry.

Ask at the administration office about permits to fish for steelhead in the Kispiox River; there is also very basic riverside camping. The B.C. Aboriginal Soccer Tournament and salmon barbecue mark summer's end.

? Kispiox Administration: Site K, Comp. 25, Kispiox, B.C., V0J 1Y0. Tel: 842-5248. At village entrance, on right. Photos of old Kispiox on display.

▼ Kisgegas: North of Kispiox, inaccessible by road. The "people of the white gulls" once lived on the north bank of the Babine River, just above its confluence with the Skeena. From the time of contact, they began to move away. By 1939, 25 remained. After World War Two, to ease administration, Indian Affairs closed the village and sent families to Kispiox and Gitanmaax. Kisgegas is now listed as a reserve of Gitanmaax people.

Gitwangak church.
CREDIT: DOROTHY HAEGERT

▼ Kuldo: Farther up the Skeena. The people of "backwoods" numbered six in 1929; one in 1939. It is now a Kispiox reserve.

West from New Hazelton on Highway 16

▮ Mission Flats: West of Hazelton High Rd. at the north edge of South Hazelton, where the Bulkley joins the Skeena. Until just over a century ago, thousands of traders from at least half a dozen nations gathered here to exchange eulachon grease, copper, herring eggs, furs, and ideas. Many probably first touched guns and cloth here, and heard about the white men—*am sii wa*, "white driftwood on the beach"—downriver, on the coast.

▮ Stii Kyo Din: South of the Skeena-Bulkley confluence, the mountain, "stands alone," is visible from all the Gitxsan villages. Says Skanu'u: "People familiar with the stories of the *wii halaits* will know how certain mountains come to be embedded with certain powers and how at certain times that power will manifest itself. There are numerous stories about why rocks will tumble down this mountain. Different stories for different places on it. There is one spot where it is said a tumble of rocks will occur shortly before the death of a high chief or the deaths of three people, one after the other."

Stii Kyo Din's greatest significance is as "the place where the goats feasted men." In the time of Tam Lax Aamid, the One-horned Goat, in human form, lured chiefs, elders and wise men, one after another over a ledge, to their deaths, because their people had forgotten the *ayok* (laws). The newcomers subsequently named the mountain Rocher Déboulé.

◢ **Seeley Lake—The Lake of Summer Pavilions:** 14 km beyond Hazelton High Rd. At an intersection of the *ada'ox* and modern science. From these waters rose the Medeek, the supernatural Grizzly who tore up mountainsides and raged through Tam Lax Aamid's Street of Chiefs, avenging the Trout *nax nok* after young women thoughtlessly adorned themselves with fish bones. In 1985 and 1986, geologists checking debris and sediment here concluded there was "a great ecological upheaval" about 3,500 years ago.

▼ **Gitsegukla:** (Pop. 700/500). 30 km beyond Hazelton High Rd. Here are the "people of Segukla ("sharp-pointed") Mountain," and grandchildren of the chiefs who led the first major Gitx̱san blockade. The 1872 Skeena "rebellion" was a curt response to the destruction of communal houses, ancient poles, and canoes after prospectors left a campfire burning and the Gitsegukla were away fishing. Until the B.C. government met with the chiefs and agreed to compensate them for the loss of what had "stood for generations . . . the honour of our forefathers," the Skeena trade artery was closed.

Around the turn of the century, new Christian faiths divided the Gitsegukla—some moved to the Salvation Army village at Andimaul, long ago "seat of astronomers." It was named for the nearby hill, where, it is said, astronomers from many tribes came in the spring and in the fall to observe the sun and discern the prospects of the coming year. Others went to the Methodist village, Carnaby. In 1926, New Gitsegukla was established near the old site and the people of Segukla Mountain began moving home. Andimaul and Carnaby are now deserted.

Poles at the lower part of the village are visible from the highway. Painted carvings of Gitsegukla's clans—Grouse, Frog, Wolf, Owl, Killer Whale, and the Medeek and Sea Bear—decorate the new elementary school and gymnasium, which visitors may also view.

❓ **Gitsegukla Administration:** 36 Cascade Ave., RR 1, South Hazelton, B.C., V0J 2R0. Tel: 849-5595.

◀ **Kitwancool Trail:** 43 km beyond Hazelton High Rd. The trail is now Hwy 37 and paved. Footworn a metre deep in places from thousands of years of use, the Kitwancool Trail is just part of a network of dozens of trails in the territory, linking the Gitx̱san to each other and to nations far away. This major north-south route connected villages here to eulachon fisheries on the Nass River, and beyond to the Stikine and Yukon rivers. In the most recent of times, Nekt (below) waged campaigns along here to control trade in metals and weapons. North to **Gitwangak**, **Kitwanga Fort** (National Historic Site), and **Gitanyow territories**.

North of Gitsegukla on the Kitwancool Trail

▼ **Gitwangak:** (Pop. 900/450). East off Hwy 37, .5 km north of Hwy 16 junction, then 2 km along unpaved road which loops to rejoin Hwy 37. In the 1830s these people came down from their *ta'awdzep* at **Kitwanga** (historic site described below), to "the place of rabbits," where the Kitwancool River flows into the Skeena. Just past the church, 12 remarkable poles, some more than a century old, some very new, describe Gitwangak's links to the warrior, Nekt, his escape from Haida Gwaii, and marvels of the fortress.

St. Paul's Anglican Church was built here in 1893, of lumber from Meanskinisht Mission. Stained-glass windows came from England. Tourist information is sometimes available here.

The Eagle clan here is working on a 250-year development plan for its old village and graveyard sites, river rafting, wilderness hiking, selective logging, and the use of hunting and fishing grounds and berry patches.

? **Gitwangak Administration:** Box 400, Kitwanga, B.C., V0J 2A0. Tel: 849-5591.

J **Kitwanga Back Road:** 6 km north of Gitwangak an unpaved road leads east. It climbs, then descends, reaching the north bank of the Skeena and the ancient site of Tam Lax Aamid. The backroad continues to Kispiox Valley Rd. just south of Glen Vowell.

I **Tam Lax Aamid:** Stop-of-interest sign 1.5 km from Hwy 37. "The land of plenty" extended all the way from here to Hazelton, maybe almost to Kispiox. Gitxsan histories relating to Tam Lax Aamid might fill libraries, but scientists are having trouble finding tangible evidence of its existence. Says Skanu'u: "I can think of no reason why it couldn't be found, except that many of our villages and municipalities are built on it. And any findings could well be misinterpreted, or may be so buried that it just hasn't been found yet." The river swirls by, washing things away.

Return to Kitwancool Trail

I **Fort Kitwanga National Historic Site:** A short distance north of Kitwanga Back Rd. A 13-m manmade hill marks the site of the fortress, or *ta'awdzep*, at this ancient crossroads of trade and warfare. History describes a series of wars probably around 1600 or 1700, culminating in the epic adventures of Nekt, a warrior who defended the Gitxsan boundaries at a time when other tribes were encroaching. He travels through Gitxsan, Nisga'a, Haisla, Tsimshian, and Haida histories, avenging the wrongs he and his Kispiox-born mother suffered.

Nekt, meaning "tongue-licked," got an early start when his mother, a Haida captive, fled, suckling her infant son on the tongue of her decapitated captor, his father. After years of wandering and warring, Nekt allied himself here with families that would later establish Gitwangak. In armour reinforced by pitch and slate, he was sometimes mistaken for a grizzly bear, allowing him to approach unidentified. His *ta'awdzep* consisted of five houses, a thousand food pits, trap doors, wooden decoys, and great log rollers. The final battle, in which Nekt was killed, probably occurred just before the arrival of Europeans to these territories. People continued to live here until the 1830s.

Parks Canada has interpretive panels in English, French, Gitxsanmx. There were also *ta'awdzep* at Kispiox and Kisgegas.

V **Gitanyow:** (Pop. 575/380). 15 km north of Fort Kitwanga. Gitanyow was Kitwancool, and before that, Gitanyow. Just as a chief will take a new name, so might a village, to reflect a shift in things. The Gitanyow were, and are again, "awesome warrior people." But for two centuries in between they were "people of a small village," recovering from their "successful" but deadly war with the Tsetsaut (Athapaskans) to the north. And since then, smallpox and the flu have taken their toll.

The only Gitxsan village not actually on the river of mists continues to set itself slightly apart. While full participants in most Gitxsan initiatives, the Gitanyow Hereditary Chiefs are pursuing treaty negotiations on their own. Their territories extend north, deep into the Nass valleys.

The poles here have been appreciated in the works of painter Emily Carr, who came up the trail by wagon in 1928 to capture what she thought was a vanishing art form. More recently, Roy Vickers has portrayed such monuments as 140-year-old *Hole in the Sky*, no longer standing. Carvers are still at work here, in the carving shed near the poles. They welcome questions about their work, and a hereditary chief may also be on site to talk about the significance of the poles to the people here. The new Gitanyow Independent School features carved doors, depicting the community's crests: Wolf and Raven, Eagle, and Killer Whale. Carvings and crafts, and travel information are in the old school near the carving shed. Also fast food, on 2nd Ave.

? Gitanyow Administration: Box 340, Kitwanga, B.C., V0J 2A0. Tel: 849-5222.

I Meziadin Lake: 130 km beyond Gitanyow. From here north almost to the Iskut River was once the range of an interior people known as the Tsetsaut. Between 1850 and 1900 they engaged in unsuccessful hostilities with the Gitanyow and other Gitxsan, and as a result ceded parts of their territory. As part of the peace settlement, they then joined the Tahltan, taking the remainder of their territory with them.

West from Kitwancool Trail on Highway 16

I Lax Wii Tdin: 9 km west of Hwy 37, at Boulder Creek Safety Rest Area, is Lax Wii Tdin, "the place where fish are caught in traps." Cultural information sign here was created by children aged 7 to 12, from Wilp Si Wilaxsinxw Hl Simgiget—"Chief's House of Learning." This bilingual school, at Gitwangak, emphasizes the Gitxsanmx language. The headwaters of Boulder Creek are in the Seven Sisters Mountains, visible to the south.

I Meanskinisht Mission: 19 km west of Hwy 37; about 1 km west of **Cedarvale Cafe** (native art for sale). In the late 1800s, Anglicans, Methodists, and the Salvation Army created their own divisions within Gitxsan territory. Here was an Anglican mission founded in 1888 by families from Gitwangak and Rev. Robert Tomlinson, who established the short-lived An'kitlaas Mission north of Kispiox nine years earlier. Modelled on the Coast Tsimshian's utopian Metlakatla, Meanskinisht, "place under the pitch pines," was also known as "the Holy City" for its extreme observation of the Sabbath.

The community's sawmill, across the river, was the region's first. The mission dissolved by the early 1900s.

B Tsimshian Territories: About 50 km west of Hwy 37 North, Hwy 16 enters Tsimshian territories (see chapter 18).

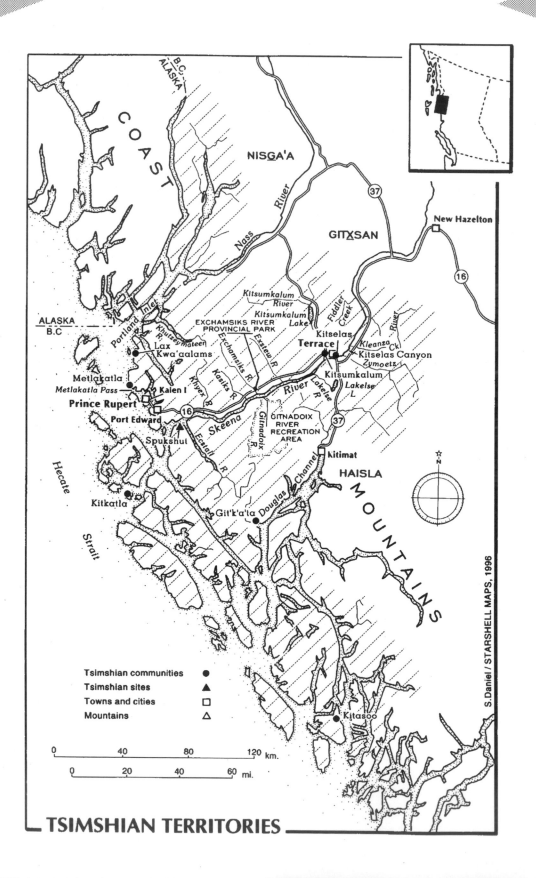

TSIMSHIAN TERRITORIES

CHAPTER 18

Tsimshian

If you walked into our village, at Kitkatla, with an open mind, and asked to meet an elder, you'd be taken. If you asked to learn a few words of Tsimshian, they would teach you.

—*Roy Vickers, artist*

Tsimshian, in the language spoken here, means "going into the river of mists" —going into the river we now call the Skeena. It's a relative description, with meaning for each of the seven communities that today occupy 150 kilometres of the river from its canyon at Kitselas, down to its mouth, and for a great distance on either side of that, on protected islands and inlets.

Just north of the Skeena's mouth on Kaien Island, the city of Prince Rupert has become, in the last few decades, the Tsimshian cultural and political centre. It is very much a Tsimshian city—overlooking the busy harbour and passes that have been, in recent millennia, the focal point for a congregation of people exceptional even for this well-populated coast. Ten Tsimshian tribes established here a dynamic corridor of winter villages so numerous it would be impossible to squeeze all their names on a map. In summer they returned up into the river of mists, to yet more villages, where they fished for salmon. Along with five other tribes—two that remained year-round

inside the Skeena and three that always stayed outside—they knew themselves as the *aluu gigyet,* "real people."

In Metlakatla Pass alone, there are hundreds of middens so deep archaeologists have only scratched the surface of their story. Among their findings: a cedar basket linking the people who live here now with the people here 5,000 years ago. It is a strong piece of evidence, but just a tiny fragment from a history that reaches far beyond that. The Tsimshian science of the past is called the *adawx*— an oral record of events, relationships, and boundaries, rigorously tested before witnesses at the feast; stored safely in the memories of one generation after another. It is here, rather than in the empty shells of middens, that we find the very precise beginnings of tribes such as the Kitselas, whose hardships brought them here from their ancient capital, Tam Lax Aamid (see chapter 17). Others found their way here from the headwaters of the Nass and Stikine rivers. Some came from Tlingit country, now Alaska, and many have their

This pictograph located between Terrace and Prince Rupert informed Skeena River travellers they were entering the trading territory of a Tsimshian chief.
CREDIT: JOHN LUTZ

of their post from the Nass to his land at Lax Kw'alaams (Port Simpson). This also drew the Tsimshian even more tightly under his reign —as all of the harbour-based tribes moved there to take advantage of new economic opportunities.

Legaic's capital, in the end, was torn apart by those who supported the age-old ways of governing as maintained by the *adawx*, and the persistent new Christian system. In 1862, Paul Legaic was among those who left Lax Kw'alaams for the Christian Utopia at Metlakatla, where everyone was equal.

But despite waves of smallpox that struck the Tsimshian hard, and schools forbidding their language, the *adawx* survives. Historians for the Tsimshian have a vast data base to work from today—supporting land claims, helping young people understand their place here. And they look to the day when their history is given as much credence as any written on paper.

Highlights and Events
⑥ First Nations Cultural Days, June   p. 195
⑥ Prince Rupert Harbour Tours   p. 195
⑥ Museum of Northern British Columbia   p. 195

INFORMATION AND PROTOCOL

Each Tsimshian tribe consists of several houses, each with its own precisely defined territories, each represented by a hereditary *sm'oogit*, "real person," or chief, of superior human qualities, both inherited and acquired. The chief of the highest-ranking house in the tribe is also the chief of the tribe.

The Kitselas, Kitsumkalum, Git'k'a'ta, Kitkatla, Kitasoo are tribes. Lax Kw'aalams and Metlakatla, on the other hand, are the names of places, and consist of members of the nine tribes: Gitzaxlaal, Ginaxangiik, Gispaxlo'ots, Gitandoiks, Gitlaan, Giluts'aaw, Gitwilgyoots,

deepest roots right where they are today.

The *adawx* holds the rise and fall of dynasties—successions of *sm'oogit*, or chiefs, such as Sebassa of the Kitkatla tribe and Legaic of the Gitspakloats. The name Legaic reigned for two centuries: by the 19th century he was the north coast's most powerful *sm'oogit*. There are many tales to be told of his mock battles up the Skeena. Legaic's power, and his boundaries, were taken very seriously, however. And it was into *his* history that European fur traders stepped. Seeing an opportunity to further expand his trading empire, Legaic arranged for the marriage of his daughter, Sudahl, to the Hudson's Bay Company chief factor, and negotiated, in 1834, the relocation

Gitando, and Gits'iis. The Tsimshian population, within and beyond these territories, is approximately 10,000.

Prince Rupert is the hub and the best place for visitors to explore Tsimshian history. None of the coastal communities are accessible by car. Kitselas and Kitsumkalum, on the Skeena, can be reached via Hwy 16.

The language here is Sm'algyax, "the real language," spoken by the peoples around Prince Rupert; a dialect, Skuumxs, prevails farther south.

? Tsimshian Tribal Council: 737-2nd Ave W., Prince Rupert, B.C., V8J 1H4. Tel: 627-8782. Members: Git'k'a'ta, Kitkatla, Kitsumkalum, Metlakatla, Kitasoo, Kitselas, and Lax Kw'alaams; also affiliated with Metlakatla Alaska. The council is pursuing treaty negotiations and administering a fisheries program.

? North Coast Tribal Council: 101-1st Ave. W., Prince Rupert, B.C., V8J 1A8. Tel: 624-4666. Tsimshian members: Kitkatla, Metlakatla, and Hartley Bay. Old Massett and Skidegate are also members.

? Allied Tsimshian Tribes Association: 2317 Victoria St., Lax Kw'alaams, B.C., V0V 1H0. Tel: 626-3297. Members: Gitlaan, Gitando, Gitandoiks, Gitzaxlaal, Giluts'aaw, Gispaxlo'ots, Ginaxangiik, Gits'iis, Gitwilgyoots.

Enter Tsimshian Territories on Highway 16

Fiddler Creek, about 50 km west of the Hwy 16/37 North junction, marks the boundary between Gitxsan and Tsimshian house territories.

V Kitselas: (Pop. 373/93). Just west of Hwy 37 South junction. The residential area and administration offices of Kitselas are now at the east end of **Terrace** (pop. 11,330/940 Ab), 4562 Queensway.

From the Gitxsan capital, Tam Lax Aamid, the ancestors of the Kitselas made their way downriver in search of a new beginning. Eventually, they came to a flat place at the bottom of the first canyon, one of few along the Skeena's route through the Coast Mountains. Salmon easily taken with gaff and spear swarmed in the pools; hunting was good. They became the "people of the canyon," and their village Tsunyow, "landing place," with its new Street of Chiefs, flourished year-round. Recent movement has been inside the 1.7-km canyon, where there have been four villages, from bottom to top. One was a fortress, on the mid-canyon terraces—spiked logs were rolled down upon invaders. Whirlpools below were guarded by canoe-eating water spirits.

From this strategic position, the Kitselas controlled coast-interior trade. The Gispaxlo'ots *sm'oogit* Legaic had the exclusive privilege (among the Tsimshian) of passing through the canyon to trade upriver. But the new white economy and a small gold rush at nearby Kleanza Creek in the 1870s finally shifted the Kitselas from their canyon stronghold. By 1885, one group lived at the cannery town, Port Essington. Others went to their current home at New Kitselas, 6 km south. Today, the Kitselas fish the river between their new home and their ancient one. To visit the canyon, ask for permission at the administration office.

Terrace is a meeting place for Tsimshian, Gitxsan, Nisga'a, and Haisla peoples. **Northern Light Studio** features First Nations art.

? Kitselas Administration: 4562 Queensway Dr., Terrace, B.C., V8G 3X6. Tel: 635-5084.

J Nisga'a Hwy (Kalum Lake Road): 3 km west of Terrace Travel Infocentre. Leads to Nisga'a territories (chapter 21).

V Kitsumkalum: (Pop. 546/207). Just west of Nisga'a Hwy, a road off Hwy 16 loops through the village at the confluence of the

Skeena, "river of mists" and the Kitsumkalum River. "We have a legend that the first dwellers here were the Robin People," says Mildred Roberts. "They taught the people who came how to catch salmon, and process them for food. Then they left. The people saw their robin feathers, so they knew who they were." These new people moved with the seasons, catching sockeye and coho salmon from the Skeena River; spring salmon from the Kitsumkalum River, which also puts the eulachon fisheries of the Nass within easy reach. Their name is often translated as "people of the plateau" and is thought to refer to the terraced cliffs behind today's village. But *kalum* also approximates a Sm'algyax word describing a place several kilometres up the Kitsumkalum River, where the water flows over a gravel bar and down a waterfall. "The family that lived there was said to talk loud, because of the falls." During the last century, many Kitsumkalum lived downriver, working at the canneries. "We never knew about welfare or unemployment insurance or credit," says Mildred.

The community hosts an **annual salmon barbecue,** on Saturday of the August long weekend. The **House of Sim-oi-ghets**, on Hwy 16, has arts and crafts, books, cards. **Kitsumkalum RV Park** offers pleasant riverside camping.

? **House of Sim-Oi-Ghets:** Box 544, Terrace, B.C., V8G 4B5. Tel: 635-6177.

Hwy 16 continues west, crossing one river after another flowing into the brooding river of mists. It's the same over on the south side. Up until the mid-1800s, there was a Tsimshian village at the mouth, or farther upriver, on virtually every one. These were the summer lands of the people who now live at Lax Kw'alaams, Metlakatla, and Prince Rupert. In a more distant past these villages were occupied year-round, as Kitselas and Kitsumkalum are still. Their former pre-eminence is reflected in

the names of rivers, parks, recreational areas, even safety rest areas.

■ **Split Mountain:** 40 km beyond Terrace. Visible from Exstew Safety Rest Area. One Kitsumkalum story is that the mountain was kicked by a great Bear. It broke, and part of it crumbled, halting the pursuit of brothers trying to rescue their sister from the Bear.

■ **Exchamsiks River Provincial Park:** 55 km beyond Terrace. The Kitsumkalum still fish at this old site on the Skeena River just across from the park. Mountain goats can be glimpsed on the cliffs; bears, lower down. This was an important hunting ground. The old highway behind it is now a trail, leading to sweeping views of the valley. In relatively recent times the Ginaxangiik, "people of the mosquitos," had a village on the Exchamsiks River's west bank opposite the park.

■ **Gitnadoix River/Recreation Area:** Across the Skeena from Exchamsiks Provincial Park, on the west bank of the Gitnadoix, lived the Gitandoiks, "people of the swift water."

■ **Kasiks Safety Rest Area:** 60 km beyond Terrace, just past the Kasiks River, was a village of that name, belonging to the Gits'iis tribe. Another Gits'iis village gave its name to the Kyex River. This tribe, with roots at Work Channel, had direct access to the Nass River eulachon fisheries. They are a strong voice at Lax Kw'alaams today.

■ **Spukshut (Port Essington):** On the opposite side of the Skeena. A Gitzaxlaal village sat at the wide mouth of the Ecstall River, and at the head of an important overland trail to southern Tsimshian and Haisla villages. The Hudson's Bay Company established a post there in 1872. By the 1890s there were two canneries supported by First Nations, Japanese, and Chinese villages. After the railway was built along the Skeena's north shore,

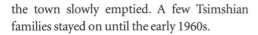

the town slowly emptied. A few Tsimshian families stayed on until the early 1960s.

I Pictograph: 100 km west of Terrace. (1 km before end of railway overpass). On the north side of Hwy 16, a short scramble leads through bush to an ancient and disregarded Tsimshian boundary marker. Two human figures and seven coppers—symbols of wealth, power, and jurisdiction—were etched onto the cliff that once faced oncoming river traffic. It is said this is how Legaic marked his Skeena River trading privilege.

I North Pacific Cannery Village Museum: 125 km beyond Terrace, turn left on road to Port Edward. The museum and national historic site is 7 km along a narrow road from Port Edward, at 1889 Skeena Dr. Tel: 628-3538. The commercial fishing industry and the establishment of some 30 salmon canneries along the lower Skeena led to yet another redistribution of the Tsimshian population. By the late 1800s, a litany of regulations limiting where, when, and how the Tsimshian could fish pushed them into employment as highly skilled cannery workers. The men delivered their fish to the canneries, where the women, children, and older people cleaned and canned them. The North Pacific cannery operated from 1889 to 1972, and at its height employed 500 to 700 workers—Tsimshian, Haida, Nisga'a, Gitxsan, Haisla, probably some Tlingit, one Plains family, Chinese, and Japanese. Exhibits shed light on their lives, and the hierarchy of living quarters here. First Nations arts and crafts for sale.

T Prince Rupert: (Pop. 16,570/2,700 Ab). 140 km beyond Terrace. On Kaien Island, north of the Skeena River mouth. Here is the largest concentration of First Nations people in B.C. Tsimshian, Haida, Nisga'a, Gitxsan, Haisla, and Tahltan peoples are employed here as teachers, administrators, artists, fishermen, longshoremen, cannery workers.

? Prince Rupert Information: Infocentre and Museum of Northern B.C., First Ave. and McBride. Tel: 624-5637. Ask about First Nations art galleries, private harbour tours and fishing charters. Also, details on **First Nations Cultural Days**, in June, when interior and coastal communities offer performances and art shows.

Harbour Tours: Operated by the Museum of Northern B.C. and the Metlakatla Development Corporation. Depart from the museum June–September for a three-hour exploration of channels that bustled with traffic from dozens of villages until the 1800s. Some had been occupied for 5,000 years. Of the hundreds of archaeological sites identified, only a few have been examined. Guides point out middens, house depressions, canoe skidways. The tour stops in at **Metlakatla** village (see below).

Museum of Northern B.C.: 100 First Ave. East. Tel: 624-3207. Established in 1924, when non-native Prince Rupert was only ten years old, this is now one of B.C.'s oldest museums. Staff and Tsimshian historians, artists, and educators work together, sharing collections and data bases. Among visitor highlights are coppers that represent a *sm'oogit's* cumulative wealth, and Chilkat blankets made from cedar-bark fibres and the wool of mountain goats. There is also a replica of the *Man Who Fell From Heaven,* the impression in rock of a young man who went to the sky world and returned with magic powers. The people at Metlakatla, who keep its actual location to themselves, say it fits anyone who lies in it. The museum offers excellent video productions, a book store, and a gift shop. Artists may be at work in the adjacent carving shed.

Chatham Village Longhouse: Across the street from the museum. The North coast Tribal Council centre blends traditional Tsimshian and modern architecture.

◎ **Self-guided Tour of Poles:** Ask for maps at the Travel Infocentre; for more detail, look for *Totem Poles of Prince Rupert* at the museum book shop. Throughout Prince Rupert are new works as well as reproductions of poles recovered from Tsimshian, Haida, and Nisga'a villages.

◎ **All Native Tournament:** First week of February. Basketball teams from all over B.C., Alaska, and Alberta converge for this major event. For tickets and information, call 627-8997.

◎ **BC Packers:** On Cow Bay Rd. Since 1870, when the first cannery was established here, this company under different names has pioneered the commercial salmon fishing and processing industry. Employees, then and now, are First Nations. Up to 2,500 people are employed in the cannery and delivering fish; 20,000 cases are produced during a 24-hour shift.

Offshore Communities

V Metlakatla: (Pop. 515/120). 5 km by boat from Prince Rupert. On the western edge of the Tsimpsean Peninsula, "between salt" overlooks the narrow passage linking the open waters of Chatham Sound with the mouth of the Skeena River. This same 5-km corridor was the strategic winter setting for the ten Tsimshian tribes that summered upriver, and in 1834 congregated at Lax Kw'alaams (Port Simpson). In 1862, 50 members of the Church Missionary Society under William Duncan returned to establish a utopian village here. They built a sawmill and a cannery and dug their gardens into middens. By 1879, the population was 1,100.

Conflicts between Duncan and the Church of England led to his formation of the Independent Native Church, and in 1887, many Metlakatlans joined him in founding yet another utopia—New Metlakatla, Alaska.

Today, the Metlakatla Development Corporation conducts harbour tours, which feature a visit here. Most of the old village was destroyed by fire in 1901.

? **Metlakatla Administration:** Box 459, Prince Rupert, B.C., V8J 3R2. Tel: 628-3234.

Harbour tours bring visitors to Metlakatla, the last of many ancient villages that once overlooked Metlakatla Pass. A Christian utopia was established here in 1862.
CREDIT: PHYLLIS BOWMAN AND THANKS TO MUSEUM NORTHERN B.C.

V Lax Kw'alaams (Port Simpson): (Pop. 1,200). 30 km north of Prince Rupert on the Tsimpsean Peninsula. Access by water taxi or seaplane. The establishment of the Hudson's Bay Company trading post here at the "place of wild roses" was an important part of Legaic's scheme to control all commerce on the north coast. Fort Simpson, established here in 1834, consisted of 18 company employees and their families inside stockaded walls, surrounded by keen traders from nine Tsimshian tribes. Over the next several years, these traders became residents of Lax Kw'alaams, as they moved here from their ancient villages in Metlakatla Pass. Other nations also came to do business here. By the late 1830s, smallpox had killed one in three Tsimshian people. The white traders thought the presence of a mission might improve conditions, and two decades later, in late 1857, William Duncan, of the Church Missionary Society, arrived. Four years after that, he left, and took his congregation with him (see Metlakatla). Twelve years later, a Methodist, Thomas Crosby, arrived, and transformed Port Simpson into a "model Christian community" following a uniquely Tsimshian-style of Christianity.

Lax Kw'alaams in 1995: the nine tribes flourish here fishing, fish processing, logging, and practising silviculture. A traditional longhouse is adjacent to the administration offices. Three churches offer revival, United Church, and Salvation Army traditions. And a road in from Prince Rupert is being planned. Bed and breakfast facilities are available.

? Lax Kw'alaams Administration: Box 992, Port Simpson, B.C., V0V 1H0. Tel: 625-3293.

? Allied Tsimshian Tribes Association: 2317 Victoria St., Lax Kw'alaams, B.C., V0V 1H0. Tel: 625-3297. Represents the nine tribes of Lax Kw'alaams.

V Kitkatla: (Pop. 1,298/400). On the north shore of Dolphin Island, about 60 km by air or private water craft south of Prince Rupert. The "people of saltwater" are the most isolated, and some say the most traditional, Tsimshian tribe—the only one that never left its ancestral home to take advantage of European opportunities. Sebassa was *sm'oogit*, descended from a line that reached back to Tam Lax Aamid. He was Legaic's greatest rival during the fur-trade period. Just as white traders came to Legaic, they came to Sebassa. There is no accommodation for visitors, but boaters do stop to admire the longhouse-style administration office. Ask here about individual artists selling work.

? Kitkatla Administration: General Delivery, Kitkatla, B.C., V0V 1C0. Tel: 848-2214.

V Gitk'a'ata (Hartley Bay): (Pop. 588/170). 120 km south of Prince Rupert by plane or boat, at the entrance to Douglas Channel. The flood carried their ancestors from Tam Lax Aamid, and delivered them into this channel, at a site some 20 km north of here. Where two rivers full of fish flowed into a tiny inlet, the *sm'oogit* placed his cane on the ground: journey's end for the "people of the ceremonial cane."

They did not join the move to Fort Simpson, but travelled far nonetheless, trading their furs at Fort McLoughlin, in Heiltsuk territories to the south. Later, many Gitk'a'ata found work in Victoria, clearing land for the new town there. And in the 1860s, they were drawn to Metlakatla. Today's village at Kulkayu is a traditional Gitk'a'ata site, re-established by the 27 who chose not to follow Duncan to Alaska. Here they maintained their Christian lifestyle, built a church, and became known for the ardour of both their industry and their singing. No tourist services.

? Gitk'a'ata Administration: General Delivery, Hartley Bay, B.C., V0V 1A0. Tel: 841-2525.

V Kitasoo (Klemtu): (Pop. 422/375). South from Prince Rupert by air. Kitasoo is the name of the people. Klemtu is where they live, on the east coast of Swindle Island. The people here speak the Tsimshian language of the peoples to the north, and the Heiltsuk language of those to the south.

"We live by the sea, on the outer edge of the Pacific Ocean," says Percy Star, born here. "Our lifestyle has been marine resources— that's what we know." There have been times over the last century when the village has emptied as people have gone to work at canneries north and south. Today, they are looking for alternatives as salmon stocks decline. There are moorage facilities, groceries, and a post office.

? Kitasoo Administration: General Delivery, Klemtu, B.C., V0T 1L0. Tel: 839-1255.

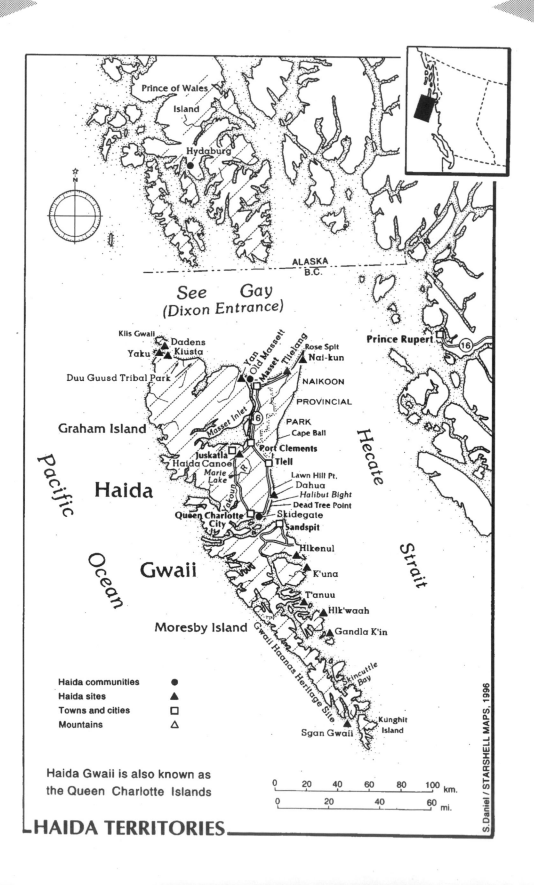

Prince of Wales
Island

Hydaburg

ALASKA
B.C.

See Gay
(Dixon Entrance)

Klis Gwaii
Yaku ▲ Dadens
Kiusta
Duu Guusd Tribal Park

Yan
Old Massett
Massett
Tllelang
Rose Spit
Nai-kun

Prince Rupert ▢ ⑯

NAIKOON

PROVINCIAL

Graham Island

Masset Inlet
⑥
PARK
Cape Ball

Juskatla
Haida Canoe
Marie
Lake
Yakoun R.

Port Clements
Tlell

Lawn Hill Pt.
Dahua
Halibut Bight
Dead Tree Point

Haida

Queen Charlotte
City
Skidegate
Sandspit

Hlkenul

K'una

Gwaii

T'anuu
Hlk'waah

Gandla K'in

Moresby Island

Gwaii Haanas Heritage Site

Skincuttle
Bay

Pacific

Ocean

Hecate

Strait

Sgan Gwaii
Kunghit
Island

Haida communities ●
Haida sites ▲
Towns and cities ▢
Mountains △

Haida Gwaii is also known as
the Queen Charlotte Islands

0   20   40   60   80   100 km.
0   20   40   60 mi.

S.Daniel / STARSHELL MAPS, 1996

HAIDA TERRITORIES

CHAPTER 19

Haida

There is a pole that holds the centre of this world—it's a cedar tree in the middle of Haida Gwaii.
—Michael Nicoll Yahgulanaas

*H*aida, in the language spoken here, means "people." *Gwaii* is their country—two very large islands and 150 smaller ones. Eighty kilometres of waves, wind, fog separate them from the mainland, which they know as Seaward Country, or, in more recent times, Canada. Their archipelago-continent, arching north to south a distance of 280 kilometres, is Inland Country. Here, at Skidegate and Old Massett, are the main centres of the Haida Nation today. Outside the limit of Canada's territorial sea, they live with their own constitution and their own flag, in defense of their sovereignty.

While archaeologists speculate about the degree and effect of fluctuating ocean levels 10,000 years ago, Haida genealogies, crests, and accounts begin with Raven, and a boundless expanse of sea and sky. He set Seaward country over there, the islands, here. When the reef, Xa'gi, appeared in the waters of Skincuttle Bay, Foam Woman was sitting upon it. At her many breasts, she nursed the future grandmothers of the Raven clan, the first of the two

great Haida clans. Some Raven families trace themselves to other shores: Those-Born-At-Qa'gials washed up on the sand spit at Skidegate Inlet in a clam shell; others, Raven cajoled from a clam shell at Nai-kun, "point town."

Many families of the other clan here, the Eagle clan, trace themselves to the supernatural woman Djila'qons. Her daughter, Swiftly-Sliding-Woman, sat up as soon as she was born to weave the first Haida cedar blanket. Swiftly-Sliding-Woman and her sisters, like the first women of the Raven clan, ventured out into Haida Gwaii, and their daughters gave birth to the first Haida towns. Their names, Sea-Lion-Town-People, Those-Born-Up-The-Inlet, and some 40 others, pinpoint the origins of today's lineages.

The first towns grew: from them, more sprang, flourishing between the sea and forests of giant cedars, straight-grained and perfect for carving poles—records of Haida journeys through time. They were ideal, too, for making the canoes that would carry their explorers

Yan village, on northern Haida Gwaii.
CREDIT: BCARS B-03593

all the way to Seaward Country, to the north, to the west, to the south, and home again.

Haida civilization expanded so much that two centuries ago, the Kaigani people of Kiis Gwaii pushed their canoes off the north tip of Haida Gwaii and, in a series of migrations, created six new towns across See Gay, "the ocean," on what are now the southern islands of Alaska, claimed by the United States.

Their departure preceded the appearance in Haida waters of the *Yaats Haade*, the "metal people." Haida travel and trade ventures had prepared them somewhat for their first encounters with Russian, European, and American traders. But the true cost of promised treasures was beyond anything they bargained for. Between the 1790s and the 1860s, smallpox struck the Gwaiian archipel-

ago three times. Whole lineages were lost. One by one, villages emptied. By 1884, the few hundred survivors from all the northern villages formed a new town at Old Massett; those from the southern villages made their way to Skidegate Mission by 1897; the Kaigani made their new town at Hydaburg, Alaska, in 1911.

Most of the old villages are quiet, but not abandoned. The *7iitlagadaa*—decision makers ("wealthy and respected")—who reside at Masset, Skidegate, southeast Alaska, and more distant urban centres still hold these sites sacred in a way not understood by newcomers. Poles have been snatched by yacht-borne raiders, some have even been sold by government officials; fallen beams from houses that once sheltered lineages have become firewood. Such actions finally prompted several members of the Haida community to return to the old villages in the 1970s, as the first Haida Gwaii Watchmen.

More than two decades later, Watchmen still preside over the islands and villages, check

HIGHLIGHTS AND EVENTS

⑥ The landscape and its ancient villages: The archipelago has two main Haida communities and a few small settlements occupied by newcomers. No cities. The draw is for visitors who are nurtured by the smell of cedar and sea-washed headlands; by solitude, or an eagle's call. And by feeling, in all of this, the inseparability of a people and their land. Some of the ancient villages, and the hot springs that may be visited are in Gwaii Hanaas Heritage Site (see p. 203) and in Duu Guusd Tribal Park (see p. 206).

⑥ Haida art: Haida Gwaii harbours one of the highest concentrations of artists in North America, and among them are some of the best in the world. Clayton Gladstone, Alfie Collinson in Skidegate; Christian White, Paul White, and Jim Hart in Old Massett, are just a few who bring traditional Haida designs into the 21st century. The most cherished are brought forth in gold, silver, cedar, and argillite, a soft-black slate found only on Haida Gwaii, and only available to Haida artists. See galleries listed below, and ask at administration offices.

⑥ Queen Charlotte Islands
Museum   p. 202

tourist permits and, when appropriate, share something of their history. Some southern villages are further protected as part of **Gwaii Haanas Heritage Site**, declared by the Council of the Haida Nation House of Assembly. As a result of the Haida stand taken in 1985, the Canadian government declared the area a national park reserve, pending settlement of an outstanding title and rights dispute.

Along the northwest coast of the archipelago is **Duu Guusd Tribal Park**, established by the House of Assembly in 1981. Here, people are actively working to reduce the impact of Canadian sports fishing on an already fragile salmon population. This conflict has already involved an armada of 200 commercial fishing boats, a collision between a 15-metre Haida canoe and a chartered airplane, and court action.

Through the Gwaii Haanas Heritage Site, Duu Guusd Tribal Park, and the Watchmen, many Haida believe some of what has been lost will be reclaimed. Says Cindy Boyco, who coordinates the Skidegate-based Watchmen, "It comes from just being there, connecting again with the land that sustains us still."

INFORMATION AND PROTOCOL

Haida Territories today include Haida Gwaii and the southern half of Prince of Wales Island, Alaska. Population on Haida Gwaii: 2,000. At Hydaburg, Alaska: 500. Total estimated population: 10,000.

The Haida language is not related to any other, anywhere: experts are convinced its independent and isolated development began at least 7,000 years ago. It is being taught in school programs for both Haida and non-Haida children. The English spoken here includes many Haida words.

The Council of the Haida Nation, formed in the 1980s, combines traditional and modern government structures. In addition to providing services to its citizens on a national and village level, it endeavours to protect a wide range of values associated with the lands and seas of the Gwaiian archipelago.

Haida Gwaii is reached by B.C. Ferries and scheduled air service from Prince Rupert, on the north coast mainland; and by scheduled air service from Vancouver.

Skidegate is at the southwest tip of the archipelago's largest island, today known as

Graham Island. Old Massett is 103 km north via Hwy 16, Haida Gwaii's only paved route. Travellers are welcome to visit galleries, shops, and studios in the two communities. But please respect their privacy, obey traffic signs. Information is at centrally located administrative offices.

The old villages at Gwaii Haanas and Duu Guusd are accessible only by private air and sea craft, or charters. Distances are great, and getting there can be dear. Visitor permits ($15) must be obtained from administration offices, the Haida Gwali Watchmen (see below), or local charter operators.

? **Haida Gwaii Watchmen:** Box 609, Skidegate, Haida Gwaii, V0T 1S0. Tel: 559-8225.

? **Council of the Haida Nation:** Box 589, Masset, Haida Gwaii, V0T 1M0. Tel: 626-5252. Fax: 626-3403.

To Haida Gwaii by Ferry from Prince Rupert

J **Ferry Terminal and Hwy 16:** At Skidegate. Route description leads west first to Queen Charlotte City, then east and north along the coast to Skidegate village and Old Massett.

T **Queen Charlotte City:** 5 km west of ferry terminal. Parks Canada administration, 598-8818, has permits and information for visiting **Gwaii Haanas Heritage Site**. At **Skidegate community-operated salmon hatchery**, 3 km west of town on Honna Forest Service Rd., coho and chum can be seen, mid-October to June; 559-4496.

V **Skidegate:** (Pop. 1,500/550). 2 km north of ferry terminal. At the west end of the beach it is still possible, at low tide, to make out "canoe runs" where stones have been cleared to allow smooth landings and launches. Four villages have, in relatively recent times, occupied Skidegate Inlet here.

Skidegate, "son of the chiton," was the leader who met the first white sea-otter fur traders here in 1787. His people were keen participants in the fur trade, and later traded with Hudson's Bay Company ships searching the islands for gold. After the people of Skidegate set a price for the return of a shipwrecked crew, trade traffic shied away. In 1853, in a search for new trade contacts, 500 people made their way from Skidegate to the emerging European centres on Vancouver Island. After that, much of the village made annual trips to Fort Victoria, returning with tales of new adventures, new wealth, and new diseases. A permanent mission (Methodist) was established here in 1883, enhancing its position as a focal point for southern Haida peoples.

The **Longhouse Gift Shop** is at 107A Front St. The **Haida Arts Coop and Carving Longhouse** sits at the end of the village. **Singaay Laa Day** is held in early June.

? **Skidegate Council:** Box 1301, Skidegate, Haida Gwaii, B.C., V0T 1S1. Tel: 559-4496. In the longhouse overlooking Rooney Bay, at the village's west end.

☉ **Queen Charlotte Islands Museum:** 2nd Beach Rd., east off Hwy 16, 1 km from ferry terminal, on Skidegate Haida reserve. Tel: 559-4643. Dramatic cedar and glass structure looks out to Hecate Strait. The site is being leased to a non-profit society in exchange for a focus on Haida culture. The museum displays an outstanding collection of antique and contemporary argillite carvings; there are ancient poles—one from Skedans tells of the great flood. Videos, Haida art and jewellery, and books are also available.

☉ **Loo Taas—"Wave Eater":** Next to the museum and Haida Gwaii Watchmen headquarters. The first Haida canoe carved since 1909 was launched at Vancouver during Expo '86. Throughout its three-week journey north

Hlkenul (Cumshewa) village today speaks of the inseparability of a people and their land.
CREDIT: JOHN LUTZ

to Haida Gwaii, coastal communities cheered its arrival. Among its passengers was one of its designers, artist Bill Reid.

? **Haida Gwaii Watchmen:** In a longhouse-style office adjacent to the museum. Permits and information for Gwaii Hanaas Heritage Site can be obtained here. Those planning to travel aboard private vessels can inquire about camping, fishing, and shellfish harvesting regulations, and the weather—very changeable. At the villages, Watchmen check permits, enforce regulations, and provide a general presence in case of emergency. Some may offer to share culture and history with visitors, but

the program's aim, after protection of sites, is, says manager Cindy Boyco, "to educate our own people."

To Gwaii Hanaas Heritage Site

Watchmen preside, during the summer, at the following five of dozens of village sites.

K'una (Skedans): Day-trip from Moresby Camp, by boat via Cumshewa Inlet to Louise Island. One of the most accessible of the ancient villages. Watchman Charley Wesley is the *7iitlagadaa* (hereditary leader) of Cumshewa village (below). Among his ancestors are those who lived here, at K'una, "point" village. He lives here from early May to late September, appearing on the beach as boats pull up on shore. He guides their passengers through the K'una of today—where deer wander peacefully through salal, and among fallen beams—and the K'una of 150 years ago, when 700 people lived here under the leader Gida'nsta (pronounced Skedans by early white traders). His house, its imprint still visible, was called "clouds sound against it as they pass over," the "biggest house on the Moresby side." Still standing: his pole marked with 13 rings, one for each of the potlatches he gave. Says Wesley: "I've stood out here in howling southeast gales, watching it sway." No one else has lived here since 1893. Logger, fisherman, environmentalist, Charley Wesley was there in 1985 when the Haida made their stand to save Gwaii Haanas from the chainsaw. A scale model of this village is on display at the Royal British Columbia Museum in Victoria (see chapter 1).

◎   **Hlkenul (Cumshewa):** Day-trip by boat from Moresby Camp. There may be no Watchman on duty, but this is often a stop for tours en route to K'una. Go'mshewah was the chief here: "Rich at the mouth of the river," for the wealth of fish, seals, and whales drawn to river mouths. Near fallen house posts sprouting new trees are rows of rocks that once bordered gardens. "The old people became very wealthy growing potatoes here," says Wesley, of one of the last villages to be abandoned.

◎   **T'anuu:** On the east shore of Tanu Island, named for the sea grass harvested near the village. Among collapsed house posts and memorial poles covered with soft green moss are signs of the missionaries—tombstones carved with hands in prayer.

◎   **Gandla K'in:** "Hot water island" was not a village site, but the healing and spiritual qualities of the natural pools have always made it sacred to the Haida. It is now one of the busiest sites for the Watchmen.

◎   **Hlk'waah (Windy Bay):** Old-growth forest here was the focus of a battle to protect Gwaii Hanaas Heritage Site from logging. To honour this, a longhouse-style cabin has been erected for the Watchmen. Elders point out where their ancestors cut holes into cedar trees selected for canoes and poles. The plagues that swept the population put an end to many carvers' plans.

◎   **Sgan Gwaii (Ninstints):** For many, this is the most evocative of the old villages. "Red Cod Island," site of Red Cod Island Village, was headquarters for the Kunghit Haida, "people to the south." Europeans called it Ninstints, after the chief, "he who is equal to two." He named his house "thunder rolls upon it," and gained prestige through the fur trade. His village in its sheltered bay was well protected from enemies by the ceaseless winds outside, but it was one of the first to be ravaged by smallpox. There are no traceable descendants of the Kunghit people, though they are remembered in the ancient poles, beams, and posts from 20 big houses, sinking slowly into the forest. They are also remembered in the designation of their ancestral home as a World Heritage Site—"of importance to the history of mankind."

Hidden in Gwaii Haanas (South Moresby) is the site where the great ancestress, Foam Woman, gave birth to all the women, the original clan mothers.

From Skidegate North on Highway 16

From Skidegate, Hwy 16 leads north to Old Massett. Before cutting inland, it traces shores facing Hecate Strait. Green, open slopes, and dark soil speckled by white shells tell where villages and campsites stood. Twelve km north of Skidegate, at Dead Tree Point, there were two villages—Raven and Eagle. On Halibut Bight, Skaigha was a seasonal fishing site. The village Dahua was at Lawn Hill, and on the reef offshore, the resting place of the chief Qoona'tik, a man of such proportions he carried the name "he-who-touches-the-sky-with-his-head-as-he-moves-about." An alternate route to Port Clements, via logging roads from Queen Charlotte City to Juskatla, provides visitors an opportunity to witness the thousands of square hectares of clearcut that grieves many Haida.

▌ Tlell: 36 km beyond Skidegate. "Place of big surf," or "land of berries," is at the rich estuary of the Tlell River. Access to the south end of Naikoon Provincial Park (see below).

▌ Yakoun River: 21 km north of Tlell, Hwy 16 cuts inland to **Port Clements** on the shores of Masset Inlet, a vast inland sea in the heart of Graham Island. Logging roads lead south from here, crossing the Yakoun, "in the middle," or "straight point." This is Haida Gwaii's longest river, flowing into the inlet. Mid-May, sockeye return here to spawn, and Haida from these islands, Prince Rupert, the Lower Mainland, and Alaska gather along the riverbanks to set their nets. Logging in the watershed threatens the five species of salmon that depend on this river, as do "on-and-off" plans to open a gold mine in the midst of what is said to be one of North America's largest deposits of mercury—a highly toxic substance.

East from Port Clements on Logging Roads

▌ Haida Canoe: About 14 km south of Port Clements via Juskatla Rd. A boardwalk and trail lead to dissolving remains of a cedar canoe left unfinished more than a century ago —one of many jobs interrupted by smallpox. The canoe's bow points to the stump of the tree from which it came. The practice was to shape the canoe on site, and tow it back to the village for completion. The largest Haida canoes were 23 m long, and had room for 40 people. The Haida Forestry Branch has located hundreds of culturally modified trees, including those used for canoes: many are in locations the B.C. Ministry of Forests has recently approved for logging.

▌ Marie Lake Salmon Hatchery: 40 km south of Port Clements on Juskatla Rd. Operated by Old Massett community; 626-5655. Marie Lake feeds Gold Creek, a tributary of the Yakoun River.

North from Port Clements on Highway 16

▌ Naikoon Provincial Park: Nai-kun, "point town," sits on the extraordinary nose of sand and gravel jutting out 12 km from the northeast tip of Graham Island, and even beyond, beneath the sea. This is where Hecate Strait meets Dixon Entrance, the ocean spumes, and tides boil. Upwelling currents bring plankton, fish, birds. This is where Raven, after the flood, "called petulantly to the empty sky and to his delight he heard an answering cry"—coming from a clamshell. Such is the story retold in what is now the centrepiece carving at Vancouver's UBC Museum of Anthropology. Raven cajoled its occupants—fearful, featherless first men—to join him in his lonely world.

While the spit helps place "point town" in our imaginations, Tow Hill, west along the coast, offers a focus for Tlielang, the largest town within these park boundaries. This 109-m basalt cliff was its fortress. Tow, "place of food," was once a glutton; he ate everything in sight, including the children of Tlielang. The nearby "blowhole," where the sea exhales through the rocks, is the whale Tow sent to swallow Hopi, the lone villager who finally defeated him. After a series of retaliatory raids between people here and from the mainland, Tlielang was abandoned—about 1860.

Along the park's southeast fringes, at Cape Ball, researchers have discovered plant remains 16,000 years old, fuelling speculation Haida Gwaii was a "refugium" during the last ice age, 12,000 years ago.

En route to Old Massett, the Delkatla Wildlife Sanctuary is a stopover for migratory birds on the Pacific flyway. This area has the second-largest concentration of waterfowl along the B.C. coast, second only to the Fraser Delta.

V Old Massett: (Pop. 2,000/650). On the eastern shore of Masset Inlet into Dixon Entrance. The people of Old Massett tell us this is where the west coast's first pole was carved. Their history records this event as coinciding with a great flood that covered the entire island, except the western mountains of Duu Guusd Tribal Park.

The present community is situated on three older villages. Atewaas or White Slope Town recalls the mounds of white clam shells deposited by wind and tide. Kayang and Jaaguhl have become part of the long rows of homes that all face south overlooking Masset Inlet.

Massett takes its name proudly as a gift from the captain of a European ship, possibly Spanish, damaged in a storm. The three villages that were here provided timbers and provisions to enable the ship to return safely home.

In 1852, Old Massett's Weah and Stastas clan leader, Albert Edward Idenso (Edenshaw), arrested a sailing ship, the *Susan Sturgess*. Her passengers, would-be gold miners, were later released to the Hudson's Bay Company.

Old Massett today is the administrative seat of the Council of the Haida Nation.

There are six poles here, all raised in the past 20 years. A longhouse community building is next to **Haida Arts and Jewelry**, overlooking the ball field. Wooden sculptures can be seen taking form in the workshop of local

artist Jim Hart. Morris White and his sons also carve poles and canoes in their large shed, along the main highway. The award-winning **Chief Matthews School** opened in 1995, with its concrete frescoes of Haida creatures delighting pupils.

Across from Old Massett is the village site of Yan. No one lives there, but a new longhouse and pole placed on the shore signal the continuity of Haida proprietorship.

? Old Massett Village Council: Box 189, Masset, Haida Gwaii, V0T 1M0. Tel: 626-3337. In the large hall on Eagle Rd. permits and information about local attractions and artists are available.

To the West Coast/Duu Guusd Tribal Park

Just over a century ago, villages stretched west along the coast from Old Massett. Today, **Duu Guusd Tribal Park** embraces the northwest coast of Graham Island from Naden Harbour to Kiusta, reaching south as far as Seal Inlet. This spectacular landscape is the site of two villages still home for many Old Massett Haida. There is currently only limited access, though the park may soon be open to visitors by special permit. Kiusta, "where the trail comes out" from Lepas Bay, is currently base for the Haida Gwaii **Rediscovery Society**. Its highly successful program, underway for nearly two decades, is being emulated by other First Nations communities. The society offers children from all communities and cultures an opportunity to participate in 10- to 14-day summer camps, where elders teach history, music and ceremony, food gathering and survival skills. For information: Haida Gwaii Rediscovery Society, Box 684, Old Massett, Haida Gwaii, V0T 1M0.

On the southern shores of Kiis Gwaii, or Langara Island, Dadens is the historical seat for the Shark House of the Yahgulanaas Clan. The strong tidal waters of Parry Passage separate Dadens from the villages of Kiusta and Yaku. This relatively sheltered area was the centre of sea-otter trading nearly two centuries ago, and bustles today with the activities of sports-fishing lodges and the comings and goings of the Haida Gwaii Rediscovery Society.

Here, in front of Dadens, 200 fishing boats recently joined with the Council of the Haida Nation in opposition to the lodges. "This fish-for-fun industry," says Michael Nicholl Yahgulanaas, "remains isolated from the communities that are suffering the decline of a once populous fishery."

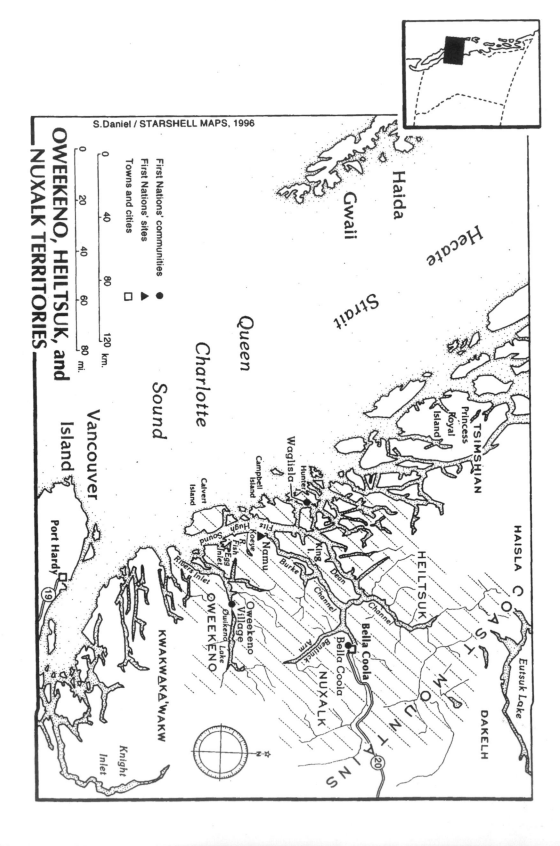

OWEEKENO, HEILTSUK, and
NUXALK TERRITORIES

S.Daniel / STARSHELL MAPS, 1996

First Nations' communities ●
First Nations' sites ▲
Towns and cities □

0   20   40   60   80 mi.
0   40   80   120 km.

Haida
Gwaii

Hecate

Strait

Queen

Charlotte

Sound

Vancouver
Island

Port Hardy 19

KWAKWAKA'WAKW

Knight
Inlet

TSIMSHIAN

Princess
Royal
Island

HAISLA

Eutsuk Lake

DAKELH

HEILTSUK

Bella Coola

NUXALK

20

COAST MOUNTAINS

Waglisla

Hunter
I.

Campbell
Island

Calvert
Island

King
I.

Burke
Channel

Dean
Channel

Bentinck
Arm

Namu

Fish
Egg
Inlet

Rivers Inlet

Hugh
Sound

Koeye
R.

Fitz
Hugh
Sound

OWEEKENO

Owikeno Lake

Oweekeno
Village

CHAPTER 20

Oweekeno, Nuxalk, and Heiltsuk

*I live beside the church and a longhouse. One day I was
watching the vehicles going left and right, and I said,
there's a job for me. One year I escorted 2,600 people
around our village.*

—*Darren Edgar, "goodwill ambassador," Bella Coola*

*We don't get any visitors here. Once every four years or
so someone comes here from one of the fishing resorts.*

—*Margaret Hanuse, Oweekeno Nation*

Between the north tip of Vancouver Island and the south tip of Haida Gwaii is the only gap where the full force of the Pacific Ocean might meet mainland B.C. But even here, as though by design, an almost unbroken chain of small islands forms a remarkable breakwater, protecting the entranceways to the long inlets of three separate peoples: the Oweekeno, Nuxalk, and Heiltsuk. Between this island chain and the mainland is a narrow but very navigable channel—the Inside Passage—offering safe passage for travellers today, as it has for thousands of years.

Just six generations ago, this broken coastline was the dynamic universe of dozens of permanent villages inhabited by the Oweekeno, Nuxalk, and Heiltsuk peoples. The fur trade, smallpox, salmon canneries, the logging industry, and the system of reserves that have swept into other shores have found their way here too. Those many villages have coalesced into just three, not always noted on maps, and creating for outsiders the illusion of a remote land with little history.

HIGHLIGHTS AND EVENTS
⑥ Tours, Nuxalk "Goodwill Ambassador" p. 211
⑥ Heiltsuk Cultural Education Centre p. 211

INFORMATION AND PROTOCOL

Only one road reaches into this region. Hwy 20 links Williams Lake in the interior to the Nuxalk centre of Bella Coola, at the head of Bentinck Arm. See chapter 14 if you plan to follow this route through Tsilhqot'in territories.

The language spoken by the Oweekeno is called Oowekayla, quite distinctive from the languages of its neighbours, though it is part of the Wakashan language family shared by the Heiltsuk and Kwakwaka'wakw neighbours to the south. The Nuxalk people, situated between the Heiltsuk and Oweekeno, speak a Coast Salish language.

▼ Oweekeno Nation: (Pop. 207/60). Oweekeno Village is 120 km northeast of Port Hardy, with access only by float plane or private boat. Oweekeno territories embrace the vast Owikeno Lake, Rivers Inlet, and Drainey Inlet, west into Fitz Hugh Sound. This has been their home since time began, and archaeologists have proven 9,000 years of continuous occupation in the area. Before Europeans arrived, the permanent villages of as many as 6,000 people stretched along the shores of the Owikeno watershed and Rivers Inlet. There were also winter camps at Fish Egg Inlet, Koeye, and on Calvert Island.

Among their ancestors were Kwa'giaxtu, "sitting on the fish weir," and Eagle, who was married to the youngest daughter of Wa'nux (Wannock), "owner of the river." They flourished on the salmon that by the 1880s drew the first of some 14 canneries to these inlet shores. The canneries' arrival, "without the prior knowledge or consent of the Oweekeno people," coincided with the establishment of three reserves. The largest, Katit Indian Reserve #1, was laid out on the north bank of the Wannock River next to land already pre-empted for the Rivers Inlet Cannery. Not long afterwards, the Oweekeno people who survived the ravages of smallpox—90 percent died between 1830 and 1862—left their villages to amalgamate here under one leader. They became, incidentally, a convenient workforce for the new cannery. More changes followed. Even on this remote coast, potlatches were banned and children were sent to residential schools.

The canneries are gone now, but the Oweekeno people remain at Katit (Oweekeno Village), slowly reclaiming their cultural heritage. The nearest store is 42 km away at Dawson's Landing: groceries arrive by barge, float plane, or with the once-a-week mail delivery. There are no tourist services at this time.

❓ Oweekeno Nation: Oweekeno Village, Rivers Inlet, c/o Bag 3500, Port Hardy, B.C., V0N 2P0. Tel: 949-2107. Fax: 949-2112.

▼ Nuxalk (Bella Coola): (Pop. 1,128/700). At the head of North Bentinck Arm of Burke Channel; 456 km west of Williams Lake via Hwy 20. At the beginning of time, the ocean lay to the east of Bella Coola, the land to the west. Drownings were frequent, so Raven turned them around. This has always been a busy place of interactions between sea, land, and people. Several dozen villages in recent centuries lined this H-shaped network of inlets right from the mountain rivers that feed them all the way to the sea.

Nuxalkimx is the name that referred specifically to the people of the rivers and creeks in the Bella Coola Valley. Nuxalk is now applied to the entire territory, and to the Coast Salish language spoken here. That their language was unintelligible to the Heiltsuk and Oweekeno peoples who live on either side did not prove to be a barrier to exchange or participation in one another's winter ceremonies. Likewise, neither language differences nor the Coast Mountain range presented a barrier to the Nuxalks' friendship with Athapaskan speakers to the east. Eulachon grease trails— well-worn trade routes—led through rainforests, and up and down steep passes to the open country, lakes, and plateaus of the Dakelh peoples. Seasons, lifetimes, generations were spent in one another's villages (see chapter 14, "Ulkatcho").

In 1793, the British fur-trade explorer Alexander Mackenzie, seeking the Pacific, was escorted here from the Fraser River. This first European across North America by land was, to the people here, just another of many visiting spirits. In order to prevent this one, whom they believed to be returned from the dead, from causing their salmon to disappear, they routed him around their fish traps as they escorted him to his destination.

Seven weeks after Mackenzie's short visit here, in which he inscribed his name in rock (a kind of pictograph to mark his accomplishment), another ghostlike visitor appeared. This one was Captain George Vancouver, travelling by sea, seeking land.

Nowadays, "goodwill ambassador" Darren Edgar is often on hand to greet visitors as they enter the village. His introduction to the Nuxalk people includes a walk through the village, a chance to meet local artists, and a stop by the Nuxalk Nation School—Acwsalcta, "the place of learning"—to meet staff, students, and elders carving in the workroom. Darren may also help arrange transportation to petroglyphs at nearby Thorsen Creek. Donations for his time are welcome.

⑤ **Sir Alexander Mackenzie Park:** 60 km west of Bella Coola on Dean Channel is the rock where the first European to cross North America by land wrote his name in grease and vermilion on a rock. Ask Darren Edgar or at band office about boat transportation.

☏ **Nuxalk Administration:** Box 65, Bella Coola, B.C., V0T 1C0. Tel: 799-5613.

V Heiltsuk (Bella Bella): (Pop. 1,823/ 1,190). On the east coast of Campbell Island. Reached from Port Hardy on Vancouver Island by B.C. Ferries' *Queen of the North* and two coastal airlines. The village of Waglisla here is the contemporary headquarters for six Heiltsuk tribes. These are the Wuyalitxv, Yisdaitxy, Wuithitxw, Quaquayaitxv, Xixis, and Kviatxv peoples, whose traditional territories stretch from Milbanke Sound in the north to Fitz Hugh Sound in the south, including Calvert Island, and reaching inland as far as the head of Dean Channel.

Their history here stretches back at least 10 millennia. Namu, a former Heiltsuk village south of Waglisla, has been declared the oldest archaeological site on this stretch of coast.

This part of the Inside Passage has long been the focus of intensive maritime trade and cultural exchanges. To take advantage of this, in 1833 the Hudson's Bay Company selected a small harbour about 3 km south of today's Waglisla for Fort McLoughlin, serving the entire northwest coast. Although the fort closed in 1843, the six tribes gradually coalesced there, served by a Hudson's Bay Company store and a Methodist mission. After the turn of the century, the Heiltsuk people moved their centre to its present location.

A century later, in the summer of 1993, they hosted what can be fairly said to be the greatest gathering ever on this coast—over 3,000 people from 30 First Nations transcending Canadian and U.S. boundaries, speaking as many languages and dialects as might be encountered in Europe. More than 1,300 participants arrived in ocean-going cedar canoes; some paddled hundreds of kilometres to get here. The event, *Qatuwas*, "people gathered together in one place," was a celebration of indigenous maritime nations. It served its purpose, as communities up and down the coast continue to reverberate with renewed cultural energy.

Since then, more non-First Nations travellers have begun to seek the beauty and spirit of these territories. The Heiltsuk people are carefully balancing their age-old tradition of welcoming respectful visitors with the need to protect their lands and resources, and the peaceful life they have chosen. For more information about Heiltsuk charter operators, visitor permits, and the **Heiltsuk Cultural Education Centre**, contact the Heiltsuk band administration office.

☏ **Heiltsuk Administration:** Box 880, Waglisla, B.C., V0T 1Z0. Tel: 957-2381.

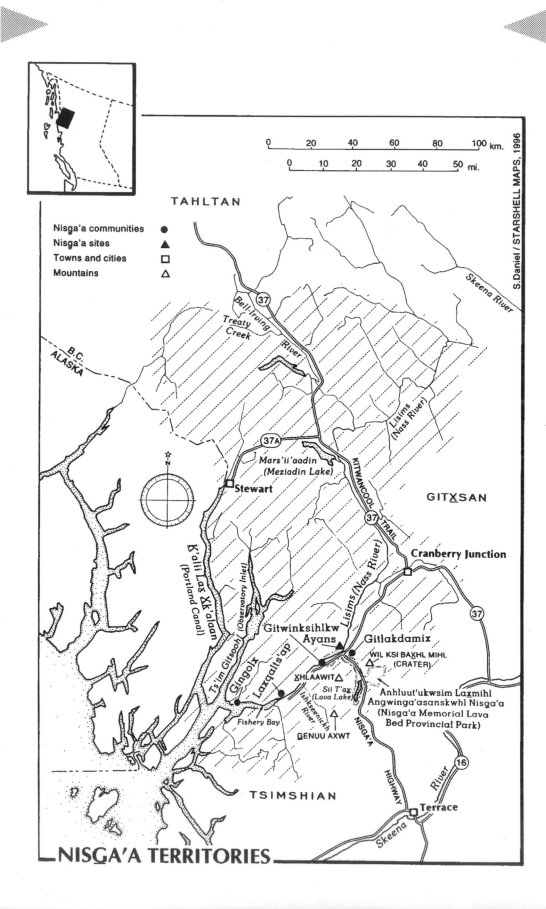

TAHLTAN

Nisg̱a'a communities ●
Nisg̱a'a sites ▲
Towns and cities □
Mountains △

Skeena River

Bell-Irving River

Treaty Creek

37

B.C.
ALASKA

37A

Mars'ii'aadin
(Meziadin Lake)

Lisims
(Nass River)

GIT X SAN

Stewart

KITWANCOOL TRAIL

K'alii Las X k'alaan
(Portland Canal)

Cranberry Junction

37

Lisims (Nass River)

Ts'im Gitsoohl (Observatory Inlet)

Gitwinksihlkw
Ayans

Gitlakdamix

WIL KSI BA X HL MIHL
(CRATER)

Gingolx

Laxqalts'ap

X HLAAWIT △

Sii T'ax
(Lava Lake)

Anhluut'ukwsim La x mihl
Angwinga'asanskwhl Nisg̱a'a
(Nisg̱a'a Memorial Lava
Bed Provincial Park)

Fishery Bay

Ishkeenickh
River

GENUU AXWT

NISGA'A

HIGHWAY

16

TSIMSHIAN

Skeena River

Terrace

NISG̱A'A TERRITORIES

CHAPTER 21

Nisga'a

What we seek is simple and straightforward. We want to negotiate our way into the economy—not take it over. We will not take away title to anyone's home. We simply want to share in the ownership of the forests, fish, and minerals of the Nass River valley, the place where our ancestors have lived for thousands of years.
—Joseph Gosnell Sr., Nisga'a Tribal Council

The Nisga'a are the people of Lisims, the river we call the Nass. In the spring, they call it Ayns Lisims, "the river of milk," its whiteness said to be the milt of eulachon mixing with pure glacial melt in the narrow canyon rapids. Four contemporary Nisga'a communities sit by Lisims, as their ancient villages always have. And still today, though many visitors come to share their wealth of resources, there are few people along all the river's 380-kilometre length, or even within their 24,862-square-kilometre traditional territories, who are not Nisga'a.

Gwinsk'eexkwm, the "village in darkness," was the first and only community on the river of milk until the supernatural man, Txamsem, brought the life-giving sun. But even as more villages flourished here, there were periods of hunger in late spring, while the Nisga'a waited for the first eulachon and salmon to arrive. So it was that Txamsem, in his canoe, descended to the underwater realm of the Eulachon People, and tricked the rich oily fish into coming sooner—in March, even as the Nass was still

cracking with ice. The Nisga'a called these tiny fish "saviours," and honoured them as chiefs. The presence of eulachon was the presence of people. The Nisga'a of the upper Nass were known to those below as Kitanwiliks, "people staying temporarily," referring to their migration downriver at fishing time. Haida, Tlingit, Gitxsan, and Tsimshian peoples crossed dangerous straits, or trekked great distances overland to reach Fishery Bay, just below Laxqalts'ap, "dwelling place comprised of other dwelling places"—"the heart of the people." At the river's wide mouth, year after year, they were welcomed by the Nisga'a. Each had their own village site where they netted the silvery fish, then stirred and skimmed vast cauldrons of strong-tasting oil.

The Nisga'a live by the principle of *Ts'a-k'hl Nisga'a*, the "common bowl." It is superseded only by laws which hold them—"the real people"—stewards of their territories. Their history, the land itself, holds stark reminders of times when they forgot this. There have been famines, and floods—the mountain,

Fishery Bay, on the Nass River, 1903 or before. At the end of winter, Haida, Tlingit, Gitxsan, and Tsimshian people travelled great distances to share the eulachon harvest.
CREDIT: RBCM 4279

Xlaawit, is where people once took refuge. Standing below Gitłakdamix, it is still possible to feel the heat blowing across the barren expanse where two centuries ago the crater Wil Ksi Baxl Mihl spewed a 23-kilometre swathe of lava. Two villages were incinerated, and the molten executioner pursued those who tried to cross the Nass in their canoes. This was a lesson to fit the times, when children amused themselves by sticking smouldering bits of birch bark into the backs of humpback salmon.

Nisga'a stewardship did not suddenly stop in 1775 when Spain's Juan Francisco de Bodega Y Quadra appeared, perhaps coincidentally with the eruption of Wil Ksi Baxl Mihl. Nor in 1793 when the British Captain, Vancouver, sailed into Ts'im Gitsoohl asking for directions. The Nisga'a people's responsibility to the land, combined with a willingness to share and trade resources and insights, continued to direct their new relationships with Hudson's Bay Company fur traders and missionaries.

But, just as Chief Sgat'inn said "Sayeen! Sayeen! Get out of my land" to white surveyors in 1886, the Nisga'a message to those who attempt to take their land and resources is no. It resounds through this century, in the formation of the First Nisga'a Land Committee in 1908; in the 1913 Nisga'a Petition, in the 1949 election of Nisga'a chief Frank Calder to the provincial legislature.

In 1973, the Nisga'a took the question of title—"never surrendered by treaty, or otherwise extinguished"—to the Supreme Court of Canada. Of the seven judges, three ruled firmly in support of the Nisga'a's "long-time occupation, possession and use" of these territories; three ruled all such rights have been extinguished by a century of colonial law. The seventh ruled against the Nisga'a on a technicality. For the Nisga'a and peoples across Canada, however, the outcome was hailed a landmark. Aboriginal rights and title at long last held some standing in Canadian courts. The time was nigh for governments, federal and provincial, to meet their own obligations as stewards, to work with First Nations, to clearly define their rights to land and resources.

In 1976, the Nisga'a became the first in B.C. to sit down at the negotiating table, honouring the principle of "the common bowl." Two decades later, the federal and provincial government, and a generation of Nisga'a men and women "grown old at the negotiating table," are on the verge of an historic settlement. When their agreement-in-principle—signed in February 1996—is finalized, B.C. will have negotiated its first major treaty in 140 years. The Nisga'a hope to gain control of 1,930 square kilometres of land and a greater share of the Nass River's salmon resource. They have plans for their own government, police force, and courts. "We are ready, and willing," says Harry Nyce Jr., to step into the next millennium. In native and non-native communities throughout B.C., all eyes are on the Nisga'a.

HIGHLIGHTS AND EVENTS

⑥ Nisga'a Lava Bed Memorial Park   p. 216

INFORMATION AND PROTOCOL

Nisga'a territories are comprised of 60 House Territories, *ango'osk,* precisely defined by streams, rivers, markers. Traditionally, each was controlled by an extended family represented by a hereditary *sim'oogit.* Early this century, the *sim'oogit* agreed all land would be held in common. The principle of "the common bowl" was extended to the whole ter-

ritory. Today, the Nisga'a Tribal Council is recording, on computer, their *Ayuukhl Nisga'a,* ancient laws and customs, all grounded in compassion. Their language, Nisga'a, is an accredited second language at B.C. universities and colleges. School District 92, the first in the province to be administered by a First Nation, sustains Nisga'a language and culture.

The Nisga'a population within these territories is 2,500; outside (in Terrace, Prince Rupert, Vancouver, and urban areas around the world) it is 3,500.

The Nisga'a Hwy from Terrace is paved as far as Lava Lake, then good gravel; it passes through Nisga'a Memorial Park to the heart of Nisga'a territories. Entry is also possible by good gravel road from Cranberry Junction on Hwy 37, 73 km north of Hwy 16. Gitlakdamix (Sii Ayans/New Aiyansh) has a gas station and food services. Laxqalts'ap has a gas station and bed-and-breakfast accommodation. There is also camping in the park.

Questions may be directed to tribal council and community administration offices, and group tours and talks can be arranged. The Nisga'a are planning a cultural centre. "We would like to send a message that people are welcome. We would like to speak with people, explain our world, through our eyes," says Harry Nyce Jr.

? Nisga'a Tribal Council: General Delivery, New Aiyansh, B.C., V0J 1A0. Tel: 633-2234. Fax: 633-2367.

? Nisga'a Public Education Working Group: 712 Yates St., Fifth Floor, Victoria, B.C., V8V 1X5.

Enter Nisga'a Territories via the Nisga'a Highway north from Terrace

Three km west of Terrace, the Nisga'a Hwy (Hwy 152) leads north from Hwy 16, tracing the Tsimshians' Kitsumkalum River. Ninety-two km beyond Hwy 16, Sii T'axl, "lava lake," marks entry into the Nass watershed, Nisga'a territories.

I   **Anhluut'ukwsim Laxmahl Angwinga'a-sanskwhl Nisga'a—"Nisga'a Lava Bed Memorial Provincial Park":** Entrance at south end of Lava Lake. The Nisga'a Hwy transects the first park jointly managed by a First Nation and B.C. government, designated in 1992. It protects a fragile ecosystem and honours the memory of two villages and as many as 2,000 people buried by lava when the volcano Wil Ksi Baxl Mihl erupted two centuries ago. Some people fled up the mountain, Genuu Axwt (Oscar Peak). Those trying to cross the Nass perished, and the river itself was pushed off course. The destruction only ceased when the giant Gwa Xts'agat appeared: for days he fought back the lava flow with his nose. Today, just below the village of Gitlakdamix, where there would be forest, is a crisp black plain stretching 10 km along the Tseax and Nass rivers, like the end, or beginning, of the world. Here and there are thin patches of forgiving soil delivered by streams, where new life clings. It is possible that the Spanish explorer Juan Francisco de Bodega Y Quadra, sailing up the coast in 1775, witnessed the eruption. The park has camping and picnic areas; an 8-km trail leads to the crater—the volcano's fury destroyed the original cone and created a new one.

J   **Road to villages:** 94 km beyond Hwy 16, at the Nass River, the road forks: it is 2 km northeast to Gitlakdamix, service centre for the park; southwest to Gitwinksihlkw, Laxqalts'ap, and Gingolx.

Tracing the Nass Seaward

Below Gitlakdamix, the Nass widens and slows after its descent through the Coast Mountains.

I   **Dedication Site:** 8 km from the Gitlakdamix turnoff, within the park. Amid wind-blown barrens, a plaque commemorates the lost villages, Lax Wii Laxx Abit and Lax Ksiluux.

V   **Gitwinksihlkw (Canyon City):** (Pop. 380/220). 9 km from New Aiyansh turnoff to new bridge. Drive across, or park on the south bank and walk across the old foot bridge suspended 15 m over the rippling Nass. It offers stunning views: the milky river's canyons to the north; to the south, volcanic plains, the open river, and one of three Nass fish wheels counting salmon. From 1969 to late 1995 this was *the* way across. Before that, each family took its own boat or crossed by ice bridge. The river was fuller, more navigable in those days. The Gitwinksihlkw built gill-net fishing boats here; picked up their groceries and supplies down at Prince Rupert. Now they drive to Terrace.

Their name, "people of the place of lizards," reaches even farther back along the story of changes here. In traditional times, explains Harry Nyce Jr., the Nass flowed not along the north side of the valley as now, but to the south. That's where his ancestors lived. "Here, there was a creek where our people came to fish. The area was inhabited by lizards. They were about three feet long, with human-like hair growing on their backs." The eruption of Wil Ksi Baxl Mihl moved the Nass, buried and shifted villages. And "those lizards left, became extinct."

The Gitwinksihlkw's search for a new village site spanned a century. Their original few families shifted from floodplain to floodplain, finally settled here, and grew. The Ts'ohl Ts'ap Memorial Centre, built in 1992, is named for one of the villages where they lived after the eruption. It honours those "who gave their today for our tomorrow"— seven brothers of the Wolf clan, the grandfathers of today's Gitwinksihlkw. The pole in front of the centre was the first raised in more than a century. In 1995 it was joined by four new poles—celebrating their new bridge across the Nass.

On the suspension bridge to Gitwinksihlkw. Until 1995, this was the community's link to the rest of the world.

❓ Gitwinksihlkw Administration: Box 400, Gitwinksihlkw, B.C., V0J 3T0. Tel: 633-2294.

🔻 Laxqalts'ap (Greenville): (1,350/600). 44 km south of the Gitlakdamix (New Aiyansh) turnoff. Accessible by road since 1984, "dwelling place comprised of other dwelling places" sits just above the tidal waters of Fishery Bay, the rich eulachon fishery that still draws the Nisga'a and their neighbours. In former times, as soon as the ice began to thaw, these shores were cheek-by-jowl with Nisga'a, Haida, Tsimshian, and Gitx̱san villages.

Opposite Laxqalts'ap, the Ishkheenickh River pours into the Nass. The people of Laxqalts'ap predict its pristine forests, glacial blue lakes, rivers full of steelhead, grizzlies, wild berries, grease trails, and camps will be the future draw for visitors here seeking recreation. They say this is also the habitat of certain *nax nox*, messengers between animals and people who bring good luck. A swamp at the foot of "serpent mountain" at the river mouth is said to be home of a supernatural serpent.

The people of Laxqalts'ap have long been known for their strength of conviction. Methodist missionary Alfred Green, who arrived in 1877, reported how many villagers resisted the temptations of traditional life by staying indoors "while messengers from a distant community announced their forthcoming winter ceremonies and departed." Meantime, others here, opposed to children being taught to reject traditional ways, "gathered at the school and beat drums to drown out the voice of the teacher." By the early 1880s, the people of Laxqalts'ap had earned a reputation down in Victoria as being "troublesome" and "saucy." Their letter to the Victoria *Colonist* in 1885 is testimony to a century of treaty demands. The descendants of those who signed it are still being heard today.

Contact the administration office for information on bed-and-breakfast accommodation, arts and crafts, and recreational opportunities.

? Laxqalts'ap Administration: General Delivery, Greenville, B.C., V0J 1X0. Tel: 621-3213.

V Gingolx (Kincolith): (1,550/300). 25 km south of Laxqalts'ap, by water. Access is by regular float plane and ferry service from Prince Rupert. A road that will change their village forever is under construction.

Gingolx, "place of skulls," is the first village on the way up the Nass. In times past the people here mounted skulls on sticks to scare away other nations who thought to steal their river. A century ago, the Tsimshian chief Legaic made his way here with a fleet of canoes from Fort Simpson. Aiming to take over the Ayns Lisims (Nass) and its rich resource of eulachon, he challenged Chief Kindzadux of the Gingolx to combat—a fierce battle of wealth. From his canoe, he struck the first blow, throwing his copper shield into the sea. Kindzadux retaliated from shore, launching his own copper into the depths. Copper after copper was released, and its name called out in song, until at last Kindzadux was forced to call upon all the Nisga'a to help him, for he was about to lose the Lisims. Legaic held sway. Kindzadux looked upon his very last copper. And then, from among the crowd on shore, a

young woman emerged, a Nisga'a married to a Tsimshian, who keenly observed what none other had. Legaic had a line attached to his copper; it was the same one going into the sea, over and over again. "With this defeat of Legaix [sic], he now gave up the fight and this was the last time any attempt was made to capture the [Lisims]."

All said and done, the people of Gingolx are known up the river and down the coast for their friendliness, and they encourage visitors. "March or April is a specially good time to visit," says Alvin Nelson, "when the eagles, sea lions, killer whales come to life after a long winter's sleep, to follow the eulachon." Today, the gleaming structure of the Anglican Christ Church, dedicated in 1900, serves as a landmark for arrivals. There's hotel accommodation; fishing for spring salmon, sockeye, and steelhead right off the dock. Nisga'a, European, and Chinese history can be found at the nearby cemetery.

? Kincolith Administration: General Delivery, Kincolith, B.C., V0V 1Y0. Tel: 624-3651.

Return to Gitlakdamix

V Gitlakdamix (New Aiyansh): (1,634/825). On the east side of the Nass, at the junction of the Nisga'a Hwy and the gravel road from Hwy 37. The people here lived just across the river in former times. Their important village sat at the junction of grease trails from the northeast and the south, and at the head of navigation for riverborne travellers. Just above, the Nass plunges through narrow Coast Mountain canyons.

The village and its people have been known by many names. Gitlakdamix, "the people of the ponds," describes a prominent physical feature of the place. In pre-contact times, they were also called Gitmidiik, "people of the grizzly bears," describing the community spirit. It is said that without seeming to do much work, when the time came to host a major function the people were prepared. The elders likened their behaviour to the great bears which were a familiar sight in the Nass Valley: unobtrusive, deliberate, consistent, and impressive when the time came for them to be visible.

One of the first missionaries to arrive here, J.B. McCullagh, created a new Anglican community about 10 km downriver. He called it Ayans, Nisga'a for "there's always spontaneous, natural growth." Although, says Shirley Morvin, born at Gitlakdamix, "he translated it Valley of Eternal Bloom." Gospel Road linked the new and old villages: converts went back and forth. "Winter was when traditional feasting started. McCullagh used this time to recruit Christians. There would be colourful marches, people preaching and persuading. It was very effective—it took him less than 40 years to yank the original culture out from under the Nisga'a."

In 1917, Ayans flooded: everyone moved back to Gitlakdamix, and it then became Ayans. The Nass flooded again in 1936, but did no serious damage. However, in 1961 there was another devastating flood—logging and a forest fire upriver left little to check the runoff of autumn rains. "It washed houses right off their lots." And so, finally, it was arranged the people of the ponds and grizzly bears would move across the Nass to New Aiyansh. "It sits on blue clay," says Shirley, "not much blooms here."

People still go back to the "old village." In summer, they cure salmon right by the river; harvest fruit and berries from gardens planted by their grandmothers.

And New Aiyansh—now called Gitlakdamix to honour its Nisga'a origins—is administrative headquarters for the Nisga'a Tribal Council. The Nisga'a Valley Health Board and school district are here, as well as the University of Northern British Columbia's satellite, Wilp Wilxo'oskwhl, "house of wisdom." Gitlakdamix is also service centre for Nisga'a Lava Bed Memorial Park, offering bed and breakfast, gas and groceries.

? Gitlakdamix Administration: Box 333, New Aiyansh, B.C., V0J 1A0. Tel: 633-2215.

J Road to Cranberry Junction: From Gitlakdamix, a forest service road traces a grease trail about 65 km east to join the Kitwancool Trail. Boxes of eulachon grease, copper, and obsidian were carried along this route to the Skeena River. Sheep, goat, and moose products were carried in. The Nass, unnavigable beyond here, is hidden from view by the forest.

J Kitwancool Trail (Hwy 37): From the Cranberry Junction the trail leads north through Gitanyow territories to Tahltan country. This was once the range of the Tsetsaut, "those of the interior," an Athapaskan-speaking people. By the 1900s, most of the few survivors were taken in by the Nisga'a.

B Treaty Creek: Roughly 70 km north of Meziadin Lake, this creek flows into the Bell-Irving River, marking the boundary between Nisga'a and Tahltan territories.

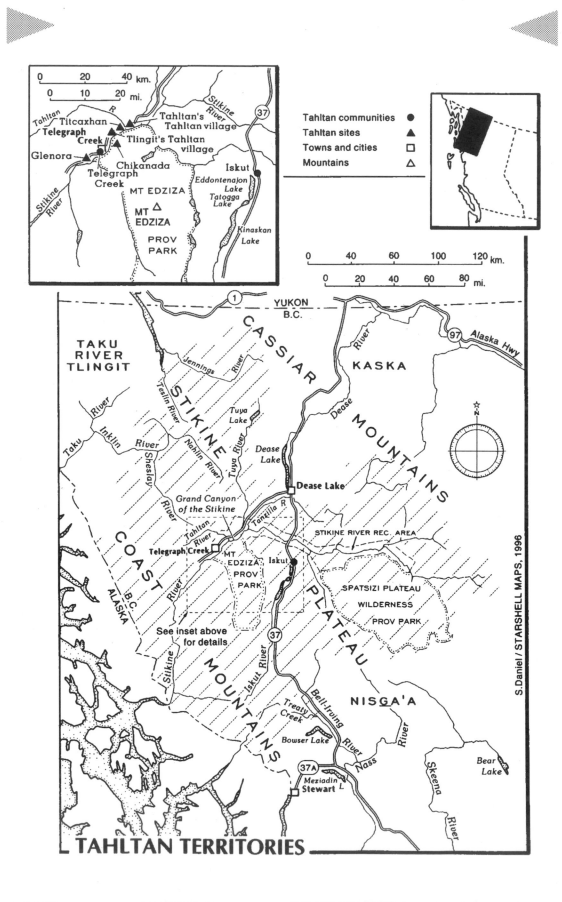

Legend:
- Tahltan communities ●
- Tahltan sites ▲
- Towns and cities □
- Mountains △

Inset map labels:

0 20 40 km.
0 10 20 mi.

Tahltan R
Titcaxhan
Telegraph Creek
Tahltan's Tahltan village
Tlingit's Tahltan village
Glenora
Chikanada
Telegraph Creek
Stikine River
37
Stikine River
MT EDZIZA
MT EDZIZA
PROV PARK
Iskut
Eddontenajon Lake
Tatogga Lake
Kinaskan Lake

Main map labels:

0 40 60 100 120 km.
0 20 40 60 80 mi.

1 YUKON B.C.
97 Alaska Hwy
TAKU RIVER TLINGIT
CASSIAR
KASKA
River
Jennings River
STIKINE
Teslin River
Taku
Inklin
River
Sheslay
River
Nahlin River
Tuya River
Tuya Lake
Dease River
Dease Lake
MOUNTAINS
Dease Lake
Grand Canyon of the Stikine
Tahltan River
Tanzilla R
STIKINE RIVER REC. AREA
Telegraph Creek
MT EDZIZA PROV PARK
Iskut
COAST
B.C.
ALASKA
Stikine River
PLATEAU
SPATSIZI PLATEAU WILDERNESS PROV PARK
37
MOUNTAINS
Iskut River
Treaty Creek
Bell-Iruing River
NISGA'A
Bowser Lake
Nass River
Skeena River
Bear Lake
37A
Meziadin L
Stewart

See inset above for details

S.Daniel / STARSHELL MAPS, 1996

TAHLTAN TERRITORIES

CHAPTER 22

Tahltan and Iskut

Non-native people have got to understand the history, the real history. It's a pretty dirty history in terms of this province's relationship with First Nations people. They've got to realize, maybe the history being taught in the schools isn't right.

—Curtis Ratry, Tahltan

The Tahltan are the people for whom the Stikine River is life's blood. They live at Telegraph Creek, just upriver from their ancestral homeland deep in the canyons, and at Dease Lake, business centre for the Tahltan people. A third community, at Iskut, often considered Tahltan by outsiders, consists of relative newcomers to these territories. Over the last two centuries, their journeys from the south and east have brought them also to the Stikine watershed.

The story of the name Tahltan has its origins where the Stikine canyons are steepest and narrowest. It begins with the flood, and two mountains here, Takitstsi'tla and Tse'toxtle—the only relief in a vast and watery expanse. When the waters receded, those who had found refuge journeyed on, some to the north, some to the sea, others here and there, to become the ancestors of many clans and peoples.

Time made a circle of things. One day, two sisters—one who had married into the Nassgottin clan to the south, and one into the Thlagoteena clan to the north—came face to face on opposite banks of the Tahltan River where it pours into the Stikine. Their first words to each other were in wonder of the salmon swarming up the river between them. And here together they founded Titcaxhan, "salmon ascending the creek."

Others from inland and the coast converged, so that soon there were many villages around Titcaxhan. These people were hunters. They trained small Tahltan bear dogs to drive caribou from the world's largest herds into corrals. And they were fish harvesters. The warm canyon breezes of Titcaxhan were ideal for drying salmon. They were appealing also to the Tlingit, who lived to the west, down the river beyond the Coast Mountains. Year after year, they paddled their heavy sea-going canoes up the "great river," Stikine, to make camp at "bowl-shaped" place—in their language, *Tahltan.*

Later, the Tlingit buffered their upper Stikine trading partners against direct contact with Europeans on the coast. It was not until

Old Tahltan village.
CREDIT: JOHN LUTZ

1874 that miners in pursuit of Cassiar gold swept through, bringing smallpox, a new economy based on trade and work for wages, and towns. The short-lived scheme to string a telegraph line from North America to Europe gave rise to Telegraph Creek. Glenora, just downriver, emerged as head of navigation for steamboats on the Stikine. Gold in the Klondike brought more miners in 1898, tracing an "all-Canadian route" via the Tahltan's ancient hunting-trading trail up to Teslin Lake.

Meanwhile, the Stikine villages under the powerful chief, Nanok, drew together and formed a new village 2 km downriver from old Titcaxhan. They named it Tahltan, and from their unity was born the "Declaration of the Tahltan Tribe," in 1910, countering crown claims upon their territories.

Since their move to Telegraph Creek a few

years later, the Tahltan have continued to be buffeted by development schemes. Construction of the Alaska Highway in 1942 brought employment. Its completion brought isolation until the Stewart-Cassiar Highway, in 1972, traced their old trails. Generally, says Curtis Ratry, more development by outsiders means more limitations for the Tahltan people. Commercial gill-netting fleets in what is now Alaska have already reduced fish stocks, as would hydroelectric projects proposed for the Stikine and Iskut rivers. A legislative squeeze on their own fisheries inevitably follows. Even wilderness parks and recreational corridors, making up about one-quarter of their territories, keep them from their traditional hunting and trapping activities.

The Tahltan people are not averse to mining or logging in their territories—as long as they can share the benefits and limit environmental costs. Says Ratry: "People say the Tahltans have never mined—they are too primitive. But we've been miners for a long long time. We mined obsidian [see below], which we traded as far north as the Yukon, as far south as Oregon, and east as far as Saskat-chewan."

"We would like to have defined, our rights to evolve and progress. If white people were limited the way we have been, they never would have put a man on the moon."

INFORMATION AND PROTOCOL

Tahltan territories were traditionally managed by the leaders of six clans who held informal council together. Today, the communities of Telegraph Creek and Iskut are served by elected chiefs and councils.

Tahltan, an Athapaskan language, is spoken here.

? **Tahltan Administration:** Box 46, Telegraph Creek, B.C., V0J 2W0. Tel: 235-3241.

North from Gitxsan Territories on Highway 37

This route over ancient grease trails leads through Gitanyow and Gitxsan territories (chapter 17). Thirty-two kilometres beyond Meziadin Lake, Hwy 37 crosses the first bridge over the Bell-Irving River, named for Henry Bell-Irving, president of the Anglo B.C. fish-canning corporation, who once said: "It is the destiny of the white man to be worked for by inferior races." About 40 km north of here, the Bell-Irving River is joined by Treaty Creek: Tahltan territories lie to the north; Nisga'a territories to the south.

V **Iskut:** (Pop. 500/300). 252 km beyond Meziadin Junction. A century of proximity has drawn the people of Iskut into political, cultural, and family alliances with the Tahltan

people. In the early to mid-1800s they were known as the Bear Lake nomads—Sekani and Gitxsan families that had come together at Fort Connelly on the northeastern frontier of Gitxsan territories. After the fort closed at the end of the century, they began trading at Telegraph Creek, and by the 1950s they had a village on the opposite bank of the Stikine. A decade later, the Iskut re-established themselves as trappers and traders in the vicinity of Eddontenajon Lake. Today, they are incorporating their old trapping and transportation trails into **Iskut Trail and River Adventures**. Raft trips launch from the Grand Canyon of the Stikine; trail rides lead to former settlements of Caribou Hide and Metsantan. Contact them at 1103-207 West Hastings St., Vancouver, B.C., V6B 1H7; 669-5175, or call 234-3406 in Iskut. Co-op store has food, hardware, gas.

? **Iskut Administration:** Box 30, Iskut, B.C., V0J 1K0. Tel: 234-3331.

I **Mt. Edziza:** 267 km from Meziadin Junction is a viewing area for this 2,787-m volcano. At its base is the obsidian motherlode that fuelled the original Tahltan mining industry. Formed about 1 million years ago, this glass-like substance used to make blades is so sharp today's surgeons use it for their most delicate operations. It was usually collected during late summer–early fall hunting expeditions, then traded: obsidian from here has travelled great distances, to sites estimated to be over 10,000 years old. That was about the time of the last great eruption, which covered much of northern B.C. with ash. On the mountain's north flank is a lava bed 80 km wide. A smaller eruption occurred 1,300 years ago.

I **Stikine River:** 284 km beyond Meziadin Junction, Hwy 37 crosses the "great river." A short distance downstream it pours into its Grand Canyon, and for 80 km surges between 304-m walls of sedimentary and volcanic earth. Most of the ancient Tahltan villages were located along these steep banks. Near where Telegraph Creek Rd. meets the Stikine, directly below its confluence with Tanzilla River, the canyon narrows to form a gap of less than 2 m, giving a fierce demonstration of the power of water. The Tahtlan travelled these parts overland. B.C. Hydro has proposed two dams, one 90 stories high, the other 85 stories, to create a reservoir covering 120 km. It would displace mountain goats, caribou, Tahltan traplines, and trappers. How this would affect the salmon of Titcaxhan is unclear.

▮ Spatsizi Plateau Wilderness Park: No road access. This 656,785-hectare wilderness east of Hwy 37 is traditional Tahltan hunting land. It is named "red goat," for the white mountain goats that rolled in iron oxide dust. The Tahltan people, like their Gitxsan neighbours, knew the consequences of mistreating goats (see chapter 17).

T Dease Lake: 345 km north of Meziadin Junction. From 1838 to 1841, Dease Lake was the site of a Hudson's Bay Company trading post which recorded an incident involving a high-status woman of the Thlagoteena clan referred to as the "Nahanni Chief" (a Kaska name for the Tahltan people). She is said to have defied the powerful Tlingit chief, Shakes, and saved the lives of trader-explorer Robert Campbell and his men. Dease Lake is a new business centre for the Tahltan Nation; the Tahltan Development Corporation is involved primarily in construction.

J Telegraph Creek Road: Cuts southwest from Dease Lake toward the heart of Tahltan country. It is 113 km to Telegraph Creek. This was an ancient foot trail, then a dog-sledge trail, horse trail, and wagon trail. "They put a little more gravel on it," says Ratry, and now it's a road—with roller-coaster moments.

Southwest from Dease Lake to Telegraph Creek

▮ Grand Canyon: About 80 km beyond Dease Lake, the road begins its dramatic descent, following the Tanzilla River into the canyon. There was a village on the north bank where the road crosses the Tuya River.

▮ The Tlingit's Tahltan Village: On the east side of the bridge across the Tahltan River. This is the "bowl-shaped" place where the Tlingit camped year after year, to dry fish and trade their eulachon and salmon oils for Tahltan fur and leather goods.

▮ Titcaxhan: On the west side of the bridge across the Tahltan River. This is the ancestral home of the Tahltan people, and headquarters for all clans—though it might have been two or three years between visits for some families.

V The Tahltan's Tahltan Village: On a high terrace, 2 km down the Stikine from the Tahltan River mouth. By 1875, with only 250 adult Tahltan survivors of the plagues— smallpox, the flu—their leader, Nanok, brought all the clans together here in a measure to preserve their culture. There was an Anglican mission here after 1897, but the people remained devoted to their own spiritual practices. In the early 1900s, after a forest fire, people began moving down to Telegraph Creek. Sports-fishing permits are available: ask at the Tahltan Band Council, Telegraph Creek. Camping is not permitted on the reserve.

▮ Chikanada: At the foot of the Grand Canyon, 12 km below Tahltan. This was an important fishing station and meeting place for the Nassgotin and Thelgtotin clans of the Tahltan people.

▼ Tahltan Community at Telegraph Creek: (Pop. 1,300/250). 113 km from Dease Lake the road enters this quiet community on a high terrace, then descends sharply to the riverbank setting of the only non-Tahltan community on the Stikine. Before the Alaska Highway swept inland traffic away, this was the debarkation point for adventures farther north. Telegraph Creek bustled with missionaries, government officials, First Nations, and Metis peoples. During the gold rushes, the Tlingit ran a lucrative canoe-freight service between here and Glenora, where the steamers stopped. The Hudson's Bay Company moved its store up from Glenora after 1900: this is now the **Stikine Riversong general store and cafe** with a lodge, showers.

? Tahltan Administration: Box 46, Telegraph Creek, B.C., V0J 2W0. Tel: 235-3241.

▮ Village of the Bear Lakers: On a low platform immediately across the Stikine from Telegraph Creek. The people who now live at Iskut had a settlement here from the mid-1950s to mid-1960s.

▮ Six Mile Forestry Campsite: On the Stikine River a few kilometres below Telegraph Creek. This public campsite is beside a Tahltan fishing site and smokehouse. Respect private property.

▮ Glenora: Road ends/begins about 19 km below Telegraph Creek. In the late 1800s, this site of former Tahltan and Tlingit fishing camps became the head of navigation for white traders and miners coming up from the coast. The Hudson's Bay Company opened a store here in 1874, altering old trade relationsips between Tlingit and Tahltan peoples. During the rush for Klondike gold, thousands of miners camped here, preparing for their tough trek north. But time makes a circle of things. Glenora is once again a Tahltan summer fish camp and gathering place, much like Titcaxhan in centuries past. Families come from all over, with their tents and trailers. They sit in lawn chairs around fires, keeping an eye on propane stoves cooking up jars full of salmon. There are also smokehouses on the riverbank, closer to their nets and cutting boards. The Stikine River runs swiftly by.

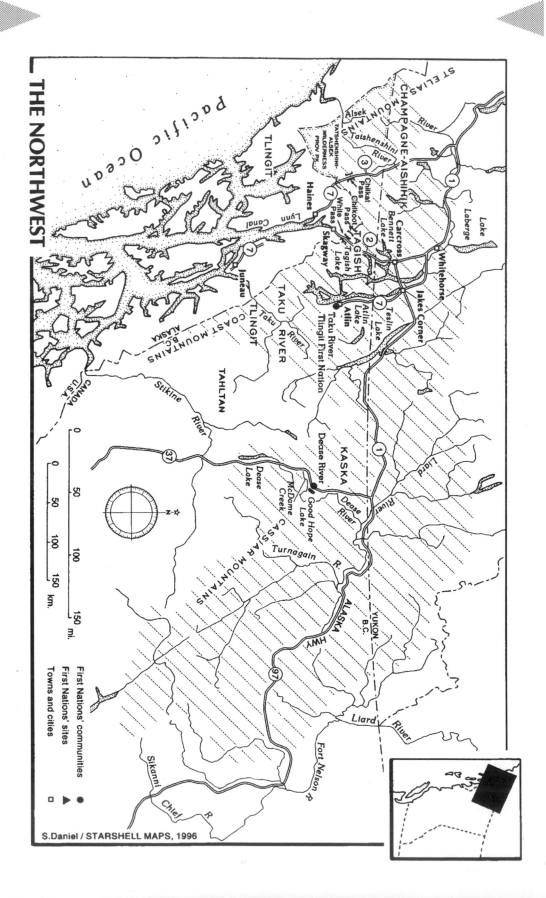

THE NORTHWEST

Pacific Ocean

ST ELIAS MOUNTAINS

CHAMPAGNE-AISHIHIK

Alsek River
Taishenshini River
Taishenshini
Alsek River

TATSHENSHINI-
ALSEK
WILDERNESS
PROV. PK.

TLINGIT

Haines
Lynn Canal
Skagway

Chilkat Pass
Chilkoot Pass
White Pass

TAGISH
Bennett Lake
Carcross

Tagish Lake

TAKU RIVER
Taku River
TLINGIT

Juneau

COAST MOUNTAINS
ALASKA
B.C.

Atlin Lake
Atlin
Taku River Tlingit First Nation

Teslin
Teslin Lake

Whitehorse
Jakes Corner

Lake Laberge

TAHLTAN

Stikine River

CANADA
U.S.A.

Dease River

KASKA

Liard River

Dease Lake
McDame Creek
Good Hope Lake
Dease River

CASSIAR MOUNTAINS
Turnagain R.

ALASKA HWY

YUKON
B.C.

Liard River

Fort Nelson R.

Sikanni Chief R.

First Nations' communities
First Nations' sites
Towns and cities

□ ▶ ●

0
50
100
150 km.

0
50
100
150 mi.

N

37

1

1

2

3

7

7

7

97

S.Daniel / STARSHELL MAPS, 1996

CHAPTER 23

The Northwest:
Kaska, Taku River Tlingit, Tagish, Champagne-Aishihik, and Tlingit

If only you were taken by boat along the Taku River,
you could write the whole story down in a book.
—*Elizabeth Nyman, in*
The Legacy of a Taku River Tlingit Clan

The double-edged boundary separating British Columbia, the Yukon Territory, and Alaska cuts awkwardly into the territories and histories of five peoples. The bottom quarters of four Yukon First Nations—and only two communities—lie on the south side of the 60th parallel. At their southernmost frontiers are the mountain passes that once bound them closely with the coastal Tlingit people.

Eastward, where the gentle forests of the Peace River give way to the sub-arctic, are the Kaska. Their home is the Liard River, its tributary, the Dease, and its tributaries. Kaska is their name for one of these, McDame Creek, which is now their southwest centre—the village here is Good Hope Lake. From Kaska comes our Cassiar, the name given to this once-booming fur-trading and mining region.

The southern territories of the Taku River Tlingit and Tagish peoples embrace the three vast lakes—Teslin, Atlin, and Tagish. These are the headwaters of the "great river," Yu-kun-ah or Yukon, which flows 3,185 kilometres to the

Bering Sea. Tagish is from *ta gizi*, "it [spring ice] is breaking up," referring to the lake, and the old village, northeast of Carcross. Most Tagish moved to Carcross around 1900, for the amenities, and there are no Tagish communities in what is now northern B.C. The Taku River Tlingit, like the Tagish, are Athapaskan peoples, although in relatively recent times they have adopted the language of their coastal Tlingit neighbours. Their homeland is plateaus, icefields, the Taku River, the 135-kilometre Atlin Lake, and 120-kilometre Teslin Lake. Most live at Atlin today.

Farther west, the southern territories of the Athapaskan Champagne-Aishihik peoples are the triangle of St. Elias Mountains—North America's highest peaks, reaching 3,000 to 4,000 metres to the sky. Their 350 glaciers form part of the largest non-polar ice cap on earth. Cutting through them, to the sea, are the Alsek and Tatshenshini rivers.

Only the boundaries of the Tlingit, "the people" of what is now called the Alaskan Panhandle, coincide with modern international

Champagne-Aishihik
woman cleaning salmon.
CREDIT: CATHIE ARCHBOULD

divisions. But even they, from the coast side of the St. Elias and Coast Mountain ranges, maintained close trade and family ties with their northern Athapaskan-speaking neighbours. Their highways were the mountain passes—Chilkat, Chilkoot, White—and the rivers—Alsek and Taku. Their "great river" to the south, the Stikine, bound them to the Tahltan people.

The peoples northeast of the mountains, especially, offer very similar accounts of how this world came to take its current shape. At the height of the flood, there was Crow, the Transformer—tired of flying. He persuaded Sea Woman (sometimes reported to be Sea Lion, or Beaver, Muskrat, or Otter) to dive beneath the seas and bring up a clump of mud, which he took and flattened. This became the world. Here, Game Mother, in her time, gave birth to all the game animals. Some

say she rocked them to sleep in a giant moose-hide hammock suspended from four mountain peaks near Teslin.

It was the small, thick-furred animals—beavers, minks, wolves—that became the focus of the European fur trade in the mid-1800s. Until this point, the Tlingit had kept the new market to themselves, trading their prized sea-otter furs to Russians sailing down the north coast. But, as the otters dwindled to near extinction, the Tlingit shifted their attention to resources farther inland. Barring the Russians from direct access to the interior, they intensified their own, ancient trading relationships with the peoples beyond the mountain passes—so much so that the Taku River and Tagish peoples became, fully, speakers of Tlingit. This is why they are referred to as Taku River Tlingit, or Inland Tlingit peoples.

Meanwhile, the British Hudson's Bay

Company was making its way across the plateaus from the east. They were intent upon buying furs from the Yu-kun-ah people before they reached Russian hands. It was this scenario—the British on the inside, east of the mountains; the Tlingit, filtering through the passes and limiting the Russians to the coast—that became the basis of boundaries determined by the Anglo-Russian Treaty of 1825, when the two great white nations came to negotiate their respective shares of the new world. The Russian portion was sold to the United States, as Alaska, in 1867.

By this time, it was no longer the drive for furs reshaping the world. Now it was gold prospectors, scouring the north since the 1860s. They had sparked rushes at Telegraph Creek and McDame Creek. But it was in 1898, some 800 kilometres north on a tributary of the Klondike River, that a Tagish man named Skookum Jim (Keish) and his nephew, Dawson Charlie (Kaa Goox), found the lode that brought 100,000 newcomers through these corridors. Some came inland from the coast via the Stikine River, through Tahltan territories, to Atlin Lake, where more gold was found. Some came through Champagne-Aishihik country, via the Dalton Trail. Most struggled over the Tlingit-Tagish mountain passes—the Chilkoot and the White.

The Kaska, Tagish, Taku River, Champagne-Aishihik, and Tlingit peoples joined the fray, making their fortunes—up to $100 a day—packing, selling meat and fish, building, navigating the river, cutting firewood to fuel riverboat steam engines. Within a year the newcomers were gone: the mountain passes were quieter than before. Two generations passed until construction of the Alaska Highway in 1942 brought another influx—34,000 road builders along its 2,400-kilometre length from Dawson Creek, B.C., to Fairbanks, Alaska. But this time, after they were gone, there was the highway itself, bringing constant change.

INFORMATION AND PROTOCOL

In the northwest corner there are two First Nations communities: the Kaska people at Dease River, on Good Hope Lake, and the Taku River Tlingit, at Atlin.

Whitehorse is administrative and cultural centre for the Yukon peoples.

The original languages spoken here were Athapaskan. The coastal Tlingit language has prevailed in the last century.

Council for Yukon First Nations: 11 Nisutlin Dr., Whitehorse, Yukon, Y1A 3S4. Tel: 403-667-7631. Fax: 403-668-6577. The Champagne-Aishihik First Nations are among 14 member nations.

Kaska Tribal Council: Box 530, Watson Lake, Yukon, Y0A 1C0. Tel: 403-536-2805. Fax: 403-536-2806. B.C.'s members are Dease River and Fort Ware.

North From Dease Lake on Highway 37

Departing from Dease Lake in Tahltan territories, Hwy 37 soon enters Kaska territories.

Dease River: (Pop. 150). 140 km beyond Dease Lake, on Good Hope Lake. As early as the 1820s, the Kaska people traded at the Hudson's Bay Company's Fort Halkett to the northeast, then moved from trading post to trading post as they opened and closed. There was a Hudson's Bay Company trading post and mission near here at McDame Creek. In 1873, the gold rush swept into this region, which became known to outsiders as "the Cassiar"—derived from Kaska, thought to be the local name for McDame Creek. Trappers and traders became guides and suppliers, continuing in this role through the Klondike days of 1898. Half a century later, the Alaska Highway's construction boom again drew them in. The road itself was punched through within only a few hundred yards of their relatives living at Lower Post. Today, most of the Dease Lake band lives here. There are also small communities to the north, at Camp Creek, 28 Mile, and French Creek.

? Dease River Administration: General Delivery, Good Hope Lake, B.C., V0C 2Z0. Tel: 239-3000.

J Alaska Highway: 234 km north of Dease Lake. West to Taku River Tlingit country embracing Teslin Lake. Gravel road follows the east shores of Atlin Lake to Atlin, home base for the Taku River Tlingit today.

V Taku River Tlingit First Nation: 96 km south of Jakes Corner on the Alaska Hwy, at the south edge of the town of Atlin. Their original villages were concentrated to the south along the Taku River, the salmon there being superior. To reach the old villages the fish travelled a short distance from the sea. To reach *this* side of the continental divide, salmon make their way 3,000 km up the Yukon River and, some say, are "only good for dog food." The Taku River Tlingit today offer visitors an exquisite taste of their landscape—at a summer concession stand, serving salmon flown up from their seasonal village on the Taku River. There are no roads. In times past they travelled back and forth on foot. There are signs here of ancient trails and camps. A pictograph marks the end of a caribou-hunting fence that stretched from a hilltop to the shore of Atlin Lake; another commemorates the arrival of a coastal canoe to this lake, brought overland from the Taku River.

It was the superior furs of this more northern plateau that entrenched the Taku River Tlingit here early in the fur trade. After that they worked packing loads and supplying meat for Klondike and Atlin gold miners. Chief Taku Jack is said to have mined 5.4 kg of gold from a creek bed somewhere between Atlin and Surprise Lake.

Meanwhile, down at the Taku River, schemes to develop a copper-lead-zinc-gold-silver mine and a 160-km road linking the site and Juneau, Alaska, to Atlin are being held up, in part, by the slow advance of the Taku Glacier across Taku Inlet.

? Taku River Tlingit First Nation: Box 132, Atlin, B.C., V0W 1A0. Tel:651-7615.

☉ Atlin Museum: Third and Trainor in Atlin. Taku Tlingit tools, bentwood boxes, photos.

I Chilkoot Trail National Historic Trail: 53-km trek from Dyea, Alaska, to Bennett, B.C., over ancient Tlingit-Tagish trail. For information on preparedness, transportation, recommended reading, and regulations, write: Superintendent, Yukon National Historic Sites, Canadian Parks Service, 205-300 Main Rd., Whitehorse, Yukon, Y1A 2B5. Tel: 403-668-2116.

I Tatshenshini-Alsek Wilderness Provincial Park: 958,000 hectares, occupying the Haines Triangle of the St. Elias Mountains. This is the territory of the Champagne and Aishihik First Nations, peoples of southern Tutchone (Athapaskan) and Tlingit descent whose villages a century ago sat on the banks of the salmon-rich Tatshenshini and Alsek rivers. North America's highest mountains here are the source of the copper nuggets, ochre, and obsidian they used. Klukshu, in the Yukon Territory, is still occupied, and visitors are welcome to visit there. Shawshe (Dalton Post), the largest of several historic fishing villages along the Tatshenshini River, is departure point for 250-km river trips destined for Dry Bay in the Gulf of Alaska. These territories were designated provincial park in 1993, sparing them from an open-pit mining scheme that threatened the fisheries and a rare diversity of wildlife. Now, more than 1,000 wilderness rafters a year use the river. And the Champagne and Aishihik First Nations are currently negotiating an agreement for future ownership and management of these lands and resources.

They have also published *Trail to Highway,* a guide to their territories from Whitehorse, Yukon, to Haines, Alaska. It covers the Hwy 3 route through B.C. An even more detailed account of their story is being researched and prepared.

? Champagne-Aishihik First Nations: Box 5309, Haines Junction, Yukon, Y0B 1L0. Tel: 403-634-2288.

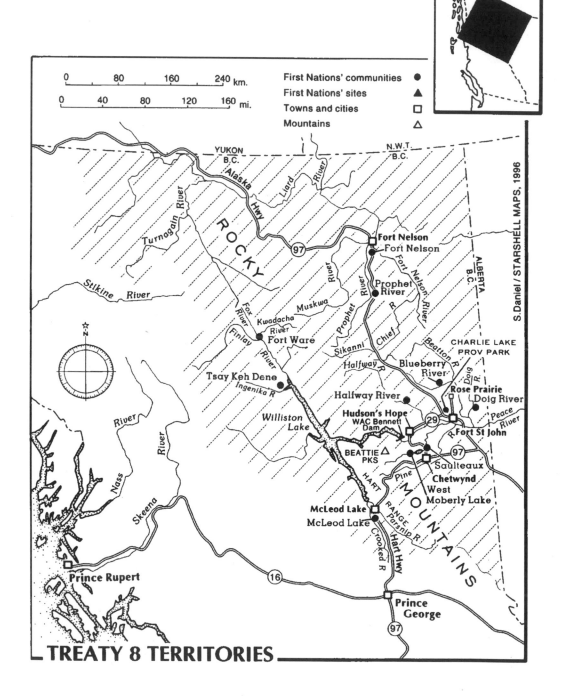

First Nations' communities ●
First Nations' sites ▲
Towns and cities ☐
Mountains △

S.Daniel / STARSHELL MAPS, 1996

0   80   160   240 km.
0   40   80   120   160 mi.

YUKON
B.C.

N.W.T.
B.C.

Alaska Hwy

Liard River

Turnagain River

ROCKY

97

Fort Nelson
Fort Nelson

Stikine River

Muskwa River

Prophet River

Fort Nelson River

Prophet River

ALBERTA
B.C.

Fox River

Kwadacha River

Finlay River

Fort Ware

Sikanni

Chief R

CHARLIE LAKE
PROV PARK

Halfway R

Blueberry River

Beatton R

Doig R.

Tsay Keh Dene

Ingenika R

Rose Prairie
Doig River

Williston Lake

Halfway River

Peace River

Hudson's Hope
WAC Bennett Dam

29

R Fort St John

97

BEATTIE
PKS

Saulteaux

Nass River

Skeena River

HART

Pine

Chetwynd
West
Moberly Lake

McLeod Lake
McLeod Lake

RANGE

Parsnip R.

Crooked R

Hart Hwy

MOUNTAINS

Prince Rupert

16

Prince George

97

TREATY 8 TERRITORIES

CHAPTER 24

Treaty 8:

Sekani, Dunne-za, Dene-thah, Saulteaux, and Cree

Identities are situational. Treaty 8 permeates the identity of these people in their relations with non-natives —it is the singular most important event in their cultural and political lives. But in their relations to each other, their language, tribal affiliation, and families are more important. If you are Salteaux, you are Salteaux. Your cousin might be Dunne-za, or Cree.

—Jim Webb, Treaty 8 Tribal Association

In what we refer to now as the northeast corner of British Columbia, boundaries offer only a general sense of who lives within them. There are maps marking out the lands occupied by the seven communities who signed Treaty 8 between 1899 and 1914. There are still other maps defining traditional territories of the Sekani, Dunne-za, Dene-thah, Saulteaux, and Cree peoples who make up those communities. What they don't show is that each community is actually its own particular blend of the five peoples.

Here, on the far side of the Rocky Mountains, is a much more fluid universe than that of the salmon-fishing peoples south and west. Ancient links flow eastward, like the Peace River, cutting its wide swathe across northern Alberta. Here are foothills, muskeg, and prairie, a habitat like none other, for moose, great rivers of elk, caribou, deer, even buffalo once. And long, long before these giants, there were dinosaurs flourishing in swampy forests.

Some say this is the ancestral home of those who are hunters: the Athapaskan-speaking peoples who have spread throughout the continent, subdividing into dozens of related languages. The Dunne-za speak of Saya, the first man who followed the trails of animals. He overcame the gigantic beasts that ate people, and turned them into the ones we see today. They say his trail is the trail to heaven. For the Dunne-za, hunting was the knowledge of trails—trails made by animals, people, celestial bodies. Where and when these trails intersected was the particular knowledge that came through dreams—dreams that still guide these hunters today.

These are not simple societies, but civilizations, built upon intangibles we are coming to value increasingly: insight, knowledge, skill, flexibility, mobility, and respect for the environment.

The configuration of people we find now is mostly the result of shifts on the plains and eastern woodlands nearly three centuries ago. Cree peoples there—trappers, guides, and middlemen for European fur traders—began

Spruce-bark canoe under construction.
CREDIT: RBCM 3240

expanding west. With newly acquired guns, they pushed before them the people they called Awokanak, the "timid people" or "slaves" whose homeland was at Lake Athabasca. These people, who knew themselves as Dene-thah, "the people," re-established themselves where the muskeg and permafrost of the Mackenzie drainage are thickest, in the north of the northeast corner. In their sweep west, the Cree also pushed the Tsattine, "dwellers among the beavers," farther toward the headwaters of their "river of beavers"—the one we now call the Peace. These are the dreamers who know themselves as the Dunne-za, "real people." They, in turn, acquired guns and bumped the Sekani, "the dwellers on the rock," from their eastern foothill hunting grounds, confining them more to the heights of the Rockies and the trench on the other side.

By 1734, Cree people too had settled in the region around Fort St. John and Hudson's Hope. The migrations continued: more than a century later, in the aftermath of the Northwest and Red River rebellions of the 1870s and 1880s in Manitoba and Saskatchewan, more Crees came, along with Metis and Saulteaux from the Lake Winnipeg area.

Alexander Mackenzie of the North West Company, among the first white emissaries of the fur trade, didn't catch up until 1793. Here, the Sekani people he met directed him onward to the Fraser River, as he sought a route to the Pacific Ocean. In his wake, Rocky Mountain House, near present-day Fort St. John, was established, the first fur-trading post in what is now mainland B.C. It was Simon Fraser, 12 years behind him, who triggered yet another series of relocations. In 1805, he established Rocky Mountain Portage, at the foot of the Peace River Canyon, near present-day Hudson's Hope. This was, more or less, a buffer zone between Sekani and Dunne-za rivals. But both were drawn here to trade. Fort St. John, opened the same year, also drew Sekani and Dunne-za, while the Trout Lake Post later known as Fort McLeod brought Sekani and Dakelh families together. Fort Nelson amalgamated Dene-thah, Sekani, Kaska, and Cree peoples. And so it came to be that these once small groups of people, who carried everything with them, gradually gave up their farthest-reaching trails for a new lifestyle anchored to the forts.

Trappers now, they provided traders with meat and furs, feeding them from their knowledge of the land. In exchange, the traders provided them with guns, ammunition, snare wires, traps. The trappers saw the arrangement as a kind of contract: each relied on the other for their very survival. In 1823, when the contract was abruptly broken by the planned closure of Fort St. John, its dependents reacted by destroying the fort and killing five employees. The retaliatory three-year closure of all upper Peace forts led to starvation throughout the land.

The passing century brought the first prospectors—for there were other resources here. And by 1898, when the Peace River delivered the first flood of gold-seekers headed for the Klondike, the peoples here knew what lay ahead. Call it experience; call it what the dreamers saw. This time, 500 Dunne-za stopped them from entering their territory. They stood their ground at Taylor Hill near Fort St. John, and pushed the miners back. Until there was a treaty in the spirit of the seven already signed in 1870–1877 by peoples from western Ontario to Alberta, there would be no peaceful entry into their hunting grounds.

For them, Treaty 8 was a guarantee they could continue to live and hunt in their ancient way, on unoccupied crown lands in treaty territory. But, "from our perspective," says Jim Webb, "it wasn't honoured at all." The people were restricted on, rather than protected by, the small reserves allocated to them. And those unoccupied lands where they would hunt became unobstructed lands— wide open to wave after wave of resource-extraction schemes. The 1920s and 1930s brought white trappers and government regulation of traplines, a violation of treaty terms. The Alaska Highway after 1942 and the John Hart Highway a decade later brought in settlement, agriculture, then the forest industry. By the 1960s, the northeast corner was "B.C.'s oil patch," with wells, pumps, and pipelines sucking out the thick black blood of the giants Saya conquered long ago. The Peace River, dammed twice for hydroelectricity, has been backed up to create the province's largest body of fresh water. It rose up over hunting grounds, ancient trails, traplines, camps.

Today the people here are pursuing all possible avenues to reinject their treaty's original spirit and intent—that there be room here in this vast prairie for them to be, and dream.

HIGHLIGHTS AND EVENTS

INFORMATION AND PROTOCOL

The seven Treaty 8 communities in northeastern B.C.—about 2,200 people—are affiliated with 32 communities in Alberta, 4 in Saskatchewan, and 6 in the Northwest Territories. They ask that visitors respect their privacy and their efforts to live as much as possible according to their own economic, cultural, and spiritual values. Visitors are encouraged to join in the Treaty Day celebrations listed above, rare opportunities to learn more about those values.

Included in this section are three Sekani communities within the official boundaries of Treaty 8, but who at this time are not signatories to it. These are McLeod Lake, Fort Ware, and Tsey Keh Dene. Their relatives to the north, around Prophet River and Fort Nelson, prefer to spell their name Thicannie, a closer reflection of the dialect spoken there.

? **Treaty 8 Tribal Association:** 10233-100th Ave, Fort St. John, B.C., V1J 1Y8. Tel: 785-

0612. Fax: 785-2021. Members: Blueberry River, Doig River, Fort Nelson, Halfway River, Prophet River, Saulteaux, West Moberly Lake.

? **Kaska Tribal Council:** Box 8, Watson Lake, Yukon, Y0A 1C0. Tel: 779-3181. Fax: 779-3371. Members: Dease River, Fort Ware in B.C., Liard and Ross River in the Yukon.

Northeast from Prince George

The Sekani (or Thicannie) who live within and just outside the treaty boundaries tell us they have occupied the river trenches for many thousands of years. In recent centuries, there were four main groups, each with its own territory along the Crooked and Parsnip, Finlay and Fox rivers, which combine to form the Peace River. The Sekani had much interaction with the Dakelh, Gitxsan and Tahltan peoples, among whom some of them now live.

V **McLeod Lake:** (Pop. 375/135). 145 km north of Prince George, at the north end of McLeod Lake. About 300 m up the hill past McLeod Lake General Store, turn left. Fort McLeod, or the Trout Lake Post, established in 1805, was the first permanent European settlement west of the Rockies. It drew the two southernmost Sekani groups, people who have lived in this area, says Verne Solonas, "since before Adam and Eve." One was called Sekani, the name now given to all who share their language; the other was Yutuwichan, "lake people" who fished for carp and trout in the lakes to the south. McLeod Lake is currently seeking inclusion in Treaty 8, hoping for a land and cash settlement that will give them greater access to educational and economic opportunities, and independence. The community operates two logging and two silviculture companies. There is an excellent **museum** in the former Hudson's Bay Company store; gas bar (has diesel fuel). Handicrafts feature work in moose hide, beads. Guide-outfitting is offered.

? **McLeod Lake Administration:** General Delivery, McLeod Lake, B.C., V0J 2G0. Tel: 750-4415.

The Far Far North

V **Tsay Keh Dene:** (Pop. 300). 567 km north of Prince George, by rough logging road. Where the Ingenika River flows into the Finlay River. These are descendants of the northern Sekani peoples who came together at Fort Graham after 1890.

In the 1960s, when the Tsay Keh Dene were informed of the scheme to construct the W.A.C. Bennett Dam on the Peace River, 400 km downstream near Hudson's Hope, they could never have imagined its effect on them. But in 1967, they watched in dismay as the Finlay River rose up to swallow their traplines, burial grounds, houses, and game. At new reserves set up for them far to the south near Mackenzie, they tried to revive their own drowning spirits. It wasn't home; there was no trapping. In 1970 they returned to their trench at the northern reaches of the reservoir. No visitor services.

? **Tsay Keh Dene Administration:** 3845-15th Ave., Prince George, B.C., V2N 1A4. Tel: 562-8882.

V **Fort Ware:** (Pop. 450/350). 500 km north of Prince George, on the Finlay River at its confluence with the Fox and Kwadacha rivers. Fort Ware, not a destination for tourists, is generally reached by air: the overland route is passable in winter—over ice bridges. This is the home of the Otzane, the "people at the end of the mountain." Old Davie, son of a Sekani woman and a French Canadian fur trader, brought his Sekani wife, four daughters, and their husbands here in 1917. Their utopia attracted others, and soon the Otzane were renowned as excellent hunters and trappers.

The community maintains administration offices in Prince George, and a member-

Fort Ware is well off the beaten track.
CREDIT: RICK BLACKLAWS

ship in the Kaska Tribal Council based in the Yukon Territory's Watson Lake. This place is remote: the only drop-in visitors are moose, mountain sheep, and goats, and pilots on the flight path up and down the Rocky Mountain Trench, landing here to fuel up. To the south, forestry provides employment for some Fort Ware residents. To the north, it is so wild, even loggers haven't gone there.

? **Fort Ware Administration:** 3-1257 4th Ave., Prince George, B.C., V2L 3J5. Tel: 563-4161.

East from McLeod Lake on Highway 97

Highway 97 winds through the Hart Range of the Rocky Mountains, descending with the Pine River into the gentle lands of the Peace River.

V **Saulteaux:** (Pop. 600/300). 21 km north of Chetwynd on Hwy 29, left onto Boucher Rd., then a short distance to the village on the north shore of east Moberly Lake. Some 2,000 km east of here, on the shores of Lake Winnipeg, two prophets shared a dream. They saw a pair of mountains—twin peaks—and a tranquil lake between them. They knew the time had come to leave behind the residue of the 1870 Riel Rebellion, and set out, across three provinces. First they settled at Sun Dance Lake, and made their peace with the Sekani, Beaver, and Cree peoples of this new land. They went on, just a short pilgrimage now, to see the Twin Sisters (Beattie Peaks) just south of the Peace and west of Moberly Lake. The Saulteaux (pronounced So-to)—Ojibwa-speaking "people of the rapids" recently from Manitoba, and from the forests around Sault St. Marie two centuries before that—were finally home.

Jim Webb speaks of trails that intersect in dreams, and of these twin mountains, also sacred to the Dunne-za and Sekani. "Most of the people here have an apocalyptic view of the future. The dreamers have spoken of a time in which brother will fight brother over water, and times will be hard. Sacred places, like Twin Sisters, are the only places where the people will survive."

Visitors are welcome at **Saulteaux Pemmican Days**, usually in late August. The Saulteaux dancers launch a full weekend of traditional skill-testing games (see West Moberly Treaty Days, below). "The whole community participates," says Rita. "We have a moose call and horse call contest for men, the cow call contest for women; even donkey and pig call, for children." Elders judge. Long-distance travellers are treated like honoured guests at the Friendship Feast. Pemmican Days derive their name from a traditional version of the granola bar, a mixture of chokecherries, blueberries, moose meat, and other ingredients—concentrated food energy that keeps well for travelling.

? Saulteaux Administration: Box 414, Chetwynd, B.C., V0C 1J0. Tel: 788-3955.

V West Moberly Lake: (Pop. 114/70). From Chetwynd, travel north on Hwy 29 for 29 km, then follow signs and a gravel road to Moberly Lake's west shores. Here are descendants of the Dunne-za who coalesced in 1805 at Rocky Mountain Portage (now Hudson's Hope), the first fur-trade post in what is now mainland B.C. When the treaty was made, the people here and at Halfway River were two communities of closely related people, administratively joined as the Hudson's Hope Band. In 1977–78 the four core families here went their own way. So many Cree and Saulteaux subsequently married that Cree is now the language spoken here and taught in summer language programs. While few here are full-blooded Dunne-za, those at Halfway River remain predominantly so. Most are employed seasonally, working with seismic, silviculture, and fire-fighting crews.

Chief George Desjarlais describes the his-

tory behind **West Moberly Lake's Treaty Days**: "When people first signed the treaty, the Indian Agent came by boat up the Peace River to Hudson's Hope to hand out our annuity payments and our rations. People from Moberly, East Moberly, Saulteaux, and Halfway River —aunts, uncles, cousins, grandparents who hadn't seen each other for a long time—would all come together here for three or four days, to celebrate, by playing games. They were very competitive, showing off their life skills— arrow-shooting, dry-meat-cutting. There was the bannock and tea-making contest—starting from scratch, to see who would finish first. Foot races, horseback wrestling, where you would start out with 15 or 20 people. The last one still on their horse wins. During the 1930s, with the Depression, and the 1940s, with the war, we got away from it. Anyway, our annuity payments came in the mail. About nine years ago, the West Moberly people said *no*. We want Indian Affairs to come to our home. In 1987, we started West Moberly Treaty Days."

Today's annual celebrations feature 27 games, including the hand game, a traditional guessing game played in teams, to the beat of the drums. Newer events include horseshoes and marathon bingo. Opening ceremonies begin with the raising of flags: Canada, B.C., Britain, the Treaty 8 Tribal Association, West Moberly. The day proceeds with performances by the West Moberly Traditional Dancers, distribution of annuities, and the Friendship Feast—moose, deer, elk, bannock, northern pike and lake trout, soups and stews, mashed potatoes and gravy. Round dancing, with drums and singers, lasts until the wee hours. Breakfast is cooked Saturday morning by the women; Sunday morning by the men. Visitors are very welcome. There is some basic camping on site, and good facilities at Moberly Lake and Charlie Lake provincial campgrounds, nearby.

? West Moberly Lake Administration: General Delivery, Moberly Lake, B.C., V0X 1X0. Tel: 788-3663.

▌ **Peace River:** 28 km beyond Moberly Lake, Hwy 29 crosses, then traces the river just as it emerges through the mountains. From its beginnings on the other side, it flows 1,923 km east and north to the Mackenzie River. And though it has changed course many times, dinosaur tracks found along the riverbanks present the awesome possibility of just how long this river was the highway here. It was called Tsades, "river of beavers," by the Athapaskan-speaking peoples who hunted along its banks, and travelled by it, for an unknown span of time. Only two centuries ago, the Cree, armed with guns, pushed their way into this region from the east. The Dunne-za eventually also gained guns, for a more even match. In 1781, smallpox further weakened the Cree and shortly thereafter, peace pipes, and an agreement, were drawn between the sovereign nations of the Cree and Dunne-za peoples at the place they named Unijigah, "peace point," near present-day Peace River, Alberta. The river, in time, became the "peace river." Now, it has been dammed twice, and many First Nations people say it won't be long until the continent's demand for water leads to conflict over such resources as this.

T **Hudson's Hope:** (Pop. 975/0 Ab). 35 km beyond Moberly Lake. This is where the Sekani and Dunne-za came together, in 1805, around Rocky Mountain Portage. **Hudson's Hope Museum**, 10506-105th Ave., opposite the Infocentre on the Peace River's north bank, occupies a turn-of-the-century Hudson's Bay Company store. First Nations crafts are for sale. Tel: 783-5735.

▌ **Charlie Lake Provincial Park:** 75 km beyond Hudson's Hope, at junction of Hwys 29 and 97. Archaeologists speculate that 10,500 years ago this region was covered by a widening of the Peace River—a vast glacial lake. Here, it narrowed between two rock outcroppings, creating a crossing place for animals and the people who hunted them. Bison

bones larger than those of historical bison, and stone artifacts, including a bead worn as adornment, have been unearthed in caves here. Several items are on display in the North Peace Museum, in Fort St. John. Despite the meagre archaeological record, it is believed the people who owned these objects possessed art, religion, and oral traditions. In more recent times, Charlie Lake has been an important fishing site.

T **Fort St. John:** (Pop. 14,040/595 Ab). 88 km east of Hudson's Hope. The northeast's largest community sits on a ridge overlooking the Peace River at the eastern gateway into the region. This is the "Energy Capital of B.C.," the "Land of New Totems"—celebrating the oil derricks darkening the horizon. For the original people here (who have no tradition of totems), this is the seat of their most vehement opposition to the unthinking extraction of resources. It was here, in 1823, that the sudden death of a young Dunne-za and planned closure of the fort led to the murder of five Hudson's Bay Company employees and agitation in forts throughout the region. It was also here, in 1898, that miners headed for the Klondike were held off by 500 Dunne-za until a treaty was promised. Today, the Treaty 8 Tribal Association makes its headquarters here.

The "Fort St. John Indians"—Dunne-za, Sekani, and Cree—have lived together here since the first post in what is now B.C. was established about 10 km upriver, shortly after Alexander Mackenzie's visit in 1793. This post, known as Rocky Mountain House, was closed in 1805, when Rocky Mountain Portage was established about 65 km west at the foot of the Peace River Canyon near Hudson's Hope.

With Treaty 8, the Fort St. John Indians were assigned the traditional gathering site, "place where happiness dwells," as their reserve. For half a century, until the end of World War Two, they called this home. Then the federal government, seeking good agricultural land for returning veterans, set its sights on the block of land it knew simply as IR-172. Eventually, its occupants were offered two new reserves—Doig and Blueberry, where they were told they would have ample room to hunt and trap on adjacent lands. Almost immediately, oil exploration began, and those adjacent lands were taken up by wells, pipelines, roads, and settlement.

V   Doig River: (Pop. 200/110). About 30 km northeast of Fort St. John, near the confluence of the Doig and Beaton rivers. This half of the former Fort St. John community makes its living trapping and operating a cattle ranch and store.

?   Doig River Administration: Box 55, Rose Prairie, B.C., V0C 2H0. Tel: 787-4849.

V   Blueberry River: (Pop. 280/150). On the Blueberry River near Rose Prairie; about 60 km northwest of Fort St. John via Hwy 97, then 20 km by back road. This is the other half of the original Fort St. John band, mostly Dunne-za and Cree: a quiet, private community with no tourist services. In 1976 a deadly sour gas or hydrogen sulphide well was opened just outside the reserve boundary, on the only road into the reserve, and 700 m from the village. The people began to complain of headaches, a general lack of well-being. Then, in 1979 a cloud of gas rolled down "like a fog" into the village. That everyone was evacuated in time was divine intervention—and the fact that the chief happened to hear the gas leaking from the well.

?   Blueberry River Administration: Box 3009, Buick Creek, B.C., V0C 2R0. Tel: 630-2584.

V   Halfway River: (Pop. 186/150). By back road north from Fort St. John. This is a private community of Dunne-za and Sekani peoples. The Halfway River is a tributary of the Peace.

?   Halfway River Administration: Box 59, Wonowon, B.C., V0C 2N0. Tel: 787-4451.

I   Sikanni Chief River Bridge: 193 km north of Fort St. John. At the headwaters of the Sikanni Chief River, according to local tradition and Treaty 8 historian Gilbert Capot Blanc, is the grave of an important "Sikanni" chief. One account guesses he may not have been Sekani, but rather a Dunne-za named Makenunatane, "his trail circles around the edge of the world." Makenunatane was said to be a Dreamer: he foresaw the arrival of white men, then guided his people in making the transition to a new way of life. He may also have been the chief known to the French-speaking traders at Rocky Mountain Fort in the late 1700s as Cigni, or Swan. This name links him with the Dunne-za hero Saya who, as a child, also held this name: his power to dream was like the flight of the swan—passing through to the land of another season, and then returning. Makenunatane prophesied his own death: wearing a white Hudson's Bay blanket, he was mistaken for an elk and shot.

V   Prophet River: (Pop. 150/100). About 110 km beyond the Sikanni Chief River Bridge. On the southern frontier of Dene-thah territories, Prophet River is home to Thicannie, Dunne-za, and Dene-thah peoples. River and community take their name from Thicannie prophet and dreamer, Zacharie Dakodoa, born in 1851. He counselled his followers to "never mind the Blackrobe." These priests he likened to "mischievous crows," saying "they will go to the fire down below, and the Slaves and Sekanais who listen to them will go after them." The prophet is probably also the man later documented as "the old Sicannie Chief," who in 1910 refused to adhere to Treaty 8: "God made the game and fur-bearing animals for the Indians, and money for the white people," he said. "My forefathers made their living in the country without white men's money and I and my people can do the same."

The following year, August 3, 1911, Dakodoa's people along with two other bands—one under Chief Mekenetcha, "Big Foot," and the "Fontas" band—adhered to the treaty. In 1961, when the Thicannies of Fort Nelson (below) finally received their treaty land, all four bands were lumped together as one. In 1974, these bands "separated" to become the Prophet River and Fort Nelson bands. There is a general store here.

? **Prophet River Administration:** Box 3250, Fort Nelson, B.C., V0C 1R0. Tel: 744-1025.

V **Fort Nelson:** (Pop. 550/300). At Mile 293, 90 km beyond Prophet River, about 6 km southwest of the town of **Fort Nelson** (pop. 3,755/115 Ab). The original name of the people who lived here was Thicannie Qwah, "people of the rocks." They also go by the name Eh-Cho Dene, "people among the big animals." They are Thicannie and Dene-thah descendants of those who traded at several North West Company and Hudson's Bay Company posts in the region dating back to 1805. The present-day town of Fort Nelson sits on the site of the last fort, established in 1864. Elders describe pulling company freight boats in along the Liard River shallows. Cree families have been here since the 1930s, and perhaps earlier, with the fur trade.

Today, Eh-Cho Dene is also the name of this bustling community's corporate arm, with a fleet of trucks, excavators, and bulldozers providing construction, welding, and engineering services for oil-field and highway projects. Individuals within the community also operate their own industrial enterprises. There is a gas bar and convenience store. People sell arts and crafts. Still others trap, fish, hunt. Some manage to blend traditional and modern lifestyles.

Fort Nelson Treaty Day Celebrations, the second weekend in August, are part of an ongoing tradition of welcoming visitors. There are games, the Sunday feast, and drummers from Northwest Territories and Alberta.

The **Fort Nelson-Liard Native Friendship Centre**, in Fort Nelson, 5012-49th Ave. next to the Anglican church, has locally made crafts: mukluks, moccasins, and tufted moose-hair wall hangings.

? **Fort Nelson Administration:** RR 1, Mile 293, Alaska Hwy, Fort Nelson, B.C., V0C 1R0. Tel: 774-7257.

Further Reading

General

Aboriginal Land Claims in Canada: A Regional Perspective, edited by Ken Coates. Toronto: Copp Clark Pitman Ltd., 1992.

Aboriginal Peoples and Politics, by Paul Tennant. Vancouver: UBC Press, 1990.

Children of the First People, by Dorothy Haegert. Vancouver: Tillacum Library, 1983.

Chinook: A History and Dictionary of the Northwest Coast Trade Jargon, by Edward Harper Thomas. Portland: Binfords & Mort, 1970.

Food Plants of Coastal First Peoples, by Nancy J. Turner. Vancouver: UBC Press, 1996.

Indian Government: Its Meaning in Practice, by Frank Cassidy and Robert L. Bish. Victoria: Oolichan Books and The Institute for Research on Public Policy, 1989.

Indian Petroglyphs of the Pacific Northwest, by Beth and Ray Hill. Saanichton: Hancock House Publishers, 1974.

Indian Rock Art of the Columbia Plateau, by James D. Keyser. Vancouver: Douglas & McIntyre, 1992.

The Legacy: Continuing Traditions of Canadian Northwest Coast Indian Art, by Macnair, Hoover and Neary. Victoria: British Columbia Provincial Museum, 1980.

Looking at Indian Art of the Northwest Coast, by Hilary Stewart. Vancouver: Douglas & McIntyre, 1979.

Looking at Totem Poles, by Hilary Stewart. Vancouver: Douglas & McIntyre, 1993.

Our Chiefs and Elders: Words and Photographs of Native Leaders, by David Neel. Vancouver: UBC Press, 1992.

Plants in British Columbia Indian Technology, by Nancy J. Turner. Victoria: Royal British Columbia Museum, 1979.

The Salish People: The Local Contributions of Charles Hill-Tout, Volumes 1–4, edited by Ralph Maud. Vancouver: Talonbooks, 1978.

Tangled Webs of History: Indians and the Law in Canada's Pacific Coast Fisheries, by Dianne Newell. Toronto: University of Toronto Press, 1993.

Totem Poles, by Marjorie M. Halpin. Vancouver: UBC Press, 1981.

Dakelh

The Carrier, My People, by Lizette Hall, 1992.

Changing Ways: Southern Carrier History, 1793–1940, by Elizabeth Furniss. Quesnel School District, 1993.

Cheryl Bibalhats: Cheryl's Potlatch, by Sheila Thompson. Vanderhoof: Yinka Dene Language Institute, 1991.

Dakelh Keyoh: The Southern Carrier of Earlier Times, by Elizabeth Furniss. Quesnel School District, 1993.

My Home Forever and *Nazko My Village*, by Laura Boyd. Nazko Indian Band, 1989.

Stoney Creek Woman: The Story of Mary John, by Bridget Moran. Vancouver: Tillacum Library, 1988.

Ulkatcho: Stories of the Grease Trail, by Sage Birchwater. Ulkatcho Indian Band, 1993.

Ulkatchot'en: the People of Ulkatcho, by Sage Birchwater. Ulkatcho Indian Band, 1991.

Gitxsan

Colonialism on Trial, by Don Monet and Skanu'u (Ardythe Wilson). Gabriola Island: New Society Publishers, 1992.

A Death Feast in Dimlahamid, by Terry Glavin. Vancouver: New Star Books, 1990.

From Mountain to Mountain: A History of the Gitxsan Village of Ans'pa Yaxw, by Maureen Cassidy. Ans'pa Yaxw School Society, 1984.

Histories, Territories and Laws of the Kitwancool, edited by Wilson Duff. Victoria: Royal British Columbia Museum, 1989.

FILMS:

Blockade, National Film Board, 1993.

Indian Land, Scope Films, 1986.

Haida

Chiefs of Sea and Sky, by George F. MacDonald. Vancouver: UBC Press, 1989.

During My Time: Florence Edenshaw Davidson, A Haida Woman, by Margaret Blackman. Vancouver: Douglas & McIntyre, 1982.

Those Born at Koona: The Totem Poles of the Haida Village Skedans Queen Charlotte Islands, by John and Carolyn Smyly. Vancouver: Hancock House Publishers, 1981.

Haisla

Tales of Kitamaat, by Gordon Robinson. Kitimat: Northern Sentinel Press, 1956.

Halq'emeylem

Hands of Our Ancestors: The Revival of Salish Weaving at Musqueam, by Elizabeth Lominska Johnson and Kathryn Bernick. Museum Note No. 16, UBC Museum of Anthropology, 1986.

Katzie Ethnographic Notes/The Faith of a Coast Salish Indian, by Wayne Suttles and Diamond Jenness. British Columbia Provincial Museum, 1986.

Legends of Vancouver, by E. Pauline Johnson-Tekahionwake. Kingston: Quarry Press, Inc., 1991.

The Mountain Goat People of Cheam, as told by Maggie Emery and Amelia Douglas. Sardis: The Stó:lo Nation, 1986.

The Story of Chehalis, as told by Ed Leon. Sardis: The Stó:lo Nation, 1983.

Hul'qumi'num

Coast Salish Essays, by Wayne Suttles. Vancouver: Talonbooks, 1987.

Legends from the Chemainus Tribe. Chemainus Tribal Council, 1992.

When the Rains Came, and Other Legends of the Salish People, as told to Dolby Bevan Turner. Victoria: Orca Book Publishers, 1992.

Ktunaxa

Kutenai Tales, by Franz Boas. Smithsonian Institution, Bureau of American Ethnology, Bulletin 59, 1918.

Kwakwa̱ka'wakw

Assu of Cape Mudge, by Harry Assu with Joy Inglis. Vancouver: UBC Press, 1989.

Guests Never Leave Hungry: The Autobiography of James Sewid, a Kwakiutl Indian, edited by James Spradley. Montreal: McGill-Queen's University Press, 1972.

Kwakwaka'wakw Settlements, 1775–1920: A Geographical Analysis and Gazetteer, by Robert Galois. Vancouver: UBC Press, 1994.

Prosecution or Persecution, by Daisy Sewid-Smith. Nu-yum-baleess Society, 1979.

FILMS:

Box of Treasures, U'Mista Cultural Centre, 1983.

Mungo Martin: A Slender Thread—the Legacy, Barb Cranmer, 1990.

Nisga'a

Nisga'a: People of the Nass River. Nisga'a Tribal Council, 1993.

Without Surrender Without Consent: A History of the Nisga'a Land Claims, by Daniel Raunet. Vancouver: Douglas & McIntyre, 1984.

Nlaka'pamux

Our Tellings: Interior Salish Stories of the Nlak7kapmx People, compiled and edited by Darwin Hanna Mamie Henry. Vancouver: UBC Press, 1996.

Stein, The Way of the River, by Michael M'Gonigle and Wendy Wickwire. Vancouver: Talonbooks, 1988.

They Write their Dreams on the Rock Forever: Rock Writings in the Stein River Valley of British Columbia, by Annie York, Richard Daly, Chris Arnett. Vancouver: Talonbooks, 1993.

FILM:

The River is Our Home, Coqualeetza Education Training Centre, 1984.

The Northwest: Kaska, Taku River Tlingit, Tagish, Champagne-Aishihik, and Tlingit

Gagiwdul.at: Brought Forth to Reconfirm: The Legacy of a Taku River Tlingit Clan, by Elizabeth Nyman and Jeff Leer. Yukon Native Language Centre and Alaska Native Language Centre, 1993.

Life Lived Like a Story: Life Stories of Three Yukon Native Elders, by Julie Cruikshank in collaboration with Angela Sidney, Kitty Smith, and Annie Ned. Vancouver: UBC Press, 1990.

Nuu-chah-nulth

Alberni Prehistory, by Alan McMillan and Denis St. Claire. Penticton: Theytus Books, 1982.

As Far As I Know: Reminiscences of an Ahousat Elder, by Peter Webster. Campbell River Museum and Archives, 1983.

Between Ports Alberni and Renfrew: Notes on West Coast Peoples by Arima, St. Claire, Clamhouse, Edgar, Jones and Thomas. Canadian Ethnology Service, Mercury Series Paper 121, Canadian Museum of Civilization, 1991.

Fables of the Tse-shaht, by George Clutesi. Port Alberni: Clutesi Agencies Ltd., 1994.

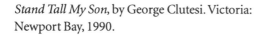
Stand Tall My Son, by George Clutesi. Victoria: Newport Bay, 1990.

Teachings of the Tides, Uses of Marine Invertebrates by the Manhousat People, by David Ellis and Luke Swan. Nanaimo: Theytus Books, 1981.

FILM:

Washing of the Tears, by Hugh Brody. National Film Board, 1994.

Okanagan

Mourning Dove: a Salishan Autobiography, edited by Jay Miller. Lincoln: University of Nebraska Press, 1990.

Nature Power: In the Spirit of an Okanagan Storyteller, by Harry Robinson. Vancouver: Douglas & McIntyre, 1992.

Okanagan Sources, edited by Jean Webber and the En'owkin Centre. Penticton: Theytus Books, 1990.

We Get Our Living Like Milk From the Land, edited by Armstrong, Derickson, Maracle, & Young-Ing. The Okanagan Rights Committee and The Okanagan Indian Education Resource Society, 1993–94.

Write it on your Heart: The Epic World of an Okanagan Storyteller, by Harry Robinson. Vancouver: Talonbooks/Theytus, 1989.

Secwepemc

Brotherhood to Nation: George Manuel and the Making of the Modern Indian Movement, by Peter McFarlane. Toronto: Between the Lines, 1993.

The Days of Augusta, by Augusta Evans and edited by Jean Speare. Vancouver: Douglas & McIntyre, 1992.

Introduction to the Shuswap. Kamloops: Secwepemc Cultural Education Society, 1986.

Shuswap History: The First 100 Years of Contact, by John Coffey, et al. Kamloops: Secwepemc Cultural Education Society, 1990.

The Shuswap: Shuswap Declaration Aug. 20, 1982. The Shuswap Nation Tribal Council, 1989.

Shíshálh

Mayuk, The Grizzly Bear: A Legend of the Sechelt People, and *How the Robin Got its Red Breast*. Nightwood Editions, 1994.

The Story of the Sechelt Nation, by Lester Petersen. Sechelt Indian Band, 1990.

Sliammon

Sliammon Life, Sliammon Lands, by Dorothy Kennedy and Randy Bouchard. Vancouver: Talonbooks, 1983.

Squamish and Tsleil Waututh

Conversations with Khahtsahlano, by Major J.S. Matthews. Vancouver City Archives, 1955.

Khot-la-cha, the Autobiography of Chief Simon Baker, edited by Verna J. Kirkness. Vancouver: Douglas & McIntyre, 1994.

My Heart Soars, by Chief Dan George. Saanichton: Hancock House, 1974.

My Spirit Soars, by Chief Dan George. Vancouver: Hancock House, 1982.

St'at'imc

Lillooet Stories, by Dorothy Kennedy and Randy Bouchard. Victoria: Provincial Archives of British Columbia, 1977.

The Same as Yesterday: The Lillooet Chronicle the Theft of Their Lands and Resources, by Joanne Drake-Terry. Lillooet Tribal Council, 1989.

Tahltan

Stikine: The Great River, by Gary Fiegehen. Vancouver: Douglas & McIntyre, 1991.

Treaty 8: Sekani, Dunne-za, Dene-thah, Saulteaux, and Cree

Little Bit Know Something, Stories in a Language of Anthropology by Robin Ridington. Vancouver: Douglas & McIntyre, 1990.

Maps and Dreams, by Hugh Brody. Vancouver: Douglas & McIntyre, 1981.

Trail to Heaven, by Robin Ridington. Vancouver: Douglas & McIntyre, 1988.

Tsilhqot'in

Nemiah: The Unconquered Country, by Terry Glavin. Vancouver: New Star Books, 1992.

The People of Alexandria, by Violet and Sharon Stump. Alexandria Indian Band, 1990.

Tsi Del Del: Redstone, by Orrie Charleyboy. Williams Lake: Chilcotin Language Committee, 1991.

Chiwid, by Sage Birchwater. Vancouver: New Star Books, 1995.

The Straits

Lauwelnew, by Earl Claxton Sr., and John Elliot, Sr. Saanich: Saanich Indian School Board, 1993.

The Saanich Year, by Earl Claxton Sr., and John Elliot, Sr. Saanich: Saanich Indian School Board, 1993.

Reef Net Technology of the Saltwater People, by Earl Claxton Sr., and John Elliot, Sr. Saanich: Saanich Indian School Board, 1994.

The Way We Were and the Way We Are, by Earl Claxton Sr., and John Elliot, Sr. Saanich: Saanich Indian School Board, 1996.

Saltwater People: As Told by Dave Elliot Sr. Saanich: School District 63, 1983.

Tsimshian

The Tsimshian: Images of the Past; Views for the Present, edited by Margaret Seguin. Vancouver: UBC Press, 1984.

Tsimshian Language Series. A series of seven books for children. First Nation Education School District 52, Prince Rupert, 1992.

Tsimshian Narratives. Volumes 1 and 2, Canadian Museum of Civilization, Mercury Series, 1987.

The Tsimshian and Their Neighbours, edited by Jay Miller and Carol M. Eastman. Seattle: University of Washington Press, 1984.

Wet'suwet'en

Eagle Down is Our Law: Witsuwit'en Law, Feasts, and Land Claims, by Antonia Mills. Vancouver: UBC Press, 1994.

The Gathering Place: A History of the Wet'suwet'en Village of Tse-kya, by Maureen Cassidy. Hagwilget Band Council, 1987.

Proud Past: A History of the Wet'suwet'en Village of Moricetown, B.C., by Maureen and Frank Cassidy. Moricetown Band, 1980.

Stories of the Moricetown Carrier Indians of Northwestern B.C., collected by Carol Naziel and Rhonda Naziel. Moricetown Indian Band Council, 1978.

Index

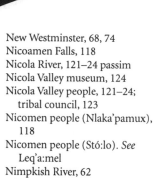

About the Author

Cheryl listens while Wsanec elder Gabriol Bartleman speaks of places on southern Vancouver Island where she now lives. This summer, Mr. Bartleman will greet thousands of First Nations people travelling from all over B.C. for the 1996 Elders Gathering. He wrote the foreword to this book.

Cheryl Coull is a third-generation British Columbian, born in Ktunaxa territories, raised in Nuu-chah-nulth territories, educated in Sney ney mux and Lekwammen territories. *A Traveller's Guide to Aboriginal B.C.* is the culmination of her nearly 20 years' experience exploring and writing about British Columbia. She is founding editor of the *Beautiful British Columbia Travel Guide*.